Using Z

C.A.R. Hoare, Series Editor

ARNOLD, A., *Finite Transition Systems*
ARNOLD, A. and GUESSARIAN, I., *Mathematics for Computer Science*
BARR, M. and WELLS, C., *Category Theory for Computing Science* (2nd edn)
BEN-ARI, M., *Principles of Concurrent and Distributed Programming*
BEN-ARI, M., *Mathematical Logic for Computer Science*
BEST, E., *Semantics of Sequential and Parallel Programs*
BIRD, R. and WADLER, P., *Introduction to Functional Programming*
BOVET, D.P. and CRESCENZI, P., *Introduction to the Theory of Complexity*
DE BROCK, B., *Foundations of Semantic Databases*
BRODA, EISENBACH, KHOSHNEVISAN and VICKERS, *Reasoned Programming*
BURKE, E. and FOXLEY, E., *Logic and Its Applications*
DAHL, O.-J., *Verifiable Programming*
DAVIES, J. and WOODCOCK, J., *Using Z: Specification, refinement and proof*
DUNCAN, E., *Microprocessor Programming and Software Development*
ELDER, J., *Compiler Construction*
ELLIOTT, R.J. and HOARE, C.A.R. (eds), *Scientific Applications of Multiprocessors*
FREEMAN, T.L. and PHILLIPS, R.C., *Parallel Numerical Algorithms*
GOLDSCHLAGER, L. and LISTER, A., *Computer Science: A modern introduction* (2nd edn)
GORDON, M.J.C., *Programming Language Theory and Its Implementation*
GRAY, P.M.D., KULKARNI, K.G. and PATON, N.W., *Object-oriented Databases*
HAYES, I. (ed.), *Specification Case Studies* (2nd edn)
HEHNER, E.C.R., *The Logic of Programming*
HINCHEY, M.G. and BOWEN, J.P., *Applications of Formal Methods*
HOARE, C.A.R., *Communicating Sequential Processes*
HOARE, C.A.R. and GORDON, M.J.C. (eds), *Mechanized Reasoning and Hardware Design*
HOARE, C.A.R. and JONES, C.B. (eds), *Essays in Computing Science*
HOARE, C.A.R. and SHEPHERDSON, J.C. (eds), *Mechanical Logic and Programming Languages*
HUGHES, J.G., *Database Technology: A software engineering approach*
HUGHES, J.G., *Object-oriented Databases*
INMOS LTD, *Occam 2 Reference manual*
JACKSON, M.A., *System Development*
JONES, C.B., *Systematic Software Development Using VDM* (2nd edn)
JONES, C.B. and SHAW, R.C.F. (eds), *Case Studies in Systematic Software Development*
JONES, G., *Programming in Occam*
JONES, G. and GOLDSMITH, M., *Programming in Occam 2*
JONES, N.D., GOMARD, C.K. and SESTOFT, P., *Partial Evaluation and Automatic Program Generation*
JOSEPH, M., *Real-time Systems: Specification, verification and analysis*
JOSEPH, M., PRASAD, V.R. and NATARAJAN, N., *A Multiprocessor Operating System*
KALDEWAIJ, A., *Programming: The derivation of algorithms*
KING, P.J.B., *Computer and Communications Systems Performance Modelling*
LALEMENT, R., *Computation as Logic*
McCABE, F.G., *Logic and Objects*
McCABE, F.G., *High-level Programmer's Guide to the 68000*
MEYER, B., *Introduction to the Theory of Programming Languages*
MEYER, B., *Object-oriented Software Construction*
MILNER, R., *Communication and Currency*
MITCHELL, R., *Abstract Data Types and Modula 2*
MORGAN, C., *Programming from Specifications* (2nd edn)
OMONDI, A.R., *Computer Arithmetic Systems*
PATON, N., COOPER, R., WILLIAMS, H. and TRINDER, P., *Database Programming Languages*
PEYTON JONES, S.L., *The Implementation of Functional Programming Languages*

Series listing continues at back of book

Using Z
Specification, refinement, and proof

Jim Woodcock and Jim Davies

PRENTICE HALL
London New York Toronto Sydney Tokyo Singapore
Madrid Mexico City Munich

First published 1996 by
Prentice Hall Europe
Campus 400, Maylands Avenue
Hemel Hempstead
Hertfordshire, HP2 7EZ
A division of
Simon & Schuster International Group

Printed and bound in Great Britain by Redwood Books, Trowbridge, Wiltshire

Library of Congress Cataloging-in-Publication Data

Available from the publishers

British Library Cataloguing-in-Publication Data

A catalogue record for this book is available from the British Library

ISBN 0-13-948472-8

1 2 3 4 5 00 99 98 97 96

Contents

Foreword

Formal methods require a soundly based specification language. Until now the emphasis in the Z literature has been on the use of Z as a specification language. In this arena, use of Z is extensive and has been fostered by its many positive aspects, including the importance that has been placed on the careful merging of text and formal material.

The construction of a clear specification is the cornerstone of any formal development and—as the authors of the current book make clear—sometimes there is little incentive to go further with formalism than to provide such a specification.

But formal methods should also include a precise notion of correctness: a formal method should pin down exactly what it means for a design to satisfy a specification and provide tractable proof obligations for use in a development which requires formal justification. This book addresses notions of development based on Z specifications.

The authors' emphasis on proof should be applauded. Although sometimes seen as a difficult undertaking, formal proofs are justified for systems on which major reliance is to be placed. There are also strong reasons for understanding notions of proof even where their use in full formality is not anticipated.

Pedagogically, experience with proof is the best route to a thorough understanding of many of the logical and data operators in a specification language. Furthermore, attempting even outline proofs about specifications and designs will inculcate good taste in the construction of specifications.

For practical purposes, perhaps the most important reason for studying proof notions is that proof obligations can be used as mental checks during reviews or inspections of stages of design even where formal proofs are not presented. It is important to remember that errors made early in the development process are extremely expensive to correct if detected late. One of the key messages then is that proof investment in the early development phases of a project can pay a dividend in terms of productivity.

I therefore find myself in full agreement with the authors of this book when they tackle the issue of data refinement proofs before methods of refining to executable code. If one intends to use proofs only on some aspects of a project, it is the early decisions on data representation which will repay the investment most clearly.

In addition to set and logic notation, Z offers a 'schema notation' whose use gives rise to some delicate issues (calculation of pre-conditions etc.) in working out an appropriate development method for Z. The reader of this book is in the hands of experts who carefully motivate their refinement rules and tackle the question of why they are correct. The authors' depth of experience is also clear from the warnings throughout the text of potential pitfalls of which the reader should be aware.

To derive maximum benefit from this book the reader should be prepared to study the material in detail. This is made easier by the careful progression of ideas and the well-chosen examples. The reader should also follow the larger case studies towards the end of the book. Such an investment will be handsomely repaid by a thorough understanding of a development method from Z specifications to code.

Cliff B Jones

Using this Book

This book contains enough material for three courses of study: a course on mathematics for software engineering, a course on formal specification, and a course on refinement. This material can be adapted in a number of ways, to support other courses or as part of a programme of self-paced learning. To make the book easier to use, we have divided it into six parts:

Introduction Chapter 1 explains the use of formal methods, and introduces the Z notation. We discuss the importance of proof and explain what makes a good specification.

Logic Chapters 2 to 4 are an introduction to mathematical logic. We explain both propositional and predicate calculus, and introduce the concepts of equality and definite description.

Relations Chapters 5 to 10 cover sets and relations. We show how to specify objects, and relationships between them, using pieces of mathematics. We show also how the mathematical logic of Chapters 2 to 4 can be used to reason about specifications.

Schemas Chapters 11 to 14 introduce the schema language. We explain how schemas can be used to structure a specification, using logical combinators, sequential composition, and promotion. We present techniques for checking for logical consistency.

Refinement Chapters 16 to 19 are concerned with refinement. We formulate a theory of refinement within the relational calculus, and extend it to cover specifications involving schemas. We then show how a concrete design may be refined to produce executable code.

Case Studies Chapter 15 and Chapters 20 to 23 contain case studies in specification and refinement. These case studies show how the Z notation can be used to produce an abstract specification, a concrete design, and a programming language implementation.

These parts can be combined to provide an appropriate introduction to using Z, whatever the background of the reader.

The material in the book has already been used in a number of taught courses, at both graduate and undergraduate levels. Examples include:

Full-time MSc in Computation (1 year)
Logic and Relations are taught as a core course; Schemas and Case Studies are taught as an optional course.

Part-time Postgraduate Diploma/MSc in Software Engineering (2 years)
Logic and Relations are taught as a single core course, Schemas as another core course, and Refinement as an optional course. Each course is delivered in a week of intensive teaching.

BA in Computer Science (3 years)
Logic and Relations are taught as part of a discrete mathematics course in the first year. Schemas are taught as part of a software engineering course in the second year.

Notice that, by omitting the development of each specification, Case Studies can be used in courses that do not cover Refinement.

Acknowledgments

This book is based upon our experience in teaching and using formal methods at the Programming Research Group, Oxford, and elsewhere. The courses that we teach draw their inspiration from the work of others: Jean-Raymond Abrial, Paul Gardiner, Ian Hayes, He Jifeng, Tony Hoare, Cliff Jones, Carroll Morgan, Jeff Sanders, Ib Holm Sørensen, Mike Spivey, and Bernard Sufrin.

We are grateful to many others for their help: John Axford, Rosalind Barden, Stephen Brien, Neil Brock, Tim Clement, David Cooper, Will Harwood, Jonathan Hoare, Fleur Howles, Roger Jones, Steve King, Peter Lupton, Andrew Martin, Colin O'Halloran, Steve Schneider, Roger Shaw, Jane Sinclair, Susan Stepney, Pete Verey, Geoff Winn, John Wordsworth, and Maureen York.

We are grateful also to the students who have attended our lectures over the years: at the Programming Research Group; at Royal Holloway, University of London; at the University of Reading; at the University of Klagenfurt; on industrial courses and summer schools in Europe, North America, and Africa. Their comments and suggestions are much appreciated.

The file system and save area case studies are based upon work carried out by Ian Hayes and Ib Sørensen; the better examples of simulation were suggested by Carroll Morgan and Paul Gardiner; the better examples of refinement owe much to the work of Cliff Jones. The diagrams in Chapter 1 were supplied by the London Transport Museum.

Jackie Harbor, Helen Martin, and Derek Moseley of Prentice Hall were professional but sympathetic at every turn. The last two years would have been less enjoyable if it had not been for their good humour, gentle tolerance, and quiet efficiency.

We would also like to thank our families, without whose love and support this book could not have been completed. This book is dedicated to them.

We would like to acknowledge the significant contribution made by the following institutions and organisations to the development of the material presented in this book:

- BNR Europe;
- British Telecom;
- Defence Research Agency, Malvern;
- Department of Computer Science, Reading;
- Department of Continuing Education, Oxford;
- Engineering and Physical Sciences Research Council;
- Formal Systems (Europe) Ltd;
- IBM UK Laboratories;
- Kellogg College, Oxford;
- Logica Cambridge;
- Pembroke College, Oxford;
- Programming Research Group, Oxford;
- Rutherford-Appleton Laboratory.

Thank you.

Chapter 1

Introduction

Today's software comes with extensive documentation: user guides, reference manuals, and design documents. There are on-line help systems, interactive tutorials, and friendly 'introductions for dummies'. Yet the behaviour of software is often a surprise to users and designers alike. Components interact and interfere, undesirable properties emerge, and systems fail to meet their requirements.

The more spectacular consequences make the headlines: aircraft have crashed, trains have collided, people have received fatal doses of radiation, and emergency telephone services have been withdrawn. The less spectacular we face every day: time is wasted, effort is expended to no avail, important projects are scrapped, and our health is damaged by sheer frustration. All of this, and more, because software fails to live up to our expectations.

There are many explanations for this: the requirements upon a piece of software are hard to define, the ways in which a system may be used are hard to anticipate, and there is always a demand for additional functionality. Indeed, the fact that many pieces of software actually work, and work well, is some indication of the skill of those whose job it is to develop them.

1.1 Formal methods

One way to improve the quality of software is to change the way in which software is documented: at the design stage, during development, and after release. Existing methods of documentation offer large amounts of text, pictures, and diagrams, but these are often imprecise and ambiguous. Important information is hidden amongst irrelevant detail, and design flaws are discovered too late, making them expensive or impossible to correct.

There is an alternative. *Formal* methods, based upon elementary mathematics, can be used to produce precise, unambiguous documentation, in which information is structured and presented at an appropriate level of abstraction. This documentation can be used to support the design process, and as a guide to subsequent development, testing, and maintenance.

It seems likely that the use of formal methods will become standard practice in software engineering. The mathematical basis is different from that of civil or mechanical engineering, but it has the same purpose: to add precision, to aid understanding, and to reason about properties of a design. Whatever the discipline, the use of mathematics can be expensive, but it is our experience that it can actually reduce costs.

Existing applications of formal methods include: the use of probability theory in performance modelling; the use of context-free grammars in compiler design; the use of the relational calculus in database theory. The formal method described in this book has been used in the specification and design of large software systems. It is intended for the description of state and state-based properties, and includes a theory of refinement that allows mathematics to be used at every stage of program development.

1.2 The CICS experience

CICS is one of the most successful pieces of software in the world: there are over 30 000 licences, and most of the world's top companies use it. CICS stands for Customer Information Control System, a family of transaction processing products produced by IBM UK Laboratories at Hursley Park. CICS provides data access, communications, integrity, and security services. Put simply, CICS manages information.

When we use an automated teller machine in San Francisco, an account at our local branch in Oxford is debited, even though the machine is thousands of miles away. During the busiest times, there may be many thousands of customers of the bank using the service all over the world, and we all expect to be served within a reasonable time. CICS offers a way of achieving this.

There have been regular releases of CICS since the mid-1970s. Each release has introduced additional features and extended the structure of the existing code. In the early 1980s, the complexity of the system started to become a serious problem for the company. A decision was made to re-design some of the CICS modules with the aim of making extensions easier. An important part of the proposed solution involved finding a more precise way to specify functionality.

Such precision requires the use of mathematical techniques that were, at that time, little known outside academia. A happy coincidence brought the CICS manager, Tony Kenny, and the Oxford professor, Tony Hoare, together at a conference. They hatched a plan to apply Oxford's ideas to Hursley's problems. Oxford advised on how formal methods could be used for the specification and design of new CICS modules. Hursley showed how the methods could be adapted to problems on an industrial scale.

A particular formal method, the *Z notation*, was used to specify the new CICS functionality. Hursley's programmers were used to writing specifications in English, and the rigorous, mathematical notation was seen as a challenge. In practice, the notation proved easy to learn and to apply, even for programmers with no previous experience of mathematics. The result was a perceived improvement in the quality and reliability of delivered code.

The first CICS product to be designed using Z was CICS/ESA version 3, announced in June 1989. In April 1992, the Queen's Award for Technological Achievement was conferred upon IBM United Kingdom Laboratories Limited and Oxford University Computing Laboratory for 'the development and use of an advanced programming method that reduces development costs and significantly enhances quality and reliability': namely, Z.

1.3 The Z notation

The Z notation is based upon set theory and mathematical logic. The set theory used includes standard set operators, set comprehensions, Cartesian products, and power sets. The mathematical logic is a first-order predicate calculus. Together, they make up a mathematical language that is easy to learn and to apply. However, this language is only one aspect of Z.

Another aspect is the way in which the mathematics can be structured. Mathematical objects and their properties can be collected together in *schemas*: patterns of declaration and constraint. The schema language can be used to describe the state of a system, and the ways in which that state may change. It can also be used to describe system properties, and to reason about possible *refinements* of a design.

A characteristic feature of Z is the use of *types*. Every object in the mathematical language has a unique type, represented as a maximal set in the current specification. As well as providing a useful link to programming practice, this notion of types means that an algorithm can be written to check the type of every object in a specification; several type-checking tools exist to support the practical use of Z.

A third aspect is the use of natural language. We use mathematics to state the problem, to discover solutions, and to prove that the chosen design meets the specification. We use natural language to relate the mathematics to objects in the real world; this job is often partly achieved by the judicious naming of variables, but additional commentary is vital. A well-written specification should be *perfectly obvious* to the reader.

A fourth aspect is refinement. We may develop a system by constructing a model of a design, using simple mathematical data types to identify the desired behaviour. We may then *refine* this description by constructing another model which respects the design decisions made, and yet is closer to implementation. Where appropriate, this process of refinement can be continued until executable code is produced.

The Z notation, then, is a mathematical language with a powerful structuring mechanism. In combination with natural language, it can be used to produce formal specifications. We may reason about these specifications using the proof techniques of mathematical logic. We may also refine a specification, yielding another description that is closer to executable code.

Z is not intended for the description of non-functional properties, such as usability, performance, size, and reliability. Neither is it intended for the description of timed or concurrent behaviour. However, there are other formal methods that are well suited for these purposes. We may use these methods in combination with Z to relate state and state-change information to complementary aspects of design.

1.4 The importance of proof

In this book, we place considerable emphasis upon proof. When we introduce the language of mathematical logic, we explain the use of a proof system. When we introduce the language of sets and relations, we explain how formal proofs may be constructed about such objects. When we introduce the language of schemas, we show how to prove that a specification is consistent, and how to prove that one specification refines another. Our intentions are two-fold: first, to show that proof adds quality to software development; second, to show that proof is a feasible part of the industrial use of formal methods.

If we reason about a specification, if we attempt to construct proofs about its properties, then we are more likely to detect problems at an early stage of system development. The process of constructing proofs can help us to understand the requirements upon a system, and can assist us in identifying any hidden assumptions. Proof at the specification stage can make a significant contribution to the quality of software.

At the design stage, a proof can show us not only that a design is correct, but also *why* it is correct. The additional insight that this affords can be invaluable: as requirements evolve and the design is modified, the consequences are easier to investigate. At the implementation stage, a proof can help us to ensure that a piece of code behaves according to the specification. Again, a significant contribution to quality can be made.

The construction of proofs is an essential part of writing a specification, just as proof-reading is an essential part of writing a book. A specification without proofs is untested: it may be inconsistent; it may describe properties that were not intended, or omit those that were; it may make inappropriate assumptions. The practice of proof makes for better specifications.

It seems to be part of software engineering folklore that proof is impossible on an industrial scale; however, our experience has been different. We have been involved in many large-scale applications of formal methods; some involved proof, others did not. We have seen that techniques involving proof are successful where formal methods are used with a light touch, and where proofs are conducted at an appropriate level of formality.

In many situations, a rigorous argument, or a semi-formal justification, will be sufficient to bring about the desired improvement in quality. In other, more critical situations, it may be necessary to increase the level of formality until the correctness of the design is beyond doubt. In some situations, a completely formal proof may be required. The trick of using formal methods effectively is to know when proofs are worth doing and when they are not.

1.5 Abstraction

An essential property of a good specification is an appropriate choice of abstraction. A good example of this is provided by the various maps of the London Underground. When the first map was published in 1908, it was faithful to the geography of the lines: all the twists and turns of the tracks and the relative distances between stations were recorded faithfully and to scale. However, the purpose of the map was to show travellers the order of stations on each line, and the various interchanges between lines; the fidelity of the map made it difficult to extract this information.

In 1933, the map was changed to a more abstract representation, called the Diagram. Here, the connectivity of stations on the network was preserved, and at last, passengers could see at a glance the route to their destination. Abstraction from superfluous detail—in this case the physical layout of the lines—was the key to the usefulness of the Diagram. Figures 1.1 and 1.2 show published versions before and after the change.

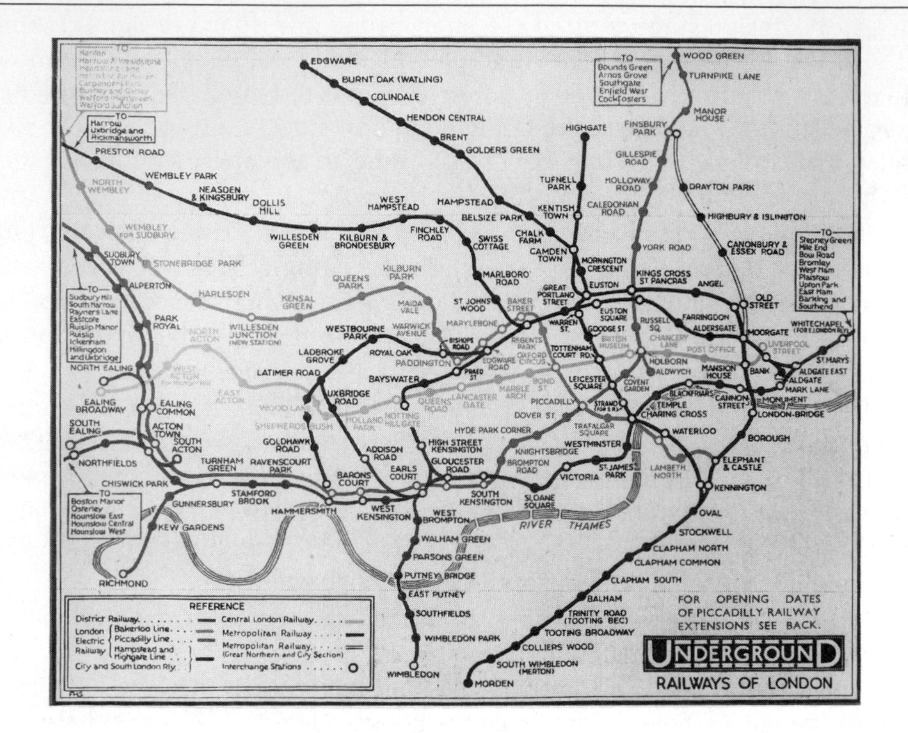

Figure 1.1: A faithful geographical representation

The Diagram was, and still is, a good specification of the London Underground network. It is

- *Abstract.* Since it records only the logical layout, not the physical reality in all its detail.
- *Concise.* Since it is printed on a single A5 sheet of card that is folded twice so that it fits into the pocket.
- *Complete.* Since every station on the London Underground network is represented.
- *Unambiguous.* Since the meaning of the symbols used is explained, and the Diagram is expressed in simple geometrical terms. It is a precise and accurate description of the Underground network.
- *Maintainable.* Since it has been successfully maintained over the last 60 years, reflecting the changes in the network as stations have opened and closed, and new lines have been added.

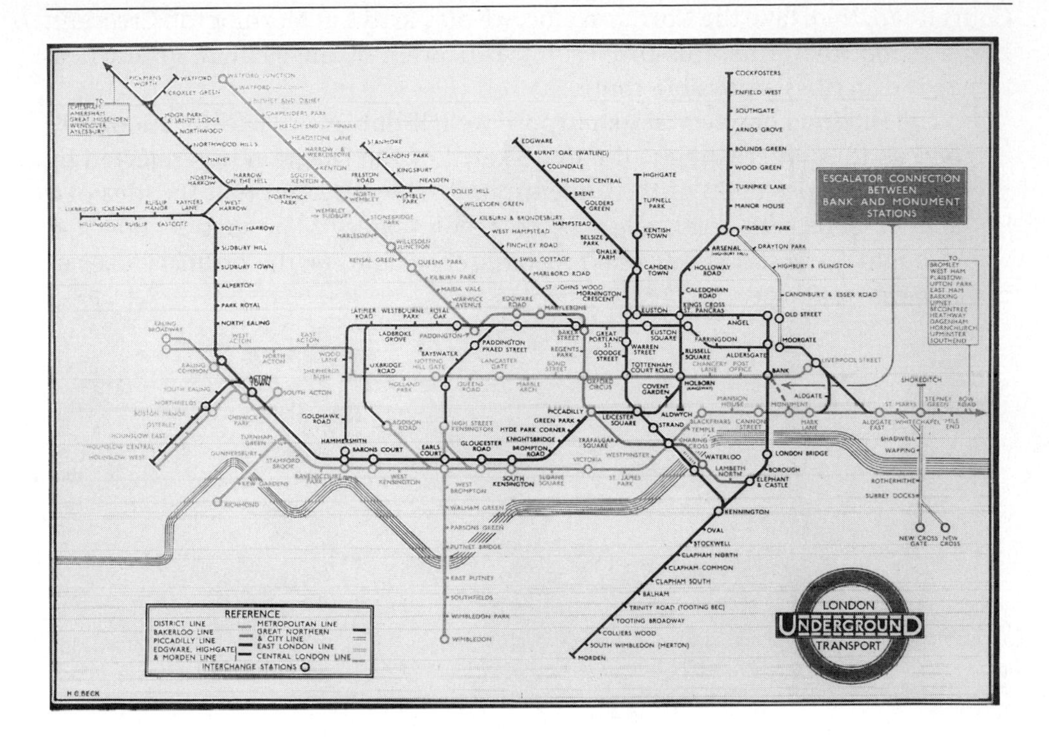

Figure 1.2: A more abstract description

- *Comprehensible.* Since it has been regarded fondly by its users from its first issue in January 1933, the Diagram must be readily understood by the general public.
- *Cost-effective.* Since it cost only five guineas to commission the specification from the engineering draughtsman Harry Beck.

The Diagram gives its users a good conceptual model; it is how Londoners and visitors see the Underground network. It embodies a specification structure that enables users to make sense out of a rather complex implementation. To do this, it uses abstract shapes, colours, and compression. All lines have been reduced to 90° or 45° angles. The various lines are coloured differently. The central area, where there are more stations, is shown in greater detail than the outlying parts, as if the Diagram were being viewed through a convex lens.

Furthermore, the Diagram may be used to predict the result of travelling on the Underground network. We might observe that if we start at Oxford Circus, travel eastbound on the Central Line and change trains at Tottenham

Court Road, then take the Northern Line, we may arrive at Mornington Crescent. In mathematical terms, this property is a theorem of the system; in practical terms, it describes a possible route.

The Diagram has served its purpose well; if only every specification were as good as this. Interestingly, the first sketch of the Diagram was rejected by the Publicity Department of the Underground. They thought that the idea of a 90° and 45° schematic treatment was too 'revolutionary'. The abstract notation was thought to be too strange and incomprehensible for the ordinary user of the Underground network.

Chapter 2

Propositional Logic

In this chapter we introduce a logical language based upon traditional propositional calculus. This language is part of the logical language of Z; other parts appear in subsequent chapters. Our presentation is based upon inference and proof: each component of the language is presented alongside rules that explain when it may be introduced or eliminated.

Collected together, these rules form a system of natural deduction: they state what may be deduced from a proposition, and under what conditions that proposition may be concluded. This provides a framework for reasoning about statements in our language, proving properties and establishing results.

2.1 Propositional logic

Propositional logic deals with the statement of alleged facts which must be either true or false, but not both.

Example 2.1 The following statements are propositions:

- A tomato is a fruit.
- An orange is a fruit.
- Oranges are not the only fruit.

□

In our logical language, propositions may be connected in various ways. The following table describes five propositional connectives, arranged in descending order of operator precedence:

$\neg$	negation	*not*
$\wedge$	conjunction	*and*
$\vee$	disjunction	*or*
$\Rightarrow$	implication	*implies*
$\Leftrightarrow$	equivalence	*if and only if*

The table gives the connective's symbol, its name, and how it is pronounced. Using the notion of precedence, we can see that the proposition

$$\neg p \wedge q \vee r \Leftrightarrow q \Rightarrow p \wedge r$$

is equivalent to the parenthesised version

$$(((\neg p) \wedge q) \vee r) \Leftrightarrow (q \Rightarrow (p \wedge r))$$

Using these connectives, we can build up *compound propositions.*

Example 2.2

- $\neg$(jaffa cakes are biscuits)
- your cat is rich $\wedge$ your dog is good looking
- the economic recovery has started $\vee$ the minister is lying
- Jim is thirty-something $\Rightarrow$ Jim is under forty
- Jim is thirty-something $\Leftrightarrow$ Jim is under forty

□

The truth of a compound proposition is uniquely determined by the truth of its constituent parts.

2.2 Conjunction

In the semantics of Z, a formal meaning is given to propositions; we don't propose to reproduce this here, but rather to give an informal understanding. For example, the conjunction $p \wedge q$ is true exactly when p is true and q is true. In case the reader thinks that this might be a sleight of hand—defining $\wedge$ in terms of 'and'—we can explain it by using a truth table:

p	q	$p \wedge q$
t	t	t
t	f	f
f	t	f
f	f	f

In the first column we describe all the situations that we are interested in: all the combinations of the possible truth values of p and q (abbreviating truth and falsity to t and f). In the second we have written down the truth value of $p \wedge q$ in each of these situations. Thus, $p \wedge q$ is true just in the case that p is true and q is true.

Now, suppose that we wanted to prove that $p \wedge q$ is true: the truth table tells us when that is so. If we follow the row that has the entry t for $p \wedge q$, we see that we must prove that both p and q are true (have the entry t). Thus, to prove $p \wedge q$, we must prove both p and also q. Now, suppose that we know that $p \wedge q$ is true, then we certainly know that p must be true; we also know that q must be true. We can summarise these observations with the following rules of inference:

$$\frac{p \quad q}{p \wedge q}\ [\wedge\text{-intro}] \qquad \frac{p \wedge q}{p}\ [\wedge\text{-elim1}] \qquad \frac{p \wedge q}{q}\ [\wedge\text{-elim2}]$$

These inference rules form part of the natural deduction system that we use to conduct our proofs.

Each inference rule is written in the following form:

$$\frac{premiss_1 \quad \ldots \quad premiss_n}{conclusion}\ [\text{name}] \qquad side\ condition$$

The list of premisses is sometimes empty; the role of the side condition will become clear later. The meaning of such a rule is that the truth of the conclusion follows from the truth of the premisses: whenever the premisses are true, then so is the conclusion.

The rules come in two flavours. For an operator *op*, the *op*-elimination rule describes what may be deduced from $p\ op\ q$; and the *op*-introduction rule describes under what conditions $p\ op\ q$ can be concluded. Using these rules to introduce and eliminate different operators, we can start from a set of propositions, or hypotheses, and derive another proposition. If the set of hypotheses is empty, then we call the derived proposition a theorem.

We now have two ways of proving things about a proposition. Consider the conjecture that conjunction is commutative. This means that it doesn't matter which way round we present the operands to the conjunction operator: $p \land q$ is the same as $q \land p$. We prove this first by constructing a truth table, and second by using the rules that we have for introducing and eliminating the conjunction operator.

Example 2.3 First, consider the two truth tables:

p	q	$p \land q$
t	t	t
t	f	f
f	t	f
f	f	f

q	p	$q \land p$
t	t	t
f	t	f
t	f	f
f	f	f

We can abbreviate the two tables by displaying them in one:

p	q	$p \land q$	$q \land p$
t	t	t	t
t	f	f	f
f	t	f	f
f	f	f	f

Notice that the columns for $p \land q$ and $q \land p$ are identical: in every situation they take the same truth value; thus, we can conclude that they are the same proposition, and so conjunction is commutative. □

Now, we shall prove that conjunction is commutative by using a natural deduction argument.

Example 2.4 We want to prove that $p \land q$ is equivalent to $q \land p$, and this may be deduced from the rule:

$$\frac{p \land q}{q \land p}$$

We prove this *derived rule* by exhibiting a proof tree, built from rules fitted together jigsaw-wise. The leaves (at the top of the tree) are instances of the premisses, and the root (at the bottom of the tree) is the conclusion.

$$\dfrac{\dfrac{p \land q}{q}\,[\land\text{-elim2}] \qquad \dfrac{p \land q}{p}\,[\land\text{-elim1}]}{q \land p}\,[\land\text{-intro}]$$

In this tree, there are three rules which have been used. Where the conclusion of one rule forms the premiss of the next, they match exactly. The tree matches the rule that we were trying to prove, since, if we take all the leaves and remove duplicates, we end up with the premiss of the rule; the root of the tree corresponds to the conclusion. □

One more piece of terminology and its notation. Some premisses are introduced during a proof: they are called *assumptions*. An assumption must be discharged during a proof, and there are certain rules (*discharge rules*) which do this. The assumption p is denoted by $\lceil p \rceil^{[]}$. In the next section we see examples of assumptions and discharge rules.

2.3 Disjunction

The disjunction $p \lor q$ is true if and only if p is true or q is true:

p	q	$p \lor q$
t	t	t
t	f	t
f	t	t
f	f	f

This is *inclusive* or: the disjunction is true in any situation in which one of the disjuncts is true, *including* the situation in which both are true. The disjunction $p \lor q$ is true if and only if either p is true or q is true. Our three rules are:

$$\frac{p}{p \lor q}\ [\lor\text{-intro1}] \qquad \frac{q}{p \lor q}\ [\lor\text{-intro2}] \qquad \frac{p \lor q \quad \begin{matrix} \lceil p \rceil^{[i]} \\ r \end{matrix} \quad \begin{matrix} \lceil q \rceil^{[i]} \\ r \end{matrix}}{r}\ [\lor\text{-elim}]^{[i]}$$

Both introduction rules hold because, if p is true, then $p \lor q$ is true; similarly for q. The elimination rule follows by supposing that $p \lor q$ is true; then, either p or q holds (we don't know which, and it might be both). Whatever follows from this (say r) must follow in both cases. Thus, the elimination rule is an example of case analysis. In the premiss

$$\begin{matrix} \lceil p \rceil^{[i]} \\ r \end{matrix}$$

the notation $\lceil p \rceil^{[i]}$ indicates that p is an assumption which may be made in order to prove r. The superscript i indicates that this assumption is justified by a step labelled i in the proof tree. It is discharged from the proof of r when the rule is applied: given a proof of $p \lor q$, a proof of r from the assumption p, and a proof of r from the assumption q, the rule concludes r.

Example 2.5 Disjunction is commutative:

p	q	$p \lor q$	$q \lor p$
t	t	t	t
t	f	t	t
f	t	t	t
f	f	f	f

The entries for $p \lor q$ and $q \lor p$ are identical. □

Example 2.6 Disjunction is commutative:

$$\frac{p \lor q}{q \lor p}$$

$$\dfrac{p \lor q \qquad \dfrac{[p]^{[1]}}{q \lor p}\;[\lor\text{-intro2}] \qquad \dfrac{[q]^{[1]}}{q \lor p}\;[\lor\text{-intro1}]}{q \lor p}\;[\lor\text{-elim}]^{[1]}$$

□

2.4 Implication

The implication $p \Rightarrow q$ may be viewed as expressing an *ordering* between the antecedent p and the consequent q: it states that the antecedent is *stronger* than (or equal to) the consequent. False is stronger than true; true is weaker than false; anything is as strong as itself. This gives the truth table

p	q	$p \Rightarrow q$
t	t	t
t	f	f
f	t	t
f	f	t

Thus, the implication is true unless the antecedent is true and the consequent is false.

The implication $p \Rightarrow q$ is true if and only if we can prove q by assuming p. Thus, in order to prove that $p \Rightarrow q$, we may assume that p is true and then prove that q is true also. If we know that $p \Rightarrow q$, then we can conclude that q is true, providing that we show that the assumption p holds. This gives us the two rules for implication:

$$\frac{\begin{array}{c}\lceil p \rceil^{[i]} \\ q\end{array}}{p \Rightarrow q}\;[\Rightarrow\text{-intro}]^{[i]} \qquad \frac{p \Rightarrow q \quad p}{q}\;[\Rightarrow\text{-elim}]$$

Example 2.7 We can replace a conjunction of antecedents in an implication by separate antecedents:

$$(p \land q \Rightarrow r) \Rightarrow (p \Rightarrow (q \Rightarrow r))$$

We may prove this by constructing a truth table:

p	q	r	$(p \land q \Rightarrow r)$		$\Rightarrow$	$(p \Rightarrow$	$(q \Rightarrow r))$
t	t	t	t	t	t	t	t
t	t	f	t	f	t	f	f
t	f	t	f	t	t	t	t
t	f	f	f	t	t	t	t
f	t	t	f	t	t	t	t
f	t	f	f	t	t	t	f
f	f	t	f	t	t	t	t
f	f	f	f	t	t	t	t

Every entry in the column underneath the major connective in the proposition is a t: thus the proposition is true in every situation. □

Example 2.8 We can replace a conjunction of antecedents in an implication by separate antecedents:

$$(p \land q \Rightarrow r) \Rightarrow (p \Rightarrow (q \Rightarrow r))$$

To see how this might be established, consider the incomplete proof tree:

$$\frac{\vdots}{(p \land q \Rightarrow r) \Rightarrow (p \Rightarrow (q \Rightarrow r))}$$

The major connective is an implication; we could consider how it got there, and try to introduce it:

$$\dfrac{\dfrac{\begin{array}{c}[p \wedge q \Rightarrow r]^{[1]}\\ \vdots\end{array}}{(p \Rightarrow (q \Rightarrow r))}}{(p \wedge q \Rightarrow r) \Rightarrow (p \Rightarrow (q \Rightarrow r))}\;[\Rightarrow\text{-intro}]^{[1]}$$

This leaves us with a new goal, $p \Rightarrow (q \Rightarrow r)$, in which the major connective is again an implication. We follow the same procedure as before; we consider how this operator may be introduced:

$$\dfrac{\dfrac{\dfrac{\begin{array}{c}[p \wedge q \Rightarrow r]^{[1]}\\ [p]^{[2]}\\ \vdots\end{array}}{q \Rightarrow r}}{(p \Rightarrow (q \Rightarrow r))}\;[\Rightarrow\text{-intro}]^{[2]}}{(p \wedge q \Rightarrow r) \Rightarrow (p \Rightarrow (q \Rightarrow r))}\;[\Rightarrow\text{-intro}]^{[1]}$$

Again the goal is an implication. Using the introduction rule a third time leaves us in the following situation:

$$\dfrac{\dfrac{\dfrac{\dfrac{\begin{array}{c}[p \wedge q \Rightarrow r]^{[1]}\\ [p]^{[2]}\\ [q]^{[3]}\\ \vdots\end{array}}{r}}{q \Rightarrow r}\;[\Rightarrow\text{-intro}]^{[3]}}{(p \Rightarrow (q \Rightarrow r))}\;[\Rightarrow\text{-intro}]^{[2]}}{(p \wedge q \Rightarrow r) \Rightarrow (p \Rightarrow (q \Rightarrow r))}\;[\Rightarrow\text{-intro}]^{[1]}$$

At this stage, the structure of the goal suggests nothing: there is no structure. Now is the time to start working forwards from the assumptions: one of them has an implication, so we should try to eliminate that:

$$\dfrac{\dfrac{\dfrac{\dfrac{\lceil p \land q \Rightarrow r \rceil^{[1]} \qquad \dfrac{\begin{matrix}\lceil p \land q \Rightarrow r \rceil^{[1]} \\ \lceil p \rceil^{[2]} \\ \lceil q \rceil^{[3]} \\ \vdots \end{matrix}}{p \land q}}{r}\,[\Rightarrow\text{-elim}]}{q \Rightarrow r}\,[\Rightarrow\text{-intro}]^{[3]}}{(p \Rightarrow (q \Rightarrow r))}\,[\Rightarrow\text{-intro}]^{[2]}}{(p \land q \Rightarrow r) \Rightarrow (p \Rightarrow (q \Rightarrow r))}\,[\Rightarrow\text{-intro}]^{[1]}$$

It is clear now how to finish this proof: the assumptions p and q can be conjoined to discharge the conjunction $p \land q$:

$$\dfrac{\dfrac{\dfrac{\dfrac{\lceil p \land q \Rightarrow r \rceil^{[1]} \qquad \dfrac{\lceil p \rceil^{[2]} \quad \lceil q \rceil^{[3]}}{p \land q}\,[\land\text{-intro}]}{r}\,[\Rightarrow\text{-elim}]}{q \Rightarrow r}\,[\Rightarrow\text{-intro}]^{[3]}}{(p \Rightarrow (q \Rightarrow r))}\,[\Rightarrow\text{-intro}]^{[2]}}{(p \land q \Rightarrow r) \Rightarrow (p \Rightarrow (q \Rightarrow r))}\,[\Rightarrow\text{-intro}]^{[1]}$$

□

2.5 Equivalence

The equivalence $p \Leftrightarrow q$ means that p and q are of the same strength; thus it might also be called bi-implication: $p \Leftrightarrow q$ means that both $p \Rightarrow q$ and $q \Rightarrow p$. Since p and q have the same strength, they must therefore have the same entries in the truth table:

p	q	$p \Leftrightarrow q$
t	t	t
t	f	f
f	t	f
f	f	t

The rules for introducing and eliminating the equivalence connective follow from the observation that $p \Leftrightarrow q$ is equivalent to $p \Rightarrow q$ and $q \Rightarrow p$ (they are reminiscent of the rules for conjunction).

$$\frac{p \Rightarrow q \quad q \Rightarrow p}{p \Leftrightarrow q}\ [\Leftrightarrow\text{-intro}] \qquad \frac{p \Leftrightarrow q}{p \Rightarrow q}\ [\Leftrightarrow\text{-elim1}] \qquad \frac{p \Leftrightarrow q}{q \Rightarrow p}\ [\Leftrightarrow\text{-elim2}]$$

Example 2.9 If p is stronger than q, then $p \wedge q$ and p have the same strength:

$$\frac{p \Rightarrow q}{p \wedge q \Leftrightarrow p}$$

To show that this is a derived rule of our system, consider the goal

$$\frac{\vdots}{p \wedge q \Leftrightarrow p}$$

The major connective is the equivalence, so let's try to introduce it:

$$\frac{\dfrac{\vdots}{p \wedge q \Rightarrow p} \quad \dfrac{\vdots}{p \Rightarrow p \wedge q}}{p \wedge q \Leftrightarrow p}\ [\Leftrightarrow\text{-intro}]$$

In the left-hand subtree, the major connective is now an implication, so let's try to introduce that:

$$\frac{\dfrac{\dfrac{\begin{array}{c}[p \wedge q]^{[1]} \\ \vdots\end{array}}{p}}{p \wedge q \Rightarrow p}\ [\Rightarrow\text{-intro}]^{[1]} \quad \dfrac{\vdots}{p \Rightarrow p \wedge q}\ [\Rightarrow\text{-intro}]}{p \wedge q \Leftrightarrow p}\ [\Leftrightarrow\text{-intro}]$$

The left-hand subtree may now be completed by conjunction elimination on the assumption. Turning now to the right-hand subtree, we should immediately introduce the implication:

$$\frac{\dfrac{\dfrac{[p \wedge q]^{[1]}}{p}\ [\wedge\text{-elim1}]}{p \wedge q \Rightarrow p}\ [\Rightarrow\text{-intro}]^{[1]} \quad \dfrac{\dfrac{\begin{array}{c}[p]^{[2]} \\ \vdots\end{array}}{p \wedge q}}{p \Rightarrow p \wedge q}\ [\Rightarrow\text{-intro}]^{[2]}}{p \wedge q \Leftrightarrow p}\ [\Leftrightarrow\text{-intro}]$$

Now, the major connective is a conjunction, so we introduce it:

$$\dfrac{\dfrac{\dfrac{[p \land q]^{[1]}}{p}\,[\land\text{-elim1}]}{p \land q \Rightarrow p}\,[\Rightarrow\text{-intro}]^{[1]} \qquad \dfrac{\dfrac{\dfrac{\begin{array}{c}[p]^{[2]}\\ \vdots\end{array}}{p} \quad \dfrac{\begin{array}{c}[p]^{[2]}\\ \vdots\end{array}}{q}}{p \land q}\,[\land\text{-intro}]}{p \Rightarrow p \land q}\,[\Rightarrow\text{-intro}]^{[2]}}{p \land q \Leftrightarrow p}\,[\Leftrightarrow\text{-intro}]$$

The left-most unfinished subtree can be closed easily, since we have to prove p from the assumption p: that is immediate. The right-most one cannot be pushed further backwards, since there is no structure to exploit; instead, we work from our premiss:

$$\dfrac{\dfrac{\dfrac{[p \land q]^{[1]}}{p}\,[\land\text{-elim1}]}{p \land q \Rightarrow p}\,[\Rightarrow\text{-intro}]^{[1]} \qquad \dfrac{\dfrac{[p]^{[2]} \quad \dfrac{p \Rightarrow q \quad \dfrac{\begin{array}{c}[p]^{[2]}\\ \vdots\end{array}}{p}}{q}\,[\Rightarrow\text{-elim}]}{p \land q}\,[\land\text{-intro}]}{p \Rightarrow p \land q}\,[\Rightarrow\text{-intro}]^{[2]}}{p \land q \Leftrightarrow p}\,[\Leftrightarrow\text{-intro}]$$

Again, the closing of this subtree is trivial, thus completing the proof:

$$\dfrac{\dfrac{\dfrac{[p \land q]^{[1]}}{p}\,[\land\text{-elim1}]}{p \land q \Rightarrow p}\,[\Rightarrow\text{-intro}]^{[1]} \qquad \dfrac{\dfrac{[p]^{[2]} \quad \dfrac{p \Rightarrow q \quad [p]^{[2]}}{q}\,[\Rightarrow\text{-elim}]}{p \land q}\,[\land\text{-intro}]}{p \Rightarrow p \land q}\,[\Rightarrow\text{-intro}]^{[2]}}{p \land q \Leftrightarrow p}\,[\Leftrightarrow\text{-intro}]$$

□

A derived rule may be used in the same way as any other inference rule; the above example gives us

$$\dfrac{p \Rightarrow q}{p \land q \Leftrightarrow p}\,[\text{subsume}]$$

This is just one of several similar inference rules involving conjunction, disjunction, and implication.

2.6 Negation

The negation $\neg p$ is true if and only if p is false. The truth table is simple:

p	$\neg p$
t	f
f	t

Our rules for negation make use of a special proposition called *false*, which stands for a contradiction: it is false in every situation. If $\neg p$ is true, then p is false; and if p is true, then $\neg p$ is false. Notice that it is not possible for $\neg p$ and p both to be true. This gives us three rules:

$$\frac{\begin{array}{c}\lceil p \rceil^{[i]} \\ \textit{false}\end{array}}{\neg p}\ [\neg\text{-intro}]^{[i]} \qquad \frac{p \quad \neg p}{\textit{false}}\ [\neg\text{-elim}] \qquad \frac{\begin{array}{c}\lceil \neg p \rceil^{[j]} \\ \textit{false}\end{array}}{p}\ [\text{false-elim}]^{[j]}$$

Our system requires three rules to deal with negation. At first sight, it might seem that the two rules that we have called [¬−intro] and [false−elim] would be sufficient, but they would give us no way of concluding *false*.

Example 2.10 One of de Morgan's Laws states that the negation of a disjunction is the conjunction of negations:

$$\frac{\neg(p \lor q)}{\neg p \land \neg q}\ [\text{de Morgan1}]$$

We start by considering the goal:

$$\frac{\vdots}{\neg p \land \neg q}$$

Clearly, we should break up the conjunction:

$$\frac{\dfrac{\vdots}{\neg p} \quad \dfrac{\vdots}{\neg q}}{\neg p \land \neg q}\ [\land\text{-intro}]$$

Let's focus on the left subtree. In order to prove the negation $\neg p$, we should assume p and then force a contradiction:

$$\dfrac{\dfrac{\dfrac{\begin{array}{c}[p]^{[1]}\\ \vdots\end{array}}{\mathit{false}}\;[\neg\text{-elim}]}{\neg p}\;[\neg\text{-intro}]^{[1]} \qquad \dfrac{\vdots}{\neg q}}{\neg p \wedge \neg q}\;[\wedge\text{-intro}]$$

Now, what should the contradiction be? We have the premiss $\neg(p \vee q)$, we could try to contradict that:

$$\dfrac{\dfrac{\dfrac{\dfrac{\begin{array}{c}[p]^{[1]}\\ \vdots\end{array}}{p \vee q} \qquad \neg(p \vee q)}{\mathit{false}}\;[\neg\text{-elim}]}{\neg p}\;[\neg\text{-intro}]^{[1]} \qquad \dfrac{\vdots}{\neg q}}{\neg p \wedge \neg q}\;[\wedge\text{-intro}]$$

We can close this subtree by noting that we can prove $p \vee q$ from p:

$$\dfrac{\dfrac{\dfrac{\dfrac{[p]^{[1]}}{p \vee q}\;[\vee\text{-intro1}] \qquad \neg(p \vee q)}{\mathit{false}}\;[\neg\text{-elim}]}{\neg p}\;[\neg\text{-intro}]^{[1]} \qquad \dfrac{\vdots}{\neg q}}{\neg p \wedge \neg q}\;[\wedge\text{-intro}]$$

The rest of the proof follows by symmetry:

$$\dfrac{\dfrac{\dfrac{\dfrac{[p]^{[1]}}{p \vee q}\;[\vee\text{-intro2}] \qquad \neg(p \vee q)}{\mathit{false}}\;[\neg\text{-elim}]}{\neg p}\;[\neg\text{-intro}]^{[1]} \qquad \dfrac{\dfrac{\dfrac{[q]^{[2]}}{p \vee q}\;[\vee\text{-intro1}] \qquad \neg(p \vee q)}{\mathit{false}}\;[\neg\text{-elim}]}{\neg q}\;[\neg\text{-intro}]^{[2]}}{\neg p \wedge \neg q}\;[\wedge\text{-intro}]$$

□

Before a natural deduction system becomes really useful, it is necessary to prove results about negation. In the next theorem we use the variant of de Morgan's law that we have just proved.

Example 2.11 The Law of the Excluded Middle states that either a proposition is true or it is false. That is,

$$p \vee \neg p$$

The major connective is a disjunction, so let's try to introduce it. Which disjunct should we throw away? Let's try $\neg p$:

$$\dfrac{\dfrac{\vdots}{p}}{p \vee \neg p}\ [\vee\text{-intro1}]$$

Now there is no structure to analyse, so we are lost, since there are no assumptions or premisses either. We must admit defeat and backtrack to the last choice that we made. Perhaps we should have thrown away p instead:

$$\dfrac{\dfrac{\vdots}{\neg p}}{p \vee \neg p}\ [\vee\text{-intro2}]$$

Now we are in the same position: we still cannot complete the proof. Again, we must backtrack to the last decision point. This time, we go right back to the start of the proof. We have tried both varieties of disjunction introduction, and there are neither assumptions nor premisses to work from. What now? One possible way forward is to try to contradict our goal: assume $\neg(p \vee \neg p)$ and force a contradiction:

$$\dfrac{\dfrac{\lceil \neg(p \vee \neg p) \rceil^{[1]} \quad \vdots}{false}}{p \vee \neg p}\ [\text{false-elim}]^{[1]}$$

Our contradiction follows by Example 2.10:

$$\dfrac{\dfrac{\dfrac{\lceil \neg(p \vee \neg p) \rceil^{[1]}}{\neg p \wedge \neg\neg p}\ [\text{de Morgan1}] \quad \vdots}{false}\ [\neg\text{-elim}]}{p \vee \neg p}\ [\text{false-elim}]^{[1]}$$

The proof tree isn't quite closed, because of the technicality that we need two separate propositions: $\neg p$ and $\neg\neg p$. We can get each from the conjunction, so we need to duplicate our work from the assumption, and use both varieties of conjunction elimination:

$$\dfrac{\dfrac{\dfrac{[\neg(p \lor \neg p)]^{[1]}}{\neg p \land \neg\neg p}\text{[de Morgan1]}}{\neg p}[\land\text{-elim1}] \qquad \dfrac{\dfrac{[\neg(p \lor \neg p)]^{[1]}}{\neg p \land \neg\neg p}\text{[de Morgan1]}}{\neg\neg p}[\land\text{-elim2}]}{\dfrac{\mathit{false}}{p \lor \neg p}[\text{false-elim}]^{[1]}}[\neg\text{-elim}]$$

Now we have finished, and the proof tree is complete. □

The last example shows an important part of the proof process: the exploration of possibilities. When we look at a proof, we see only a completed chain of reasoning; we do not see the other attempts that may have been made. Furthermore, rules like negation elimination give us a problem in a backwards proof, since p appears in the premiss, but not in the conclusion. Thus, when we match the consequent to our current goal, we still have to find an instantiation of p.

2.7 Tautologies and contradictions

Propositions which evaluate to t in every combination of their propositional variables are known as tautologies: they are always true. If, on the other hand, they evaluate to f in every combination, then they are known as contradictions. Of course, the negation of a contradiction is a tautology, and vice versa.

Example 2.12 The following propositions are tautologies:

$$p \lor \neg p$$

$$p \Rightarrow p$$

$$p \Rightarrow (q \Rightarrow p)$$

while the following are contradictions:

$$p \land \neg p$$

$$p \Leftrightarrow \neg p$$

$$\neg(p \Rightarrow (q \Rightarrow p))$$

□

To prove that a proposition is a tautology, we have only to produce a truth table and check that the major connective takes the value t for each combination of propositional variables.

Example 2.13 We prove that $\neg p \vee q \Leftrightarrow p \Rightarrow q$ is a tautology by exhibiting the following table:

p	q	$\neg p \vee q \Leftrightarrow p \Rightarrow q$
t	t	$f\ t\ \ t\ \ t$
t	f	$f\ f\ \ t\ \ f$
f	t	$t\ t\ \ t\ \ t$
f	f	$t\ t\ \ t\ \ t$

□

Tautologies involving equivalences are particularly useful in proofs; they can be used to rewrite goals and assumptions to facilitate the completion of an argument. For any pair of propositions a and b, the tautology $a \Leftrightarrow b$ corresponds to a pair of inference rules:

$$\frac{b}{a}\ [a \Leftrightarrow b] \qquad \frac{a}{b}\ [a \Leftrightarrow b]$$

If either of these propositions appears in a proof, then we may replace it with the other:

$$\dfrac{\dfrac{\dfrac{\vdots}{a}}{b}\ [a \Leftrightarrow b] \qquad \vdots}{\vdots}$$

A logical equivalence may be used to justify rewriting even when the proposition involved is only part of the goal or assumption:

$$\dfrac{\dfrac{\dfrac{\vdots}{(\neg\, q \vee p) \Rightarrow r}}{(p \Rightarrow q) \Rightarrow r}\ [(\neg b \vee a) \Leftrightarrow (a \Rightarrow b)] \qquad \vdots}{\vdots}$$

Tautologies involving implications also correspond to inference rules: if $a \Rightarrow b$ is a tautology, then

$$\frac{a}{b}\ [a \Rightarrow b]$$

may be used as a derived rule. An implication alone is not enough to justify rewriting part of a goal. To see why not, consider the following proposition:

$$(p \land q) \Rightarrow (r \lor s)$$

The proposition $(a \land b) \Rightarrow a$ is a tautology, but the proof step

$$\frac{(p \land q) \Rightarrow (r \lor s)}{p \Rightarrow (r \lor s)}\ [(a \land b) \Rightarrow a]$$

is invalid. The statement $p \Rightarrow (r \lor s)$ does not follow from $(p \land q) \Rightarrow r \lor s$: it is possible for the former to be false when the latter is true.

Example 2.14 The following tautology

$$\neg(p \land q) \Rightarrow \neg p \lor \neg q$$

corresponds to another of de Morgan's laws:

$$\frac{\neg(p \land q)}{\neg p \lor \neg q}\ [\text{de Morgan2}]$$

□

A proposition which is neither a tautology nor a contradiction is said to be a *contingency*.

Chapter 3

Predicate Logic

In this chapter we introduce another part of our logical language. The language of propositions introduced in the previous chapter allows us to make statements about specific objects, but it does not allow us to make statements such as 'Every cloud has a silver lining'. These are known as *universal* statements, since they describe properties that must be satisfied by *every* object in some universe of discourse.

Example 3.1 The following are examples of universal statements:

- Each student must hand in course work.
- Nobody knows the trouble I seen.
- Jim doesn't know anybody who can sign his bail application.

□

Sometimes we wish to state that at least one thing has a particular property, without necessarily knowing which thing it is. This leads to an *existential* statement.

Example 3.2 The following are examples of existential statements:

- I heard it from one of your friends.
- A mad dog has bitten Robert.
- Some people prefer logic.

□

To formalise such statements, we require a language that reveals the internal structure of our propositional statements, a language that allows us to take them apart and apply them to objects without proper names. The language we require is the language of *predicate calculus*.

3.1 Predicate calculus

A predicate is a statement with a place for an object. There may be many such places within a single predicate; this is often the case when the objects concerned are mathematical. When these places are filled, our predicates become statements about the objects that fill them. We could say that a predicate is a proposition with a gap for an object of some kind.

For example, the statement '$\_ > 5$' is a predicate. As it stands, it is not a proposition; we cannot say whether it is true or false until we have filled the empty place. We could turn it into a proposition by putting 0 in this place; the result would be '$0 > 5$', a proposition that happens to be false. This is not the only way to fill a gap, however. We could also choose to put an object variable in the empty place above.

The predicate '$x > 5$' is still not a proposition; we cannot say whether it is true or false without knowing what x is. The use of object variables is a powerful technique, and holds the key to expressing the universal and existential properties described above. We can make a proposition out of '$x > 5$' by adding a *quantifier* to the front of the expression. For example, we could state that 'there is an x, which is a natural number, such that $x > 5$'. Here, the quantifier is 'there is an...', and we have quantified the predicate '$x > 5$' to produce a true proposition.

In mathematics, the symbol '$\exists$' is used to denote the expression 'there is an ...'; in Z, the natural numbers are denoted by the symbol '$\mathbb{N}$'. Thus, we can write down our quantified predicate in Z as:

$$\exists x : \mathbb{N} \bullet x > 5.$$

To see that the quantified predicate is true, consider the number 6: it is a natural number, and it is greater than 5.

Existential quantification may be thought of as a generalised form of disjunction: for example,

$$\begin{array}{l} \exists x : \mathbb{N} \bullet x > 5 \\ \Leftrightarrow \\ 0 > 5 \lor 1 > 5 \lor 2 > 5 \lor 3 > 5 \lor \ldots \end{array}$$

The predicate is true for *some* natural number; it is true of 0 or it is true of 1 or it is true of 2 or it is true of 3, etcetera.

Example 3.3 The statements in Example 3.2 may be formalised as follows:

- Let *Friends* stand for the set of all your friends, and let x *told* y mean that x has told y.

$$\exists f : Friends \bullet f \ told \ me$$

- Let *MadDog* stand for the set of all mad dogs, and let x *bit* y mean that x has bitten y.

$$\exists fido : MadDog \bullet fido \ bit \ Robert$$

- Let *Person* stand for the set of all people, and let $PL(x)$ mean that x prefers logic.

$$\exists p : Person \bullet PL(p)$$

□

Another way of quantifying a predicate is to say that it is true *for every* value. We might take the predicate '$x > 5$' and prepend a *universal quantifier* to produce the statement 'for every x which is a natural number, it is the case that $x > 5$'. Here, the quantifier is 'for every x ...', and we have quantified the predicate to produce a false proposition.

In mathematics, the notation '$\forall$' is used to denote the *universal quantifier*. We can write down our new predicate in Z as follows:

$$\forall x : \mathbb{N} \bullet x > 5.$$

Again, this is the same as

$$\forall y : \mathbb{N} \bullet y > 5.$$

This predicate is false because not every natural number x is greater than 5: consider 3.

The universal quantifier may be thought of as a generalised conjunction: for example,

$$\forall x : \mathbb{N} \bullet x > 5$$
$$\Leftrightarrow$$
$$0 > 5 \land 1 > 5 \land 2 > 5 \land 3 > 5 \land \ldots$$

The predicate $\_ > 5$ would have to be true of *every* natural number; of 0 and of 1 and of 2 and of 3, etcetera. It is not true of 0, for example, and thus the whole quantified expression is false.

Example 3.4 The statements in Example 3.1 may be formalised as follows:

- Let *Student* stand for the set of all students, and let *Submit*(x) mean that x must hand in course work.

$$\forall s : Student \bullet Submit(s)$$

- Let *Person* be the set of all people, and let *knows_trouble*(x) mean that x knows the trouble I seen.

$$\forall p : Person \bullet \neg knows\_trouble(p)$$

- Again, let *Person* be the set of all people. Let x *Knows* y means that x knows y, and let x *CanBail* y mean that x can sign y's application for bail.

$$\forall p : Person \bullet Jim\ Knows\ p \Rightarrow \neg(p\ CanBail\ Jim)$$

□

3.2 Quantifiers and declarations

In the Z notation, the two kinds of quantified expressions have a similar syntax:

$$\mathcal{Q}\, x : a \mid p \bullet q$$

where

- $\mathcal{Q}$ is the *quantifier*;
- x is the *bound variable*;
- a is the *range* of x;
- p is the *constraint*; and
- q is the *predicate*.

The optional constraint p restricts the set of objects under consideration; only those objects in a that satisfy p are to be considered. The constraint takes on the role of a conjunction or an implication, depending upon the quantifier concerned, as may be seen from the following equivalences:

$$(\exists x : a \mid p \bullet q) \Leftrightarrow (\exists x : a \bullet p \wedge q)$$

$$(\forall x : a \mid p \bullet q) \Leftrightarrow (\forall x : a \bullet p \Rightarrow q)$$

The existentially quantified predicate

$$\exists x : a \mid p \bullet q$$

is pronounced 'there exists an x in a satisfying p, such that q'. The universally quantified predicate

$$\forall x : a \mid p \bullet q$$

is pronounced 'for all x in a satisfying p, q holds'.

Each quantifier introduces a 'bound variable', which is analogous to a local variable in a block-structured programming language. In the quantified predicate $\mathcal{Q}\ x : a \mid p \bullet q$ the bound variable x has a scope that is exactly the constraint p and predicate q. The quantifiers bind very loosely, so the scope of a quantified variable extends to the next enclosing bracket.

Example 3.5 In the following expression, the scope of variable x is marked by a brace:

$$(\forall x : a \mid \underbrace{p \bullet q \wedge r}_{\text{scope of } x}) \vee s \Rightarrow t$$

□

If a statement contains more than one quantifier, the scopes may overlap. This poses no problems unless the same name is chosen for two variables bound by different quantifiers; in this case, there would be a hole in one of the scopes.

Example 3.6 In the following expression, the scope of the first bound variable has a hole corresponding to the scope of the second:

$$\forall y : a \mid \underbrace{p \bullet q \wedge (\forall y : b \mid}_{\text{scope of first } y} \overbrace{r \bullet s \Rightarrow t}^{\text{scope of second } y} \underbrace{) \wedge u \vee v}_{\text{scope of first } y}$$

□

As the above example shows, there is scope for confusion whenever two different variables have the same name.

Whenever such confusion can arise, we will choose another name for one of the variables. We can change the name of a bound variable without changing the meaning of the quantified expression, as long as we avoid the names of any other variables that appear.

Example 3.7 Consider the following quantified expression, which states that every natural number x is greater than or equal to zero:

$$\forall\, num : \mathbb{N} \bullet num \geqslant 0$$

The choice of '*num*' as the variable name is not important; the following expression has the same meaning:

$$\forall\, nat : \mathbb{N} \bullet nat \geqslant 0$$

□

We must take care that the new name chosen for a bound variable has not already been used for a different variable in the same expression.

Example 3.8 Consider the following quantified expression, which states that there is some natural number *max* such that every natural number *num* must be less than or equal to *max*:

$$\exists\, max : \mathbb{N} \bullet \forall\, num : \mathbb{N} \bullet num \leqslant max$$

This statement is false: there is no greatest natural number.

If we were to change the name of the universally-quantified variable from *num* to *max*, then some confusion would result. The following expression states that there is some natural number such that every natural number is less than or equal to itself.

$$\exists\, max : \mathbb{N} \bullet \forall\, max : \mathbb{N} \bullet max \leqslant max$$

This statement is true; the meaning has changed. □

To avoid changing the meaning of a statement, we insist that a *fresh* variable name is chosen whenever such a change of name occurs. This name should not appear elsewhere in the logical expressions under consideration.

In the last example, we saw two variables quantified at the start of an expression, one immediately after the other. In this case, the quantifiers were different. Had they been the same, we could have quantified both variables at the same time, separating their declarations with a semicolon.

Example 3.9 The quantified predicate

$$\exists x : a \bullet \exists y : b \bullet p$$

could also be written as

$$\exists x : a; \ y : b \bullet p$$

□

There is a circumstance in which this is not possible: when the first quantified variable appears in the range of the second.

Example 3.10 In the expression below, the first bound variable is used as the range of the second:

$$\exists a : b \bullet \exists c : a \bullet p$$

In this case, it would make no sense to merge the two quantifications. □

If a variable x appears in a predicate p but is not bound by any quantifier, we say that x is *free* in p. Each occurrence of x that is outside the scope of a declaration of the form '$\forall x : a$' or '$\exists x : a$' is said to be a free occurrence.

Example 3.11 In the expression below, there is a single free occurrence of variable z:

$$\forall x : \mathbb{N} \bullet z \leqslant x$$

This predicate states that every natural number x is greater than z, whatever z may be. □

If we use the same name for two different variables, then we may find that a variable appears both free and bound in the same expression.

Example 3.12 There are both free and bound occurrences of variable x in the expression below:

$$\underbrace{x}_{\text{free occurrence}} = 3 \land \forall x : \mathbb{N} \bullet 0 \leqslant \underbrace{x}_{\text{bound occurrence}}$$

The occurrence of x adjacent to the quantifier is neither free nor bound; it is a *binding* occurrence. □

3.3 Substitution

If a predicate p contains a free occurrence of variable x, then p may represent a non-trivial statement about x. The choice of variable x is important: p does not, in general, represent the same statement about any other variable y. If we wish to change the subject of the statement from x to y, we must replace each *free* occurrence of x in p with an occurrence of y. This process is called *substitution*.

We write $p[y / x]$ to denote the predicate that results from substituting y for each free occurrence of x in predicate p; this new operator binds more tightly than any other. The expression y need not be another variable; it can be any expression whose possible values match those of x.

Example 3.13

1. $(x \leqslant y + 2)[0 / x] \Leftrightarrow (0 \leqslant y + 2)$
2. $(\exists x : \mathbb{N} \bullet x \leqslant y + 2)[0 / x] \Leftrightarrow (\exists x : \mathbb{N} \bullet x \leqslant y + 2)$
3. $(\exists x : \mathbb{N} \bullet x \leqslant y + 2)[5 / y] \Leftrightarrow (\exists x : \mathbb{N} \bullet x \leqslant 5 + 2)$

□

We write $p[t / x][u / y]$ to denote the predicate $p[t / x]$ with the expression u systematically substituted for free occurrences of the variable y.

Example 3.14

1. $(x \leqslant y + 2)[0 / x][5 / y] \Leftrightarrow (0 \leqslant y + 2)[5 / y] \Leftrightarrow (0 \leqslant 5 + 2)$
2. $(x \leqslant y + 2)[y / x][5 / y] \Leftrightarrow (y \leqslant y + 2)[5 / y] \Leftrightarrow (5 \leqslant 5 + 2)$

□

We write $p[t, u / x, y]$ to denote the result of *simultaneously* substituting t for x and u for y in predicate p. In general, this is different from the multiple substitution $p[t / x][u / y]$.

Example 3.15

1. $(x \leqslant y + 2)[y, 5 / x, y] \Leftrightarrow (y \leqslant 5 + 2)$
2. $(x \leqslant y + 2)[y / x][5 / y] \Leftrightarrow (y \leqslant y + 2)[5 / y] \Leftrightarrow 5 \leqslant 5 + 2$

□

A potential problem with substitution is the unintentional capture of free variables. If y is bound in p, then the substitution $p[y / x]$ might include new *bound* instances of y in place of *free* instances of x. This may change the meaning of p in a way that is not intended.

Example 3.16 Let *Person* denote the set of all people, and let m *LooksLike* n mean that person m looks like person n. The following predicate is a statement about a person o; it states that there is some person who does not look like o:

$$\exists p : Person \bullet \neg (p \; LooksLike \; o)$$

We may make the same statement about person m by substituting m for o:

$$\exists p : Person \bullet \neg (p \; LooksLike \; m)$$

However, if we substitute p for o, we obtain a different statement entirely:

$$\exists p : Person \bullet \neg (p \; LooksLike \; p)$$

The expression substituted for o contains a free occurrence of p, which is then bound by the quantifier. The new predicate states that there is someone who does not look like themself. The substitution has brought an unwanted change of meaning. □

To avoid such confusion, we may rename bound variables prior to substitution, choosing *fresh* variable names to avoid variable capture.

We can give equivalences to explain the effect of substitution into quantified expressions. In the simplest case, the variable being substituted for has the same name as the one being quantified:

$$(\forall x : a \mid p \bullet q)[t / x] \Leftrightarrow (\forall x : a[t / x] \mid p \bullet q)$$
$$(\exists x : a \mid p \bullet q)[t / x] \Leftrightarrow (\exists x : a[t / x] \mid p \bullet q)$$

In this case, the only part of the expression that may change is the range of the quantified variable. In general, this substitution will have no effect; it is poor practice to include a free variable in the declaration of a bound variable of the same name.

If the quantifier is binding some variable other than x, then the substitution will have more of an effect. If y is not free in t, then

$$(\forall y : a \mid p \bullet q)[t / x] \Leftrightarrow (\forall y : a[t / x] \mid p[t / x] \bullet q[t / x])$$
$$(\exists y : a \mid p \bullet q)[t / x] \Leftrightarrow (\exists y : a[t / x] \mid p[t / x] \bullet q[t / x])$$

If y is free in t, then we choose a fresh variable z, different from x and not appearing in t:

$$
\begin{array}{l}
(\forall\, y : a \mid p \bullet q)[t / x] \\
\qquad \Leftrightarrow\ (\forall\, z : a[t / x] \mid p[z / y][t / x] \bullet q[z / y][t / x]) \\
(\exists\, y : a \mid p \bullet q)[t / x] \\
\qquad \Leftrightarrow\ (\exists\, z : a[t / x] \mid p[z / y][t / x] \bullet q[z / y][t / x])
\end{array}
$$

By using z instead of y for the name of the quantified variable, we have avoided any possibility of unintentional variable capture.

If the major operator in an expression is not a quantifier, then the effect of substitution is easy to explain:

$$
\begin{array}{rcl}
(\neg p)[t / x] & \Leftrightarrow & \neg p[t / x] \\
(p \wedge q)[t / x] & \Leftrightarrow & p[t / x] \wedge q[t / x] \\
(p \vee q)[t / x] & \Leftrightarrow & p[t / x] \vee q[t / x] \\
(p \Rightarrow q)[t / x] & \Leftrightarrow & p[t / x] \Rightarrow q[t / x] \\
(p \Leftrightarrow q)[t / x] & \Leftrightarrow & p[t / x] \Leftrightarrow q[t / x]
\end{array}
$$

In every case, substitution distributes through the propositional operators.

3.4 Universal introduction and elimination

In general, the truth-table technique for giving meaning to connectives and reasoning about them is useless for the quantifiers, since the sets that bound variables may range over are simply too large. However, we may build upon the natural deduction system of the previous chapter by adding rules to introduce and eliminate quantifiers.

If we view universal quantification as a generalised conjunction, then we should be able to generalise the rules for conjunction to get the rules for the universal quantifier. Consider first the introduction rule. In order to prove $p \wedge q$, one needs to prove both p and q. In order to prove $\forall\, x : a \bullet p$, one must prove that p is true for each value in a. This doesn't sound terribly hopeful, as it might involve an infinite number of premisses, and therefore an infinite number of proofs.

A better approach might be to prove that p holds for an *arbitrary* member of a: if we make *no assumptions whatsoever* about which member of a we choose in order to prove p, then our proof generalises to all members. A simplified rule for introducing universal quantification is the following:

$$\frac{\begin{array}{c}\lceil x \in a \rceil^{[i]} \\ q\end{array}}{\forall\, x : a \bullet q}\ [i] \qquad \text{provided that } x \text{ is not free in the assumptions of } q$$

where $x \in a$ means that x is a member of set a.

Notice that we are required to check that x is not free in the assumptions of q. This ensures that we not making any assumptions about which member of a we are choosing. The assumptions of q are those leaves of the proof tree above q that have not been discharged: by implication-introduction, for example.

In the full form of the universal quantifier, there is also a constraint that x must satisfy; we may treat the constraint as an additional assumption:

$$\frac{\begin{array}{c}\lceil x \in a \rceil^{[1]} \\ \lceil p \rceil^{[1]} \\ q\end{array}}{\forall\, x : a \mid p \bullet q}\ [\forall\text{-intro}]^{[1]} \qquad \text{provided that } x \text{ is not free in the assumptions of } q$$

This rule may be derived from the first [$\forall$−intro] rule:

$$\cfrac{\cfrac{\cfrac{\begin{array}{c}\lceil x \in a \rceil^{[1]} \\ \lceil p \rceil^{[2]} \\ \vdots \\ q\end{array}}{p \Rightarrow q}\ [\Rightarrow\text{-intro}]^{[2]}}{\forall\, x : a \bullet p \Rightarrow q}\ [\forall\text{-intro}]^{[1]}}{\forall\, x : a \mid p \bullet q}\ [\text{defn}]$$

The constraint part of a universal quantification may be treated as the antecedent of an implication.

From a conjunction, one may conclude either of the conjuncts; by analogy, from a universally quantified predicate, one may conclude that the predicate holds for any value in the range. Suppose that we have the universally quantified predicate $\forall\, x : a \bullet p$, and that the expression t denotes a value in a; then p must be true of t.

$$\frac{t \in a \quad \forall\, x : a \bullet p}{p[t / x]}$$

We systematically substitute t for x in p.

The full form requires the equivalent of implication elimination, to demonstrate that the expression chosen satisfies the constraint:

$$\frac{t \in a \quad \forall x : a \mid p \bullet q \quad p[t/x]}{q[t/x]} \;[\forall\text{-elim}]$$

A special case of the last rule takes t as x:

$$\frac{x \in a \quad \forall x : a \mid p \bullet q \quad p}{q} \;[\forall\text{-elim}]$$

Example 3.17 The universal quantifier distributes through conjunction. We will prove this in one direction only:

$$(\forall x : a \bullet p \land q) \Rightarrow ((\forall x : a \bullet p) \land (\forall x : a \bullet q))$$

We begin the proof with the stated goal:

$$\frac{\vdots}{(\forall x : a \bullet p \land q) \Rightarrow ((\forall x : a \bullet p) \land (\forall x : a \bullet q))}$$

The major connective here is the implication, so we assume the antecedent and try to prove the consequent:

$$\frac{\dfrac{\begin{array}{c}\lceil \forall x : a \bullet p \land q \rceil^{[1]} \\ \vdots\end{array}}{(\forall x : a \bullet p) \land (\forall x : a \bullet q)}}{(\forall x : a \bullet p \land q) \Rightarrow ((\forall x : a \bullet p) \land (\forall x : a \bullet q))} \;[\Rightarrow\text{-intro}]^{[1]}$$

In order to prove this conjunction, we should prove each conjunct separately:

$$\frac{\dfrac{\dfrac{\begin{array}{c}\lceil \forall x : a \bullet p \land q \rceil^{[1]} \\ \vdots\end{array}}{\forall x : a \bullet p} \quad \dfrac{\begin{array}{c}\lceil \forall x : a \bullet p \land q \rceil^{[1]} \\ \vdots\end{array}}{\forall x : a \bullet q}}{(\forall x : a \bullet p) \land (\forall x : a \bullet q)} \;[\land\text{-intro}]}{(\forall x : a \bullet p \land q) \Rightarrow ((\forall x : a \bullet p) \land (\forall x : a \bullet q))} \;[\Rightarrow\text{-intro}]^{[1]}$$

We shall deal with the left-hand subtree. The major connective is the universal quantifier, so we introduce it.

$$
\dfrac{
  \dfrac{
    \dfrac{
      \begin{array}{c}\lceil \forall x : a \bullet p \land q \rceil^{[1]} \\ \lceil x \in a \rceil^{[2]} \\ \vdots \end{array}
    }{p}
  }{\forall x : a \bullet p}\;[\forall\text{-intro}]^{[2]}
  \quad
  \dfrac{
    \begin{array}{c}\lceil \forall x : a \bullet p \land q \rceil^{[1]} \\ \vdots \end{array}
  }{\forall x : a \bullet q}
}{
  \dfrac{(\forall x : a \bullet p) \land (\forall x : a \bullet q)}{(\forall x : a \bullet p \land q) \Rightarrow ((\forall x : a \bullet p) \land (\forall x : a \bullet q))}\;[\Rightarrow\text{-intro}]^{[1]}
}\;[\land\text{-intro}]
$$

We cannot work backwards any further, so now we must take advantage of our assumptions. If we eliminate the universal quantifier, we expose a useful conjunction:

$$
\dfrac{
  \dfrac{
    \dfrac{
      \begin{array}{c}\dfrac{\lceil x \in a \rceil^{[2]} \quad \lceil \forall x : a \bullet p \land q \rceil^{[1]}}{p \land q}\;[\forall\text{-elim}] \\ \vdots \end{array}
    }{p}
  }{\forall x : a \bullet p}\;[\forall\text{-intro}]^{[2]}
  \quad
  \dfrac{
    \begin{array}{c}\lceil \forall x : a \bullet p \land q \rceil^{[1]} \\ \vdots \end{array}
  }{\forall x : a \bullet q}
}{
  \dfrac{(\forall x : a \bullet p) \land (\forall x : a \bullet q)}{(\forall x : a \bullet p \land q) \Rightarrow ((\forall x : a \bullet p) \land (\forall x : a \bullet q))}\;[\Rightarrow\text{-intro}]^{[1]}
}\;[\land\text{-intro}]
$$

Now this subtree is finished, since we can use conjunction elimination to connect top and bottom. The right-hand subtree is symmetric with the left.

$$
\dfrac{
  \dfrac{
    \dfrac{
      \dfrac{\lceil x \in a \rceil^{[2]} \quad \lceil \forall x : a \bullet p \land q \rceil^{[1]}}{p \land q}\;[\forall\text{-elim}]
    }{p}\;[\land\text{-elim1}]
  }{\forall x : a \bullet p}\;[\forall\text{-intro}]^{[2]}
  \quad
  \dfrac{
    \dfrac{
      \dfrac{\lceil x \in a \rceil^{[3]} \quad \lceil \forall x : a \bullet p \land q \rceil^{[1]}}{p \land q}\;[\forall\text{-elim}]
    }{q}\;[\land\text{-elim2}]
  }{\forall x : a \bullet q}\;[\forall\text{-intro}]^{[3]}
}{
  \dfrac{(\forall x : a \bullet p) \land (\forall x : a \bullet q)}{(\forall x : a \bullet p \land q) \Rightarrow ((\forall x : a \bullet p) \land (\forall x : a \bullet q))}\;[\Rightarrow\text{-intro}]^{[1]}
}\;[\land\text{-intro}]
$$

□

Example 3.18 Provided that x does not occur free in the antecedent, then we can move the universal quantifier through an implication

$$(\forall x : a \bullet p \Rightarrow q) \Leftrightarrow (p \Rightarrow \forall x : a \bullet q) \qquad \text{provided } x \text{ is not free in } p$$

A suitable proof would be:

$$\dfrac{\dfrac{\dfrac{\dfrac{\lceil x \in a \rceil^{[5]} \quad \dfrac{\lceil p \Rightarrow \forall x : a \bullet q \rceil^{[4]} \quad \lceil p \rceil^{[6]}}{\forall x : a \bullet q}\;[\Rightarrow\text{-elim}]}{q}\;[\forall\text{-elim}]}{p \Rightarrow q}\;[\Rightarrow\text{-intro}]^{[6]}}{\forall x : a \bullet p \Rightarrow q}\;[\forall\text{-intro}]^{[5]}}{(p \Rightarrow \forall x : a \bullet q) \Rightarrow (\forall x : a \bullet p \Rightarrow q)}\;[\Rightarrow\text{-intro}]^{[4]}$$

$$\dfrac{\dfrac{\dfrac{\dfrac{\dfrac{\dfrac{\lceil x \in a \rceil^{[3]} \quad \lceil \forall x : a \bullet p \Rightarrow q \rceil^{[1]}}{p \Rightarrow q}\;[\forall\text{-elim}] \quad \lceil p \rceil^{[2]}}{q}\;[\Rightarrow\text{-elim}]}{\forall x : a \bullet q}\;[\forall\text{-intro}]^{[3]}}{p \Rightarrow \forall x : a \bullet q}\;[\Rightarrow\text{-intro}]^{[2]}}{(\forall x : a \bullet p \Rightarrow q) \Rightarrow (p \Rightarrow \forall x : a \bullet q)}\;[\Rightarrow\text{-intro}]^{[1]} \quad \vert}{(\forall x : a \bullet p \Rightarrow q) \Leftrightarrow (p \Rightarrow \forall x : a \bullet q)}\;[\Leftrightarrow\text{-intro}]$$

□

3.5 Existential introduction and elimination

The existential quantification $\exists x : a \mid p \bullet q$ is true if and only if there is some x in set a such that p and q are true. Of course, this object does not have to be called x; it can be any expression t such that t has a value in a and the following predicate is true:

$$p[t / x] \wedge q[t / x]$$

That is, given that we are talking about t not x, both the constraint and the quantified predicate should hold.

To introduce an existential quantifier, we must show that a suitable expression t exists: we must provide an example.

$$\dfrac{t \in a \quad p[t / x] \quad q[t / x]}{\exists x : a \mid p \bullet q}\;[\exists\text{-intro}]$$

As before, the expression $t \in a$ means that t is a member of set a.

Example 3.19 With suitable assumptions about $\mathbb{N}$, $+$, and $>$, we can prove that for any natural number x, there is some natural number y such that y is greater than x. We use existential introduction, choosing $x + 1$ as a specific value:

$$\dfrac{\dfrac{\lceil x \in \mathbb{N} \rceil^{[1]}}{x + 1 \in \mathbb{N}}\,[\text{arithmetic}] \qquad \dfrac{\dfrac{\dfrac{\lceil x \in \mathbb{N} \rceil^{[1]}}{x < x + 1}\,[\text{arithmetic}]}{(x < y)[x + 1 / y]}\,[\text{subst}]}{\exists\, y : \mathbb{N} \bullet x < y}\,[\exists\text{-intro}]}{\forall\, x : \mathbb{N} \bullet \exists\, y : \mathbb{N} \bullet x < y}\,[\forall\text{-intro}]^{[1]}$$

Two of the steps in this proof cannot be made using the rules of our natural deduction system. The validity of these steps depends upon our understanding of the natural numbers $\mathbb{N}$, and a conventional interpretation of $>$ and $+$. □

A special case of the existential-introduction rule takes expression t to be the variable x. If p and q are already true, then there is no reason to substitute another expression for x:

$$\dfrac{x \in a \quad p \quad q}{\exists\, x : a \mid p \bullet q}\,[\exists\text{-intro}]$$

Example 3.20 If, in the course of a proof, we have established that $x \in \mathbb{N}$ and $x \geqslant 0$, then we may apply the special case of existential-introduction and conclude that

$$\exists\, x : \mathbb{N} \bullet x \geqslant 0$$

□

Elimination of the existential quantifier is a more difficult affair. The predicate $\exists\, x : a \bullet s$ states that there is some object x in a for which s is true. If x appears free in p then simply removing the quantifier leaves us with an unjustified statement about a free variable x. We cannot, in general, conclude p from $\exists\, x : a \bullet p$. To use the information contained in p, we must complete any reasoning that involves x before eliminating the quantifier.

Suppose that we assume only that $x \in a$ and that p holds of x. If we are then able to derive a predicate r that does not involve x, and we know that there is some x in a for which p is true, then we may safely conclude r.

$$\dfrac{\exists\, x : a \bullet p \qquad \begin{array}{c} \lceil x \in a \wedge p \rceil^{[i]} \\ r \end{array}}{r}\,[\exists\text{-elim}]^{[i]} \qquad \text{provided } x \text{ is not free in the assumptions, and } x \text{ is not free in } r$$

It is important that nothing is assumed about x during the derivation of r, apart from the explicit assumption

$$\lceil x \in a \land p \rceil^{[i]}$$

which states that x is in a and that p holds.

The full form of the existential-elimination rule includes the optional constraint part of the quantification:

$$\frac{\exists x : a \mid p \bullet q \qquad \begin{array}{c}\lceil x \in a \land p \land q \rceil^{[i]} \\ r\end{array}}{r}\;[\exists\text{-elim}]^{[i]}$$

provided x is not free in the assumptions, and x is not free in r

These rules are generalisations of the case analysis rule given in Chapter 2 for the elimination of the $\lor$ operator. For each value of x, we must show that r follows from p and q.

Example 3.21 Existential quantifiers commute. We will prove this in one direction only:

$$(\exists x : a \bullet \exists y : b \bullet p) \Rightarrow (\exists y : b \bullet \exists x : a \bullet p)$$

provided x is not free in b, and y is not free in a.

$$\cfrac{\cfrac{\begin{array}{c}\lceil \exists x : a \bullet \exists y : b \bullet p \rceil^{[1]} \\ \vdots \end{array} \qquad \cfrac{\lceil \exists y : b \bullet p \rceil^{[2]} \qquad \cfrac{\lceil y \in b \rceil^{[3]} \qquad \cfrac{\lceil x \in a \rceil^{[2]} \quad \lceil p \rceil^{[3]}}{\exists x : a \bullet p}\;[\exists\text{-intro}]}{\exists y : b \bullet \exists x : a \bullet p}\;[\exists\text{-intro}]}{\exists y : b \bullet \exists x : a \bullet p}\;[\exists\text{-elim}]^{[3]}}{\exists y : b \bullet \exists x : a \bullet p}\;[\exists\text{-elim}]^{[2]}}{(\exists x : a \bullet \exists y : b \bullet p) \Rightarrow (\exists y : b \bullet \exists x : a \bullet p)}\;[\Rightarrow\text{-intro}]^{[1]}$$

□

The two quantifiers are related in the same way as the propositional operators they generalise. The statement 'for some x in a, predicate p is true' is the negation of 'for every x in a, predicate p is false'. In terms of equivalences:

$$\exists x : a \bullet p \Leftrightarrow \neg \forall x : a \bullet \neg p$$
$$\forall y : b \bullet q \Leftrightarrow \neg \exists y : b \bullet \neg q$$

These two equivalences are generalisations of the de Morgan laws for the $\land$ and $\lor$ operators given in Chapter 2.

3.6 Satisfaction and validity

A predicate with free variables or 'spaces' is neither true nor false; it cannot be assigned a truth value until values are chosen for these variables or the spaces are filled. Some predicates will become true whatever values are chosen: these are said to be *valid* predicates.

Example 3.22 If n denotes a natural number, then the predicate

$$n \geqslant 0$$

is valid: it will be true whichever value is chosen from the list $0, 1, 2, 3, \ldots$ □

A predicate that is true for some, but not necessarily all, choices of values is said to be *satisfiable.*

Example 3.23 If n denotes a natural number, then the predicate

$$n \geqslant 5$$

is satisfiable. There are natural numbers greater than or equal to 5. □

A predicate that is false for all choices is said to be *unsatisfiable.* Valid, satisfiable, and unsatisfiable predicates are the analogues of tautologies, contingencies, and contradictions in the language of propositions.

Chapter 4

Equality and Definite Description

In this chapter we extend our language of mathematics by adding a theory of equality between expressions. The language of predicate calculus with equality is strictly more expressive than without, since it allows us to assert the identity of two objects, or to distinguish between them. We provide inference rules to support the intuitive notion that expressions which are equal may be substituted one for the other, without affecting the truth of a statement, or the value of a larger expression. These rules form the basis of our theory of equality, and properties such as symmetry and transitivity can be derived from them.

The addition of equality allows us to formulate a simple rule for reasoning with quantifications: the *one-point rule*. We show how this rule may be used to introduce and eliminate the existential quantifier. We show also how equality may be used in statements expressing uniqueness and numerical quantity. We conclude the chapter by introducing a notation for identifying objects by using a description of their properties, rather than by referring to them by name.

4.1 Equality

The notion of *equality* is a familiar one: in arithmetic we learn that $1 + 1$ equals 2; in the Christian religion, the 25th of December equals Christmas Day. Such statements are meant to indicate that the two expressions concerned have the same value, or that they denote the same object. In a formal description, we *identify* expressions using the equality symbol:

$$1 + 1 = 2, \qquad \mathit{Christmas\,Day} = 25\mathit{th\,December}$$

We write $e = f$ when e is identical to f, in the sense that we cannot distinguish between them.

Example 4.1 In an identity parade, a witness may state that 'the man on the right is the man who stole my idea', making the following identification:

the man on the right = the man who stole my idea

That is, the man on the right is *identical to* the man who stole the idea. □

The '=' symbol is due to Robert Recorde, whose textbook on algebra *The Whetstone of Witte*, published in 1557, used the symbol for the first time. Recorde argued that a pair of parallel lines of the same length were suitable as the symbol for equality 'bicause noe 2 thynges can be moare equalle'.

We do not use equality to state that two predicates are identical: the propositional connective of equivalence is reserved for that purpose. Rather, we use equality to state that two values (such as numbers) are identical. Thus, we may write $5 + 3 = 3 + 5$, since both sides of the equation are expressions which denote values. These denoted values are the same, so the equality is true. Equalities form the atomic propositions in our logical language; the only other way of obtaining an atomic proposition is through set membership, described in Chapter 5.

Everything is identical to itself: thus, if t is any expression, then t is equal to t. This principle is known as the law of *reflection*:

$$\frac{}{t = t}\ \text{[eq-ref]}$$

It should be remarked that there are logics in which this principle does not hold. It is, however, an *axiom* of standard Z.

Example 4.2 In basic arithmetic, everybody knows that

$$1 + 1 = 1 + 1$$

whatever the properties of numbers and addition. □

Another axiom involving equality is *Leibniz's law*, or the substitution of equals: if $s = t$, then whatever is true of s is also true of t.

$$\frac{s = t \quad p[t / x]}{p[s / x]}\ \text{[eq-sub]}$$

In fact, Leibniz (1646–1716) stated the following *Principle of the Identity of Indiscernibles*: $s = t$ if and only if every property of s is a property of t, and conversely. The rule above follows from this principle.

Example 4.3 If we know that *Christmas Day* = 25*th December*, and that

> 25*th December* falls on a Sunday this year

then we may apply the [eq-sub] rule and conclude that

> *Christmas Day* falls on a Sunday this year

□

If two expressions e and f are not identical, then we write $e \neq f$. This is simply an abbreviation for $\neg(e = f)$.

Example 4.4 Expressions with different properties are themselves different:

$$\frac{p[s / x] \qquad \neg p[t / x]}{s \neq t}$$

This may be proved by

$$\cfrac{\cfrac{\cfrac{p[s / x] \qquad \cfrac{\cfrac{[s = t]^{[1]} \qquad \cfrac{\neg p[t / x]}{(\neg p)[t / x]}\,[\text{subst}]}{(\neg p)[s / x]}\,[\text{eq-sub}]}{\neg p[s / x]}\,[\text{subst}]}{\mathit{false}}\,[\neg\text{-elim}]}{\neg(s = t)}\,[\neg\text{-intro}]^{[1]}}{s \neq t}\,[\text{abbreviation}]$$

□

Using the rules [eq-ref] and [eq-sub], we are able to establish that equality is symmetric: for any expressions s and t, if $s = t$, then $t = s$. If we let x be a fresh variable, so that x does not appear in either s or t, then we may construct the following derivation:

$$\cfrac{\cfrac{s = t \qquad \cfrac{\cfrac{}{t = t}\,[\text{eq-ref}]}{(t = x)[t / x]}\,[\text{subst}]}{(t = x)[s / x]}\,[\text{eq-sub}]}{t = s}\,[\text{subst}]$$

Having derived this property, we may use it as a rule of inference in our natural deduction system; we will refer to it as [eq-symm].

Example 4.5 From the identification made in Example 4.1, we may apply the [eq-symm] rule and conclude that:

the man who stole my idea = the man on the right

□

We are also able to establish that equality is *transitive*: for any expressions s, t and u, if $s = t$ and $t = u$ then $s = u$. Again, let x be a fresh variable:

$$\dfrac{\dfrac{s = t \quad \dfrac{t = u}{(x = u)[t / x]}\,[\text{subst}]}{(x = u)[s / x]}\,[\text{eq-sub}]}{s = u}\,[\text{subst}]$$

Example 4.6 After the identity parade, it is revealed that the man on the right is Professor Plum, the prominent plagiarist:

the man on the right = Professor Plum

We may add this to the information in Example 4.5 and conclude that

the man who stole my idea = Professor Plum

□

4.2 The one-point rule

The notion of equality allows us to manipulate the existential quantifier. If the identity of a bound variable is revealed within the quantified expression, then we may replace all instances of that variable, and remove the existential quantifier. Consider the following predicate:

$$\exists x : a \bullet p \land x = t$$

This states that there is a value of x in a for which $p \land x = t$ is true. If t is in a, and p holds with t substituted for x, then t is a good candidate for this value.

This is the basis of the one-point rule for the existential quantifier, which embodies the following equivalence:

$$(\exists x : a \bullet p \land x = t) \Leftrightarrow t \in a \land p[t / x]$$

For this to work, x must not be free in t. If it were, then x would be bound on the left-hand side of the equivalence but free on the right. In this case, if we were to replace the left-hand side of the equivalence by the right-hand side, x would suddenly become a free variable.

The right-to-left implication is rather obvious: it relies on existential introduction, and the equality suggests what the term should be:

$$\dfrac{\dfrac{\dfrac{[t \in a \land p[t/x]]^{[1]}}{t \in a}[\land\text{-elim1}] \qquad \dfrac{\dfrac{\dfrac{[t \in a \land p[t/x]]^{[1]}}{p[t/x]}[\land\text{-elim2}] \quad \dfrac{}{t = t}[\text{eq-ref}]}{p[t/x] \land t = t}[\land\text{-intro}]}{(p \land x = t)[t/x]}[\text{subst}]}{\exists x : a \bullet p \land x = t}[\exists\text{-intro}]}{t \in a \land p[t/x] \Rightarrow (\exists x : a \bullet p \land x = t)}[\Rightarrow\text{-intro}]^{[1]}$$

The left-to-right direction is more interesting, since it relies on the use of existential elimination. Notice that the use of this rule is sound, due to the proviso that x is not free in t.

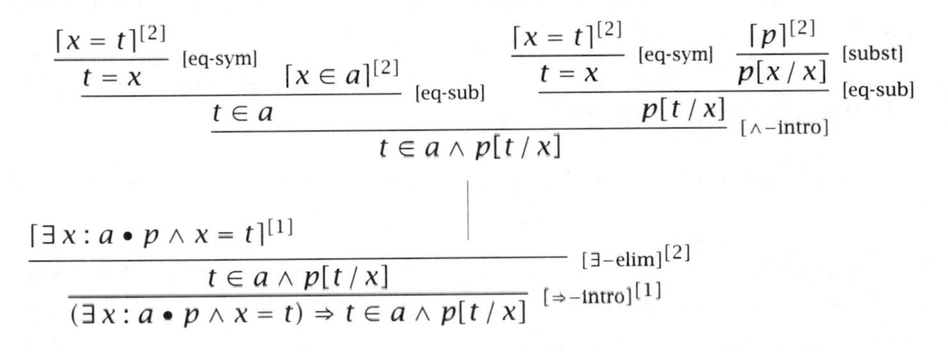

So, the existential one-point rule is a derived rule in our logic:

$$\dfrac{\exists x : a \bullet p \land x = t}{t \in a \land p[t/x]}[\text{one-point}] \qquad \text{provided that } x \text{ is not free in } t$$

It is particularly useful in specification: we know that some object x exists with a particular property, and we have identified x as t; this rule allows us to infer *immediately* that p holds of t. The fact that we have an equivalence is also very useful, in that it allows us to eliminate an existentially quantified variable without changing the strength of the predicate.

Example 4.7 The predicate

$$\exists n : \mathbb{N} \bullet 4 + n = 6 \land n = 2$$

is equivalent, by the one-point rule, and since n does not appear free in the expression '2', to the proposition

$$2 \in \mathbb{N} \land 4 + 2 = 6$$

which is, of course, true. The predicate

$$\exists n : \mathbb{N} \bullet 6 + n = 4 \land n = -2$$

is equivalent, by the one-point rule, and since n does not appear free in the expression '-2', to the proposition

$$-2 \in \mathbb{N} \land 6 - 2 = 4$$

which is, of course, false. The predicate

$$\exists n : \mathbb{N} \bullet (\forall m : \mathbb{N} \bullet n > m) \land n = n + 1$$

cannot be simplified using the one-point rule, since n is free in the expression '$n + 1$'. □

4.3 Uniqueness and quantity

Equality can be used to make our predicate calculus more expressive, by allowing us to identify and distinguish objects.

Example 4.8 Let x *loves* y mean that x is in love with y, and let *Person* be the set of all people. We may symbolise the proposition 'only Romeo loves Juliet' using a conjunction:

$$\begin{array}{l} \mathit{Romeo\ loves\ Juliet} \\ \land \\ \forall p : \mathit{Person} \bullet p\ \mathit{loves\ Juliet} \Rightarrow p = \mathit{Romeo} \end{array}$$

That is, any person who loves Juliet must be Romeo. □

A similar technique can be used to formalise statements containing the English phrases 'at most' and 'no more than'.

Example 4.9 The statement 'there is at most one person with whom Romeo is in love' may be formalised as

$$\forall p, q : \mathit{Person} \bullet \mathit{Romeo\ loves}\ p \land \mathit{Romeo\ loves}\ q \Rightarrow p = q$$

That is, if p and q are two people that Romeo loves, then they must be the same person. □

Example 4.10 The statement 'no more than two visitors are permitted' can be formalised as

$$\forall\, p, q, r : \mathit{Visitors} \bullet p = q \lor q = r \lor r = p$$

□

The notion of 'at least one' can be formalised using the existential quantifier.

Example 4.11 The statement 'at least one person has applied' could be formalised as

$$\exists\, p : \mathit{Person} \bullet p \in \mathit{Applicants}$$

□

However, to say 'at least *two*', we need equality.

Example 4.12 'There are at least two applicants' may be formalised as

$$\exists\, p, q : \mathit{Applicants} \bullet a \neq b$$

□

With the notions of 'at least' and 'at most', we have a method for formalising definite numerical propositions. This will be made easier later in the book when we have introduced finite sets. Then we shall be able to say, for example, that there are 29 distinct things with property p.

Example 4.13 The statement 'there is exactly one book on my desk' may be formalised as

$$\exists\, b : \mathit{Book} \bullet b \in \mathit{Desk} \land (\forall\, c : \mathit{Book} \mid c \in \mathit{Desk} \bullet c = b)$$

where '*Book*' denotes the set of all books, and '$x \in \mathit{Desk}$' means that 'x is on my desk'. □

Specifying that there is exactly one object with a given property occurs so often that there is a special notation for it: *the unique quantifier.* We write

$$\exists_1\, x : a \bullet p$$

when there exists exactly one element x of set a such that p holds. This new quantifier can be defined in terms of the two forms of quantifier introduced in

Chapter 3:

$$\exists_1 x : a \mid p \bullet q \Leftrightarrow \exists x : a \mid p \bullet q \\ \land \\ \forall y : a \bullet p[y / x] \land q[y / x] \Rightarrow y = x$$

The predicate $\exists_1 x : a \mid p \bullet q$ is true under two conditions: there must be an element x of a satisfying p and q *and* any element y of a that satisfies p and q is identical to x.

4.4 Definite description

We often use a descriptive phrase to denote an object, rather than a name. For example, when a crime has been committed, and the police have not yet learned who committed it, the tabloids are not silenced for want of a name—the individual in question is referred to as 'the driver of the white car' or 'the cat in the hat'. In both of these examples, it is the word 'the' that is important; it is used to indicate *existence* and *uniqueness.*

Example 4.14 Each of the following phrases indicates that there is a unique object with a certain property:

- The man who shot John Lennon
- The woman who discovered radium
- The oldest college in Oxford

□

In our mathematical language, there is a special notation for this *definite description* of objects: the μ-notation. We write

$$(\mu x : a \mid p)$$

to denote the unique object x from a such that p.

Example 4.15 The phrases in Example 4.14 can be formalised as above:

- $(\mu x : \mathit{Person} \mid x$ shot John Lennon $)$
- $(\mu y : \mathit{Person} \mid y$ discovered radium $)$
- $(\mu z : \mathit{Colleges} \mid z$ is the oldest college in Oxford $)$

□

To say that y is equal to the expression $(\mu x : a \mid p)$ is to say that y is the unique element of a such that p holds.

Example 4.16 The statement that Marie Curie is the person who discovered radium could be formalised as

$$\mathit{Marie\ Curie} = (\mu y : \mathit{Person} \mid y \text{ discovered radium})$$

This is equivalent to the following proposition:

$$\exists x : \mathit{Person} \bullet x \text{ discovered radium} \land x = \mathit{Marie\ Curie}$$

□

Such a statement makes sense only if there exists a *unique* object with the specified property. This requirement is reflected in the proof rules for the μ operator:

$$\frac{\exists_1 x : a \bullet p \quad t \in a \land p[t/x]}{t = (\mu x : a \mid p)} \; [\mu\text{-intro}] \qquad \text{provided that } x \text{ does not appear free in } t$$

and

$$\frac{\exists_1 x : a \bullet p \quad t = (\mu x : a \mid p)}{t \in a \land p[t/x]} \; [\mu\text{-elim}] \qquad \text{provided that } x \text{ does not appear free in } t$$

If there is a unique x from a such that p holds, and t is such an object, then we may infer that t is equal to the μ-expression $(\mu x : a \mid p)$. Conversely, if t is equal to this expression and uniqueness is guaranteed, then we may infer that t is an element of a such that p holds.

Example 4.17 The following proposition states that 2 is the natural number that yields a result of 6 when added to 4:

$$2 = (\mu n : \mathbb{N} \mid 4 + n = 6)$$

It may be proved by

$$\frac{\dfrac{}{\exists_1 n : \mathbb{N} \bullet 4 + n = 6} \; [\text{arithmetic}] \qquad \dfrac{}{2 \in \mathbb{N} \land 4 + 2 = 6} \; [\text{arithmetic}]}{2 = (\mu n : \mathbb{N} \mid 4 + n = 6)} \; [\text{defdesc}]$$

In both left and right subtrees, the required result follows from the properties of $\mathbb{N}$ and $+$. □

To prove that an object is not equal to a given μ-expression we must show that the μ-expression denotes a unique object, and that this isn't it.

Example 4.18 The following proposition states that 3 is not the natural number that yields a result of 6 when added to 4:

$$3 \neq (\mu\, n : \mathbb{N} \mid 4 + n = 6)$$

It may be proved by

$$\dfrac{\dfrac{\dfrac{\dfrac{\dfrac{\dfrac{}{\exists_1\, n : \mathbb{N} \bullet 4 + n = 6}\,[\text{arithmetic}] \qquad \lceil 3 = (\mu\, n : \mathbb{N} \mid 4 + n = 6) \rceil^{[1]}}{\exists\, n : \mathbb{N} \mid 4 + n = 6 \bullet 3 = n}\,[\mu\text{-elim}]}{3 \in \mathbb{N} \land 4 + 3 = 6}\,[\text{one-point}]}{4 + 3 = 6}\,[\land\text{-elim2}]}{\mathit{false}}\,[\text{arithmetic}]}{3 \neq (\mu\, n : \mathbb{N} \mid 4 + n = 6)}\,[\neg\text{-intro}]^{[1]}$$

□

If there is no unique object with the specified property, then our attempts at proving equality may fail.

Example 4.19 The following proposition states that 1 is the unique natural number that satisfies $n = n + 0$:

$$1 = (\mu\, n : \mathbb{N} \mid n = n + 0)$$

There is no unique number with this property—every number has it—so we should not be surprised if we encounter problems during the proof.

An application of the μ-introduction rule leaves us with two subtrees to investigate:

$$\dfrac{\exists_1\, n : \mathbb{N} \bullet n = n + 0 \qquad 1 \in \mathbb{N} \land 1 = 1 + 0}{1 = (\mu\, n : \mathbb{N} \mid n = n + 0)}\,[\mu\text{-intro}]$$

The right-hand subtree seems quite easy to prove, but the left-hand one is impossible. At this point, we might decide that our proposition is false, and attempt to prove its negation.

$$\dfrac{\dfrac{\dfrac{\exists_1\, n : \mathbb{N} \bullet n = n + 0 \qquad \lceil 1 = (\mu\, n : \mathbb{N} \mid n = n + 0) \rceil^{[1]}}{\vdots}\,[\mu\text{-elim}]}{\mathit{false}}}{1 \neq (\mu\, n : \mathbb{N} \mid n = n + 0)}\,[\neg\text{-intro}]^{[1]}$$

This proof is also problematic: we must derive a contradiction, and the only assumption that we have is that

$$1 = (\mu n : \mathbb{N} \mid n = n + 0)$$

We cannot use this assumption unless we prove that

$$\exists_1 n : \mathbb{N} \bullet n = n + 0$$

which is not true, and even if we could, it would be no use, since it does not lead to a contradiction. In conclusion, we cannot prove that

$$1 = (\mu n : \mathbb{N} \mid n = n + 0)$$

nor can we prove its negation. In this respect, our proof system is *incomplete*, and deliberately so.

There is no unique number n which has the property that $n = n + 0$, there are many; we refer to the descriptive phrase

$$(\mu n : \mathbb{N} \mid n = n + 0)$$

as being *improper*. We do not know what value it has, and we can prove very little about it. □

Example 4.20 The following proposition states that 1 is the unique natural number which is equal to its own successor:

$$1 = (\mu n : \mathbb{N} \mid n = n + 1)$$

No natural number has this property, and our attempts to prove this proposition or its negation will fail. □

Sometimes we wish to refer not to the unique object with some property, but to some object or expression associated with it. A more general form of μ-expression allows this: we write

$$(\mu x : a \mid p \bullet e)$$

to denote the expression e such that there is a unique x from a satisfying p.

Example 4.21 The date upon which University College, Oxford, was founded might be given by the expression:

$$(\mu z : Colleges \mid z \text{ is the oldest in Oxford} \bullet date\_of\_foundation(z))$$

□

The proof rules for this form of definite description are simple generalisations of those given above:

$$\frac{\exists_1 x : a \bullet p \quad \exists x : a \mid p \bullet t = e}{t = (\mu x : a \mid p \bullet e)} \text{[defdesc]}$$

provided that x does not appear free in t

and

$$\frac{\exists_1 x : a \bullet p \quad t = (\mu x : a \mid p \bullet e)}{\exists x : a \mid p \bullet t = e} \text{[defdesc]}$$

provided that x does not appear free in t

Notice that since the object x is unique, so too is the value of the expression e.

Chapter 5

Sets

Mathematical objects are often seen as collections of other objects: a square is a collection of points in a plane; a function is a collection of pairs linking arguments with values. These collections are called *sets*, and their theory is a fundamental part of mathematics. As mathematics forms the basis of modern software engineering, we should not be surprised to find that sets are important to our understanding of formal specification and design.

The Z notation is based upon set theory; specifications in Z find their meanings as operations upon sets. In this chapter, we present the foundations of elementary set theory: the notions of set membership, extension, and comprehension; the power set and Cartesian product constructors. This will be all the set theory we require for specification, refinement, and proof in Z.

At the end of the chapter we will introduce a system of *types* based upon maximal sets, a system used throughout the rest of the book. This will help us to ensure that expressions and variables are used consistently within a specification, and will also ensure that our formal language does not support the definition of paradoxical sets such as those of Cantor and Russell.

5.1 Membership and extension

Intuitively, a set is any well-defined collection of objects; what we mean by 'well-defined' will be explained later. The objects in a set can be anything—numbers, people, letters, days—they may even be sets themselves.

Example 5.1 The following are all examples of sets:

- the four oceans of the world

- the individuals who have been appointed to the post of secretary-general of the United Nations
- the passwords that may be generated using eight lower-case letters
- the prime numbers
- the collection of programs written in C^{++} that halt if run for a sufficient time on a computer with unlimited storage

□

We impose no restriction upon the number of elements that there may be in a set. Neither do we insist upon an effective procedure for deciding whether an arbitrary object is a member; the collection of programs in the last example is a set, although no algorithm can determine whether or not an arbitrary program will halt.

If a set is sufficiently small, we may define it by *extension*. To do this, we produce a list of its elements; a set s containing three elements a, b, and c could be defined by

$$s == \{a, b, c\}$$

Whenever we write out a set in such an explicit fashion, we use commas to separate the elements of the list, and braces to mark the beginning and end. The notation $n == e$ means that n is by definition a name for, and hence equal to, the expression e. We say that n is a *syntactic abbreviation* for e. This notation is fully explained in Chapter 6.

Example 5.2 The first two sets in Example 5.1 can be defined by extension:

$$\begin{aligned} \mathit{Oceans} &== \{\mathit{Atlantic},\ \mathit{Arctic},\ \mathit{Indian},\ \mathit{Pacific}\} \\ \mathit{Secretaries\text{-}General} &== \{\ \mathit{Trygve\ Lie},\ \mathit{Dag\ Hammarskjöld},\ \mathit{U\ Thant}, \\ &\qquad \mathit{Kurt\ Waldheim},\ \mathit{Javier\ Pérez\ de\ Cuéllar}, \\ &\qquad \mathit{Boutros\ Boutros\ Ghali}\} \end{aligned}$$

□

We write $x \in s$ to indicate that object x is an element of set s. This is pronounced 'x belongs to s', or 'x is in s'. If x is not a member of s, then we write $x \notin s$: clearly,

$$x \notin s \Leftrightarrow \neg(x \in s)$$

Example 5.3 If *Primes* denotes the set of all prime numbers, then the following propositions are true:

$$3 \in Primes$$

$$5 \in Primes$$

$$8 \notin Primes$$

□

The idea of set membership allows us to characterise equality between sets. Two sets s and t are *equal* if and only if they have the same elements: that is, every member of s is also a member of t and every member of t is also a member of s.

$$\frac{(\forall x : t \bullet x \in u) \land (\forall x : u \bullet x \in t)}{t = u} \text{ [ext]} \quad \text{provided that } x \text{ is free in neither } u \text{ nor } t$$

This rule expresses an equivalence known as the *axiom of extension*, one of the axioms of Zermelo-Fraenkel set theory—the variety of set theory upon which the Z notation is based.

An expression belongs to a set described in extension if and only if it is equal to one of the set's elements:

$$\frac{t = u_1 \lor \ldots \lor t = u_n}{t \in \{u_1, \ldots, u_n\}} \text{ [ext-mem]}$$

Again, an inference can be made in both directions. Used in conjunction with the axiom of extension, this rule allows us to discover an important property of sets: that the order and multiplicity of listed elements is unimportant.

Example 5.4 If we define

$$s == \{2, 2, 5, 5, 3\}$$
$$t == \{2, 3, 5\}$$

then

$$s = t$$

That is, the list expressions used to define s and t denote the same set.

This may be proved using the two inference rules given above:

$$
\dfrac{
\dfrac{
\dfrac{\dfrac{\dfrac{\dfrac{\lceil x \in s \rceil^{[1]}}{x \in \{2,2,5,5,3\}}\;[\text{eq-sub}]}{x = 2 \lor x = 3 \lor x = 5}\;[\text{ext-mem}]}{x \in \{2,3,5\}}\;[\text{ext-mem}]}{x \in t}\;[\text{eq-sub}]}{\forall x : s \bullet x \in t}\;[\forall\text{-intro}]^{[1]}
\qquad
\dfrac{\dfrac{\dfrac{\dfrac{\dfrac{\lceil x \in t \rceil^{[2]}}{x \in \{2,3,5\}}\;[\text{eq-sub}]}{x = 2 \lor x = 3 \lor x = 5}\;[\text{ext-mem}]}{x \in \{2,2,5,5,3\}}\;[\text{ext-mem}]}{x \in s}\;[\text{eq-sub}]}{\forall x : t \bullet x \in s}\;[\forall\text{-intro}]^{[2]}
}{(\forall x : s \bullet x \in t) \land (\forall x : t \bullet x \in s)}\;[\land\text{-intro}]
}{s = t}\;[\text{ext}]
$$

Notice that, having defined s and t through syntactic abbreviations, we are able to assume that they are equal and substitute accordingly. □

Some sets are so useful that they are given special names, and regarded as permanent features of our formal language: one such set is $\mathbb{N}$, the set of all natural numbers:

$$\mathbb{N} \;=\; \{0, 1, 2, 3, 4, 5, \ldots\}$$

This is not a formal definition of the set $\mathbb{N}$; such a definition is provided later in the book: see Example 6.8.

Another useful set is the set with no elements: the empty set. We write $\varnothing$ to denote such a set.

Example 5.5 If we let *Rockallers* be the set of people who live and work on Rockall, a small uninhabited island in the Atlantic Ocean, then

$$\mathit{Rockallers} \;=\; \varnothing$$

□

Another axiom of Zermelo-Fraenkel set theory states that the empty set exists, and has no elements:

$$\dfrac{}{\forall x : a \bullet x \notin \varnothing}\;[\text{empty}]$$

Whatever set a that we consider, none of the values x in a will appear in the empty set.

Example 5.6 Any universal quantification over the empty set is valid:

$$\forall x : \varnothing \bullet p$$

This may be proved by

$$\dfrac{\dfrac{\dfrac{[x \in \varnothing \wedge p]^{[1]}}{x \in \varnothing}\,[\text{dec-mem}] \qquad \dfrac{\dfrac{}{\forall x \in a \bullet x \notin \varnothing}\,[\text{empty}]}{\neg (x \in \varnothing)}\,[\forall\text{-elim}]}{p}\,[\neg\text{-elim}]}{\forall x : \varnothing \bullet p}\,[\forall\text{-intro}]^{[1]}$$

□

We may generalise our notion of set equality to allow us to compare two sets containing the same kind of objects. If every element from set s is also present in set t, we say that s is a subset of t, written $s \subseteq t$.

Example 5.7 Let *Benelux* denote the set of countries in the Benelux economic union, and let *Europe* denote the set of all countries in the European Union. Since the formation of the EU, it has been true that $Benelux \subseteq Europe$. There were other partners when the EU (then the EEC) was formed in 1957, so it is also true that $\neg (Europe \subseteq Benelux)$. □

We may prove that one set is a subset of another by establishing a universal quantification:

$$\frac{\forall x : s \bullet x \in t}{s \subseteq t}\,[\text{subset}] \qquad \text{provided that } x \text{ is not free in } t$$

This rule may be used in both directions; it is easy to establish that

$$s \subseteq t \wedge t \subseteq s \Leftrightarrow s = t$$

If s is a subset of t and t is a subset of s, then s and t are the same set.

5.2 Set comprehension

Given any non-empty set s, we can define a new set by considering only those elements of s that satisfy some property p. This method of definition is called *comprehension*. We write

$$\{ x : s \mid p \}$$

to denote the set of elements x in s that satisfy predicate p.

Example 5.8 Suppose that a red car is seen driving away from the scene of a crime. In this case, the authorities might wish to talk to anyone who owns such a vehicle. If *Person* denotes the set of all people, then the set to consider is given by

$$\{ x : Person \mid x \text{ drives a red car} \}$$

□

A simple comprehension term $\{ x : s \mid p \}$ has two parts: a declaration part $x : s$ and a predicate part p. The declaration part may be seen as a generator, providing a range s of possible values for x; the predicate part may be seen as a filter, picking out only those values of x that satisfy p.

It may be that we are interested in some expression formed from the values satisfying the predicate, and not in the values themselves. In this case, we add a term part to our set comprehension: we write

$$\{ x : s \mid p \bullet e \}$$

to denote the set of all expressions e such that x is drawn from s and satisfies p. The expression e will usually involve one or more free occurrences of x.

Example 5.9 In order to pursue their investigation of the crime, the authorities require a set of addresses to visit. This set is given by

$$\{ x : Person \mid x \text{ drives a red car} \bullet address(x) \}$$

□

If we have no restrictions upon the choice of values, we can still use a set comprehension to generate a set of expressions: we write

$$\{ x : s \bullet e \}$$

to denote the set of all expressions e such that x is drawn from s.

Example 5.10 Without the information that a red car was involved, the authorities would be left with the following set of addresses:

$$\{ x : Person \bullet address(x) \}$$

This set contains every address associated with an element of *Person*. □

We may treat the short forms of comprehension as abbreviations. A comprehension without a term part is equivalent to one in which the term is the same as the bound variable:

$$\{ x : s \mid p \} = \{ x : s \mid p \bullet x \}$$

Similarly, a comprehension without a predicate part is equivalent to one with the predicate *true*:

$$\{ x : s \bullet e \} = \{ x : s \mid \mathit{true} \bullet e \}$$

as the predicate *true* places no restriction upon the choice of values.

The declaration part of a comprehension may introduce more than one variable: we write

$$\{ x : a; \ y : b \mid p \bullet e \}$$

to denote the set of expressions e formed as x and y range over a and b, respectively, and satisfy predicate p.

Example 5.11 An eyewitness account has established that the driver of the red car had an accomplice, and that this accomplice left a copy of the *Daily Mail* at the scene. The authorities are now interested in tracing the following set of potential criminals:

$$\begin{aligned} \{ x : \mathit{Person}; \ y : \mathit{Person} \mid\ & x \text{ is associated with } y \land \\ & x \text{ drives a red car} \land \\ & y \text{ reads the } \textit{Daily Mail} \bullet x \} \end{aligned}$$

□

The variables declared in a set comprehension are bound in the same way as variables declared in a quantified expression. We may change their names provided that we choose names that are not already used in the comprehension.

Example 5.12 There is nothing special about the names chosen for the driver and his or her accomplice. The set in Example 5.11 could equally well have been written as

$$\begin{aligned} \{ v : \mathit{Person}; \ w : \mathit{Person} \mid\ & v \text{ is associated with } w \land \\ & v \text{ drives a red car} \land \\ & w \text{ reads the } \textit{Daily Mail} \bullet v \} \end{aligned}$$

□

If a set a has been defined by comprehension, then expression f is an element of a if and only if there is some expression e in a such that $e = f$.

$$\frac{\exists x : s \mid p \bullet e = f}{f \in \{ x : s \mid p \bullet e \}} \text{ [compre]} \qquad \text{provided that } x \text{ is not free in } f$$

Our use of this inference rule is supported by two axioms of Zermelo–Fraenkel set theory: the axiom of *specification* justifies the predicate part; the axiom of *replacement* justifies the term.

The one-point rule of Chapter 4 leads to a pair of derived rules for set comprehensions without a term part:

$$\frac{f \in s \quad x \in s \quad p[f / x]}{f \in \{ x : s \mid p \}} \text{ [compre-s]} \qquad \text{provided that } x \text{ is not free in } f$$

and

$$\frac{f \in \{ x : s \mid p \}}{f \in s \land p[f / x]} \text{ [compre-s]} \qquad \text{provided that } x \text{ is not free in } f$$

Example 5.13 If we replace the predicate part of a set comprehension with a weaker condition, then we obtain a larger set.

$$\frac{\forall x : a \bullet p \Rightarrow q}{\{ x : a \mid p \} \subseteq \{ x : a \mid q \}}$$

This may be proved by

$$\cfrac{\cfrac{\cfrac{\cfrac{\cfrac{\begin{matrix}\vdots \\ y \in a\end{matrix} \quad \forall x : a \bullet p \Rightarrow q}{p[y/x] \Rightarrow q[y/x]} \text{ [}\forall\text{-elim]} \qquad \cfrac{\cfrac{\lceil y \in \{ x : a \mid p \} \rceil^{[1]}}{\exists x : a \mid p \bullet x = y} \text{ [compre]}}{p[y/x]} \text{ [one-point]}}{q[y/x]} \text{ [}\forall\text{-elim]}}{\exists x : a \mid q \bullet x = y} \text{ [one-point]}}{y \in \{ x : a \mid q \}} \text{ [compre]}}{\forall y : \{ x : a \mid p \} \bullet y \in \{ x : a \mid q \}} \text{ [}\forall\text{-intro]}^{[1]}}{\{ x : a \mid p \} \subseteq \{ x : a \mid q \}} \text{ [subset]}$$

We have not justified the assertion $y \in a$ above. We could assert that this follows immediately from the assumption $\lceil y \in \{ x : a \mid p \} \rceil^{[1]}$. For the purposes of this example, however, we can achieve a greater degree of formality by exhibiting the following derivation:

$$\dfrac{\dfrac{[y \in \{\, x : a \mid p \,\}]^{[1]}}{\exists x \in a \mid p \bullet x = y}\,[\text{compre}] \qquad \dfrac{\dfrac{[x : a \mid p \land x = y]^{[2]}}{x \in a}\,[\text{dec-mem}] \quad \dfrac{[x : a \mid p \land x = y]^{[2]}}{x = y}\,[\land\text{-elim2}]}{y \in a}\,[\text{subst}]}{y \in a}\,[\exists\text{-elim}]^{[2]}$$

□

5.3 Power sets

If a is a set, then the set of all subsets of a is called the *power set* of a, and written $\mathbb{P}\,a$. For example, if a is the set $\{x, y\}$ then

$$\mathbb{P}\,a = \{\varnothing, \{x\}, \{y\}, \{x, y\}\}$$

This new set has four elements: the empty set, the set a itself, and the two other subsets of a. In general, if a set a has n elements, then the power set $\mathbb{P}\,a$ has 2^n.

Example 5.14 Four friends have been invited to dinner: Alice, Bill, Claire, and David. If their names are abbreviated to A, B, C, and D, then the set of people that actually arrive will be an element of the power set

$$\begin{aligned}\mathbb{P}\{A, B, C, D\} = \{\, &\varnothing, \{A\}, \{B\}, \{C\}, \{D\}, \{A, B\}, \{A, C\}, \{A, D\},\\ &\{B, C\}, \{B, D\}, \{C, D\}, \{A, B, C\}, \{A, B, D\},\\ &\{A, C, D\}, \{B, C, D\}, \{A, B, C, D\} \,\}\end{aligned}$$

□

A set s belongs to the power set of a if and only if s is a subset of a:

$$\dfrac{s \subseteq a}{\overline{s \in \mathbb{P}\,a}}\,[\text{power}]$$

This inference rule corresponds to the *power set* axiom of Zermelo-Fraenkel set theory, which states that a power set exists for any set a.

Example 5.15 For any set a, the empty set is an element of $\mathbb{P}\, a$:

$$\varnothing \in \mathbb{P}\, a$$

This follows from the result of Example 5.6, that any universal quantification over the empty set is valid:

$$\cfrac{\cfrac{\overline{\forall x : \varnothing \bullet x \in a}\;\text{[Example 5.6]}}{\varnothing \subseteq a}\;\text{[subset]}}{\varnothing \in \mathbb{P}\, a}\;\text{[power]}$$

□

The Z notation has a second power set symbol; we write $\mathbb{F}\, a$ to denote the set of *finite* subsets of a; this symbol is defined in Chapter 10.

5.4 Cartesian products

In a formal description of a software system, we may wish to associate objects of different kinds: names; numbers; various forms of composite data. We may also wish to associate two or more objects of the same kind, respecting order and multiplicity. To support this structuring of information, the Z notation includes *Cartesian products*. These are sets of *tuples*: ordered lists of elements, one drawn from each of the component sets.

If a and b are sets, then the Cartesian product $a \times b$ consists of all tuples of the form (x, y), where x is an element of a and y is an element of b. A tuple with exactly two elements is called an *ordered pair*; a tuple with exactly n elements, where n is greater than 2, is called an n-tuple.

Example 5.16 In the game of *Cluedo*™, it is assumed that a murder has been committed. The players are then invited to guess the identity of the person responsible, the room in which the crime was committed, and the weapon used. If we define the set of guests, the set of locations, and the set of potential weapons,

$$\begin{aligned} Guests == \{ & Mrs\ Peacock, Miss\ Scarlett, Reverend\ Green, \\ & Mrs\ White, Colonel\ Mustard, Professor\ Plum \} \\ Rooms == \{ & Library, Study, Lounge, Hall, Kitchen, \\ & Billiard\ Room, Ballroom, Conservatory, Dining\ Room \} \\ Weapons == \{ & Rope, Dagger, Revolver, Candlestick, \\ & Lead\ Pipe, Spanner \} \end{aligned}$$

then the set of possible solutions is given by the Cartesian product:

$$Guests \times Rooms \times Weapons$$

and a typical guess would be

$$(Colonel\ Mustard, Library, Revolver)$$

It was Colonel Mustard, in the library, with the revolver. □

An n-tuple $(x_1, \ldots, x_n)$ is present in the Cartesian product $a_1 \times \ldots \times a_n$ if and only if each element x_i is an element of the corresponding set a_i.

$$\frac{x_1 \in a_1 \land \ldots \land x_n \in a_n}{(x_1, \ldots, x_n) \in a_1 \times \ldots \times a_n} \text{ [cart-mem]}$$

In the case where $n = 2$, this rule expresses the following equivalence:

$$(x, y) \in a \times b \Leftrightarrow x \in a \land y \in b$$

The ordered pair (a, b) is an element of the product set $a \times b$ if and only if x is in a and y is in b.

The order of components in a Cartesian product is important: if a and b are different sets, then $a \times b \neq b \times a$. A similar consideration applies to the elements of a product set: two tuples are the same if and only if they agree in every component:

$$\frac{x_1 = y_1 \land \ldots \land x_n = y_n}{(x_1, \ldots, x_n) = (y_1, \ldots, y_n)} \text{ [cart-eq]}$$

To refer to a particular component of a tuple t, we use a projection notation: the first component of the tuple is written $t.1$; the second component $t.2$, and so on.

$$\frac{t.1 = x_1 \land \ldots \land t.n = x_n}{t = (x_1, \ldots, x_n)} \text{ [cart-proj]}$$

Example 5.17 If *guess* is an element of $Guests \times Rooms \times Weapons$, then

- *guess*.1 is the name of the murderer
- *guess*.2 is the suggested location
- *guess*.3 is the weapon used

If *guess* is the tuple $(Colonel\ Mustard, Library, Revolver)$ then these would be *Colonel Mustard*, *Library*, and *Revolver*, respectively. □

The product set is so called because the size of the set $a \times b$ is the product of the size of a and the size of b.

Example 5.18 There are 6 guests, 9 rooms, and 6 weapons in *Cluedo*™. There are $6 \times 9 \times 6 = 234$ elements in the set

$$Guests \times Rooms \times Weapons$$

There are 234 possible solutions to the mystery. □

5.5 Union, intersection, and difference

If a and b are sets, then we write $a \cup b$ to denote the *union* of a and b; this is the smallest set that contains all of the elements of a and b.

$$\frac{x \in (a \cup b)}{x \in a \lor x \in b} \text{ [union]}$$

We may generalise the union operator as follows: if s is a set of sets $\{a, b, c, \ldots\}$ then we write $\bigcup s$ to denote the smallest set containing all of the elements that appear in at least one of a, b, c, ...

$$\frac{x \in \bigcup s}{\exists a : s \bullet x \in a} \text{ [Union]}$$

The *union* axiom of Zermelo-Fraenkel set theory guarantees the existence of $\bigcup s$ for any set of sets s.

Example 5.19 Edward, Fleur, and Gareth have each been given an assignment consisting of 7 questions. Edward has attempted the questions numbered 1, 2, and 4; Fleur has attempted all but questions 5 and 6; Gareth has attempted only those questions with even numbers. We may record this information as follows:

$$E == \{1, 2, 4\}$$
$$F == \{1, 2, 3, 4, 7\}$$
$$G == \{2, 4, 6\}$$

We may discover which questions have been attempted by examining the union of these three sets:

$$\bigcup\{E, F, G\} = \{1, 2, 3, 4, 6, 7\}$$

This is the set of numbers n such that question n was attempted by at least one of the three. □

We write $a \cap b$ to denote the *intersection* of two sets a and b; this is the set that contains only those elements that are common to a and b.

$$\frac{x \in (a \cap b)}{x \in a \land x \in b} \text{ [inter]}$$

We may generalise the intersection operator as follows: if s is a set of sets $\{a, b, c, \ldots\}$, then $\bigcap s$ denotes the set containing only those elements that appear in every one of a, b, c, ...

$$\frac{x \in \bigcap s}{\forall a : s \bullet x \in a} \text{ [Inter]}$$

If s is the empty set of sets, then the universal quantification above will be true for any x; the set $\bigcap \varnothing$ contains all of the elements of the appropriate type: see Section 5.6.

Example 5.20 Using the information of Example 5.19, we may discover which questions were attempted by all three students by examining the intersection

$$\bigcap\{E, F, G\} = \{2, 4\}$$

This is the set of numbers n such that question n was attempted by every one of the three. □

If a and b are sets, then we write $a \setminus b$ to denote the set difference *a minus b*; this is the set containing only those elements that appear in a but not in b.

$$\frac{x \in (a \setminus b)}{x \in a \land x \notin b} \text{ [diff]}$$

Example 5.21 The set of questions which have been attempted by both Edward and Fleur, but have not been attempted by Gareth, is given by

$$(E \cap F) \setminus G = \{6\}$$

and the set of questions attempted by Fleur alone is given by

$$F \setminus (E \cup G) = \{3, 7\}$$

□

5.6 Types

When people use set theory to specify software systems, they often include some notion of types. In Z, this notion is a simple one: a *type* is a maximal set, at least within the confines of the current specification. This has the effect of ensuring that each value x in a specification is associated with exactly one type: the largest set s present for which $x \in s$.

The Z notation has a single built-in type: the set of all integers $\mathbb{Z}$. Any other types will be constructed from $\mathbb{Z}$, or from *basic types* of values. A basic type is a set whose internal structure is invisible. We may introduce elements of such a set, and associate properties with them, but we can assume nothing about the set itself.

Example 5.22 A computer system used by the United States Immigration Service might store information about foreign nationals presently in the United States. In a specification of this system, the set of all people would be a good choice for a basic type. The set of all UK nationals would be a poor choice, as we are likely to consider supersets of this set. □

Additional types can be created using the power set constructor $\mathbb{P}$ and the Cartesian product $\times$. If T is a type, then the power set $\mathbb{P}\,T$ is the type of all subsets of T. If T and U are types, then $T \times U$ is the type of all pairs formed from elements of T and elements of U.

Example 5.23 The power set $\mathbb{P}\,\mathbb{Z}$ is the type of all sets of integers,

$$\{1, 2, 3\} \in \mathbb{P}\,\mathbb{Z}$$

while the Cartesian product $\mathbb{Z} \times \mathbb{Z}$ is the type of all number pairs:

$$(1, 2) \in \mathbb{Z} \times \mathbb{Z}$$

□

The fact that each value in a specification is associated with exactly one type is most useful. We can apply type-checking algorithms to the mathematical text of a Z document to reveal any inconsistencies in the use of variable names and expressions. Such algorithms can verify neither the interpretation of these names nor the inferences made using them, but they are a powerful means of increasing confidence in a formal specification.

Our use of types imposes restrictions upon the ways in which we may define and use sets. For example, the statement $x \in s$ is valid only if the type of s is the power set of the type of x. If this is not the case, then the statement is meaningless and cannot be used in specifications. Such restrictions are welcome, in that they help us to avoid certain forms of logical paradox.

Example 5.24 Suppose that types were not important in the use of $\in$. In this case, we could define R, the set of sets of some type T that are not members of themselves:

$$R == \{s : T \mid \neg\, s \in s\}$$

We would then be faced with a logical paradox.

$$\cfrac{\cfrac{R \in T \land \neg\,(R \in R)}{R \in \{s : T \mid \neg\, s \in s\}}\;[\text{compre-s}]}{R \in R}\;[\text{defn of } R]$$

The set R is an element of itself if it isn't an element of itself, and vice versa; to define R would be to introduce a contradiction into our specification. □

Chapter 6

Definitions

A formal specification should contain a significant amount of prose; this should relate the mathematical objects to features of the design: system states, data structures, properties, and operations. Of course, if the statements in the mathematics are to be meaningful, then we must ensure that the objects concerned are properly defined.

In the Z notation, there are several ways of defining an object. We may simply *declare*, we may define *by abbreviation*, or we may define *by axiom*. In addition, there are special mechanisms for *free types* and *schemas*, discussed later in the book. In this chapter, we explain the use of declarations, abbreviations, and axiomatic definitions. We also present rules for reasoning with the information that they contain.

6.1 Declarations

The simplest way to define an object is to declare it. If the object is a given set, or basic type, then we do this by writing its name between brackets: for example, the declaration

$$[\mathit{Type}]$$

introduces a new basic type called *Type*. If the object is a variable, then we give the name of a set that it comes from. The declaration

$$x : A$$

introduces a new variable x, drawn from the set A. If this set is not $\mathbb{Z}$, the type of integers, then it must be defined elsewhere in the specification.

Example 6.1 A hotel switchboard uses a software package to maintain a record of call charges to current guests. A formal specification of this system could include the declaration

$$[Guests, Rooms]$$

introducing two basic types to represent the set of all guests and the set of all rooms. A variable of the type *Guest* is introduced by the following declaration:

$$x : Guest$$

□

A declaration of the form $x : t$, where t is a type, is called a *signature*: it makes explicit the underlying type of the object being introduced. Any other declaration may be replaced by a signature and a constraint, the constraint defining the subset of the underlying type that the object is drawn from. If the declaration is local—part of a set comprehension, quantification, or μ-expression—then the constraint follows a vertical bar:

$$x : t \mid x \in s$$

If the declaration is global—introducing a constant that may be used throughout the specification—then an axiomatic definition is required: see Section 6.4.

6.2 Abbreviations

Another way to define an object is to exhibit an existing object and state that the two are the same. The abbreviation definition

$$symbol \; == \; term$$

introduces a new name for *term*, a mathematical object that must be defined elsewhere in the specification. The new name *symbol* is a global constant of the specification, with the same type and value as the expression *term*.

Example 6.2 The abbreviation definition

$$Additive \; == \; \{red, green, blue\}$$

introduces a set *Additive*, as another name for the set described in enumeration above. The names *red*, *green*, and *blue* must be defined elsewhere, they are not introduced by the abbreviation. If they are declared as elements of a type *Colours*, then *Additive* is a constant of type $\mathbb{P}\, Colours$. □

Any symbol defined by abbreviation may be eliminated from a specification by replacing each instance with the expression on the right of the definition. Accordingly, the notation may not be used to make recursive definitions.

Example 6.3 The recursive acronym gnu could *not* be defined using the abbreviation notation:

$$\mathsf{gnu} == \mathsf{gnu}'s\ not\ unix$$

This is not a valid abbreviation, as gnu appears also on the right. □

An abbreviation definition is quite benign: it asserts nothing, it simply provides a more convenient way of referring to something that is already defined.

Example 6.4 Given the basic type *Person*, representing the set of all people, we may introduce abbreviations for the set of all people who take sugar in tea:

$$English == \{p : Person \mid p \text{ drinks tea} \land p \text{ takes sugar}\}$$

and the set of all people who put salt on their porridge:

$$Scots == \{q : Person \mid q \text{ eats porridge} \land q \text{ adds salt}\}$$

Provided that the constraining predicates are properly introduced, the two sets above are bound to be well defined. □

6.3 Generic abbreviations

In the course of a formal specification, we may wish to define a *family* of symbols, one for each value of a particular index or parameter. Rather than present a series of similar definitions, we employ a generic form of abbreviation:

$$symbol\ parameters == term$$

This defines a global constant *symbol* parameterised by a list of sets, each of which may appear in the expression *term*.

The simplest example is the definition of the empty set symbol $\varnothing$. In a Z specification, there may be many empty sets, one for each type. We must distinguish between empty sets of different types; no expression can have a value that belongs to more than one type. To define the empty set of objects from a set S, we write

$$\varnothing[S] == \{ x : S \mid false \}$$

The generic parameter S may be any set, although in the case of $\varnothing$, it is likely to be a type. The parameter list may be enclosed in brackets, as above, or omitted altogether where the values chosen are obvious from the context.

Example 6.5 For any set T, we may define the set of all non-empty subsets of T as follows:

$$\mathbb{P}_1 T \;==\; \{ a : \mathbb{P}\, T \mid a \neq \varnothing \}$$

We are happy to omit the brackets from the parameter list in the definition and in instantiations:

$$\mathbb{P}_1 \{0, 1\} \;==\; \{\{0\}, \{1\}, \{0, 1\}\}$$

A second generic symbol appears in the definition above: the $\varnothing$ symbol. From the context, it is clear that this denotes the empty set of elements from T. □

For the convenience of the reader, we allow the definition of infix generic symbols. The abbreviation

parameters symbol parameters == *term*

defines a global constant *symbol* which may appear inside a list of parameters.

Example 6.6 We may define a generic symbol *rel* such that, for any sets s and t, the set s *rel* t is the power set of $s \times t$:

$$s \mathrel{rel} t \;==\; \mathbb{P}(s \times t)$$

Each element of s *rel* t is a set of pairs; the first component of each pair is an element of s; the second is an element of t. □

Once an abbreviation definition has been made, we may conclude that the symbol on the left is equal to the term on the right. Each abbreviation adds an inference rule to our specification:

$$\frac{}{s = e}\;[\text{abbrev}] \qquad \text{given the abbreviation } s == e$$

A generic abbreviation adds a family of rules, one for each instantiation.

Example 6.7 From the definition of the empty set symbol given in the text, we may establish that, for any n in $\mathbb{N}$, n is not an element of the empty set of numbers.

$$\dfrac{\dfrac{\dfrac{\dfrac{\dfrac{\lceil n \in \varnothing[\mathbb{N}] \rceil^{[2]}}{n \in \{\, n : \mathbb{N} \mid \mathit{false} \,\}}\;\text{[eq-sub]} \qquad \dfrac{\dfrac{}{\varnothing[\mathbb{N}] = \{\, n : \mathbb{N} \mid \mathit{false} \,\}}\;\text{[abbrev]}}{\{\, n : \mathbb{N} \mid \mathit{false} \,\} = \varnothing[\mathbb{N}]}\;\text{[eq-symm]}}{n \in \mathbb{N} \land \mathit{false}}\;\text{[compre-s]}}{\mathit{false}}\;[\land\text{-elim2}]}{n \notin \varnothing[\mathbb{N}]}\;[\neg\text{-intro}]^{[2]}}{\forall n : \mathbb{N} \bullet n \notin \varnothing[\mathbb{N}]}\;[\forall\text{-intro}]^{[1]}$$

□

6.4 Axiomatic definitions

A third form of definition includes a constraint upon the object being introduced. Such definitions are said to be *axiomatic*, as the constraint is assumed to hold whenever the symbol is used: it is an axiom for the object. In the Z notation, an axiomatic definition takes the form

| *declaration*
|———————
| *predicate*

where the predicate expresses the constraints upon the object or objects introduced in the declaration.

The definition

| $x : s$
|———————
| p

introduces a new symbol x, an element of s, satisfying predicate p. The predicate part of the definition may place constraints upon the values that x can take; it may even constrain x to the point where there is only one object that x can denote.

Example 6.8 We may use an axiomatic definition to define the set of natural numbers:

| $\mathbb{N} : \mathbb{P}\,\mathbb{Z}$
|———————
| $\forall z : \mathbb{Z} \bullet z \in \mathbb{N} \Leftrightarrow z \geqslant 0$

This introduces a new object $\mathbb{N}$, a subset of $\mathbb{Z}$, containing only those integers that are greater than or equal to zero. There is exactly one subset of $\mathbb{Z}$ with this property. □

If this is not the case, if there are several values of the underlying type that meet the constraints, then we say that the definition is *loose*.

Example 6.9 We may define a constant *maxsize* as follows:

$$\begin{array}{|l} maxsize : \mathbb{N} \\ \hline maxsize > 0 \end{array}$$

That is, *maxsize* is a natural number, and it is strictly greater than zero. □

The declaration and predicate parts of an axiomatic definition may be used to support reasoning about the symbol they define. If the symbol x is introduced as above, then we are free to apply the inference rule:

$$\frac{}{x \in s \wedge p}\,[\text{axdef}]$$

There will be a rule like this for each axiomatic declaration.

Example 6.10 The definition of *maxsize* can be used to establish the truth of the following predicate:

$$\exists\, n : \mathbb{N} \bullet n = maxsize - 1$$

The proof is as follows:

$$\cfrac{\cfrac{\cfrac{\cfrac{\cfrac{\cfrac{}{maxsize \in \mathbb{N} \wedge maxsize > 0}\,[\text{axdef}]}{maxsize > 0}\,[\wedge\text{-elim2}]}{maxsize \geq 1}\,[\text{arith}]}{maxsize - 1 \geq 0}\,[\text{arith}]}{maxsize - 1 \in \mathbb{N}}\,[\text{arith}]}{\exists\, n : \mathbb{N} \bullet n = maxsize - 1}\,[\text{one-point-s}]$$

□

We must take care that our axiomatic definitions do not introduce inconsistencies into a specification. Such a definition asserts that some object exists with the stated property; this may contradict other parts of the specification, or even well-known mathematical results.

Example 6.11 If *Primes* has been defined as the set of all prime numbers, then we may define *maxprime*, the largest prime number, as follows:

$$\begin{array}{|l} maxprime : \mathbb{N} \\ \hline \forall\, p : Primes \bullet maxprime \geq p \end{array}$$

This would be an unfortunate definition, as it can be shown that such a number cannot exist. □

In some cases, we may wish to precede an axiomatic definition with a proof of existence: a proof of $\exists\, x : s \bullet p$.

If the predicate part of an axiomatic definition is *true*, then it may be omitted, leaving a definition of the form

$$\begin{array}{|l} x : s \end{array}$$

This is a declaration of a *global* constant x; it introduces a corresponding inference rule into the current specification:

$$\frac{}{x \in s}\ \text{[axdef]}$$

Such a definition may still be contradictory: the set s may be empty.

6.5 Generic definitions

A generic form of axiomatic definition may be used to define a family of global constants, parameterised by some set X. The definition

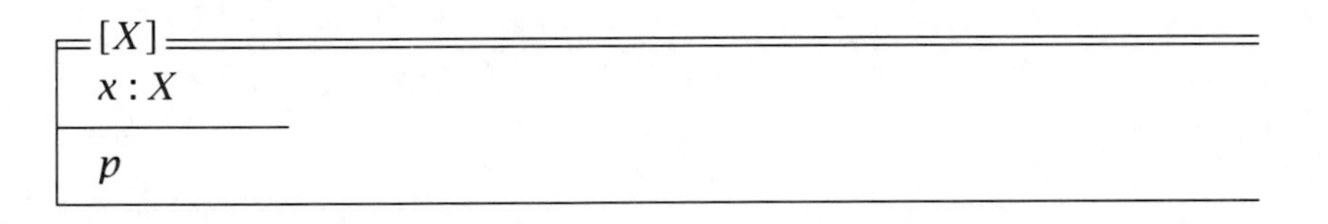

introduces a generic constant x of type X, satisfying predicate p. The set X is a formal parameter; it can be regarded as a basic type whose scope is the body of the definition.

Any value given to this parameter when the definition is used must be of set type. As in the case of generic abbreviations, the actual parameter list may be enclosed in brackets, or omitted altogether when the instantiation is obvious from the context.

Example 6.12 The generic non-empty power set constructor defined using an abbreviation in Example 6.5 may also be defined using a generic definition:

$$
\begin{array}{l}
[X] \\
\hline
\mathbb{P}_1 : \mathbb{P}(\mathbb{P}\,X) \\
\hline
\mathbb{P}_1 = \{\, s : \mathbb{P}\,X \mid s \neq \varnothing \,\}
\end{array}
$$

In applications, the brackets around the generic parameter are optional: the forms $\mathbb{P}_1[s]$ and $\mathbb{P}_1\, s$ are equally acceptable. □

Example 6.13 We can use a generic definition to define the subset symbol:

$$
\begin{array}{l}
[X] \\
\hline
\_ \subseteq \_ : \mathbb{P}\,X \leftrightarrow \mathbb{P}\,X \\
\hline
\forall\, s, t : \mathbb{P}\,X \bullet \\
\qquad s \subseteq t \Leftrightarrow \forall\, x : X \bullet x \in s \Rightarrow x \in t
\end{array}
$$

The $\subseteq$ symbol denotes a *relation* between two sets of the same type $\mathbb{P}\,X$ (relations are mathematical objects discussed in Chapter 7). In applications, we omit the parameter list altogether:

$$\{2,3\} \subseteq \{1,2,3,4\}$$

□

The rule for introducing facts about a generic definition is similar to that for axiomatic ones, with the obvious addition of a mechanism for instantiating parameters. In the general case, if S is an expression including X—$\mathbb{P}\,X$, for example—and the specification contains the declaration

$$
\begin{array}{l}
[X] \\
\hline
x : S \\
\hline
p
\end{array}
$$

then we may apply the following rule:

$$\frac{}{(x \in S \wedge p)[t, x[t] \,/\, X, x]} \text{ [gendef]}$$

where t is the value being given to the formal generic parameter X. Again, this is a family of inference rules, for each definition in the specification, and for each possible instantiation of X.

Example 6.14 The definition of $\mathbb{P}_1$ in Example 6.12 gives us the property of its declaration and its axiom; we can use the latter to prove that

$$\varnothing[\mathbb{N}] \notin \mathbb{P}_1[\mathbb{N}]$$

A suitable proof of this result might be

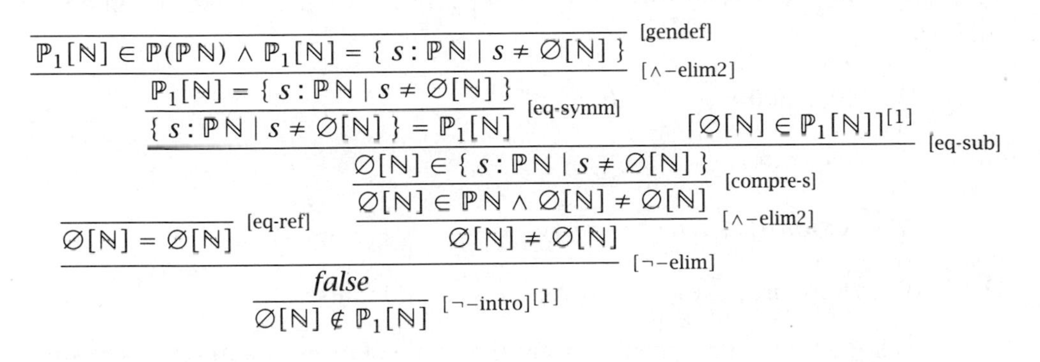

□

6.6 Sets and predicates

All of the objects that we define in Z are *sets* of one kind or another. A reader with some experience of mathematical logic might be excused for asking: how do we define a predicate symbol? How do we introduce a symbol such as *good*, so that *good* x is true for some values of x and false for others? The answer is simple: we define a predicate in terms of the set of objects that satisfy it.

If p is a predicate with a free variable x of type t, and

$$c = \{ x : t \mid p \}$$

then we say that c is the *characteristic set* of p: it is the set of values of x for which p is true.

If we wished to define a predicate *good*, then we could define it as a set of values:

$$\begin{array}{|l} good : \mathbb{P}\, t \\ \hline \ldots \end{array}$$

We can now write $x \in good$ to represent the statement 'x is good'.

Example 6.15 We wish to formalise the predicate 'is a crowd' upon sets of people. To do this, we introduce a set of sets:

$$\begin{array}{|l} crowds : \mathbb{P}(\mathbb{P}\, Person) \\ \hline crowds = \{\, s : \mathbb{P}\, Person \mid \# s \geqslant 3 \,\} \end{array}$$

The expression '$\#s$' denotes the number of elements in set s—it is defined formally in Section 8.6. With this definition of *crowds*, we may make statements such as

$$\{Alice, Bill, Claire\} \in crowds$$

and

$$\{Dave, Edward\} \in crowds$$

The first of these propositions is true, the second is false. □

It is sometimes convenient to treat the name of a set as a unary operator: in this case, the definition will include an underscore to indicate the position of the argument.

Example 6.16 For a number of reasons, it is not a good idea to have Alice and Bill in the room at the same time. Thus, a set of people is *safe* if it contains Alice, or Bill, or neither, but *not* both. We may define *safe* as a property of sets of people:

$$\begin{array}{|l} safe\_ : \mathbb{P}\, Person \\ \hline \forall\, s : \mathbb{P}\, Person \bullet safe\ s \Leftrightarrow \neg(\{Alice, Bill\} \subseteq s) \end{array}$$

We treat *safe s* as an abbreviation of $s \in safe$. We are then free to decide the truth of such statements as

$$safe\ \{Alice, Claire, Dave\}$$

and

$$\neg\ (safe\ \{Alice, Bill, Edward\})$$

□

Chapter 7

Relations

In a formal specification, it is often necessary to describe relationships between objects: this record is stored under that key; this input channel is connected to that output channel; this action takes priority over that one. These relationships, and others like them, can be described using simple mathematical objects called *relations*.

In this chapter, we explain how to define relations, and how to extract information from them. We explain that relations may be classified: as *homogeneous* or *heterogeneous*; as *reflexive*, *symmetric*, or *transitive*. We describe how relations may be inverted or composed to form new objects, and explain what these objects represent.

7.1 Binary relations

Although we may define relations that express links between any finite number of objects, it is enough to employ *binary relations*: relations that express links between pairs of objects. In our mathematical language, a relation is a set of ordered pairs, a subset of a Cartesian product.

If X and Y are sets, then $X \leftrightarrow Y$ denotes the set of all relations between X and Y. The relation symbol may be defined by generic abbreviation:

$$X \leftrightarrow Y == \mathbb{P}(X \times Y)$$

Any element of $X \leftrightarrow Y$ is a set of ordered pairs in which the first element is drawn from X, and the second from Y: that is, a subset of the Cartesian product set $X \times Y$.

Example 7.1 The set of relations $\{a, b\} \leftrightarrow \{0, 1\}$ is the set of sets of pairs

$$\{\varnothing, \{(a,0)\}, \{(a,1)\}, \{(b,0)\}, \{(b,1)\}, \{(a,0),(a,1)\}, \{(a,0),(b,0)\}, \{(a,0),(b,1)\}, \{(a,1),(b,0)\}, \{(a,1),(b,1)\}, \{(b,0),(b,1)\}, \{(a,0),(a,1),(b,0)\}, \{(a,0),(a,1),(b,1)\}, \{(a,0),(b,0),(b,1)\}, \{(a,1),(b,0),(b,1)\}, \{(a,0),(a,1),(b,0),(b,1)\}\}$$

A typical element of this set is $\{(a,0),(a,1),(b,0)\}$: the relation that associates a with 0, a with 1, and b with 0. □

Where ordered pairs are being used as elements of relations, we will often write them using a *maplet* notation. The expression $x \mapsto y$ is another way of writing (x, y).

Example 7.2 The relation *drives* is used to record which makes of car are driven by the members of a small group of people. If the group of people is defined by

$$Drivers == \{helen, indra, jim, kate\}$$

and the choice of cars is defined by

$$Cars == \{alfa, beetle, cortina, delorean\}$$

then *drives* is an element of $Drivers \leftrightarrow Cars$, and the statement 'Kate drives a cortina' could be formalised as $kate \mapsto cortina \in drives$. □

We may also choose to introduce a relation as an infix symbol: a symbol that sits between its arguments. Many familiar relations are written in this way: the less-than-or-equal-to relation $\leqslant$ on numbers; the subset relation $\subseteq$ on sets. If the pair (x, y) is an element of the infix relation R, then we may write $x\ R\ y$. When we define an infix relation, we include underscores to indicate where the arguments should go.

Example 7.3 The relation *drives* could be defined by

$$\_drives\_ : Drivers \leftrightarrow Cars$$

$$drives = \{helen \mapsto beetle, indra \mapsto alfa, jim \mapsto beetle, kate \mapsto cortina\}$$

That is, Helen and Jim drive Beetles, Indra drives an Alfa, Kate drives a Cortina, and nobody drives a DeLorean. □

Simple relations can be illustrated using diagrams with arrows, or *graphs*. The graph of *drives* is shown in Figure 7.1.

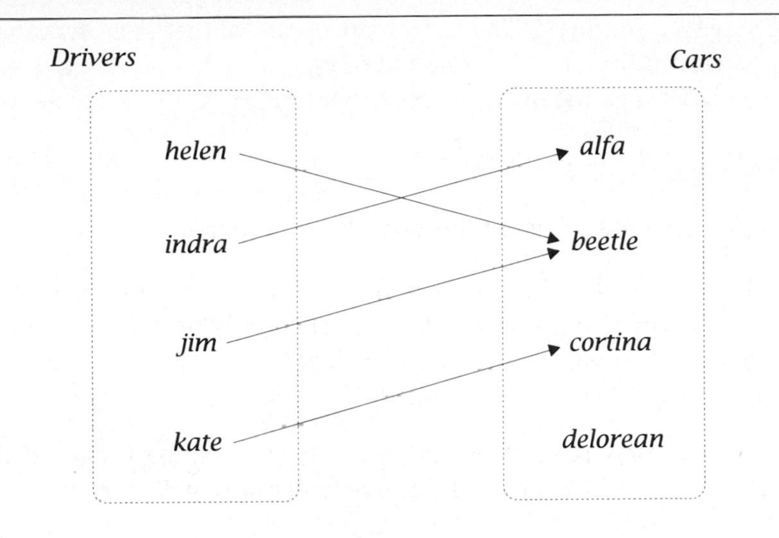

Figure 7.1: The relation *drives*

7.2 Domain and range

A relation may contain a great deal of information; often, we require only a small part. To enable us to extract the information that we need, a number of basic functions are included in our mathematical language. The simplest examples are the *domain* and *range* functions, 'dom' and 'ran'. If R is a relation of type $X \leftrightarrow Y$, then the domain of R is the set of elements in X related to something in Y:

$$\operatorname{dom} R = \{ x : X;\ y : Y \mid x \mapsto y \in R \bullet x \}$$

The range of R is the set of elements of Y to which some element of X is related:

$$\operatorname{ran} R = \{ x : X;\ y : Y \mid x \mapsto y \in R \bullet y \}$$

Example 7.4 The set of people that drive is the domain of *drives*:

$$\operatorname{dom} \mathit{drives} = \{\mathit{helen}, \mathit{indra}, \mathit{jim}, \mathit{kate}\}$$

The set of cars that are driven is the range:

$$\operatorname{ran} \mathit{drives} = \{\mathit{alfa}, \mathit{beetle}, \mathit{cortina}\}$$

□

We may focus upon part of the domain, or part of the range, by considering a subset of the relation. If R is a relation of type $X \leftrightarrow Y$, and A is any subset of X, then $A \lhd R$ denotes the *domain restriction* of R to A; this is the set of pairs

$$\{ x : X;\ y : Y \mid x \mapsto y \in R \land x \in A \bullet x \mapsto y \}$$

Any maplet whose first element lies outside A is ignored.

Example 7.5 In Example 7.2, we presented information about cars driven by members of the set *Drivers*. If we are concerned only with Jim and Kate, then it is enough to examine the relation$\{jim, kate\} \lhd drives$, which contains the maplets $jim \mapsto beetle$ and $kate \mapsto cortina$. □

Alternatively, we may restrict our attention to part of the range. If B is any subset of Y, then $R \rhd B$ denotes the *range restriction* of R to B: this is the set of pairs

$$\{ x : X;\ y : Y \mid x \mapsto y \in R \land y \in B \bullet x \mapsto y \}$$

Any maplet whose second element lies outside B is ignored.

Example 7.6 If we are interested only in sports cars, then it is enough to consider the relation $drives \rhd \{alfa, delorean\}$ which contains the single maplet $indra \mapsto alfa$. □

The position of the arguments is different for the two forms of restriction. In domain restriction, the set argument appears to the left of the operator; in range restriction, it appears to the right. This corresponds to the position of domain and range in the Cartesian product underlying the relation.

To exclude the set A from the domain of a relation, we could consider the domain restriction $(X \setminus A) \lhd R$. However, this occurs so frequently that an abbreviated form is provided. We write $A \ndres R$ to denote the *domain subtraction* of A from R, where

$$A \ndres R \;=\; \{ x : X;\ y : Y \mid x \mapsto y \in R \land x \notin A \bullet x \mapsto y \}$$

This includes only those maplets whose first element does not lie in A.

Similarly, we may exclude the set B from the range of a relation. We write $R \nrres B$ to denote the *range subtraction* of B from R, where

$$R \nrres B \;=\; \{ x : X;\ y : Y \mid x \mapsto y \in R \land y \notin B \bullet x \mapsto y \}$$

This includes every maplet whose second element does not lie in B.

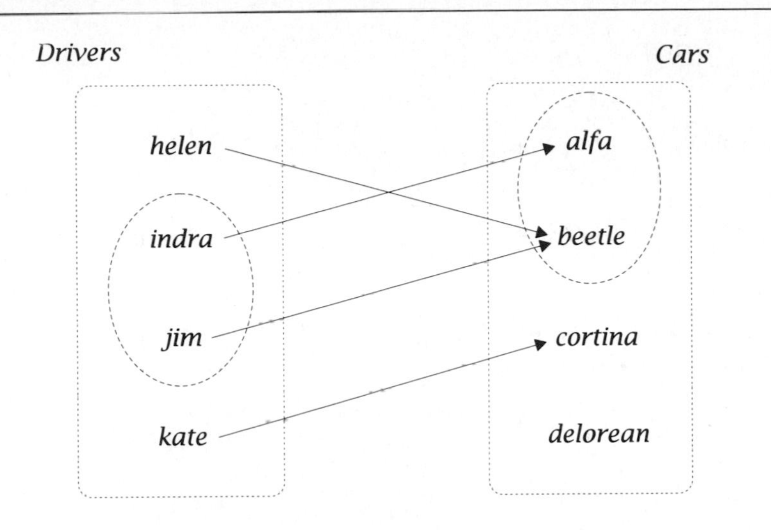

Figure 7.2: Relational image of $\{indra, jim\}$

Example 7.7 If we are concerned only with people who are not called 'Jim', then the relation $\{jim\} \mathbin{⩤} drives$ tells us all that we want to know. It is a relation with three elements:

$$\{helen \mapsto beetle, indra \mapsto alfa, kate \mapsto cortina\}$$

□

It may be that we are interested in the effect of a relation upon a particular set of elements. If R is an element of $X \leftrightarrow Y$, and A is a subset of X, then we write $R(\!|\ A\ |\!)$ to denote the *relational image* of A under R. This is the set of all elements in Y to which some element of A is related. We may observe that

$$R(\!|\ A\ |\!) = \operatorname{ran}(A \lhd R)$$

The relational image is simply the range of R domain restricted to A.

Example 7.8 The set of all cars that are driven by either Indra or Jim is given by the relational image of the set $\{indra, jim\}$ under $drives$. That is,

$$drives\ (\!|\ \{indra, jim\}\ |\!) = \{alfa, beetle\}$$

as shown in Figure 7.2. □

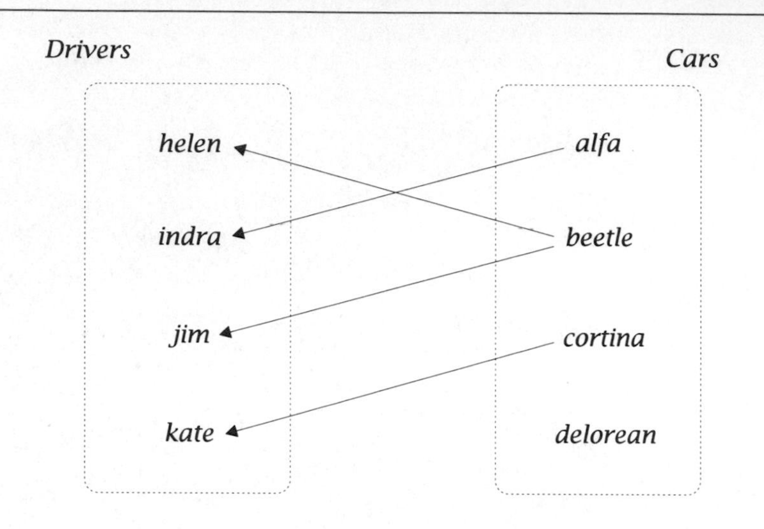

Figure 7.3: The relation *drives*$^\sim$

7.3 Relational inverse

If R is an element of the set $X \leftrightarrow Y$, then we say that X and Y are the *source* and *target* sets of R. The choice of terminology reminds us that relations are directional: they relate objects of one set *to* objects of another. It is always possible to reverse this direction, and thus present the same information in a different way.

The relational inverse operator $^\sim$ does exactly this. Source and target are exchanged, and so are the elements of each ordered pair; the result is an element of $Y \leftrightarrow X$ such that

$$\forall x : X;\ y : Y \bullet x \mapsto y \in R^\sim \;\Rightarrow\; y \mapsto x \in R$$

The relation $R^\sim$ maps y to x exactly when R maps x to y.

Example 7.9 The inverse of the relation *drives*, defined in Example 7.2, relates cars to their drivers:

$$drives^\sim \;=\; \{alfa \mapsto indra, beetle \mapsto helen, beetle \mapsto jim, cortina \mapsto kate\}$$

The graph of this relation is shown in Figure 7.3. □

If the source and target of a relation have the same type, then we say that the relation is *homogeneous*; if they are different, then we say that the relation is *heterogeneous*.

Example 7.10 The relation $<$ on natural numbers is homogeneous: the source and the target sets are the natural numbers $\mathbb{N}$. The relation *drives* is heterogeneous: the source is *Drivers*, the target is *Cars*. □

An important homogeneous relation is the *identity relation*, defined by

$$\mathrm{id}\, X == \{ x : X \bullet x \mapsto x \}$$

That is, it associates each element of X with itself, and makes no other associations. The identity relation is useful in reasoning about other relations and in classifying them. If a homogeneous relation contains the identity relation, we say that it is *reflexive*. The set of all reflexive relations on X is given by

$$Reflexive[X] == \{ R : X \leftrightarrow X \mid \mathrm{id}\, X \subseteq R \}$$

That is, R is reflexive if $\forall x : X \bullet x \mapsto x \in R$.

Example 7.11 The relation $\leqslant$ upon natural numbers is reflexive; the relation $<$ is not. □

Another useful property of homogeneous relations is symmetry: we say that a relation is *symmetric* if whenever it relates x to y, it also relates y to x.

$$Symmetric[X] == \{ R : X \leftrightarrow X \mid \forall x, y : X \bullet x \mapsto y \in R \Rightarrow y \mapsto x \in R \}$$

Example 7.12 At a business meeting, we might use a relation to record the fact that one person shook hands with another. This relation will be symmetric: if a shook hands with b, then b shook hands with a. □

A symmetric relation is its own inverse:

$$S \in Symmetric[X]$$

$$\vdots$$

$$\dfrac{\lceil a \mapsto b \in S \rceil^{[1]} \quad a \mapsto b \in S \Rightarrow b \mapsto a \in S}{b \mapsto a \in S}\ [\Rightarrow\text{-elim}]$$

$$\vdots$$

$$\dfrac{\dfrac{\dfrac{\dfrac{b \mapsto a \in S \Rightarrow a \mapsto b \in S^{\sim}}{a \mapsto b \in S^{\sim}}\ [\Rightarrow\text{-elim}]}{a \mapsto b \in S \Rightarrow a \mapsto b \in S^{\sim}}\ [\Rightarrow\text{-intro}]^{[1]}}{\forall a, b : X \bullet a \mapsto b \in S \Rightarrow a \mapsto b \in S^{\sim}}\ [\forall\text{-intro}] \qquad \vdots}{S = S^{\sim}}\ [\text{ext}]$$

Some parts of this derivation have been omitted. To complete the proof, we would expand the definition of *Symmetric*, refer to the generic definition of relational inverse in Section 8.3, and construct a matching derivation of the proposition $\forall a, b : X \bullet a \mapsto b \in S^{\sim} \Rightarrow a \mapsto b \in S$.

A homogeneous relation may be *antisymmetric*. In this case, it is impossible for two different elements to be related in both directions.

$$Antisymmetric[X] == \\ \{ R : X \leftrightarrow X \mid (\forall x, y : X \bullet x \mapsto y \in R \wedge y \mapsto x \in R \Rightarrow x = y) \}$$

If a relation is antisymmetric, we may use it to prove equality between two objects; we have only to show that the relationship holds in both directions.

Example 7.13 The subset relation $\subseteq$ is antisymmetric. For any two sets s and t, if $s \subseteq t$ and $t \subseteq s$, then $s = t$. This fact is often used to show that two sets are equal. □

A homogeneous relation R may be *asymmetric*. In this case, the statements $x \mapsto y \in R$ and $y \mapsto x \in R$ are mutually exclusive.

$$Asymmetric[X] == \\ \{ R : X \leftrightarrow X \mid \forall x, y : X \bullet (x \mapsto y \in R) \Rightarrow \neg(y \mapsto x \in R) \}$$

That is, $x \mapsto y \in R$ and $y \mapsto x \in R$ cannot both be true.

Example 7.14 The strict subset relation is asymmetric: it is impossible to find two sets s and t such that $s \subset t$ and $t \subset s$. □

These three categories—symmetric, antisymmetric, and asymmetric—are not exhaustive; it is quite possible for a relation to be none of the three.

Example 7.15 Three people—Louise, Martin, and Natalie—live together in a shared house. A homogeneous relation *likes* records their feelings for each other:

$$\begin{aligned} likes = \{ & Louise \mapsto Martin, Louise \mapsto Louise, \\ & Martin \mapsto Louise, Martin \mapsto Martin, \\ & Martin \mapsto Natalie, Natalie \mapsto Natalie \} \end{aligned}$$

This relation tells us that Louise likes Martin, that Martin likes Louise, and Martin likes Natalie: see Figure 7.4.

Although *likes* is reflexive relation, each member of the household likes him- or herself, it is not symmetric: Martin likes Natalie, but Natalie does not

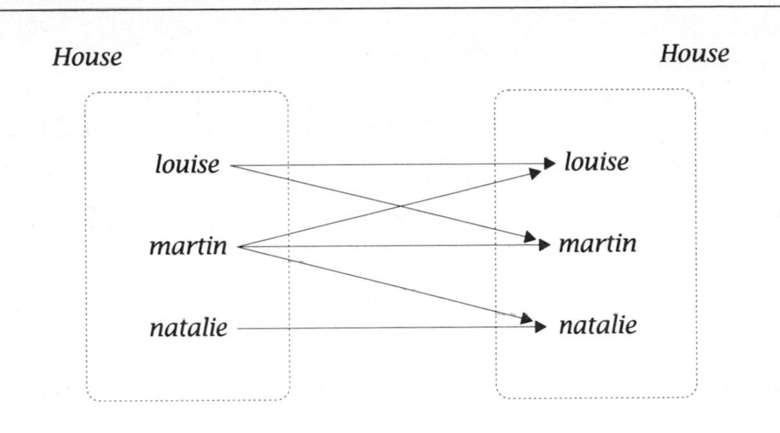

Figure 7.4: The relation *likes*

like Martin. Neither is it antisymmetric: Martin and Louise like each other, but they are not the same person.

Finally, as a reflexive relation, it cannot be asymmetric. Even if we subtract the identity relation, the reciprocal relationship between Louise and Martin would break asymmetry. □

7.4 Relational composition

If the target type of one relation matches the source type of another, then they may be combined to form a single relation. If R is an element of $X \leftrightarrow Y$, and S is an element of $Y \leftrightarrow Z$, then we write $R \mathbin{;} S$ to denote the *relational composition* of R and S. This is the element of $X \leftrightarrow Z$ such that

$$x \mapsto z \in R \mathbin{;} S \Leftrightarrow \exists y : Y \bullet x \mapsto y \in R \wedge y \mapsto z \in S$$

That is, two elements x and z are related by the composition $R \mathbin{;} S$ if there is an intermediate element y such that x is related to y and y is related to z.

Example 7.16 The relation *uses* of type *Cars* $\leftrightarrow$ *Fuels* tells us which fuel is used by each of the cars in Example 7.2:

$$\begin{array}{|l} uses : Cars \leftrightarrow Fuels \\ \hline uses = \{alfa \mapsto unleaded, alfa \mapsto leaded, beetle \mapsto leaded, \\ \qquad cortina \mapsto leaded, delorean \mapsto electricity\} \end{array}$$

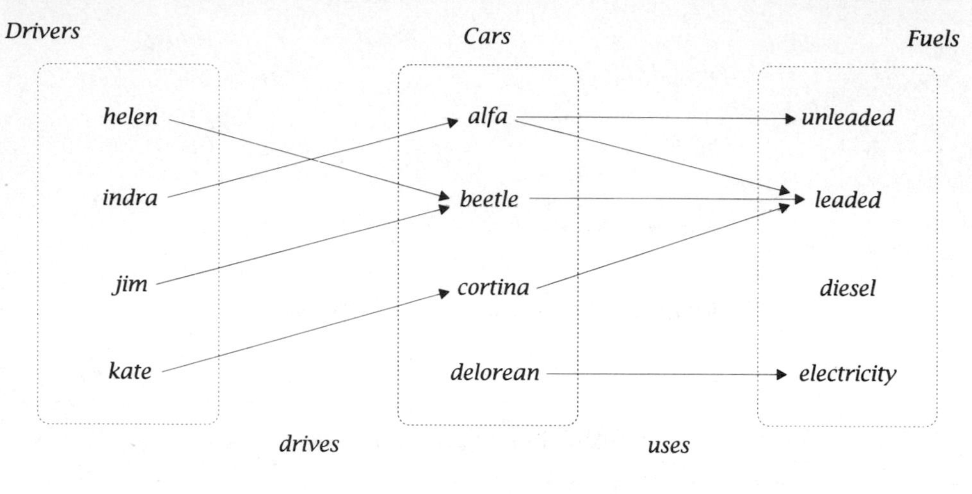

Figure 7.5: Which fuel to buy?

An Alfa can use either leaded or unleaded petrol, the older cars—Beetles and Cortina—require leaded petrol, and the DeLorean in question runs on large amounts of electricity.

We may compose the *drives* and *uses* relation to find out which the fuel or fuels that each driver may purchase. If $buys = drives \mathbin{;} uses$ then *buys* is a relation of type $Drivers \leftrightarrow Fuels$ such that

$$\begin{aligned} buys \;=\; & \{helen \mapsto leaded, jim \mapsto leaded, kate \mapsto leaded, \\ & \quad indra \mapsto unleaded, indra \mapsto leaded\} \end{aligned}$$

This composition of relations is illustrated in Figure 7.5. Note that the maplet $delorean \mapsto electricity$ makes no contribution to the new relation. □

In the previous section, we presented two useful properties of homogeneous relations: reflexivity and symmetry. A relation is reflexive if it includes the identity relation, and symmetric if it includes its own inverse. The inclusion of a relational composition is associated with a third property: transitivity.

A homogeneous relation R is *transitive* if every pair of connecting maplets $x \mapsto y$ and $y \mapsto z$ in R has a corresponding maplet $x \mapsto z$ in R.

$$\begin{aligned} & Transitive[X] \;==\; \\ & \qquad \{ R : X \leftrightarrow X \mid \forall x, y, z : X \bullet x \mapsto y \in R \land y \mapsto z \in R \Rightarrow x \mapsto z \in R \} \end{aligned}$$

Example 7.17 The greater-than relation on natural numbers $\mathbb{N}$ is transitive: whenever $a > b$ and $b > c$, we know that $a > c$. □

Example 7.18 The *likes* relation is not transitive: it contains $louise \mapsto martin$ and $martin \mapsto natalie$ but not $louise \mapsto natalie$. Louise likes Martin, and Martin likes Natalie, but Louise does not like Natalie. □

If a homogeneous relation is reflexive, symmetric, and transitive, then it is an *equivalence* relation:

$$Equivalence[X] == Reflexive[X] \cap Symmetric[X] \cap Transitive[X]$$

Example 7.19 The relation *same_sign* holds between two people if and only if they have the same birth sign. Assuming that each person has exactly one birth sign, this is an equivalence relation:

- any person a has the same sign as themselves, so *same_sign* is reflexive;
- if a has the same sign as b, then b has the same sign as a, so *same_sign* is symmetric;
- if a has the same sign as b, and b has the same sign as c, then a has the same sign as c, so *same_sign* is transitive.

□

An equivalence relation E upon a set X divides that set into a number of disjoint subsets, each consisting of elements that are related to one other, according to E. For each element a, the *equivalence class* of a is the set

$$\{x : X \mid x \mapsto a \in E\}$$

That is, the set of elements that are related to a.

Example 7.20 The relation *same_sign* divides *Person* into twelve equivalence classes, corresponding to the twelve signs of the zodiac. If *Marina* was born on 28th January, then the equivalence class of *Marina* will be the set of all Aquarians (20th January - 18th February). □

7.5 Closures

A principle that is often useful in specification is that of *closure*: given a certain amount of information, we may consider what may be obtained by using this information to its fullest extent, or by adding to it in a well-defined way. When

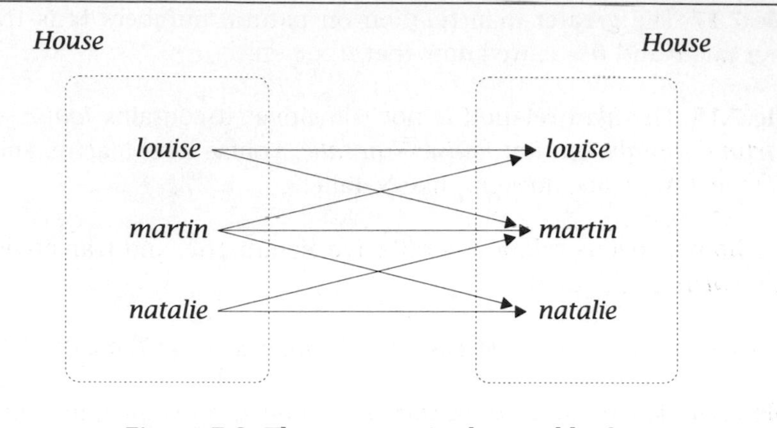

Figure 7.6: The symmetric closure $likes^s$

applied to relations, this principle involves adding maplets to a relation until some useful property is achieved.

The simplest form of closure is obtained by adding the identity relation. If R is a homogeneous relation, we write R^r to denote its *reflexive closure*, where

$$R^r = R \cup \mathrm{id}\, X$$

A reflexive relation is its own reflexive closure.

Example 7.21 The reflexive closure $<^r$ is the relation $\leqslant$. □

Example 7.22 The *likes* relation of Example 7.15 is its own reflexive closure: the maplets $louise \mapsto louise$, $martin \mapsto martin$, and $natalie \mapsto natalie$ are already present. □

Another form of closure is obtained by adding just enough maplets to produce a symmetric relation. If R is a homogeneous relation, we write R^s to denote the *symmetric closure* of R, where

$$R^s = R \cup R^\sim$$

Any symmetric relation containing R must also contain $R^\sim$; the smallest such relation is obtained by adding the maplets in $R^\sim$.

Example 7.23 The *likes* relation is not symmetric: Martin likes Natalie, but Natalie does not like Martin. To obtain the symmetric closure $likes^s$, we must add the maplet $natalie \mapsto martin$: the result is shown in Figure 7.6. □

If R is a homogeneous relation, it is useful to consider the result of composing R with itself some finite number of times. If the maplet $x \mapsto z$ is present in $R \circ R$, then we know that x and z are related by precisely two applications of R: that is, x is related to some y, and that y is related to z. Similarly, the maplet $x \mapsto w$ is present in $R \circ R \circ R$ if x and w are related by precisely three applications of R.

For any positive natural number n, we may write R^n to denote the composition of n copies of R: that is,

$$\begin{aligned} R^1 &= R \\ R^2 &= R \circ R \\ R^3 &= R \circ R \circ R \\ &\vdots \end{aligned}$$

We may extend this idea of *iteration* to cover all integers by taking R^{-n} to be the inverse of R^n and R^0 to be the identity relation.

The information obtained from all finite iterations of R may be combined to form the relation R^+, where

$$R^+ = \bigcup \{ n : \mathbb{N} \mid n \geqslant 1 \bullet R^n \}$$

This is a transitive relation. To see why, suppose that $x \mapsto y$ and $y \mapsto z$ are both elements of R^+. There must then be natural numbers a and b such that $x \mapsto y \in R^a$ and $y \mapsto z \in R^b$. But then $x \mapsto z$ is an element of $R^a \circ R^b$, and this is the same relation as R^{a+b}, another element of R^+. Thus $x \mapsto z$ is also in R^+. We say that R^+ is the *transitive closure* of R; it is the smallest transitive relation containing R.

Example 7.24 If *likes* is the relation introduced in Example 7.15, then

$$\begin{aligned} likes^2 &= likes \cup \{louise \mapsto natalie\} \\ likes^3 &= likes^2 \\ likes^4 &= likes^2 \\ &\vdots \end{aligned}$$

and the transitive closure $likes^+$ is given by

$$likes^+ = likes \cup \{louise \mapsto natalie\}$$

□

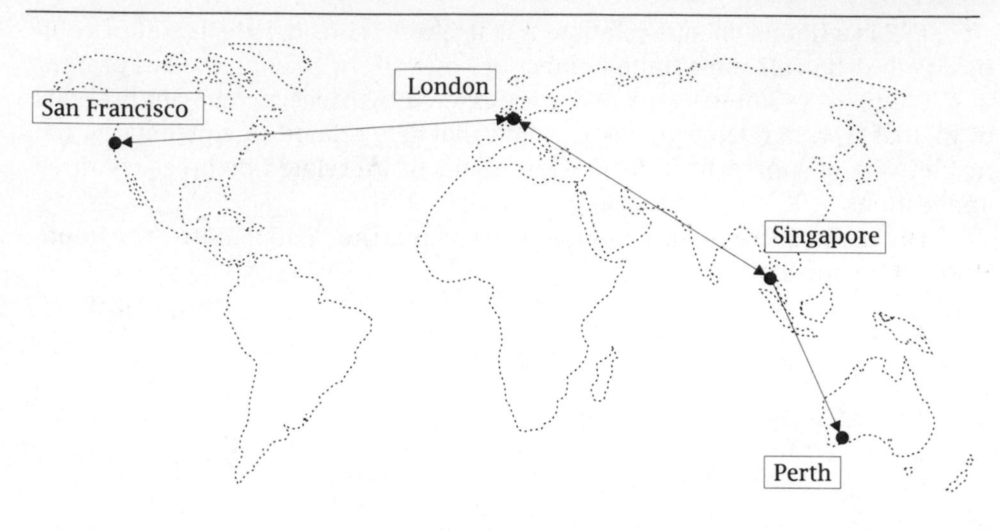

Figure 7.7: Direct flights

Example 7.25 We may use a relation *direct* to record the availability of a direct flight between two airports. For the four airports shown in Figure 7.7, this relation is given by

$$\begin{aligned} direct = \{ & singapore \mapsto london, london \mapsto singapore, singapore \mapsto perth, \\ & london \mapsto san\_francisco, san\_francisco \mapsto london\} \end{aligned}$$

The composition $direct \mathbin{\text{⨾}} direct$ comprises all of the possibly indirect flights that involve at most one stop *en route*:

$$\begin{aligned} direct \mathbin{\text{⨾}} direct = \{ & singapore \mapsto singapore, singapore \mapsto san\_francisco, \\ & london \mapsto london, san\_francisco \mapsto singapore, \\ & london \mapsto perth, san\_francisco \mapsto san\_francisco\} \end{aligned}$$

It is now possible to reach Perth from London. With a second stop, we may reach Perth from San Francisco using only the flights shown in *direct*:

$$\begin{aligned} direct \mathbin{\text{⨾}} direct \mathbin{\text{⨾}} direct = \{ & singapore \mapsto london, london \mapsto san\_francisco, \\ & london \mapsto singapore, san\_francisco \mapsto london, \\ & san\_francisco \mapsto perth\} \end{aligned}$$

No more journeys are added by considering further iterations: it is possible to show that $direct^4 = direct^2$ and that $direct^5 = direct^3$. □

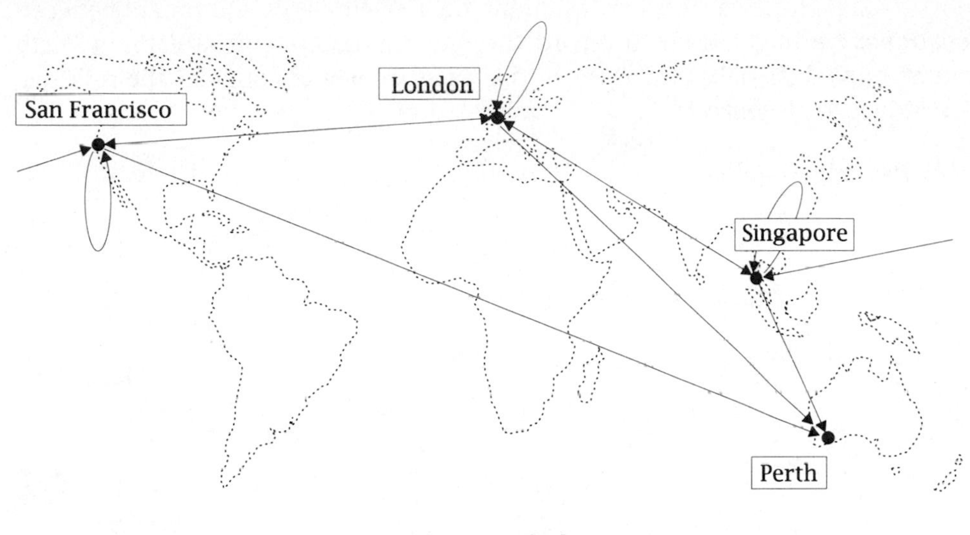

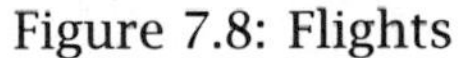
Figure 7.8: Flights

Example 7.26 The transitive closure of *direct* relates two airports exactly when there is a route between them consisting of some number of direct flights: see Figure 7.8.

$$\begin{aligned} direct^+ = \{ & singapore \mapsto singapore, singapore \mapsto london, \\ & singapore \mapsto san\_francisco, singapore \mapsto perth, \\ & london \mapsto singapore, london \mapsto london, \\ & london \mapsto san\_francisco, london \mapsto perth, \\ & san\_francisco \mapsto singapore, san\_francisco \mapsto london, \\ & san\_francisco \mapsto san\_francisco, san\_francisco \mapsto perth\} \end{aligned}$$

□

It is sometimes useful to consider the *reflexive transitive closure* of a homogeneous relation. If R is a relation of type $X \leftrightarrow X$, then we write R^* to denote the smallest relation containing R that is both reflexive and transitive, given by

$$R^* = R^+ \cup \operatorname{id} X$$

Example 7.27 In the $direct^+$ relation of Example 7.26, there is no way to travel from Perth to Perth: in our small collection of routes, there is not one flight that starts there. However, if we are planning the movement of equipment between locations, we might wish to record the fact any equipment already at Perth can be moved (trivially) to Perth. In this case, we would consider the reflexive transitive closure *direct** of our flights relation:

$$direct^* \;=\; direct^+ \cup \{perth \mapsto perth\}$$

□

Chapter 8

Functions

Some relationships can be modelled by a special kind of relation. If each object of one set is related to at most one object of another, then the relation between the two sets is said to be a *function*: a term that should be familiar from any introduction to mathematics or computation.

In this chapter, we introduce a notation for functions and their application. We show how this notation can be used to produce concise definitions for many of the basic operators in our language. We examine properties of functions, and consider the case in which the domain of a function is finite.

8.1 Partial functions

A partial function from X to Y is a relation that maps each element of X to at most one element of Y; we write $X \rightarrowtail\!\!\!\!\!+\ Y$ to denote the set of all such relations, and define

$$X \mathrel{+\!\!\!\!\rightarrow} Y == \\ \{f : X \leftrightarrow Y \mid \forall x : X; \ y_1, y_2 : Y \bullet x \mapsto y_1 \in f \land x \mapsto y_2 \in f \Rightarrow y_1 = y_2\}$$

Whenever a function appears to relate an element of X to two elements of Y, these two elements must be the same.

Example 8.1 An organisation has a system for keeping track of its employees while they are on the premises. Each employee is issued with an *active badge* which reports their current position to a central database. If the set of all people is *Person*, and the set of all locations is *Location*, then the information provided by the system may be described by a relation *where_is* of type

Person ↔ *Location*. It is impossible for an employee to be in two places at once, so this relation will be a partial function:

$$where\_is \in Person \rightarrowtail\!\!\!\!\!\!\!+ \; Location$$

□

These relations are called *partial* functions because there may be elements of X that are not related to any element of Y. If each element of X is related to some element of Y, then the function is said to be *total*; we write $X \rightarrow Y$ to denote the set of all total functions from X to Y, where

$$X \rightarrow Y \;==\; \{f : X \nrightarrow Y \mid \mathrm{dom}\, f = X\}$$

The domain of a total function must be the whole of the source set.

Example 8.2 We may define a relation *double* on the set of natural numbers $\mathbb{N}$ as follows:

$$\begin{array}{|l} double : \mathbb{N} \leftrightarrow \mathbb{N} \\ \hline \forall\, m, n : \mathbb{N} \bullet m \mapsto n \in double \Leftrightarrow m + m = n \end{array}$$

This relation is a total function: for every natural number m there is a unique number n such that $m \mapsto n \in double$. □

If a lies within the domain of a function f, we write $f(a)$ to denote the unique object that is related to x. We say that $f(a)$ is the result of *applying* function f to argument a. There are two inference rules associated with function application. The first rule states that if there is a unique maplet in f with a as its first element and b as its second, then $b = f(a)$.

$$\frac{\exists_1\, p : f \bullet p.1 = a \quad a \mapsto b \in f}{b = f(a)}\,[\text{app-intro}] \qquad \text{provided that } b \text{ does not appear free in } a$$

The second states that if $b = f(a)$ and there is a unique pair whose first element is a, then $a \mapsto b \in f$.

$$\frac{\exists_1\, p : f \bullet p.1 = a \quad b = f(a)}{a \mapsto b \in f}\,[\text{app-elim}] \qquad \text{provided that } b \text{ does not appear free in } a$$

In either case, we must be sure that there are no free occurrences of b in a.

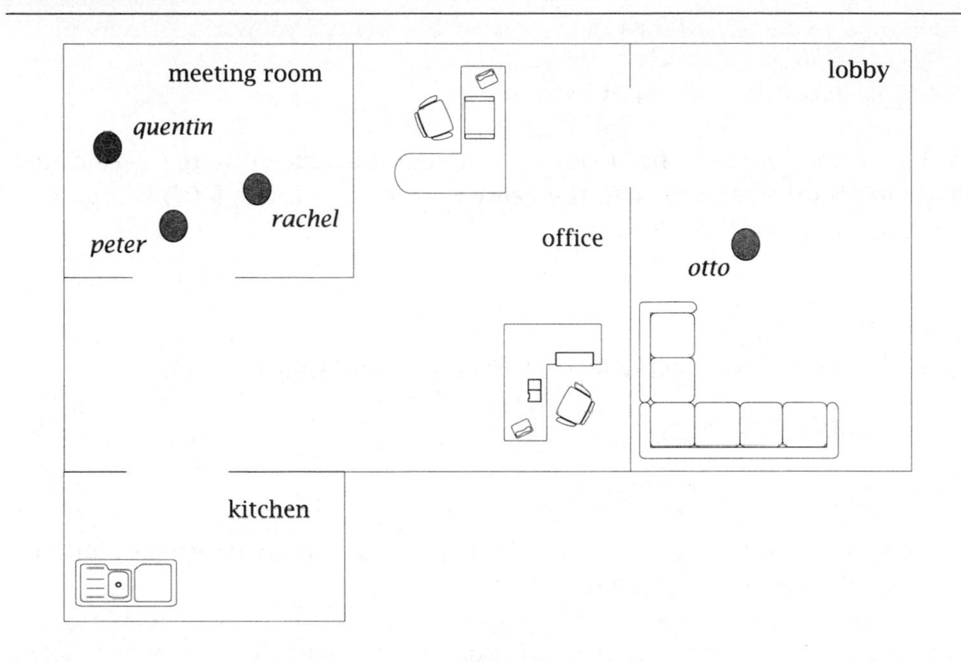

Figure 8.1: Where is Rachel?

Example 8.3 If Rachel is an employee, then we may write *where_is rachel* to denote her current location. This expression makes sense only if the database has a unique record of Rachel's whereabouts. If *where_is* is the function

$$\{otto \mapsto lobby, peter \mapsto meeting, quentin \mapsto meeting, rachel \mapsto meeting\}$$

(see Figure 8.1) then we may observe that

$$where\_is\ rachel = meeting$$

□

8.2 Lambda notation

Suppose that f is a function whose domain is precisely those elements of X that satisfy a constraint p. If the result of applying f to an arbitrary element x can be written as the expression e, then f can be described as

$$f = \{x : X \mid p \bullet x \mapsto e\}$$

The *lambda notation* offers a more concise alternative; we write

$$\lambda\ declaration \mid constraint \bullet result$$

to denote the function that maps each object introduced by the *declaration* that satisfies the *constraint* to the expression *result*. Using lambda notation, our function f could be described as

$$f = \lambda x : X \mid p \bullet e$$

Example 8.4 The function *double* could also be defined by

$$\begin{array}{|l} double : \mathbb{N} \leftrightarrow \mathbb{N} \\ \hline double = \lambda m : \mathbb{N} \bullet m + m \end{array}$$

As the domain of this function is the whole of the source, the constraint part of the lambda expression is omitted. □

Example 8.5 The function *approx* takes a number n and a set of numbers s and returns the closest approximation to a in s, in the sense that

$$a \leqslant n \land \forall y : s \bullet y \leqslant n \Rightarrow y \leqslant a$$

The approximation a is the greatest element of s that remains less than or equal to n. This function may be defined as follows:

$$\begin{array}{|l} approx : (\mathbb{N} \times \mathbb{P}\,\mathbb{N}) \leftrightarrow \mathbb{N} \\ \hline approx = \lambda n : \mathbb{N};\ s : \mathbb{P}\,\mathbb{N} \mid s \neq \varnothing \bullet \\ \qquad \mu(x : s \mid x \leqslant n \land \forall y : s \bullet y \leqslant n \Rightarrow y \leqslant x) \end{array}$$

The discrete nature of the natural numbers means that a unique approximation to n exists in every non-empty set. □

If the declaration part of a lambda expression introduces more than one variable, then the source type of the function is given by the resulting *characteristic tuple*. For example, the source of the function

$$\lambda a : A;\ b : B;\ c : C \bullet \ldots$$

would be the Cartesian product set $A \times B \times C$; we would expect to apply this function to objects of the form (a, b, c), where $a \in A$, $b \in B$, and $c \in C$.

Example 8.6 The function *pair* takes two functions f and g as arguments, each of which must be a homogeneous relation on $\mathbb{N}$. The result is a function that takes a natural number x and returns the pair formed by applying each of f and g to x:

$$
\begin{array}{|l}
pair : ((\mathbb{N} \pfun \mathbb{N}) \times (\mathbb{N} \pfun \mathbb{N})) \fun (\mathbb{N} \pfun (\mathbb{N} \times \mathbb{N})) \\
\hline
pair = \lambda f, g : \mathbb{N} \pfun \mathbb{N} \bullet (\lambda n : \mathbb{N} \mid n \in \operatorname{dom} f \cap \operatorname{dom} g \bullet (f\,x, g\,x))
\end{array}
$$

Because f and g may be any partial function on the natural numbers, *pair* is a total function. □

Functional application is left associative: the expression $f\;g\;a$ should be read as $(f\;g)\;a$. The function arrow, on the other hand, is right associative: $A \to B \to C$ has the same meaning as $A \to (B \to C)$.

Example 8.7 Let *triple* be the function $\lambda n : \mathbb{N} \bullet n + n + n$. The expression

$$
\begin{aligned}
pair\,(double, triple)\;3 &= (pair\,(double, triple))\;3 \\
&= (\lambda n : \mathbb{N} \bullet (double\,n, triple\,n))\;3 \\
&= (double\,3, triple\,3) \\
&= ((\lambda n : \mathbb{N} \bullet n + n)\;3, (\lambda n : \mathbb{N} \bullet n + n + n)\;3) \\
&= (6, 9)
\end{aligned}
$$

□

8.3 Functions on relations

In the previous chapter, we introduced the operators that form the basis of a calculus of relations: domain, range, inverse, composition, and closure. These may all be seen as examples of functions upon relations.

Example 8.8 The domain and range operators may be defined by

$$
\begin{array}{|l}
[X, Y] \\
\hline
\operatorname{dom} : (X \rel Y) \fun \mathbb{P}\,X \\
\operatorname{ran} : (X \rel Y) \fun \mathbb{P}\,Y \\
\hline
\forall R : X \rel Y \bullet \\
\quad \operatorname{dom} R = \{ x : X \mid \exists y : Y \bullet x \mapsto y \in R \} \\
\quad \operatorname{ran} R = \{ y : Y \mid \exists x : X \bullet x \mapsto y \in R \}
\end{array}
$$

□

If a function takes more than one argument, then it may be defined as an infix symbol; we use underscores to indicate the intended position of the arguments.

Example 8.9 The restriction operators may be defined by

$$
\begin{array}{l}
[X, Y] \\
\_ \lhd \_ : \mathbb{P} X \times (X \leftrightarrow Y) \rightarrow (X \leftrightarrow Y) \\
\_ \rhd \_ : (X \leftrightarrow Y) \times \mathbb{P} Y \rightarrow (X \leftrightarrow Y) \\
\hline
\forall R : X \leftrightarrow Y;\ A : \mathbb{P} X;\ B : \mathbb{P} Y \bullet \\
\quad A \lhd R = \{ x : X;\ y : Y \mid x \in A \land x \mapsto y \in R \bullet x \mapsto y \} \\
\quad R \rhd B = \{ x : X;\ y : Y \mid y \in B \land x \mapsto y \in R \bullet x \mapsto y \}
\end{array}
$$

□

In the declarations above, we have assumed an order of precedence: by convention, the Cartesian product symbol binds more tightly than the function or relation symbols.

Example 8.10 The relational composition operator may be defined by

$$
\begin{array}{l}
[X, Y, Z] \\
\_ \fatsemi \_ : (X \leftrightarrow Y) \times (Y \leftrightarrow Z) \rightarrow (X \leftrightarrow Z) \\
\hline
\forall R : X \leftrightarrow Y;\ S : Y \leftrightarrow Z \bullet \\
\quad R \fatsemi S = \{ x : X;\ y : Y;\ z : Z \mid x \mapsto y \in R \land y \mapsto z \in S \bullet x \mapsto z \}
\end{array}
$$

The pair $x \mapsto z$ is present in the relational composition $R \fatsemi S$ exactly when there is some y such that $x \mapsto y \in R$ and $y \mapsto z \in S$. □

We may use a single underscore to indicate that a function is intended as a suffix symbol.

Example 8.11 The relational inverse operator may be defined by

$$
\begin{array}{l}
[X, Y] \\
\_^{\sim} : (X \leftrightarrow Y) \rightarrow (Y \leftrightarrow X) \\
\hline
\forall R : X \leftrightarrow Y \bullet \\
\quad R^{\sim} = \{ x : X;\ y : Y \mid x \mapsto y \in R \bullet y \mapsto x \}
\end{array}
$$

Given any two sets X and Y, the inverse operator is a total function on the set $X \leftrightarrow Y$ which yields relations in the set $Y \leftrightarrow X$. □

Example 8.12 The transitive closure operators may be defined by

$$
\begin{array}{l}
[X] \\
\hline
\_^{+} : (X \leftrightarrow X) \rightarrow (X \leftrightarrow X) \\
\_^{*} : (X \leftrightarrow X) \rightarrow (X \leftrightarrow X) \\
\hline
\forall R : X \leftrightarrow X \bullet \\
\quad R^{+} = \bigcap \{ T : X \leftrightarrow X \mid R \subseteq T \land (T \fatsemi T) \subseteq T \} \\
\quad R^{*} = \bigcap \{ T : X \leftrightarrow X \mid (R \cup \mathrm{id}\, X) \subseteq T \land (T \fatsemi T) \subseteq T \}
\end{array}
$$

These definitions rely upon the fact that a relation T is transitive if and only if it contains the composition $T \fatsemi T$. □

8.4 Overriding

To combine the information contained in functions f and g, we could simply write $f \cup g$. However, there may be objects that are mapped to one value under f, and to another under g; if this is the case, then $f \cup g$ is not a function. To ensure that the combination of two functions is also functional, we must resolve any conflicts that arise.

If f and g are functions of the same type, we write $f \oplus g$ to denote the relational overriding of f with g. This is a relation that agrees with f everywhere outside the domain of g; but agrees with g where g is defined:

$$
\begin{array}{l}
[X, Y] \\
\hline
\_ \oplus \_ : (X \leftrightarrow Y) \times (X \leftrightarrow Y) \rightarrow (X \leftrightarrow Y) \\
\hline
\forall f, g : X \leftrightarrow Y \bullet \\
\quad f \oplus g = (\mathrm{dom}\, g \mathbin{⩤} f) \cup g
\end{array}
$$

Although the operator is usually employed for functions, it may be applied to any two relations of the same type.

Example 8.13 Suppose that a partial update arrives from the staff location system, informing us that Rachel and Sally are in the lobby and that Tim is in the office. This update may be represented by a partial function from *Person* to *Location*:

$$update = \{rachel \mapsto lobby, sally \mapsto lobby, tim \mapsto office\}$$

The union of this function with our original information would not be functional. The expression (*where_is* ∪ *update*) *rachel* is not defined, as there are two locations associated with *rachel* in this relation.

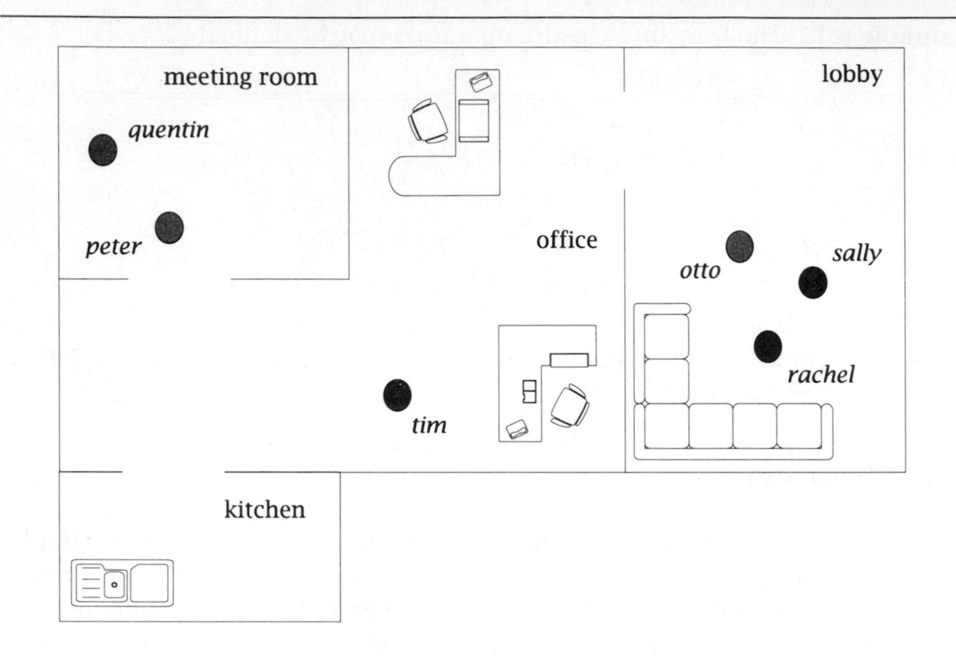

Figure 8.2: Where is Rachel now?

If the information obtained from the update function takes precedence, then we may use

$$where\_now = where\_is \oplus update$$

as our new location relation. The result is shown in Figure 8.2. The information that Quentin and Peter are in the meeting room comes from *where_is*, the others are within the domain of *update*. □

If two functions have disjoint domains, then there is no conflict between them, and overriding behaves as the union operator:

$$\mathrm{dom}\, f \cap \mathrm{dom}\, g = \varnothing \Rightarrow f \oplus g = f \cup g$$

In this case, the overriding operator is commutative:

$$\mathrm{dom}\, f \cap \mathrm{dom}\, g = \varnothing \Rightarrow f \oplus g = g \oplus f$$

Example 8.14 If we were to receive two pieces of information, one locating Quentin and Peter,

$$information\_1 = \{quentin \mapsto meeting, peter \mapsto meeting\}$$

and the other locating Rachel and Sally, then

$$information\_2 = \{rachel \mapsto lobby, sally \mapsto office\}$$

then we could combine them in either order:

$$information\_1 \oplus information\_2 = information\_2 \oplus information\_1$$

as the domains are disjoint. □

8.5 Properties of functions

It is extremely helpful to categorise functions according to whether or not they are *total*, and whether or not they possess three key properties: injectivity, surjectivity, and bijectivity. Our mathematical language has a special symbol associated with each category:

$\mathrel{\rightarrowtail\!\!\!\!\!\!+}$	partial, injective functions
$\rightarrowtail$	total, injective functions
$\mathrel{+\!\!\!\!\!\twoheadrightarrow}$	partial, surjective functions
$\twoheadrightarrow$	total, surjective functions
$\mathrel{\rightarrowtail\!\!\!\!\!\!+\!\!\!\!\!\twoheadrightarrow}$	partial, bijective functions
$\rightarrowtail\!\!\!\!\!\twoheadrightarrow$	total, bijective functions

When we introduce a function using one of these arrows, an important property is made explicit.

The characteristic property of a function is a lack of *diverging* arrows in its graph: no element of the source is mapped to more than one element of the target. If in addition there are no *converging* arrows, then the relation is said to be an *injective* function, or an *injection*. Formally, f is an injection if

$$\forall x_1, x_2 : \mathrm{dom}\, f \bullet f\, x_1 = f\, x_2 \Rightarrow x_1 = x_2$$

Example 8.15 The location function of Example 8.3 is not injective. According to *where_is*, there are at least two different people in the meeting room:

$$where\_is\ quentin = meeting$$
$$where\_is\ peter = meeting$$

and $quentin \neq peter$. □

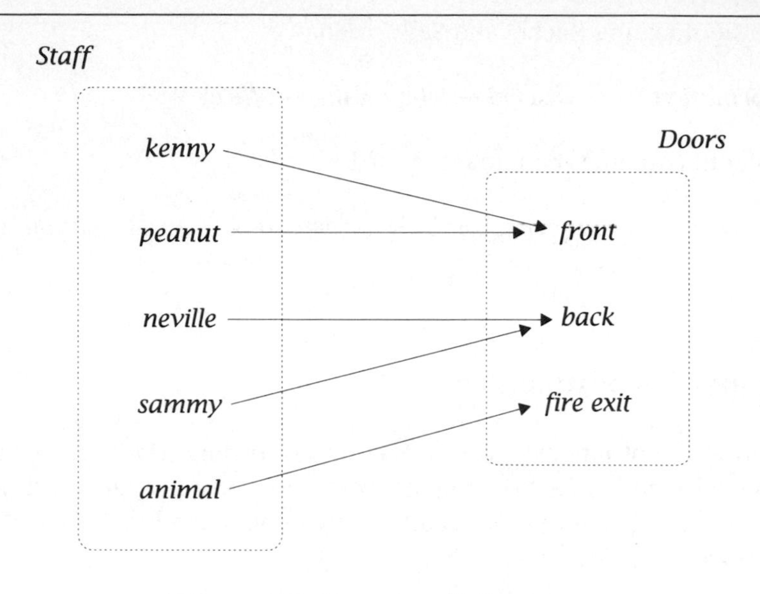

Figure 8.3: Covering all the exits

If the range of a function is the whole of the target, then it is said to be a *surjective* function, or a *surjection*. If the target of function f is B, then f is a surjection if $\operatorname{ran} f = B$.

Example 8.16 There are three entrances to the *Pink Flamingo*: the front door, the back door, and the fire exit. Kenny and Peanut are paid to stand at the front door, Neville and Sammy are watching the back, and Animal is leaning on the fire exit. This situation is represented by a surjective function,

$$\begin{aligned} \mathit{bouncers} = \{ & \mathit{kenny} \mapsto \mathit{front}, \mathit{peanut} \mapsto \mathit{front}, \\ & \mathit{neville} \mapsto \mathit{back}, \mathit{sammy} \mapsto \mathit{back}, \\ & \mathit{animal} \mapsto \mathit{fire\,exit} \} \end{aligned}$$

in which every door is covered: see Figure 8.3. □

A *bijective* function, or *bijection*, is a function which is both injective and surjective: no two elements of the domain are mapped to the same object, and the range is the whole of the target set.

Example 8.17 It is Senior Citizens Night at the *Pink Flamingo*, so Reg Thorpe, the owner, decides that he needs just one bouncer on each door. Peanut and

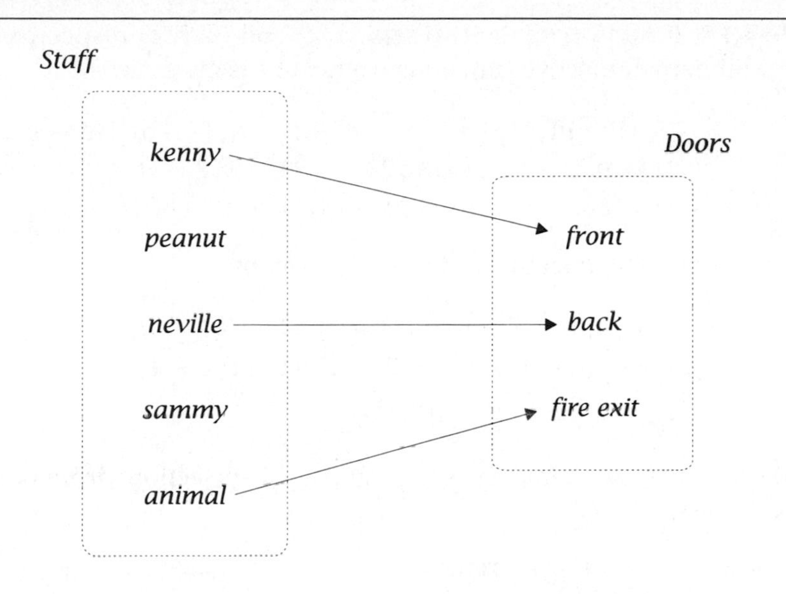

Figure 8.4: Senior Citizens Night

Sammy are given the night off, and the relaxed state of security is described by the following mapping, pictured in Figure 8.4:

$$\{kenny \mapsto front, neville \mapsto back, animal \mapsto fire\ exit\}$$

This is a partial bijection from the set of bouncers

$$\{kenny, peanut, neville, sammy, animal\}$$

to the set of doors

$$\{front, back, fire\_exit\}$$

□

We define the set of all partial injective functions by generic abbreviation: if A and B are sets, then

$$A \rightarrowtail\!\!\!\!\!\!\!+ B == \{f : A \nrightarrow B \mid \forall x_1, x_2 : \operatorname{dom} f \bullet f\,x_1 = f\,x_2 \Rightarrow x_1 = x_2\}$$

$$A \rightarrowtail B == (A \rightarrow B) \cap (A \rightarrowtail\!\!\!\!\!\!\!+ B)$$

A total injective function is any member of this set which is also a total function from A to B.

Example 8.18 If s and t are the two sets $\{1, 2\}$ and $\{a, b, c\}$ respectively, then the set of all partial injective functions from s to t is given by:

$$\begin{aligned} s \mathrel{⤔} t \;=\; & \{\varnothing, \{1 \mapsto a\}, \{1 \mapsto b\}, \{1 \mapsto c\}, \{2 \mapsto a\}, \{2 \mapsto b\}, \{2 \mapsto c\}, \\ & \{1 \mapsto a, 2 \mapsto b\}, \{1 \mapsto a, 2 \mapsto c\}, \{1 \mapsto b, 2 \mapsto a\}, \\ & \{1 \mapsto b, 2 \mapsto c\}, \{1 \mapsto c, 2 \mapsto a\}, \{1 \mapsto c, 2 \mapsto b\}\} \end{aligned}$$

and the set of all total injective functions is given by

$$\begin{aligned} s \rightarrowtail t \;=\; & \{\{1 \mapsto a, 2 \mapsto b\}, \{1 \mapsto a, 2 \mapsto c\}, \{1 \mapsto b, 2 \mapsto a\}, \\ & \{1 \mapsto b, 2 \mapsto c\}, \{1 \mapsto c, 2 \mapsto a\}, \{1 \mapsto c, 2 \mapsto b\}\} \end{aligned}$$

□

If A and B are sets, we define the set of all partial surjections from one to the other as follows:

$$A \mathrel{⤀} B == \{f : A \mathrel{⇸} B \mid \operatorname{ran} f = B\}$$

$$A \twoheadrightarrow B == (A \rightarrow B) \cap (A \mathrel{⤀} B)$$

A total surjective function is any element of this set that is also a total function from A to B.

Example 8.19 If s and t are as defined in Example 8.18, then there are no surjective functions from s to t:

$$s \mathrel{⤀} t = \varnothing$$

The source s has fewer elements than the target t, and for a function to be surjective, there must be at least as many elements in the domain—a subset of the source—as there are in the target. □

Finally, if A and B are sets, we define the set of all partial bijections from A to B by generic abbreviation:

$$A \mathrel{⤗} B == (A \mathrel{⤔} B) \cap (A \mathrel{⤀} B)$$

$$A \mathrel{⤖} B == (A \mathrel{⤗} B) \cap (A \rightarrow B)$$

A total bijection is any element of this set that is also a total function.

Example 8.20 As none of the functions from s and t are surjections, there can be no bijections between these two sets. If we replace t with the set $\{a, b\}$, then two bijections are possible:

$$s \mathrel{⤗} \{a, b\} = \{\{1 \mapsto a, 2 \mapsto b\}, \{1 \mapsto b, 2 \mapsto a\}\}$$

Both of these are total: for a function to be bijective, the domain and the target must have the same number of elements. □

8.6 Finite sets

Our mathematical language can be used to talk about any set, regardless of the number of elements it contains; indeed, infinite sets are often a more convenient abstraction. However, it is worth considering the properties of finite sets, if only because they form the basis of our theory of finite *sequences*—the subject of the next chapter.

A finite set is one whose elements are countable up to some natural number n: that is, a set that may be seen as the range of a total bijection from

$$1, 2, \ldots, n$$

Example 8.21 The set $\{a, b, c\}$ is finite: it may be seen as the range of a bijection from the set $\{1, 2, 3\}$,

$$\{1 \mapsto a, 2 \mapsto b, 3 \mapsto c\}$$

in which a, b, and c, correspond to 1, 2, and 3, respectively. □

Our mathematical language includes a familiar piece of notation for defining finite sets of numbers. The *number range* operator is a function on pairs of natural numbers, defined by

$$\_\,..\,\_ : \mathbb{N} \times \mathbb{N} \to \mathbb{P}\,\mathbb{N}$$

$$\forall\, m, n : \mathbb{N} \bullet m \,..\, n = \{i : \mathbb{N} \mid m \leq i \leq n\}$$

If m and n are natural numbers, then $m \,..\, n$ is the set consisting of all numbers between m and n, inclusive.

We can now introduce a second power set symbol: if X is a set, then the set of all finite subsets of X is given by

$$\mathbb{F}\,X == \{s : \mathbb{P}\,X \mid \exists\, n : \mathbb{N} \bullet \exists\, f : 1 \,..\, n \rightarrowtail\!\!\!\!\twoheadrightarrow s \bullet \mathit{true}\}$$

If X is a finite set, then $\mathbb{F}\,X$ and $\mathbb{P}\,X$ are equal.

Example 8.22

- There are a finite number of oceans: we can exhibit a total bijection from the range $1 \mathinner{\ldotp\ldotp} 4$ to the set of all *Oceans*:

  $$\{1 \mapsto \mathit{Atlantic}, 2 \mapsto \mathit{Arctic}, 3 \mapsto \mathit{Indian}, 4 \mapsto \mathit{Pacific}\}$$

- There is only one Jose Feliciano: we can exhibit a total bijection from the range $1 \mathinner{\ldotp\ldotp} 1$ to the set of all Jose Felicianos:

  $$\{1 \mapsto \mathit{jose\ feliciano}\}$$

- The set of all inhabitants of Rockall is finite, despite being empty. The empty function is a total bijection from the empty number range $1 \mathinner{\ldotp\ldotp} 0$ to the empty set:

  $$\varnothing \in 1 \mathinner{\ldotp\ldotp} 0 \rightarrowtail\!\!\!\!\!\twoheadrightarrow \mathit{Rockallers}$$

- The set of prime numbers is not finite. Given any natural number n, any total injection

  $$\mathit{inj} \in 1 \mathinner{\ldotp\ldotp} n \rightarrowtail \mathit{Primes}$$

  can be used to generate another element of *Primes* that is outside the range of *inj*. Whatever n we choose, there is no hope of finding a surjective function from $1 \mathinner{\ldotp\ldotp} n$ to *Primes*.

□

If s is a finite set, we write $\#s$ to denote the number of elements in s. This operator, called *size* or *cardinality*, is defined as follows:

$$
\begin{array}{l}
[X] \\
\hline
\# : \mathbb{F} X \rightarrow \mathbb{N} \\
\hline
\forall s : \mathbb{F} X;\ n : \mathbb{N} \bullet \\
\quad n = \#s \Leftrightarrow \exists f : (1 \mathinner{\ldotp\ldotp} n) \rightarrowtail\!\!\!\!\!\twoheadrightarrow s \bullet \mathit{true}
\end{array}
$$

For any finite set s, there is exactly one natural number n such that we can define a bijection from $1 \mathinner{\ldotp\ldotp} n$ to s.

Example 8.23

- $\#Oceans = 4$
- $\#Jose\ Felicianos = 1$
- $\#Rockallers = 0$
- $\#Primes$ is undefined

□

If the domain of a function is a finite set, then that function is itself finite; we write $A \nrightarrow\!\!\!\!\nrightarrow B$ to denote the set of all finite functions from A to B:

$$A \twoheadrightarrow\!\!\!\!\shortmid B \;==\; \{ f : A \twoheadrightarrow\!\!\!\!\shortmid\, B \mid \operatorname{dom} f \in \mathbb{F} A \}$$

This set is important: it corresponds to the set of all finite collections of B, indexed by elements of A. Also of interest is the set of all finite injections,

$$A \rightarrowtail\!\!\!\!\shortmid\!\!\shortmid B \;==\; A \twoheadrightarrow\!\!\!\!\shortmid\!\!\shortmid B \cap A \rightarrowtail\!\!\!\!\shortmid B$$

This corresponds to the set of all finite collections of B, indexed by elements of A, without repetition.

Example 8.24 The mapping from bouncers to doors described in Example 8.16 is a finite function:

$$bouncers \in Staff \twoheadrightarrow\!\!\!\!\shortmid\!\!\shortmid Doors$$

Once Peanut and Sammy are given the night off, as in Example 8.17, the mapping becomes a finite injection: the entrances are indexed by bouncers, without repetition. □

Chapter 9

Sequences

It is sometimes necessary to record the order in which objects are arranged: for example, data may be indexed by an ordered collection of keys; messages may be stored in order of arrival; tasks may be performed in order of importance. In this chapter, we introduce the notion of a sequence: an ordered collection of objects. We examine the ways in which sequences may be combined, and how the information contained within a sequence may be extracted. We show that the resulting theory of sequences falls within our existing theory of sets, and provide formal definitions for all of the operators used. The chapter ends with a proof method for universal statements about sequences.

9.1 Sequence notation

A sequence is an ordered collection of objects. If there are no objects in the collection, the sequence is the *empty sequence*, and is written '$\langle\rangle$'. Otherwise, the sequence is written as a list of objects between angle brackets: for example, the expression $\langle a, b, c\rangle$ denotes the sequence containing objects a, b, and c, in that order.

A useful way of composing sequences is *concatenation*, in which two sequences are combined in such a way that the elements of one follow the elements of the other, and order is maintained. If s and t are sequences, we write $s \frown t$ to denote the concatenation of s and t. For example,

$$\langle a, b, c\rangle \frown \langle d, e\rangle = \langle a, b, c, d, e\rangle$$

Example 9.1 The ticket office in a railway station has a choice of two counters at which tickets may be purchased. There are two queues of people, one at each counter; these may be modelled as sequences:

$$\begin{aligned} queue\_a &= \langle sally, tim, ulla \rangle \\ queue\_b &= \langle vicky, wilson, xavier \rangle \end{aligned}$$

Sally and Vicky are at the head of their respective queues, but—just as Vicky is about to be served—the ticket machine at Counter b breaks down, and the people waiting there join the end of other queue. Order is maintained, so the result is given by $queue\_a \frown queue\_b$, the sequence

$$\langle sally, tim, ulla, vicky, wilson, xavier \rangle$$

A queue of six people forms at Counter a. □

A sequence contains information about a collection of elements and the order in which they occur. It may be that not all of this information concerns us: we may restrict our attention to elements from a given set using the *filter* operator: if s is a sequence, then $s \upharpoonright A$ is the largest subsequence of s containing only those objects that are elements of A:

$$\langle a, b, c, d, e, d, c, b, a \rangle \upharpoonright \{a, d\} = \langle a, d, d, a \rangle$$

The order and multiplicity of elements is preserved.

Example 9.2 In the station, there is a destination board displaying a list of trains, arranged in order of departure: see Figure 9.1. This may be modelled as a sequence of pairs, each recording a time and a destination:

$$\begin{aligned} trains == \langle &(10.15, london), (10.38, edinburgh), (10.40, london), \\ &(11.15, birmingham), (11.20, reading), (11.40, london) \rangle \end{aligned}$$

Sally is interested only in those trains that are going to London; she would be content with the filtered sequence

$$trains \upharpoonright \{ t : Time \bullet (t, london) \}$$

that is,

$$\langle (10.15, london), (10.40, london), (11.40, london) \rangle$$

□

DEPARTURES	
10 15	LONDON PADDINGTON via READING
10 38	EDINBURGH
10 40	LONDON PADDINGTON
11 15	BIRMINGHAM NEW STREET
11 20	READING via DIDCOT PARKWAY
11 40	LONDON PADDINGTON

Figure 9.1: Destination board

It may be that we need to refer to the first element of a sequence, or to the part of the sequence that follows the first element; these are called the *head* and *tail*, respectively. For example,

$$\begin{aligned} head\,\langle a, b, c, d, e\rangle &= a \\ tail\,\langle a, b, c, d, e\rangle &= \langle b, c, d, e\rangle \end{aligned}$$

Notice that the head of a sequence is an element, while the tail is another sequence. If s is any non-empty sequence, then

$$s = \langle head\ s\rangle \frown tail\ s$$

Neither of these operators is defined upon the empty sequence.

Example 9.3 Sally wants to take the first train to London. From the list of trains on the destination board, she knows that this is the 10:15,

$$head(trains \upharpoonright \{\, t : Time \bullet (t, london)\,\}) = (10.15, london)$$

Tim is still waiting to buy a ticket, and the first train is about to leave. If we assume that he will not reach the platform in time, then the list of available trains is given by '*tail trains*', the sequence

$$\langle (10.38, edinburgh), (10.40, london), (11.15, birmingham), \\ (11.20, reading), (11.40, london)\rangle$$

□

The number of elements in a sequence is often of interest: if s is a sequence, then we write '$\#s$' to denote the length of s. For example,

$$\#\langle a, b, c, d, e, f \rangle = 6$$

Recall that the same notation was used in Section 8.6 to denote the size of a finite set.

Example 9.4 The total number of trains on the destination board is given by

$$\#trains = 6$$

and the total number of trains to London is given by

$$\#(trains \upharpoonright \{ t : Time \bullet (t, london) \}) = 3$$

□

A distributed version of the concatenation operator maps a sequence of sequences to a single sequence; this process is sometimes called *flattening*. For example,

$$\frown/\langle\langle a, b, c\rangle, \langle d, e\rangle, \langle f, g, h\rangle\rangle = \langle a, b, c, d, e, f, g, h\rangle$$

When a sequence of sequences is flattened, the result consists of the constituent sequences concatenated in order.

Example 9.5 The names and addresses of Sally's friends are stored in 26 files, `address.a`, `address.b`, ..., `address.z`, according to the first letter of the person's surname. Within each file, the records are ordered alphabetically: e.g., `address.h` contains the records

```
Robert Harris, 15 Royal Crescent, ...
Guy Hart-Davis, 38 Bridge Street, ...
Alison Harvey, 56 West Street, ...
```

Sally would prefer to have just one file containing all of the records. Using the DOS copy command, she types:

```
copy address.a + address.b + ... + address.z address.all
```

If we model each file as a sequence of addresses—for example, the first file might be represented by a sequence *address.a*, where

$$\begin{aligned} address.a \;=\; & \langle\text{'Gregory Abowd, 1126 Pacific Street, \ldots'}, \\ & \text{'Laurence Arnold, 9 Acacia Avenue, \ldots'}, \\ & \ldots\rangle \end{aligned}$$

—then we may describe the effect of the copy command using distributed concatenation:

$$address.all \;=\; {}^\frown/\langle address.a, address.b, \ldots, address.z\rangle$$

The result is exactly what Sally requires: a file address.all containing all of the names and addresses, arranged in alphabetical order. □

9.2 A model for sequences

The operators introduced above have not been formally defined; we have no way of proving anything about sequences, nor can we be sure that mathematical objects exist with the specified properties. For example, we stated that for any non-empty sequence s,

$$s \;=\; \langle head\, s\rangle {}^\frown tail\, s$$

but how can we be sure that this is the case? Clearly, we must find a formal basis for our theory of sequences.

Such a basis already exists within our mathematical language. A sequence may be regarded as a function from the natural numbers to a collection of objects: the object associated with 1 comes first in the sequence, the object associated with 2 comes second, and so on. Thus, in our mathematical language, a finite sequence is a function defined upon some *initial segment* of the natural numbers: a number range starting at 1.

If X is a set, then the set of all finite sequences of objects from X is defined by the following abbreviation:

$$\mathrm{seq}\, X \;==\; \{s : \mathbb{N} \twoheadrightarrow\!\!\!\!\!\!\shortmid\;\; X \mid \exists\, n : \mathbb{N} \bullet \mathrm{dom}\, s = 1 \,..\, n\}$$

This definition makes explicit an assumption about sequences: that every element of a given sequence must share the same type. The expression

$$\langle 1, (1, 2)\rangle$$

makes no sense to us: the first element is an element of $\mathbb{N}$, while the second is an element of $\mathbb{N} \times \mathbb{N}$.

In this book, we will restrict ourselves to sequences with finite length. Such sequences are easier to reason about, and are sufficient for most applications. However, certain properties are impossible to describe without infinite sequences; *fairness* is an obvious example; it is perfectly possible to add a theory of infinite sequences to our mathematical language.

If a sequence is to be a special kind of function, then we are free to re-use the notation introduced in Chapters 7 and 8. For example, we can use functional application to refer to objects according to their position: if s is a sequence of at least n objects, then the expression '$s\ n$' denotes the nth object in s.

Example 9.6 The third person in the queue at Counter b is Wilson:

$$queue\_b\ 3 = wilson$$

and the second train on the destination board is the 10.38 to Edinburgh:

$$trains\ 2 = (10.38, edinburgh)$$

□

Furthermore, the practice of using '#' to denote both the cardinality of a set and the length of a sequence now makes perfect sense: if we regard a sequence s as a function, then the length of s is equal to the number of maplets in s.

If s and t are sequences and i is a number in the range $1 \mathinner{..} \#s$, then the ith element of $s \frown t$ is the ith element of s:

$$(s \frown t)\ i = s\ i$$

and if j is a number in the range $1 \mathinner{..} \#t$, then the $(j + \#s)^{\text{th}}$ element of $s \frown t$ is the jth element of t:

$$(s \frown t)\ (j + \#s) = t\ j$$

As $s \frown t$ is a sequence of length $\#s + \#t$, this is enough to provide a unique definition of the concatenation operator:

$$
\begin{array}{|l}
[X] \\
\hline
\_ \frown \_ : \operatorname{seq} X \times \operatorname{seq} X \to \operatorname{seq} X \\
\hline
\forall s, t : \operatorname{seq} X \bullet \\
\quad \#(s \frown t) = \#s + \#t \\
\quad \forall i : 1 \mathinner{..} \#s \bullet (s \frown t)\ i = s\ i \\
\quad \forall j : 1 \mathinner{..} \#t \bullet (s \frown t)\ (j + \#s) = t\ j \\
\hline
\end{array}
$$

The restriction operator is harder to define. Not only must we remove any maplets which point to objects outside the chosen set, but we must also make sure that the result is a sequence. The first task is accomplished using range restriction, while the second requires an auxiliary function:

$$s \upharpoonright A \;=\; squash\,(s \rhd A)$$

The auxiliary function *squash* takes a finite function defined upon the natural numbers and returns a sequence. It compacts the domain to remove any spaces created by range restriction, while preserving the order of the remaining maplets: for example,

$$squash\,\{1 \mapsto a, 3 \mapsto c, 6 \mapsto f\} \;=\; \{1 \mapsto a, 2 \mapsto c, 3 \mapsto f\} \;=\; \langle a, c, f \rangle$$

A suitable definition of *squash* would be:

$$
\begin{array}{l}
[X] \\
\hline
squash : (\mathbb{N}_1 \twoheadrightarrow\!\!\!\!\!\!+\;\, X) \to \mathrm{seq}\, X \\
\hline
\forall f : (\mathbb{N}_1 \twoheadrightarrow\!\!\!\!\!\!+\;\, X) \bullet \\
\quad squash\, f = (\mu\, g : 1\,..\,\#f \rightarrowtail\!\!\!\!\!\twoheadrightarrow \mathrm{dom}\, f \mid g^{\sim} \fatsemi (\_ + 1) \fatsemi g \subseteq (\_ < \_)) \\
\qquad\qquad \fatsemi \\
\qquad\qquad f \\
\hline
\end{array}
$$

For any function f whose domain is a finite set of numbers, we consider the unique function g that enumerates the domain of f in ascending order. The composition of g with f is then the sequence we require.

Our generic definition of restriction is then:

$$
\begin{array}{l}
[X] \\
\hline
\_ \upharpoonright \_ : \mathrm{seq}\, X \times \mathbb{P}\, X \to \mathrm{seq}\, X \\
\hline
\forall s : \mathrm{seq}\, X;\; A : \mathbb{P}\, X \bullet \\
\quad s \upharpoonright A \;=\; squash\,(s \rhd A) \\
\hline
\end{array}
$$

The head operator is easily described:

$$
\begin{array}{l}
[X] \\
\hline
head : \mathrm{seq}\, X \nrightarrow X \\
\hline
\forall s : \mathrm{seq}\, X \mid s \neq \langle\rangle \bullet \\
\quad head\, s = s\, 1 \\
\hline
\end{array}
$$

but the tail operator requires a translation:

$$
\begin{array}{l}
[X] \\
\hline
tail : \mathrm{seq}\, X \rightarrow\!\!\!\!\!\rightarrow \mathrm{seq}\, X \\
\hline
\forall s : \mathrm{seq}\, X \mid s \neq \langle\rangle \bullet \\
\quad \# tail\, s = \# s - 1 \\
\quad \forall i : 1 \mathinner{\ldotp\ldotp} \# s - 1 \bullet (tail\, s)\ i = s\,(i + 1)
\end{array}
$$

These definitions make it clear that '*head*' and '*tail*' are strictly partial: the empty sequence has neither a head nor a tail. Because this sequence is exceptional, we give a name to the set of all non-empty sequences over X,

$$\mathrm{seq}_1\, X == \{s : \mathrm{seq}\, X \mid s \neq \langle\rangle\}$$

Observe that '*head*' and '*tail*' are total when defined upon this set.

Another special set of sequences is the set of all *injective* sequences: sequences in which no element appears more than once. We write $\mathrm{iseq}\, X$ to denote the set of all injective sequences over set X, where

$$\mathrm{iseq}\, X == \{\, s : \mathrm{seq}\, X \mid s \in \mathbb{N} \rightarrowtail X \,\}$$

Such sequences are used to represent ordered collections of distinct objects.

9.3 Functions on sequences

In the course of a specification, we may wish to describe new operations upon sequences. For example, it might be necessary to reverse the order in which objects appear, or to select every other object in a sequence. We can, of course, define these new operations in terms of their effect upon finite functions, but there is a more convenient alternative.

We may introduce an operation f by describing its effect upon the empty sequence, and also its effect upon a sequence starting with an arbitrary element:

$$
\begin{aligned}
f\ \langle\rangle &= k \\
f\ (\langle x\rangle \frown s) &= g\,(x, f(s))
\end{aligned}
$$

In this description, k is a constant expression, while g may be any function of x and $f\, s$. The fact that these equations define a unique function f on finite sequences is a consequence of the *recursion principle* for the natural numbers, which will be discussed in Section 10.4.

Example 9.7 The function '*reverse*' returns a sequence in which the elements appear in reverse order. The two equations

$$reverse\,\langle\rangle = \langle\rangle \qquad \text{(reverse.1)}$$

$$reverse(\langle x\rangle \frown s) = (reverse\,s) \frown \langle x\rangle \qquad \text{(reverse.2)}$$

are enough to describe the effect of '*reverse*' upon any finite sequence. In this case, the constant k is simply $\langle\rangle$, and the function g is given by

$$\begin{array}{l} [X] \\ g : X \times \operatorname{seq} X \to \operatorname{seq} X \\ \hline \forall x : X;\ s : \operatorname{seq} X \bullet \\ \quad g\,(x, s) = (reverse\,s) \frown \langle x\rangle \end{array}$$

□

However an operator is defined, we will find it useful to identify a set of laws: equations that express important properties of the operator in question. For example, the restriction operator admits the law

$$\langle\rangle \upharpoonright A = \langle\rangle \qquad \text{(filter.1)}$$

which states that the empty sequence is unaffected by an application of the filter operator, and the law

$$(\langle x\rangle \frown s) \upharpoonright A = \begin{cases} \langle x\rangle \frown (s \upharpoonright A) & \text{if } x \in A \\ s \upharpoonright A & \text{otherwise} \end{cases} \qquad \text{(filter.2)}$$

which describes the effect of $\upharpoonright$ upon an arbitrary non-empty sequence.

A proof by equational reasoning is a series of expressions, each obtained from the previous one by substitution. Each substitution is justified by an appropriate equation or law.

Example 9.8 Using laws 'reverse.1' and 'filter.1', we may construct a proof that '$reverse(\langle\rangle \upharpoonright A) = (reverse\,\langle\rangle) \upharpoonright A$' for any set A. We proceed as follows:

$$\begin{array}{ll} reverse(\langle\rangle \upharpoonright A) & \\ \quad = reverse\,\langle\rangle & \text{[filter.1]} \\ \quad = \langle\rangle & \text{[reverse.1]} \\ \quad = \langle\rangle \upharpoonright A & \text{[filter.1]} \\ \quad = (reverse\,\langle\rangle) \upharpoonright A & \text{[reverse.1]} \end{array}$$

□

A common property of functions on sequences is *distributivity*. We say that a function f is distributive if

$$f\,(s \frown t) \;=\; (f\,s) \frown (f\,t)$$

for any sequences s and t. That is, if it distributes through concatenation.

Example 9.9 The function *add_one* is defined on sequences of numbers by the following pair of equations:

$$\begin{aligned} add\_one\,\langle\rangle &= \langle\rangle \\ add\_one\,(\langle n\rangle \frown s) &= \langle n+1\rangle \frown (add\_one\,s) \end{aligned}$$

The effect of applying *add_one* is to increase each number in the sequence by precisely one: for example, $add\_one\,\langle 2,4,6\rangle = \langle 3,5,7\rangle$. This function is distributive, as $add\_one\,(s \frown t) = (add\_one\,s) \frown (add\_one\,t)$. □

The filter operator $\upharpoonright$ is also distributive, but this cannot be established by equational reasoning using the laws given above. We would need to show that

$$(s \frown t) \upharpoonright A \;=\; (s \upharpoonright A) \frown (t \upharpoonright A)$$

for arbitrary sequences s and t. If s is empty, or a singleton sequence, then we may construct a proof using 'filter.1' or 'filter.2', respectively. If s has two or more elements, say

$$s \;=\; \langle x_1, x_2, x_3, \ldots\rangle$$

then we must rewrite s as $\langle x_1\rangle \frown \langle x_2, x_3, \ldots, \rangle$ before we can apply 'filter.2'. To produce a formal proof, we must write s in extension.

To establish that $\upharpoonright$ is distributive by equational reasoning, it seems that we require an infinite family of proofs: a proof for when s is empty, a proof for when s has length 1, a proof for when s has length 2, and so on. The proof for length n will require n applications of the law 'filter.2', followed by a single application of 'filter.1'. Fortunately, there is another way.

9.4 Structural induction

The set of natural numbers $\mathbb{N}$ has an important property. If $P\,\_$ is a predicate on natural numbers such that

- $P\,0$ is true, and
- if $i \in \mathbb{N}$ and $P\,i$ is true, then $P\,(i+1)$ is also true

then $P\,n$ is true for all natural numbers n. This is an *induction principle* for the natural numbers, and it can be extremely useful in proofs of universal properties.

Example 9.10 The cumulative sum of the first n natural numbers has the value $x = (n^2 + n) \operatorname{div} 2$. Assuming a suitable definition of the function 'sum', and using the induction principle as a proof rule, we define a predicate

$$\begin{array}{|l} P\_ : \mathbb{P}\,\mathbb{N} \\ \hline \forall n : \mathbb{N} \bullet P\,n \Leftrightarrow \mathrm{sum}\{\, i : 0 \mathinner{..} n \,\} = (n^2 + n) \operatorname{div} 2 \end{array}$$

to be our *inductive hypothesis*. We construct a proof of the following form:

$$\dfrac{\dfrac{\begin{array}{c}\vdots \\ P\,0\end{array} \qquad \begin{array}{c}\vdots \\ \forall m : \mathbb{N} \bullet P\,m \Rightarrow P\,(m+1)\end{array}}{\forall n : \mathbb{N} \bullet P\,n}\;[\text{induction}]}{\forall n : \mathbb{N} \bullet \mathrm{sum}\{\, i : 0 \mathinner{..} n \,\} = (n^2 + n) \operatorname{div} 2}\;[\text{axdef}]$$

The left-hand branch of the proof is called the *base case*; the right-hand branch is called the *inductive step*. □

The set of all finite sequences over X has a similar property. If P is a predicate on sequences such that

- $P\,\langle\rangle$ is true
- if $x \in X$, $t \in \mathrm{seq}\,X$, and $P\,t$ is true, then $P\,(\langle x \rangle \frown t)$ is also true

then $P\,s$ is true for all sequences s in $\mathrm{seq}\,X$. This is an induction principle for finite sequences over X; it can be written as a proof rule:

$$\dfrac{P\,\langle\rangle \qquad \forall x : X;\ t : \mathrm{seq}\,X \bullet P\,t \Rightarrow P\,(\langle x \rangle \frown t)}{\forall s : \mathrm{seq}\,X \bullet P\,s}\;[\text{induction}]$$

This form of reasoning is called *structural induction*. Our induction principle is based upon the structure of a sequence; every non-empty sequence may be built up from the empty sequence by adding the appropriate elements, one at a time. If a property is true of $\langle\rangle$, and remains true whatever elements we add, then it is true of every finite sequence.

We are now able to construct a proof that $\upharpoonright$ is distributive: we can use structural induction to show that

$$\forall s, t : \mathrm{seq}\,X;\ A : \mathbb{P}\,X \bullet (s \frown t) \upharpoonright A = (s \upharpoonright A) \frown (t \upharpoonright A)$$

There are two sequence variables in the above predicate, but we will need to consider only one of them. Our inductive hypothesis is described by the following predicate:

$$\begin{array}{|l} P\_ : \mathbb{P}\,\mathrm{seq}\,X \\ \hline \forall s : \mathrm{seq}\,X \bullet \\ \qquad P\,s \Leftrightarrow \forall t : \mathrm{seq}\,X;\ A : \mathbb{P}\,X \bullet (s \frown t) \restriction A = (s \restriction A) \frown (t \restriction A) \end{array}$$

and the proof proceeds as follows:

$$\dfrac{\dfrac{}{P\,\langle\rangle}\,[\text{Lemma 1}] \qquad \dfrac{\dfrac{\dfrac{\lceil x \in X \wedge r \in \mathrm{seq}\,X \rceil^{[1]} \quad \lceil S\,r \rceil^{[2]}}{S\,(\langle x \rangle \frown r)}\,[\text{Lemma 2}]}{S\,r \Rightarrow S\,(\langle x \rangle \frown r)}\,[\Rightarrow\text{-intro}]^{[2]}}{\forall x : X;\ r : \mathrm{seq}\,X \bullet S\,r \Rightarrow S\,(\langle x \rangle \frown r)}\,[\forall\text{-intro}]^{[1]}}{\dfrac{\forall s : \mathrm{seq}\,X \bullet P\,s}{\dfrac{\forall s : \mathrm{seq}\,X \bullet \forall t : \mathrm{seq}\,X;\ A : \mathbb{P}\,X \bullet (s \frown t) \restriction A = (s \restriction A) \frown (t \restriction A)}{\forall s, t : \mathrm{seq}\,X;\ A : \mathbb{P}\,X \bullet (s \frown t) \restriction A = (s \restriction A) \frown (t \restriction A)}\,[\text{law of } \forall]}\,[\text{axdef}]}\,[\text{induction}]$$

The base case and inductive step in this proof have been reduced to simpler inferences: Lemma 1 and Lemma 2. These can be established by equational reasoning, using the following laws:

$$\langle\rangle \frown s = s \qquad \text{(cat.1)}$$

$$s \frown (t \frown u) = (s \frown t) \frown u \qquad \text{(cat.2)}$$

The first of these confirms that $\langle\rangle$ is a unit for the concatenation operator; the second states that concatenation is associative.

The first lemma can be proved using the unit law of concatenation and law 'filter.1', which describes the effect of applying the filter operator to the empty sequence.

$$\begin{aligned} &(\langle\rangle \frown t) \restriction A \\ &\quad = t \restriction A && [\text{cat.1}] \\ &\quad = \langle\rangle \frown (t \restriction A) && [\text{cat.1}] \\ &\quad = (\langle\rangle \restriction A) \frown (t \restriction A) && [\text{filter.1}] \end{aligned}$$

The inductive step—Lemma 2—depends upon the associative property of concatenation and the law 'filter.2'.

$$((\langle x \rangle \frown r) \frown t) \restriction A$$

$$
\begin{aligned}
&= ((\langle x\rangle \frown (r \frown t)) \upharpoonright A && \text{[cat.2]}\\
&= \langle x\rangle \frown ((r \frown t) \upharpoonright A) \quad \text{if } x \in A && \text{[filter.2]}\\
&\quad\ (r \frown t) \upharpoonright A \quad \text{otherwise} &&\\
&= \langle x\rangle \frown ((r \upharpoonright A) \frown (t \upharpoonright A)) \quad \text{if } x \in A && [P\,r]\\
&\quad\ (r \upharpoonright A) \frown (t \upharpoonright A) \quad \text{otherwise} &&\\
&= ((\langle x\rangle \frown (r \upharpoonright A)) \frown (t \upharpoonright A) \quad \text{if } x \in A && \text{[cat.2]}\\
&\quad\ (r \upharpoonright A) \frown (t \upharpoonright A) \quad \text{otherwise} &&\\
&= (((\langle x\rangle \frown r) \upharpoonright A) \frown (t \upharpoonright A) && \text{[filter.2]}
\end{aligned}
$$

The step marked $P\,t$ is justified by our inductive assumption that the result holds for sequence r.

Example 9.11 For any set A and sequence s, the sequences '$reverse(s \upharpoonright A)$' and '$(reverse\,s) \upharpoonright A$' are equal, provided that the types of s and A are compatible:

$$\forall\, s : \mathrm{seq}\,X;\ A : \mathbb{P}\,X \bullet reverse(s \upharpoonright A) = (reverse\,s) \upharpoonright A$$

The order in which reverse and filter are applied makes no difference.

This result is easily established by structural induction, with the following predicate as an inductive hypothesis:

$$
\begin{array}{|l}
P\_ : \mathrm{seq}\,X\\
\hline
\forall\, s : \mathrm{seq}\,X \bullet\\
\qquad P\,s \Leftrightarrow \forall\, A : \mathbb{P}\,X \bullet reverse(s \upharpoonright A) = (reverse\,s) \upharpoonright A
\end{array}
$$

The base case of the induction has already been established; it was the subject of a proof in Example 9.8.

$$
\dfrac{\dfrac{}{P\,\langle\rangle}\ \text{[Example 9.8]} \qquad \dfrac{\dfrac{\dfrac{\lceil x \in X \wedge r \in \mathrm{seq}\,X\rceil^{[1]} \quad \lceil P\,r\rceil^{[2]}}{P\,(\langle x\rangle \frown r)}\ \text{[see below]}}{P\,t \Rightarrow P\,(\langle x\rangle \frown r)}\ [\Rightarrow\text{-intro}]^{[2]}}{\forall\, x : X;\ r : \mathrm{seq}\,X \bullet P\,r \Rightarrow P\,(\langle x\rangle \frown r)}\ [\forall\text{-intro}]^{[1]}}{\dfrac{\dfrac{\forall\, s : \mathrm{seq}\,X \bullet P\,s}{\forall\, s : \mathrm{seq}\,X \bullet \forall\, A : \mathbb{P}\,X \bullet reverse(s \upharpoonright A) = (reverse\,s) \upharpoonright A}\ \text{[axdef]}}{\forall\, s : \mathrm{seq}\,X;\ A : \mathbb{P}\,X \bullet reverse(s \upharpoonright A) = (reverse\,s) \upharpoonright A}\ [\text{law of } \forall]}\ \text{[induction]}
$$

As in the proof that the filter operator is distributive, the inductive step can be completed using equational reasoning:

$$
\begin{array}{lll}
\multicolumn{2}{l}{reverse((\langle x \rangle \frown r) \upharpoonright A)} & \\
\quad = reverse(\langle x \rangle \frown (r \upharpoonright A)) & \text{if } x \in A & \text{[filter.2]} \\
\quad reverse(r \upharpoonright A) & \text{otherwise} & \\
\quad = reverse(r \upharpoonright A) \frown \langle x \rangle & \text{if } x \in A & \text{[reverse.2]} \\
\quad reverse(r \upharpoonright A) & \text{otherwise} & \\
\quad = ((reverse\, r) \upharpoonright A) \frown \langle x \rangle & \text{if } x \in A & \text{[P r]} \\
\quad (reverse\, r) \upharpoonright A & \text{otherwise} & \\
\quad = ((reverse\, r) \upharpoonright A) \frown (\langle x \rangle \upharpoonright A) & & \text{[filter.2]} \\
\quad = ((reverse\, r) \frown \langle x \rangle) \upharpoonright A & & \text{[filter is distributive]} \\
\quad = (reverse\,(\langle x \rangle \frown r)) \upharpoonright A & & \text{[reverse.2]}
\end{array}
$$

As with ordinary formal proofs, once an equational result has been established, it may be used as a law in subsequent proofs. Here, we have been able to exploit the fact that the filter operator is distributive. □

9.5 Bags

A sequence stores information about the *multiplicity* and *ordering* of its elements. In the sequence $\langle a, b, c, a, b, c \rangle$, we can see that there are exactly two occurrences of a, and that these occupy the first and fourth positions in the sequence. Sometimes this is more information than we need.

Suppose that only the number of occurrences of a is important. If this is the case, then the sequence above contains more detail than is necessary: it is not a *fully abstract* representation. The set $\{a, b, c\}$, on the other hand, is not an *adequate* representation: it records that a is present, but does not record how many times it occurs.

If we wish to record multiplicities, but not ordering, then we may represent a collection of objects as a *bag*. We write $[\![a, a, b, b, c, c]\!]$ to denote the bag containing two copies of a, two copies of b, and two copies of c. The order in which elements are written is not important: the expression $[\![a, b, b, a, c, c]\!]$ denotes exactly the same bag.

Example 9.12 Four friends—Alice, Bill, Claire, and David—are sitting in a café, waiting for their drinks to arrive. Alice and Claire have asked for espresso, Bill has asked for fruit tea, and David has asked for grape juice. Their requests can be represented by a bag:

$$\llbracket espresso, espresso, fruit\_tea, grape\_juice \rrbracket$$

The order in which these drinks are to be delivered is left unspecified; the group will be content with any ordering that includes two *espresso*s, one *fruit_tea*, and one *grape_juice*. □

If B is a bag of elements from set X, then B may be regarded as a partial function from X to $\mathbb{N}$. Any element of X that appears in B is associated with a natural number, recording the number of instances that are present. For example, the bag $\llbracket a, a, b, b, c, c \rrbracket$ contains the same information as the function $\{a \mapsto 2, b \mapsto 2, c \mapsto 2\}$, which associates each element with the number 2.

If X is a set, then the set of all bags of elements from X may be defined by the following generic abbreviation:

$$\mathrm{bag}\,X \;==\; X \pfun \mathbb{N} \setminus \{0\}$$

where $\mathbb{N}$ denotes the set of all natural numbers. A bag is a finite partial function from X to $\mathbb{N}$; elements of X that do not appear in the bag are left out of the domain, rather than mapped to zero.

If we wish to know how many instances of an object there are in a given bag, then we could simply apply the bag as a function. However, if the object is not present in the bag, the effect of this functional application is undefined. To avoid this, we employ the total function *count*:

$$\begin{array}{l}
[X] \\
\hline
count\,B : \mathrm{bag}\,X \rightarrowtail\!\!\!\twoheadrightarrow (X \rightarrow \mathbb{N}) \\
\hline
\forall B : \mathrm{bag}\,X \bullet \\
\quad count\,B = (\lambda\, x : X \bullet 0) \oplus B
\end{array}$$

If B is a bag of elements from set X, then $count\,B$ associates each element of X with the number of times that it occurs in B, even if that number is zero.

For convenience, we define an infix version: if x is an element of X, then $B \sharp x$ is the number of occurrences of x in B:

$$\begin{array}{l}
[X] \\
\hline
_ \sharp _ : \mathrm{bag}\,X \times x \rightarrow \mathbb{N} \\
\hline
\forall B : \mathrm{bag}\,X;\; x : X \bullet \\
\quad B \sharp x = count\,B\,x
\end{array}$$

The number of occurrences of a in the bag $[\![a, a, b, b, c, c]\!]$ could be written either as $count\ [\![a, a, b, b, c, c]\!]\ a$ or as $[\![a, a, b, b, c, c]\!] \sharp a$.

Example 9.13 If *drinks* denotes the collection of drinks requested by the four friends in Example 9.12, then

$$count\ drinks\ espresso = 2$$

reflecting the fact that two people have asked for an espresso. It is also possible to order decaffeinated coffee in the café, but no-one has asked for it. This information may be expressed using the prefix function *count*,

$$count\ drinks\ decaffeinated\_coffee = 0$$

or the infix function $\sharp$,

$$drinks \sharp decaffeinated\_coffee = 0$$

□

We define bag membership and sub-bag relations, similar to the set membership and subset relations introduced in Chapter 5:

$$
\begin{array}{l}
[X] \\
\hline
\_ \sqsubset \_ : X \leftrightarrow \text{bag}\, X \\
\_ \sqsubseteq \_ : \text{bag}\, X \leftrightarrow \text{bag}\, X \\
\hline
\forall x : X;\ B : \text{bag}\, X \bullet \\
\quad x \sqsubset B \Leftrightarrow x \in \text{dom}\, B \\
\forall B, C : \text{bag}\, X \bullet \\
\quad B \sqsubseteq C \Leftrightarrow \forall x : X \bullet B \sharp x \leqslant C \sharp x \\
\hline
\end{array}
$$

An element x is a member of bag B if it appears in the domain of B, considered as a function. A bag B is a sub-bag of another bag C of the same type if each element occurs no more often in B than it does in C.

Example 9.14 At least one grape juice has been requested,

$$grape\_juice \sqsubset drinks$$

and two of the group have asked for espresso,

$$[\![espresso, espresso]\!] \sqsubseteq drinks$$

□

We define also bag union and bag difference operators. If B and C are bags of the same type, then their union $B \uplus C$ contains as many copies of each element as B and C put together:

$$
\begin{array}{l}
[X] \\
\hline
\_ \uplus \_, \_ \cup\!\!\!\!-\ \_ : \text{bag}\, X \times \text{bag}\, X \rightarrow \text{bag}\, X \\
\hline
\forall B, C : \text{bag}\, X;\ x : X \bullet \\
\qquad B \uplus C \sharp x = B \sharp x + C \sharp x \\
\qquad B \cup\!\!\!\!-\ C \sharp x = \max\{B \sharp x - C \sharp x, 0\}
\end{array}
$$

If there are m copies of some element in bag B, and n copies of the same element in bag C, then the bag difference $B \cup\!\!\!\!-\ C$ contains $m - n$ copies, provided that $m \geqslant n$. If there are more copies in C than in B, then the count of this element is zero in the difference.

Example 9.15 No sooner have the drinks been asked for than two more friends arrive—Edward and Fleur—and take their places at the table. Edward asks for a cappucino; Fleur asks for a mineral water. If we define

$$more\_drinks == [\![cappucino, mineral\_water]\!]$$

then the collection of requests is a bag union:

$$requests == drinks \uplus more\_drinks$$

A few minutes later, a tray of drinks is brought over. It holds a mineral water, a grape juice, a decaffeinated coffee, and an espresso:

$$tray == [\![mineral\_water, grape\_juice, decaffeinated\_coffee, espresso]\!]$$

The collection of outstanding requests is a bag difference:

$$remainder == requests \cup\!\!\!\!-\ tray$$

No-one has asked for a decaffeinated coffee, $decaffeinated\_coffee \not\sqsubset requests$, so its inclusion on the tray has no effect upon the remainder, which is equal to the bag $[\![fruit\_tea, espresso, cappucino]\!]$. □

If s is a sequence, then we may extract the multiplicity information from s using the function *items*, which turns sequences into bags:

$$
\begin{array}{l}
[X] \\
\hline
items : \mathrm{seq}\, X \to \mathrm{bag}\, X \\
\hline
\forall s : \mathrm{seq}\, X;\ x : X \bullet \\
\quad (items\ s) \sharp x = \#(s \rhd \{x\})
\end{array}
$$

The ordering information present in the sequence is discarded.

Example 9.16 Another tray is brought over with the remaining drinks; these are placed on the table in front of our friends. The order in which the drinks are placed upon the table is recorded in the following sequence,

$$
\begin{array}{rcl}
arrive & == & \langle grape\_juice, mineral\_water, espresso, fruit\_tea, cappucino, \\
& & cappucino, espresso\rangle
\end{array}
$$

but only the *count* of each drink is important. The group at the table will be content, as *items arrive* = *drinks*. □

Chapter 10

Free Types

In the course of a specification we may define a variety of data structures: lists, arrays, or trees of elements drawn from one or more basic types. These structures could be modelled using a combination of sets and relations, but the resulting definitions would be quite verbose. A more elegant, concise alternative is offered by *free types*: sets with explicit structuring information.

In this chapter we show how free types are used to model enumerated collections, compound objects, and recursively defined structures. We examine the motivation behind free type definitions by attempting to describe a recursive data structure resembling the natural numbers. We then explain the consequences of such definitions, giving inference rules for reasoning about the objects that are introduced.

10.1 The natural numbers

The set of all natural numbers, $\mathbb{N}$, is already part of our mathematical language; it has been defined as a subset of the built-in type $\mathbb{Z}$. However, the construction of a set similar to $\mathbb{N}$ will prove a useful illustration of the properties of a free type. Thus we attempt to define such a set, beginning with a basic type *nat*, a zero element, and a partial function called succ:

$$\begin{array}{|l} \mathsf{zero} : nat \\ \mathsf{succ} : nat \rightarrowtail\!\!\!\!\rightarrow nat \\ \hline \forall\, n : nat \bullet n = \mathsf{zero} \lor \exists\, m : nat \bullet n = \mathsf{succ}\, m \end{array}$$

Every element n is either the constant zero or the result of applying the successor function succ to an element m.

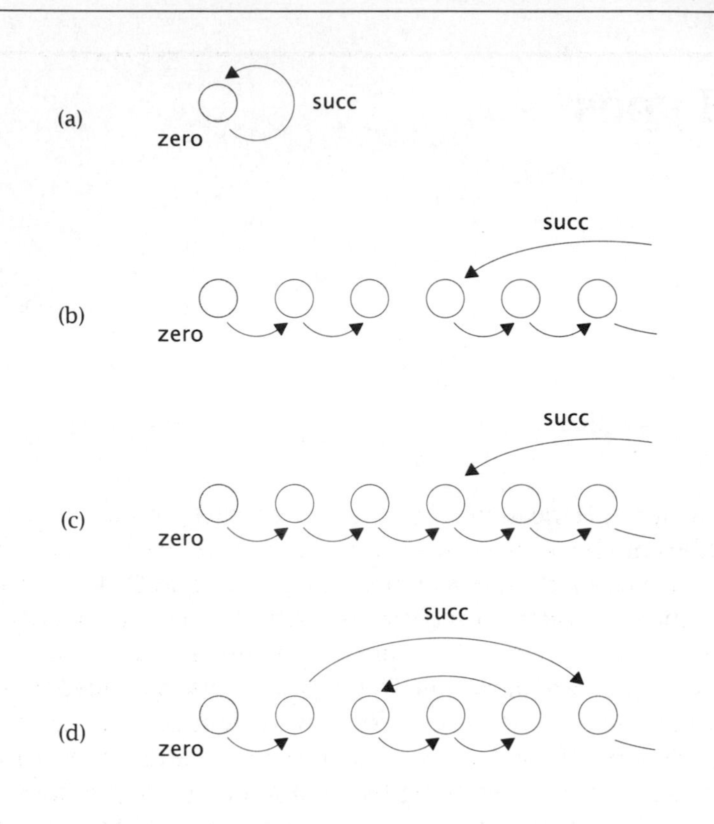

Figure 10.1: Four sets that are not the natural numbers

Unfortunately, this is not enough to capture the essence of $\mathbb{N}$. The set pictured in Figure 10.1(a) satisfies the above definition, but is quite unlike the set of natural numbers. Accordingly, we decide to exclude **zero** from the range of **succ**; however, even this is not enough. Consider the following:

$$\begin{array}{|l} \mathsf{zero} : nat \\ \mathsf{succ} : nat \twoheadrightarrow nat \\ \hline \forall n : nat \bullet n = \mathsf{zero} \lor \exists m : nat \bullet n = \mathsf{succ}\, m \\ \mathsf{zero} \cap \operatorname{ran} \mathsf{succ} = \varnothing \end{array}$$

This definition fails to exclude the set shown in Figure 10.1(b): it is quite possible to have elements of *nat* that have no successor. Having realised that the function used to construct the natural numbers must be total, we try again:

$$
\begin{array}{|l}
\mathsf{zero} : nat \\
\mathsf{succ} : nat \to nat \\
\hline
\forall n : nat \bullet n = \mathsf{zero} \lor \exists m : nat \bullet n = \mathsf{succ}\, m \\
\mathsf{zero} \cap \operatorname{ran} \mathsf{succ} = \varnothing
\end{array}
$$

And still this is not enough. We have failed to exclude the possibility that some element is the successor of two or more others: see Figure 10.1(c). There is nothing that allows us to conclude that *nat* is an infinite set.

We must thus add a fourth requirement: that the function used to construct the natural numbers is *injective*. This leads us to the following definition:

$$
\begin{array}{|l}
\mathsf{zero} : nat \\
\mathsf{succ} : nat \rightarrowtail nat \\
\hline
\{\mathsf{zero}\} \cap \operatorname{ran} \mathsf{succ} = \varnothing \\
\{\mathsf{zero}\} \cup \operatorname{ran} \mathsf{succ} = nat
\end{array}
$$

With this, we are guaranteed an infinite set with the familiar structure of the natural numbers. There is one more requirement to consider; the above definition fails to exclude the set shown in Figure 10.1(d). The set *nat* must contain a copy of the natural numbers $\mathbb{N}$, or at least a set with exactly the same structure, but it may contain more besides. The final requirement is that *nat* should be the *smallest* set that meets the conditions laid down above.

10.2 Free type definitions

Our mathematical language has a special mechanism for introducing sets such as *nat*: the free type definition. To begin with, consider the special case in which the set to be introduced has a small, finite number of elements. An example might be the set of colours of the rainbow: red, orange, yellow, green, blue, indigo, and violet. In the programming language Pascal, this set may be introduced as an enumerated type:

```
Colours = {red,orange,yellow,green,blue,indigo,violet}
```

We could take a similar approach in Z, writing

$$Colours == \{red, orange, yellow, green, blue, indigo, violet\}$$

However, this abbreviation does not *define* the constants in the set. It not only fails to introduce the names, it also fails to make them distinct: there is no guarantee that *red* is different from *green*.

The following *free type* definition has a different effect; it introduces a set *Colours*, and seven distinct constants:

$$Colours ::= \mathsf{red} \mid \mathsf{orange} \mid \mathsf{yellow} \mid \mathsf{green} \mid \mathsf{blue} \mid \mathsf{indigo} \mid \mathsf{violet}$$

Once this definition has been made, we may infer that *Colours* is the smallest set containing the seven distinct elements 'red', 'orange', 'yellow', 'green', 'blue', 'indigo', and 'violet'. The order in which these elements are introduced is unimportant: the definition

$$Colours ::= \mathsf{violet} \mid \mathsf{indigo} \mid \mathsf{blue} \mid \mathsf{green} \mid \mathsf{yellow} \mid \mathsf{orange} \mid \mathsf{red}$$

would have the same effect.

Example 10.1 The people in charge of Oxford colleges are given a variety of titles. We may represent this variety as a free type:

$$\begin{aligned} Titles ::= {} & \mathsf{dean} \mid \mathsf{master} \mid \mathsf{president} \mid \mathsf{principal} \mid \\ & \mathsf{provost} \mid \mathsf{rector} \mid \mathsf{warden} \end{aligned}$$

From this definition we can conclude that 'dean' and 'warden' are elements of the set *Titles* and that $\mathsf{dean} \neq \mathsf{warden}$. A dean and a warden are quite different animals. □

We may include copies of other sets as part of a free type, using *constructor* functions. The notation

$$FreeType ::= \mathsf{constructor} \langle\!\langle source \rangle\!\rangle$$

introduces a collection of constants, one for each element of the set *source*. constructor is an injective function whose target is the set *FreeType*.

Example 10.2 The University of Oxford awards a number of different degrees; four of the most common are: *BA*, bachelor of arts; *MSc*, master of science; *D.Phil*, doctor of philosophy; *MA*, master of arts. For ceremonial purposes, these degrees are ordered as follows: an *MA* is the highest ranking; a *D.Phil* takes second place, followed by an *MSc* and a *BA*, in that order.

Suppose that we wish to represent this ordered collection of degrees as a free type. The ordering of elements is similar to the one imposed upon the first four natural numbers by the less-than-or-equal to relation. Importing these numbers into a free type, we define

$$Degree ::= \mathsf{status} \langle\!\langle 0 \mathinner{..} 3 \rangle\!\rangle$$

and give names to the four elements of the set *Degree*:

$$ba, msc, dphil, ma : Degree$$

$$\begin{aligned} ba &= \mathsf{status}\ 0 \\ msc &= \mathsf{status}\ 1 \\ dphil &= \mathsf{status}\ 2 \\ ma &= \mathsf{status}\ 3 \end{aligned}$$

We are then free to define the University's ordering of degrees in terms of the $\leqslant$ ordering on $0 \mathbin{..} 3$:

$$\leqslant_{status} : Degree \leftrightarrow Degree$$

$$\begin{aligned} &\forall d_1, d_2 : Degree \bullet \\ &\qquad d_1 \leqslant_{status} d_2 \Leftrightarrow \mathsf{status}^\sim d_1 \leqslant \mathsf{status}^\sim d_2 \end{aligned}$$

Because status is an injection, we can be sure that its inverse is a function, and hence that $\mathsf{status}^\sim d$ is well-defined. □

Constants and constructor functions may be used together in the same definition, as in the following free type:

$$FreeType ::= \mathsf{constant} \mid \mathsf{constructor} \langle\langle source \rangle\rangle$$

What is more, the source type of a constructor function may refer to the free type being defined. The result is a recursive type definition: *FreeType* is defined in terms of itself.

Example 10.3 The set *nat* discussed in the previous section could be introduced by the following free type definition:

$$nat ::= \mathsf{zero} \mid \mathsf{succ} \langle\langle nat \rangle\rangle$$

Every element of *nat* is either zero or the successor of a natural number, zero is not a successor, and every element of *nat* has a unique successor. The set *nat* is the smallest set containing the following collection of distinct elements: zero, succ zero, succ(succ zero), succ(succ(succ zero)), and so on. □

Example 10.4 We may define a free type of binary trees, in which every element is either a leaf or a branching point.

$$Tree ::= \mathsf{leaf} \langle\langle \mathbb{N} \rangle\rangle \mid \mathsf{branch} \langle\langle Tree \times Tree \rangle\rangle$$

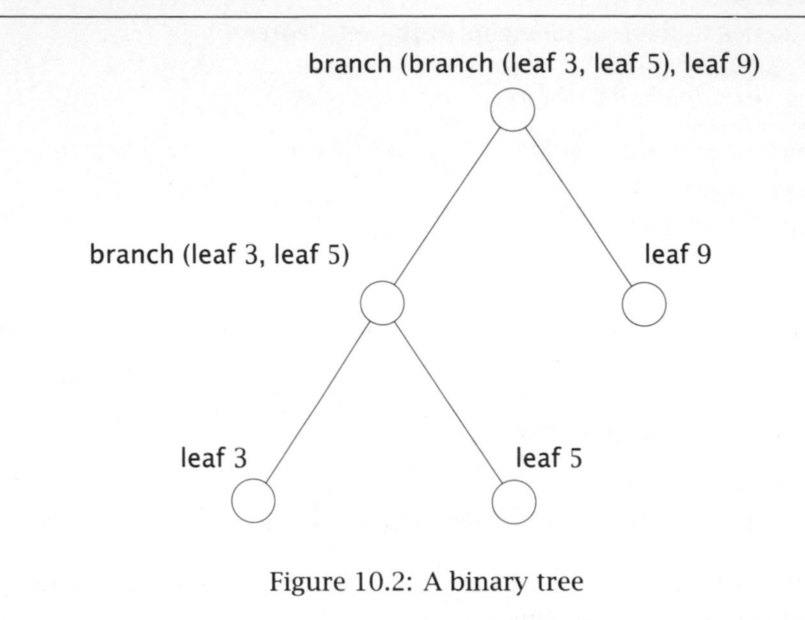

Figure 10.2: A binary tree

Each leaf contains a number; each branching point joins a pair of sub-trees. For example, one element of *Tree* is given by

$$\mathsf{branch}\,(\mathsf{branch}\,(\mathsf{leaf}\,3,\ \mathsf{leaf}\,5),\ \mathsf{leaf}\,9)$$

in which three different leaves are joined together to form the structure pictured in Figure 10.2. □

Example 10.5 The following definition introduces a more complex free type, in which every element is a tree: a pair whose first component is a natural number and whose second component is a sequence of trees.

$$SequenceTree ::= \mathsf{tree}\langle\langle \mathbb{N} \times \mathrm{seq}\, SequenceTree\rangle\rangle$$

This is a particularly involved data structure, one element of which is shown below:

$$(1, \langle (2, \langle\rangle), (3, \langle\rangle), (4, \langle (2, \langle\rangle)\rangle)\rangle)$$

□

Suppose that $E_1, E_2, \ldots, E_n$ are expressions that may depend on set T, and that c_1, c_2, ..., c_m are constant expressions. The definition

$$T ::= c_1 \mid \ldots \mid c_m \mid d_1 \langle\langle E_1 \rangle\rangle \mid \ldots \mid d_n \langle\langle E_n \rangle\rangle$$

introduces a new basic type T, with constant elements $c_1, \ldots, c_m$ and constructor functions $d_1, \ldots, d_n$. The same effect could be achieved by introducing T as a basic type and making the following axiomatic definition:

$$\begin{array}{|l}
c_1 : T \\
\vdots \\
c_m : T \\
d_1 : E_1 \rightarrowtail T \\
\vdots \\
d_n : E_n \rightarrowtail T \\
\hline
\mathrm{disjoint}\ \langle \{c_1\}, \ldots, \{c_m\}, \mathrm{ran}\, d_1, \ldots \mathrm{ran}\, d_n \rangle \\
\forall S : \mathbb{P}\, T \bullet \\
\qquad (\{c_1, \ldots, c_m\} \cup d_1 (\!| E_1[S / T] |\!) \cup \ldots \cup d_n (\!| E_n[S / T] |\!)) \subseteq S \\
\qquad\qquad \Rightarrow S = T
\end{array}$$

Such a definition adds two inference rules to a specification. The first states that the constants are distinct and that the ranges are disjoint:

$$\frac{}{\mathrm{disjoint}\ \langle \{c_1\}, \ldots, \{c_m\}, \mathrm{ran}\, d_1, \ldots \mathrm{ran}\, d_n \rangle}$$

Example 10.6 In the case of *nat*, we may infer that the constant zero is not the successor of any natural number,

$$\mathrm{disjoint}\ \langle \{zero\}, \mathrm{ran}\, succ \rangle$$

□

Example 10.7 From the definition of *Tree*, we may conclude that leaves and branches are different objects:

$$\mathrm{disjoint}\ \langle \mathrm{ran}\, leaf, \mathrm{ran}\, branch \rangle$$

A tree may be either a leaf or a branch, but not both. □

The second rule is an induction principle: it is essential to reasoning about the elements of a recursive type.

$$\frac{S \subseteq T \quad \{c_1, \ldots, c_m\} \cup d_1 (\!| E_1[S / T] |\!) \cup \ldots \cup d_n (\!| E_n[S / T] |\!) \subseteq S}{S = T}$$

Any subset of T that contains all of the constants and is *closed* under the constructors must be the whole of T. A set S is closed under d and E if the image of $E[S / T]$ under d is within S itself.

Example 10.8 The free type definition of *nat* can be used to justify the following assertion:

$$\forall s : \mathbb{P}\, nat \bullet (\{\mathsf{zero}\} \cup \mathsf{succ}(\!|\, s \,|\!) \subseteq s) \Rightarrow s = nat$$

Any subset of *nat* which contains zero and is closed under succ must be equal to *nat* itself. □

10.3 Proof by induction

The second inference rule above can be rewritten to match the induction principles given in the previous chapter. Suppose that P is a predicate upon elements of a free type T, and define the characteristic set

$$S == \{t : T \mid P\, t\}$$

that is, S is the set of elements of T that satisfy P. Since S is a subset of T, the inference rule gives us that

$$\frac{(\{\mathsf{c}_1, \ldots, \mathsf{c}_m\} \cup \mathsf{d}_1(\!|\, E_1[S / T] \,|\!) \cup \ldots \mathsf{d}_n(\!|\, E_n[S / T] \,|\!)) \subseteq S}{S = T}$$

We may use properties of the union and subset operators to separate the antecedent part of the rule into a list of inequalities. Furthermore, Each of the expressions involving $\subseteq$ may be rewritten:

$$\begin{aligned} & \mathsf{d}_i (\!|\, E_i[S / T] \,|\!) \subseteq S \\ & \quad \Leftrightarrow E_i[S / T] \subseteq \mathsf{d}_i^{\sim} (\!|\, S \,|\!) \\ & \quad \Leftrightarrow \forall e : E_i[S / T] \bullet e \in \mathsf{d}_i^{\sim} (\!|\, S \,|\!) \\ & \quad \Leftrightarrow \forall e : E_i[S / T] \bullet \mathsf{d}_i\, e \in S \end{aligned}$$

That is, whenever a constructor d_i is applied, the result is an element of S.

If we may replace each instance of the statement $e \in S$ with the abbreviated form $P\, e$, then we obtain an induction principle that matches those given for sequences:

$$\frac{\begin{array}{l} P\,\mathsf{c}_1 \\ \vdots \\ P\,\mathsf{c}_m \\ \forall\, e : E_1[S \,/\, T] \bullet P\,(\mathsf{d}_1\, e) \\ \vdots \\ \forall\, e : E_n[S \,/\, T] \bullet P\,(\mathsf{d}_n\, e) \end{array}}{\forall\, t : T \bullet P\, t} \text{ [induction principle]}$$

The appearance of S in the source set of e corresponds to the condition that P holds for any elements of the free type used in the construction of e.

Example 10.9 The definition of *nat* involved a single constant zero and a single constructor function succ:

$$nat \; ::= \; \mathsf{zero} \mid \mathsf{succ}\,\langle\!\langle nat \rangle\!\rangle$$

This type has a single constant and a single constructor function; the definition yields an inference rule of the form

$$\frac{S \subseteq T \quad (\{\mathsf{c}\} \cup \mathsf{d}(\!|\, E[S \,/\, nat] \,|\!)) \subseteq S}{S = T}$$

In this instance: the constant c is zero; the constructor function d is succ; and the expression E is *nat* itself.

If P is a predicate on *nat*, we may take S to be the characteristic set

$$S \; == \; \{n : nat \mid P\, n\}$$

and obtain the following induction principle:

$$\frac{\begin{array}{l} P\,\mathsf{zero} \\ \forall\, m : nat \bullet P\, m \Rightarrow P\,(\mathsf{succ}\, m) \end{array}}{\forall\, n : nat \bullet P\, n}$$

To establish that P holds of every natural number, we must show that it holds for zero and that it is preserved by the successor function: if it is true of m, then it is also true of succ m. □

Example 10.10 The definition of *Tree* in Example 10.4 leads to the following induction principle:

$$\frac{\begin{array}{l}\forall\, n : \mathbb{N} \bullet P\,(\mathsf{leaf}\; n) \\ \forall\, t_1, t_2 : Tree \bullet \\ \qquad P\, t_1 \wedge P\, t_2 \Rightarrow P\,(\mathsf{branch}\,(t_1, t_2))\end{array}}{\forall\, t : Tree \bullet P\, t}$$

To show that a property P is true of all trees, we must show that it holds for any leaf, whatever value is stored there. We must show also that the property is preserved when trees are joined using branch: if it is true of both components, then it is true of their combination. □

10.4 Primitive recursion

A function defined upon the elements of a free type may have a number of different parts: one for each clause in the type definition. For example, suppose that f is a function upon elements of a free type T, introduced by

$$T ::= \mathsf{c} \mid \mathsf{d}\langle\langle E \rangle\rangle$$

There may be two parts to the definition of f: one explaining the effect of f upon constant c, the other explaining the effect of f upon an element of the set $\mathsf{d}(\!|\, E \,|\!)$.

If the expression E contains a copy of the free type T, the function definition will be recursive. It will describe the result of applying f to an element of $\mathsf{d}(\!|\, E \,|\!)$ in terms of the result of applying f to one or more components.

Example 10.11 We may define a function *fact* upon *nat* by giving a case for zero and a case for successors:

$$\begin{aligned} fact\; 0 &= 1 \\ fact\,(\mathsf{succ}\; n) &= (n + 1) * (fact\; n) \end{aligned}$$

If $+$ and $*$ correspond to addition and multiplication, respectively, then this defines the ubiquitous factorial function upon *nat*. □

The fact that such functions are well defined follows from a *recursion principle* for the type in question. In the case of the natural numbers, this principle may be stated as follows: for every value k and operator g, there is a unique total function f from the natural numbers such that

$$f\,0 = k$$
$$f(n+1) = g(n+1)(f\ n)$$

This may be used to justify the use of recursively defined functions upon $\mathbb{N}$. A similar principle applies to arbitrary free types, provided that their definitions are *consistent*, a condition discussed in the next section.

Example 10.12 We may define a function *flatten* that takes a binary tree and produces a sequence by *traversing* the tree from left to right.

$$flatten : Tree \rightarrow \operatorname{seq} \mathbb{N}$$
$$\forall n : \mathbb{N} \bullet flatten\ \mathsf{leaf}\ n = \langle n \rangle$$
$$\forall t_1, t_2 : Tree \bullet flatten\ \mathsf{branch}\,(t_1, t_2) = flatten\ t_1 \frown flatten\ t_2$$

Whenever it is applied to a branch, it will produce a sequence in which all of the elements of the left branch appear before those of the right.

Furthermore, we may define a function *flip* which transforms on binary trees by swapping the position of any two trees that meet at the same branch.

$$flip : Tree \rightarrow Tree$$
$$\forall n : \mathbb{N} \bullet flip\ \mathsf{leaf}\ n = \mathsf{leaf}\ n$$
$$\forall t_1, t_2 : Tree \bullet flip\ \mathsf{branch}\,(t_1, t_2) = \mathsf{branch}\,(flip\ t_2, flip\ t_1)$$

In both cases, the fact that the given equations define a unique function is a consequence of the recursion principle for binary trees. □

Recursion and induction go hand-in-hand. If a function has been defined using recursion, then induction may be required when we come to reason about its properties.

Example 10.13 Using the induction principle for binary trees, we may prove that flipping and flattening is the same as flattening and then reversing. To be more precise, if we apply *flip* to a binary tree and then *flatten* the result, we obtain the same sequence that appears when we *flatten* the tree and apply the *reverse* function. Formally,

$$\forall t : Tree \bullet (flip \mathbin{;} flatten)\ t \;=\; (flatten \mathbin{;} reverse)\ t$$

where '*reverse*' is the function on sequences defined in Chapter 9.

The proof of this result proceeds as follows. We begin by identifying our inductive hypothesis:

$$P(t) \Leftrightarrow (\mathit{flip} \,⨾\, \mathit{flatten})\, t = (\mathit{flatten} \,⨾\, \mathit{reverse})\, t$$

and then check that the base case is valid. Suppose that n is an arbitrary natural number:

$$\begin{aligned}
&(\mathit{flip} \,⨾\, \mathit{flatten})\, \mathsf{leaf}\, n \\
&\quad = \mathit{flatten}(\mathit{flip}\, \mathsf{leaf}\, n) && [\text{property of } ⨾] \\
&\quad = \mathit{flatten}(\mathsf{leaf}\, n) && [\text{definition of } \mathit{flip}] \\
&\quad = \langle n \rangle && [\text{definition of } \mathit{flatten}] \\
&\quad = \mathit{reverse}\, \langle n \rangle && [\text{definition of } \mathit{reverse}] \\
&\quad = \mathit{reverse}(\mathit{flatten}\, \mathsf{leaf}\, n) && [\text{definition of } \mathit{flatten}] \\
&\quad = (\mathit{flatten} \,⨾\, \mathit{reverse})\, \mathsf{leaf}\, n && [\text{property of } ⨾]
\end{aligned}$$

This piece of equational reasoning can be incorporated into a simple deductive proof of the base case:

$$\dfrac{\dfrac{\dfrac{\lceil n : \mathbb{N} \rceil^{[1]}}{(\mathit{flip} \,⨾\, \mathit{flatten})\, \mathsf{leaf}\, n = (\mathit{flatten} \,⨾\, \mathit{reverse})\, \mathsf{leaf}\, n}\; [\text{equational reasoning}]}{P(\mathsf{leaf}\, n)}\; [\text{definition of } P]}{\forall\, n : \mathbb{N} \bullet P(\mathsf{leaf}\, n)}\; [\forall\text{-intro}]^{[1]}$$

We then proceed to show that the inductive step is also valid. Suppose that the hypothesis P is true for trees t_1 and t_2:

$$\begin{aligned}
&(\mathit{flip} \,⨾\, \mathit{flatten})\, \mathsf{branch}\, (t_1, t_2) \\
&\quad = \mathit{flatten}(\mathit{flip}\, \mathsf{branch}\, (t_1, t_2)) && [\text{property of } ⨾] \\
&\quad = \mathit{flatten}(\mathsf{branch}\, (t_2, t_1)) && [\text{definition of } \mathit{flip}] \\
&\quad = (\mathit{flatten}\, t_2) \frown (\mathit{flatten}\, t_1) && [\text{definition of } \mathit{flatten}] \\
&\quad = \mathit{reverse}((\mathit{flatten}\, t_1) \frown (\mathit{flatten}\, t_2)) && [\text{property of } \mathit{reverse}] \\
&\quad = \mathit{reverse}(\mathit{flatten}\, \mathsf{branch}\, (t_1, t_2)) && [\text{definition of } \mathit{flatten}] \\
&\quad = (\mathit{flatten} \,⨾\, \mathit{reverse})\, \mathsf{branch}\, (t_1, t_2) && [\text{property of } ⨾]
\end{aligned}$$

The property of *reverse* used in this proof is easy to establish.

As before, we may incorporate this reasoning into a deductive proof:

$$\dfrac{\dfrac{\dfrac{\lceil t_1, t_2 : Tree \rceil^{[1]}}{(flip \mathbin{;} flatten)\ \mathsf{branch}\ (t_1, t_2) = (flatten \mathbin{;} reverse)\ \mathsf{branch}\ (t_1, t_2)}\ \text{[equational reasoning]}}{P(\mathsf{branch}\ (t_1, t_2))}\ \text{[definition of } P\text{]}}{\forall\, t_1, t_2 : Tree \bullet P\, t_1 \wedge P\, t_2 \Rightarrow P\,(\mathsf{branch}\ (t_1, t_2))}\ [\forall\text{-intro}]^{[1]}$$

The equality that we were trying to prove now follows immediately, with a single application of the induction principle for *Tree*. □

10.5 Consistency

It is possible to use a free type definition to introduce a contradiction into any specification. To see how it might happen, consider the following definition:

$$T ::= \mathsf{d}\langle\langle \mathbb{P}\, T \rangle\rangle$$

The free type T contains an element $\mathsf{d}\, s$ for each element s of $\mathbb{P}\, T$. Since d is injective, T must be at least as big as its power set. This is impossible, as for any α, if T has α elements, then $\mathbb{P}\, T$ has 2^{α}.

The problem lies in our use of the power set construction. This generates too many new elements at each application, producing a set that is bigger than itself. The same problem may occur with any construction using the relation symbol $\leftrightarrow$ or the function symbol $\rightarrow$. Such constructions are not *finitary*, and we cannot be sure that they will produce a consistent definition.

More formal definitions of *finitary* can be found in the literature, but for most applications it is enough to know that any construction involving only Cartesian products and finite power sets is finitary, and that any free type definition that uses only finitary constructions will be consistent. That is, the free type definition

$$T ::= \mathsf{c}_1 \mid \ldots \mid \mathsf{c}_m \mid \mathsf{d}_1\langle\langle E_1 \rangle\rangle \mid \ldots \mid \mathsf{d}_n\langle\langle E_n \rangle\rangle$$

will be consistent if each of the constructions

$$E_1, \ldots, E_n$$

involves only Cartesian products, finite power sets, finite functions, and finite sequences.

Example 10.14 The free type definition

$$Fun ::= \mathsf{atom}\langle\langle \mathbb{N} \rangle\rangle \mid \mathsf{fun}\langle\langle Fun \rightarrow Fun \rangle\rangle$$

may not be consistent, as the construction $Fun \rightarrow Fun$ is not finitary. □

Example 10.15 The free type definition

$$List ::= \mathsf{nil} \mid \mathsf{atom}\langle\langle \mathbb{N} \rangle\rangle \mid \mathsf{cat}\langle\langle List \times List \rangle\rangle$$

must be consistent, as both constructions are finitary. □

Chapter 11

Schemas

In the Z notation there are two languages: the mathematical language and the schema language. The mathematical language is used to describe various aspects of a design: objects, and the relationships between them. The schema language is used to structure and compose descriptions: collating pieces of information, encapsulating them, and naming them for re-use.

Re-usability is vital to the successful application of a formal technique. By identifying and sharing common components, we keep our descriptions both flexible and manageable. In the schema language, we see specifications sharing parts, proofs sharing arguments, theories sharing abstractions, problems sharing common aspects.

We believe that the use of schemas helps to promote a good specification style. However, as with any notation, the language of schemas requires careful and judicious application if it is not to be abused. We should take care to develop simple theories and to use schemas to present them in an elegant and comprehensible fashion.

This chapter is an informal introduction to schemas: their appearance, and the information they contain. We see how they may be used as types, as declarations, and as predicates. In subsequent chapters, we present a language of schema operators, and show how schemas may be used in reasoning about formal descriptions.

11.1 The schema

The mathematical language of Z is powerful enough to describe most aspects of system behaviour. However, the unstructured application of mathematics soon results in descriptions that are difficult to understand. To avoid this, we must present mathematical descriptions in a sympathetic fashion, explaining small parts in the simplest possible context, and then showing how to fit the pieces together to make the whole.

One of the most basic things that we can do to help the reader—or indeed the writer—of a specification is to identify commonly used concepts and factor them out from the mathematical description of a system. In this way, we can encapsulate an important concept and give it a name, thus increasing our vocabulary—and our mental power.

In formal specifications, we see a pattern occurring over and over again: a piece of mathematical text which is a *structure* describing some variables whose values are constrained in some way. We call this introduction of variables under some constraint a *schema*.

Example 11.1 The set comprehension term, lambda expression, and quantified predicates below each exhibit this pattern of introduction and constraint:

$$\{m, n : \mathbb{N} \mid n = 2 \times m \bullet m \mapsto n\}$$

$$\lambda\, s : seq[X] \mid s \neq \langle\rangle \bullet (\text{tail}\ s) \frown \langle head\ s\rangle$$

$$\forall\, x, y : \mathbb{N} \mid x \neq y \bullet x > y \vee y > x$$

$$\exists\, z : \mathbb{N} \mid z \neq 1 \bullet z < 2$$

□

Example 11.2 A concert hall uses a software system to keep track of bookings for performances. Inside the hall is a certain amount of seating, some or all of which may be made available to customers for a given performance. At this level of abstraction, we have no need to consider the representation of seats and customers, so we introduce them as given sets:

$$[Seat, Customer]$$

The box office maintains a record of which seats have been sold, and to whom. This relationship should be functional: that is, no seat can be sold to two different customers:

$$sold : Seat \nrightarrow Customer$$

To allow for the possibility that seats may be added to or removed from the hall, we introduce a set *seating*, a subset of *Seat*, to represent the seating allocated for the performance.

It should not be possible to book seating that has not been allocated; the following predicate should be true at all times

$$\mathrm{dom}\ sold \subseteq seating$$

That is, the domain of *sold* should be a subset of *seating*. This property, together with the declarations of *sold* and *seating*, forms a schema which we shall call *BoxOffice*. □

A schema consists of two parts: a *declaration* of variables; and a *predicate* constraining their values. We can write the text of a schema in one of two forms: horizontally

[*declaration* | *predicate*]

or vertically

declaration
predicate

In the horizontal form, the declaration and predicate are separated by a vertical bar, and the schema text is delimited by brackets. In the vertical form, the declaration and predicate are separated by a horizontal bar, and the schema text is delimited by a broken box.

Example 11.3 We can write the box office schema in horizontal form, as

$$[seating : \mathbb{P}\, Seat;\ sold : Seat \twoheadrightarrow Customer \\ \mid \mathrm{dom}\ sold \subseteq seating]$$

or in vertical form, as

$seating : \mathbb{P}\, Seat;\ sold : Seat \twoheadrightarrow Customer$
$\mathrm{dom}\ sold \subseteq seating$

□

In the declaration part of a schema, the order in which variables are introduced is unimportant. In the above example, it would make no difference if *sold* were to be declared before *seating*.

The schema language includes a special operator for associating names with schemas. We may name a schema by writing

$$Name \mathrel{\widehat{=}} [declaration \mid predicate]$$

or by embedding the name in the top line of the schema box

```
┌─ Name ──────────────────────────────
│ declaration
├──────────
│ predicate
└─────────────────────────────────────
```

In either case, we are introducing a syntactic equivalence between *Name* and the schema text. We may use *Name* to refer to this text in the remainder of a formal description.

Example 11.4 We can name the box office schema text by writing

$$BoxOffice \mathrel{\widehat{=}} [seating : \mathbb{P}\, Seat;\ sold : Seat \mathrel{+\!\!\!\!\twoheadrightarrow} Customer \mid \operatorname{dom} sold \subseteq seating]$$

or by writing

```
┌─ BoxOffice ─────────────────────────
│ seating : ℙ Seat; sold : Seat ⇸ Customer
├──────────
│ dom sold ⊆ seating
└─────────────────────────────────────
```

□

Two schemas are equivalent if they introduce the same variables, and place the same constraints upon them. When considering equivalence, remember that some constraints may be hidden in the declaration part.

Example 11.5 The declaration part of the box office schema includes the constraint that the relation *sold* between *Seat* and *Customer* must be functional. The following schema, in which this constraint appears as part of the predicate, is entirely equivalent:

```
┌─────────────────────────────────────
│ seating : ℙ Seat; sold : Seat ↔ Customer
├──────────
│ dom sold ⊆ seating ∧ sold ∈ Seat ⇸ Customer
└─────────────────────────────────────
```

□

To make a schema more readable, we may put each declaration on a new line, and leave out the semicolons. Similarly, we may put each conjunct on a new line, and leave out the conjunction symbols. For example, the predicate

$$a \Rightarrow b$$
$$c \vee d$$

is another way of writing $(a \Rightarrow b) \wedge (c \vee d)$. Of course, this is not the case where the line is broken with another operator: for example, the predicate

$$\begin{aligned} &\exists\, y : T \bullet \\ &\qquad x < y \;\vee \\ &\qquad y < x \end{aligned}$$

means $\exists\, y : T \bullet x < y \;\vee y < x$.

Example 11.6 The schema of Example 11.5 could be written in the following form:

$$\begin{array}{|l} seating : \mathbb{P}\, Seat \\ sold : Seat \leftrightarrow Customer \\ \hline \operatorname{dom} sold \subseteq seating \\ sold \in Seat \twoheadrightarrow Customer \end{array}$$

□

If the schema text introduces components, but places no constraints upon them, then we may omit the predicate part.

Example 11.7 The following schema text has a single component, a set of seats called *stalls*, with no constraints:

$$\begin{array}{|l} stalls : \mathbb{P}\, Seat \end{array}$$

This is equivalent to the text

$$\begin{array}{|l} stalls : \mathbb{P}\, Seat \\ \hline true \end{array}$$

□

11.2 Schemas as types

In our mathematical language, there are four ways of introducing a type: as a given set, as a free type, as a power set, or as a Cartesian product. If we require a composite type, one with a variety of different components, then the schema language offers a useful alternative. The schema below corresponds to a composite data type with two components: an integer called a, and a set of integers called c.

```
┌─ SchemaOne ──────────────────────────
│ a : ℤ
│ c : ℙ ℤ
└──────────────────────────────────────
```

We may introduce elements of this type in the usual way: the declaration s : *SchemaOne* introduces an object s of schema type *SchemaOne*.

To write an object of schema type in extension, we list the component names and the values to which they are bound. This requires a new piece of notation:

$$\langle\!| a \rightsquigarrow 2, c \rightsquigarrow \{1, 2, 3\} |\!\rangle$$

is a *binding* in which a is bound to 2 and c is bound to the set $\{1, 2, 3\}$. The schema type *SchemaOne* is the set of all bindings in which a and c are bound to an integer and a set of integers, respectively.

Example 11.8 The declaration b : *BoxOffice* introduces an object b with two components: a set called *seating* and a relation called *sold*. The type of b is a schema type:

$$[\mathit{seating} : \mathbb{P}\, \mathit{Seat};\ \mathit{sold} : \mathit{Seat} \leftrightarrow \mathit{Customer}]$$

The schema *BoxOffice* appears as a subrange type; it describes only those bindings in which *sold* is a partial function, and the domain of *sold* is a subset of *seating*. □

Example 11.9 A date is an object consisting of two named components: the name of a month and the number of a day. We may define *Month* as a free type with twelve constants:

$$\mathit{Month} ::= \mathsf{jan} \mid \mathsf{feb} \mid \mathsf{mar} \mid \mathsf{apr} \mid \mathsf{may} \mid \mathsf{jun} \mid \mathsf{jul} \mid \mathsf{aug} \mid \mathit{sep} \mid \mathsf{oct} \mid \mathsf{nov} \mid \mathsf{dec}$$

The set of all valid dates may be represented as a schema type:

$$\begin{array}{l} \textit{Date} \\ \hline \textit{month} : \textit{Month} \\ \textit{day} : 1 \,..\, 31 \\ \hline \textit{month} \in \{\mathsf{sep}, \mathsf{apr}, \mathsf{jun}, \mathsf{nov}\} \Rightarrow \textit{day} \leqslant 30 \\ \textit{month} = \mathsf{feb} \Rightarrow \textit{day} \leqslant 29 \\ \hline \end{array}$$

A binding $\langle\!| \textit{month} \rightsquigarrow m, \textit{day} \rightsquigarrow d \,|\!\rangle$ is a valid date provided that there are at least d days in month m. □

A schema type differs from a Cartesian product in that the components are stored not by position but by name. To refer to a particular component, we employ a selection operator '_._'. For example, if s is an object of schema type *SchemaOne*, we may write $s.a$ and $s.c$ denote the integer component and set component of s, respectively.

Example 11.10 In a token ring or Ethernet network, information is transmitted in the form of data frames. Each frame has a source address, a destination, and a data component. The type of all frames is a schema type:

$$\begin{array}{l} \textit{Frame} \\ \hline \textit{source}, \textit{destination} : \textit{Address} \\ \textit{data} : \textit{Data} \\ \hline \end{array}$$

where *Address* is the set of all addresses in the network, and *Data* is the set of all possible data components. If f is an object of type *Frame*, then we write $f.\textit{source}$ to denote its source, $f.\textit{destination}$ to denote its destination, and $f.\textit{data}$ to denote its data component. □

Example 11.11 We may declare an object of subrange type *Date* to represent Fleur's birthday:

$$\mid \textit{Fleur's\_birthday} : \textit{Date}$$

Following such a declaration, we may refer to name of the month in which Fleur was born as $\textit{fleur's\_birthday.month}$, and to the day on which she was born as $\textit{fleur's\_birthday.day}$. □

11.3 Schemas as declarations

A schema may be used whenever a declaration is expected: in a set comprehension, in a lambda expression, or following a logical quantifier. The effect is to introduce the variables mentioned in the declaration part of the schema, under the constraint of the predicate part.

To illustrate this, we introduce a second schema with the same components as *SchemaOne*, but under some constraint:

$$
\begin{array}{|l}
\textit{SchemaTwo} \\
\hline
a : \mathbb{Z} \\
c : \mathbb{P}\,\mathbb{Z} \\
\hline
c \neq \varnothing \land a \in c \\
\hline
\end{array}
$$

This describes a subset of the bindings described by *SchemaOne*: number a must be an element of set c.

The following set consists of those sets of integers c that contain the integer 0:

$$\{ \textit{SchemaTwo} \mid a = 0 \bullet c \}$$

The same effect could be achieved by replacing *SchemaTwo* with a list of declarations and a constraint:

$$\{ a : \mathbb{Z};\ c : \mathbb{P}\,\mathbb{Z} \mid a \in c \land c \neq \varnothing \land a = 0 \bullet c \}$$

or by declaring an object of subrange type *SchemaTwo* and selecting the two components:

$$\{ s : \textit{SchemaTwo} \mid s.a = 0 \bullet s.c \}$$

The first expression, in which *SchemaTwo* is used as a declaration, is both more concise and more readable.

Example 11.12 If *Date* is the schema named in Example 11.9, then the set comprehension

$$\{ \textit{Date} \mid \textit{day} = 31 \bullet \textit{month} \}$$

describes the set of all months that have 31 days:

$$\{\mathsf{jan}, \mathsf{mar}, \mathsf{may}, \mathsf{jul}, \mathsf{aug}, \mathsf{oct}, \mathsf{dec}\}$$

□

If a set comprehension has no term part, then the type of objects in the set depends upon the characteristic tuple of the declaration. For example, in the set

$$\{ a : \mathbb{Z};\ c : \mathbb{P}\,\mathbb{Z} \mid a \in c \land a = 0 \}$$

the characteristic tuple is the pair (a, c), and the type of objects in the set is $\mathbb{Z} \times \mathbb{P}\,\mathbb{Z}$. The set consists of every pair (a, c) that meets the stated constraint.

In a schema, the order in which components are declared is unimportant, so the characteristic tuple of

$$\{ \mathit{SchemaTwo} \mid a = 0 \}$$

is quite different from (a, c). A typical element of this set is a binding associating a with 0 and c with some set containing 0; the characteristic tuple has one component: the binding $\langle\!| a \leadsto a, c \leadsto c |\!\rangle$.

This is a binding in which component a is bound to the value of variable a, and component c is bound to the value of variable c:

$$\langle\!|\ a \leadsto a,\ \underbrace{c}_{\text{component name}} \leadsto \overbrace{c}^{\text{variable value}}\ |\!\rangle$$

Such a binding, in which each component of a schema is bound to a value of the same name, is called a *characteristic binding*.

If S is the name of a schema, then we write θS to denote the characteristic binding of components from S. For example,

$$\theta \mathit{SchemaTwo} \;=\; \langle\!| a \leadsto a, c \leadsto c |\!\rangle$$

Whenever this expression is used, variables a and c must already have been declared. Furthermore, the types of these variables must match those given in the declaration part of *SchemaTwo*, although any predicate information in the schema is ignored.

Example 11.13 If *Date* is the schema named in Example 11.9, then $\theta \mathit{Date}$ denotes the characteristic binding

$$\langle\!| \mathit{month} \leadsto \mathit{month}, \mathit{day} \leadsto \mathit{day} |\!\rangle$$

Whenever this expression is used, variables *month* and *day* must be in scope, and their types must match those given in the declaration part of *Date*. □

There is a close relationship between our use of schemas as types and our use of the θ notation. As an illustration of this, consider the schema

$$
\begin{array}{l}
\text{SchemaThree} \\
\hline
a : \mathbb{Z} \\
c : \mathbb{P}\,\mathbb{Z} \\
\hline
c \neq \varnothing \land a \in c \\
c \subseteq \{0, 1\} \\
\hline
\end{array}
$$

This introduces the same variables as *SchemaOne* and *SchemaTwo*, but under a more restrictive set of constraints.

If we use *SchemaThree* to describe a set of bindings, then this set will have exactly four elements:

$$
\begin{aligned}
\mathit{SchemaThree} = {} & \{\langle\!| a \rightsquigarrow 0, c \rightsquigarrow \{0\} |\!\rangle, \langle\!| a \rightsquigarrow 0, c \rightsquigarrow \{0,1\} |\!\rangle, \\
& \langle\!| a \rightsquigarrow 1, c \rightsquigarrow \{1\} |\!\rangle, \langle\!| a \rightsquigarrow 1, c \rightsquigarrow \{0,1\} |\!\rangle\}
\end{aligned}
$$

The same set of bindings is described by the set comprehension

$$\{ a : \mathbb{Z};\ c : \mathbb{P}\,\mathbb{Z} \mid c \neq \varnothing \land a \in c \land c \subseteq \{0,1\} \bullet \langle\!| a \rightsquigarrow a, c \rightsquigarrow c |\!\rangle \}$$

which is equal to $\{ \mathit{SchemaThree} \bullet \theta \mathit{SchemaThree} \}$.

When a schema name is used where a set or type would be expected, we take it to represent the corresponding set of bindings. For any schema S, the declaration $a : S$ is an abbreviated form of

$$a : \{ S \bullet \theta S \}$$

The variable a is declared to be a binding of appropriate type that meets the constraint part of schema S. Thus we see that bindings, not schema types, are the primitive notion.

Example 11.14 When used in a variable declaration, the schema name *Date* represents the set of all valid dates: bindings in which there are at least *day* days in month *month*. This set of bindings could also be written as a set comprehension:

$$\{ \mathit{Date} \bullet \theta \mathit{Date} \}$$

Notice that, although $\theta \mathit{Date}$ is the default term of this set comprehension, we include it here to avoid confusion. It is not immediately obvious that the expression $\{\mathit{Date}\}$ denotes a set comprehension. □

A schema may be used as the declaration part of a lambda expression. If *SchemaOne* is as defined above, then

$$FunctionOne == \lambda\, SchemaOne \bullet a^2$$

introduces a function defined upon objects of schema type, mapping any binding of a and c to the square of the value of a. For example,

$$FunctionOne\, \langle\!| a \leadsto 2, c \leadsto \{1,2,3\} |\!\rangle = 4$$

As in Section 8.2, the source type of a lambda expression is given by the characteristic tuple of the declaration. In this case, the characteristic tuple has a single component: $\theta SchemaOne$.

Example 11.15 An object of schema type *BoxOffice* has two components: a set of seats allocated for the performance, and a record of which seats have been sold, and to whom. Given such an object, we may be interested in the set of seats that have yet to be sold. The function

$$free == \lambda\, BoxOffice \bullet \#(seating \setminus \mathrm{dom}\, sold)$$

maps an object of type *BoxOffice* to the number of unsold seats, calculated as the size of the set difference between *seating* and dom *sold*. □

A schema may be used as the declaration part of a quantified expression; this has the effect of introducing the components of the schema and then constraining them. For example,

$$\exists\, SchemaTwo \bullet a = 0 \Leftrightarrow \exists\, a : \mathbb{Z};\ c : \mathbb{P}\,\mathbb{Z} \mid c \neq \emptyset \land a \in c \bullet a = 0$$

In such expressions, the order in which the components are declared is unimportant: there are no characteristic tuples to consider.

These expressions may be used to make statements about objects of the corresponding schema type. For example, the following predicate states that, for any object of type *SchemaOne*, the a components must be an element of the c component:

$$\forall\, SchemaOne \bullet a \in c$$

This predicate is false, as the binding $\langle\!| a \leadsto 1, c \leadsto \{2,3\} |\!\rangle$ is an object of type *SchemaOne*. On the other hand, the predicate

$$\forall\, SchemaTwo \bullet a \in c$$

is true, as any binding of subrange type *SchemaTwo* must satisfy precisely this constraint.

Example 11.16 The following predicate states that there is an object of schema type *Date* such that the value of *month* is feb and the value of *day* is 29:

$$\exists\, Date \bullet month = \mathsf{feb} \land day = 29$$

This is true: there can be 29 days in February. □

Example 11.17 The following predicate states that, for any object of schema type *Date*, the value of *day* must be less than or equal to 30:

$$\forall\, Date \bullet day \leqslant 30$$

This is false, as the binding $\langle\!| month \rightsquigarrow \mathsf{mar}, day \rightsquigarrow 31 |\!\rangle$ satisfies the predicate part of *Date*. March is a month with 31 days. □

Whenever a schema appears as the declaration part of a quantified expression, the same result could be achieved by declaring an object of schema type. For example, the quantified predicate

$$\forall\, SchemaTwo \bullet a \in c$$

is logically equivalent to

$$\forall\, s : SchemaTwo \bullet s.a \in s.c$$

Both predicates insist that there is a binding of type *SchemaTwo* such that a is an element of c.

11.4 Schemas as predicates

A schema may be used as a predicate, provided that each component of the schema has already been declared as a variable of the correct type. The effect is to introduce a constraint equivalent to the predicate information stored in the schema. The following quantified expression states that any integer a and set of integers c satisfying the predicate *SchemaThree* must also satisfy the predicate *SchemaTwo*.

$$\forall\, a : \mathbb{Z};\ c : \mathbb{P}\,\mathbb{Z} \mid SchemaThree \bullet SchemaTwo$$

This is logically equivalent to the following statement:

$$\forall a : \mathbb{Z};\ c : \mathbb{P}\,\mathbb{Z} \mid c \notin \varnothing \land a \in c \land c \subseteq \{0,1\} \bullet c \notin \varnothing \land a \in c$$

The declaration parts are discarded; only the constraints remain.

Example 11.18 If *A* is an element of type *Address*, the set of all addresses within a network, then the following schema represents the set of all frames whose source address is *A*:

```
┌─ FromA ─────────────────────────────
│ source, destination : Address
│ data : Data
├─────────────
│ source = A
└─────────────────────────────────────
```

Used as a predicate, this schema asserts that the value of *source* is *A*. □

When we use a schema as a predicate, we should remember that the declaration part may include some constraint information. At first glance, the following schema appears equivalent to *SchemaTwo*:

```
┌─ SchemaFour ────────────────────────
│ a : ℕ
│ c : ℙ ℕ
├─────────────
│ a ∈ c ∧ c ≠ ∅
└─────────────────────────────────────
```

but this is not the case: an additional constraint upon a and c has been imposed by the declarations $a : \mathbb{N}$ and $c : \mathbb{P}\,\mathbb{N}$.

To avoid confusion, we may choose to rewrite a schema so that all of the constraint information appears in the predicate part. This process is called *normalisation*; the declaration part has been reduced to a unique, canonical form. For example, the above schema may be rewritten as

```
┌─ SchemaFourNormalised ──────────────
│ a : ℤ
│ c : ℙ ℤ
├─────────────
│ a ∈ ℕ
│ c ∈ ℙ ℕ
│ a ∈ c ∧ c ≠ ∅
└─────────────────────────────────────
```

It is now obvious that this schema contains strictly more information that *SchemaTwo*. When used as a predicate, it will insist that a, and every element of c, is greater than or equal to 0.

Example 11.19 At first glance, it might seem that any set *seating* of seats, and any relation *sold* between seats and customers, such that

$$\operatorname{dom} sold \subseteq seating$$

would meet the constraint of schema *BoxOffice*. We would expect to be able to show that

$$\forall\, seating : \mathbb{P}\, Seat;\ sold : Seat \leftrightarrow Customer \bullet \\ \quad \operatorname{dom} sold \subseteq seating \Rightarrow BoxOffice$$

However, this is not the case. The declaration part of *BoxOffice* includes the additional requirement that *sold* is a partial function. □

Example 11.20 The schema *Date* introduces two variables, *month* and *day*, in such a way that they correspond to a date in the Gregorian calendar. Using this schema as a predicate, we can show that

$$\forall\, month : Month;\ day : \mathbb{Z} \bullet Date \Rightarrow day \in 1 \mathinner{..} 31$$

The necessary constraint upon the range of *day* is included in the declaration part of the schema. If we consider the normalised form of *Date*,

$$
\begin{array}{|l}
\hline
\textit{DateNormalised} \\
month : Month \\
day : \mathbb{Z} \\
\hline
day \in 1 \mathinner{..} 31 \\
month \in \{\mathsf{sep}, \mathsf{apr}, \mathsf{jun}, \mathsf{nov}\} \Rightarrow day \leqslant 30 \\
month = \mathsf{feb} \Rightarrow day \leqslant 29 \\
\hline
\end{array}
$$

then the truth of the implication becomes obvious. □

11.5 Renaming

It is sometimes useful to rename the components of a schema; in this way, we are able to introduce a different collection of variables with the same pattern of declaration and constraint. If *Schema* is a schema, then we write

$$Schema[new / old]$$

to denote the schema obtained from *Schema* by replacing component name *old* with *new*. For example, we might wish to introduce variables q and s under the constraint of *SchemaTwo*: the schema

$$SchemaTwo[q/a, s/c]$$

is equivalent to the schema

$$\begin{array}{|l}
q : \mathbb{Z} \\
s : \mathbb{P}\,\mathbb{Z} \\
\hline
s \neq \varnothing \land q \in s
\end{array}$$

The new predicate part is obtained by systematically substituting q and s for free occurrences of a and c.

Example 11.21 The variables *start_month* and *start_day* represent the month and the day on which a contract of employment is due to start. The requirement that this should be a valid date can be encapsulated by an appropriate renaming of the schema *Date*:

$$Date[start\_month/month, start\_day/day]$$

This is equivalent to the following schema:

$$\begin{array}{|l}
\multicolumn{1}{l}{StartDate} \\
start_month : Month \\
start_day : 1\,..\,31 \\
\hline
start_month \in \{sep, \mathsf{apr}, \mathsf{jun}, \mathsf{nov}\} \Rightarrow start_day \leqslant 30 \\
start_month = \mathsf{feb} \Rightarrow start_day \leqslant 29
\end{array}$$

The types of the variables, and the constraints upon them, are unaffected by the renaming operation. □

Renaming the components of a schema produces a new schema type. For example, the schema type

$$SchemaOne[q/a, s/c]$$

consists of all bindings of q and s to values in $\mathbb{Z}$ and $\mathbb{P}\,\mathbb{Z}$. This is quite different from the schema type *SchemaOne*, which consists of bindings of a and c. In a schema type, component names are important.

Example 11.22 We may use another renaming to describe the set of all valid finish dates for our contract:

$$FinishDate \mathrel{\widehat{=}} Date[finish\_month / month, finish\_day / day]$$

A start date and a finish date are quite different objects, although each has a component of type *Month* and another of type $\mathbb{Z}$. If $s \in StartDate$ and $f \in FinishDate$, then the value of $s = f$ is undefined: these are variables of different types. However, it still makes sense to state that

$$s.start\_day = f.finish\_day$$

as both expressions are of type $\mathbb{Z}$. □

11.6 Generic schemas

Although we may rename the components of a schema, we cannot change their types. If we wish use the same structure for a variety of different types, we may define a generic schema: a schema with one or more formal parameters. The following schema introduces two variables, a and c, under the constraint that a is an element of c:

```
┌─ SchemaFive[X] ─────────────────
│ a : X
│ c : ℙX
├──────────
│ a ∈ c
└─────────────────────────────────
```

The types of a and c are parameterised by formal parameter X, which may be instantiated with any set.

This schema may be used whenever we wish to introduce two objects that are related in this way. If we choose $\mathbb{Z}$ to be the actual parameter, we obtain a schema that is equivalent to *SchemaTwo*:

```
┌─────────────────────────────────
│ a : ℤ
│ c : ℙℤ
├──────────
│ a ∈ c
└─────────────────────────────────
```

and if we choose $\mathbb{N}$, we obtain a schema that is equivalent to *SchemaFour*.

Example 11.23 The booking system could be generalised to describe a system which monitors the sale of unspecified items to a client base.

$$\begin{array}{|l}
\multicolumn{1}{l}{\textit{System}[\textit{Items}, \textit{Client}]} \\
\hline
\textit{seating} : \mathbb{P}\,\textit{Items} \\
\textit{sold} : \textit{Items} \mathrel{+\!\!\!\!\rightarrow} \textit{Client} \\
\hline
\operatorname{dom} \textit{sold} \subseteq \textit{seating} \\
\hline
\end{array}$$

We may obtain the familiar *BoxOffice* system by instantiating *Items* with *Seat* and *Client* with *Customer*.

$$\textit{System}\,[\textit{Seat}, \textit{Customer}] = \textit{BoxOffice}$$

□

Chapter 12

Schema Operators

In this chapter we see how the information contained in schemas may be combined in a variety of different ways. We introduce a language of logical schema operators: conjunction, disjunction, negation, quantification, and composition. To illustrate the use of this language, we explain how schemas may be used to describe the behaviour of a computing system.

This application of the schema language revolves around the concept of an abstract data type: a collection of variables, and a list of operations that may change their values. We encapsulate these variables within a schema, so that an object of the corresponding schema type represents a state of the system.

An operation that affects the state can be seen as a relation upon objects of schema type: bindings of the state variables. The schema notation provides a convenient way of describing such a relation: we may use a schema to express the relationship between the state before and the state after an operation.

12.1 Conjunction

We may combine the information contained in two schemas in a variety of ways: the simplest of these is conjunction. Suppose that S and T are the schemas introduced by

```
┌─ S ──────────────          ┌─ T ──────────────
│ a : A                      │ b : B
│ b : B                      │ c : C
├──────────                  ├──────────
│ P                          │ Q
└──────────────────          └──────────────────
```

where P and Q are predicates upon the corresponding variables.

We write $S \wedge T$ to denote the conjunction of these two schemas: a new schema formed by merging the declaration parts of S and T and conjoining their predicate parts:

$$
\begin{array}{|l}
a : A \\
b : B \\
c : C \\
\hline
P \wedge Q
\end{array}
$$

If the same variable is declared in both schemas, as with b above, then the types must match, or the schema $S \wedge T$ will be undefined.

The result of a schema conjunction is a schema that introduces both sets of variables and imposes both constraints. Schema conjunction allows us to specify different aspects of a specification separately, and then combine them to form a complete description. This makes for simple, well-structured descriptions, in which each individual component can be easily understood.

Example 12.1 Our theatre company presents *premieres*: special performances of new productions. Only those customers who have signed up as *friends* of the theatre may buy seats for these shows. To include this information in our formal description, we add a new variable of type *Status*:

$$Status ::= \mathsf{standard} \mid \mathsf{premiere}$$

A show may be a standard performance, or it may be a premiere. We require also a set *friends*, to represent the set of all customers who are currently registered as friends of the theatre.

The necessary enhancement to the box office system is described by the following schema:

$$
\begin{array}{|l}
\multicolumn{1}{l}{\textit{Friends}} \\
\hline
friends : \mathbb{P}\, Customer \\
status : Status \\
sold : Seat \leftrightarrow\!\!\!\!\!\!\rightarrow Customer \\
\hline
status = \mathsf{premiere} \Rightarrow \operatorname{ran} sold \subseteq friends
\end{array}
$$

If the current performance is a premiere, then seats may be sold only to friends of the theatre.

To describe the enhanced box office, we have only to conjoin this schema with the original:

$$FriendlyBoxOffice \mathrel{\widehat{=}} BoxOffice \land Friends$$

The same effect could have been achieved by defining:

```
┌─ FriendlyBoxOffice ──────────────────────
│ status : Status
│ friends : ℙ Customer
│ sold : Seat ⇸ Customer
│ seating : ℙ Seat
├──────────
│ dom sold ⊆ seating
│ status = premiere ⇒ ran sold ⊆ friends
└──────────────────────────────────────────
```

In such a small example, there is little to be gained from the separate description of different features. In larger, more realistic examples, such a *separation of concerns* is essential if we are not to be overwhelmed by complexity. □

We may also conjoin two schemas by including one in the declaration part of the other. This has the same effect as schema conjunction, in that the declarations are merged and the predicates conjoined, but suggests a more hierarchical structure. This is particularly useful if we wish to describe an enhanced state.

Example 12.2 The friendly box office could have been introduced by including *BoxOffice* in the declaration part of a schema:

```
┌─ FriendlyBoxOffice ──────────────────────
│ BoxOffice
│ status : Status
│ friends : ℙ Customer
├──────────
│ status = premiere ⇒ ran sold ⊆ friends
└──────────────────────────────────────────
```

or by including both *BoxOffice* and *Friends*:

```
┌─ FriendlyBoxOffice ──────────────────────
│ BoxOffice
│ Friends
└──────────────────────────────────────────
```

□

Example 12.3 An alternative enhancement to the box office provides a variable *available*, which represents the number of seats available for the current performance. If we take *free* to be the function defined in Example 11.15, then this enhancement is described by

$$\begin{array}{|l}
\hline \textit{EnhancedBoxOffice} \\
\textit{BoxOffice} \\
\textit{available} : \mathbb{N} \\
\hline
\textit{available} = \textit{free}\ \theta \textit{BoxOffice} \\
\hline
\end{array}$$

To obtain the number of seats available, we have only to apply *free* to the binding θ*BoxOffice*, representing the values of *seating* and *sold*. □

12.2 Decoration

Suppose that the state of a system is modelled by a schema *State* with two components a and b, and that these are introduced under a constraint P.

$$\begin{array}{|l}
\hline \textit{State} \\
a : A \\
b : B \\
\hline
P \\
\hline
\end{array}$$

Each object of schema type *State* represents a valid state: a binding of a and b in which predicate P is satisfied. We say that P forms part of the state invariant for the system: a constraint that must always be satisfied.

Example 12.4 The set of all valid states of our box office system is described by the schema type *BoxOffice*, where

$$\begin{array}{|l}
\hline \textit{BoxOffice} \\
\textit{seating} : \mathbb{P}\ \textit{Seat} \\
\textit{sold} : \textit{Seat} \pfun \textit{Customer} \\
\hline
\mathrm{dom}\ \textit{sold} \subseteq \textit{seating} \\
\hline
\end{array}$$

Each state is a binding of variables *seating* and *sold*; the state invariant insists that only allocated seats are sold, and that the relationship between seats and customers remains functional. □

To describe an operation upon the state, we use two copies of *State*: one representing the state before the operation; the other representing the state afterwards. To distinguish between the two, we decorate the components of the second schema, adding a single prime to each name: that is,

$$\begin{array}{|l}
\textit{State}' \\
\hline
a' : A \\
b' : B \\
\hline
P[a' / a, b' / b] \\
\hline
\end{array}$$

The predicate part of the schema is modified to reflect the new names of the state variables.

Example 12.5 To describe the state of the box office system after some operation, we could use the following schema:

$$\begin{array}{|l}
\textit{BoxOffice}' \\
\hline
\textit{seating}' : \mathbb{P}\, \textit{Seat} \\
\textit{sold}' : \textit{Seat} \twoheadrightarrow \textit{Customer} \\
\hline
\mathrm{dom}\, \textit{sold}' \subseteq \textit{seating}' \\
\hline
\end{array}$$

This introduces two variables, *seating′* and *sold′*, corresponding to the seat seating and the sales record after the operation has been performed. □

We may describe an operation by including both *State* and *State′* in the declaration part of a schema. For example,

$$\begin{array}{|l}
\textit{Operation} \\
\hline
\textit{State} \\
\textit{State}' \\
\hline
\ldots \\
\hline
\end{array}$$

This is a schema with four components, two of them primed. The inclusion of *State* and *State′* indicates that a and b constitute a valid state of the system, and that the same is true of a' and b'.

The predicate part of such a schema characterises the operation: it describes its effect upon the values of the state variables; it states what must be true of the state if the effect of the operation is to be fully defined. In the above example, we would expect the predicate part of *Operation* to include free occurrences of a, a', b and b'.

Example 12.6 One operation upon the state of the box office system is the purchasing of a single seat for the current performance. Suppose that this seat is denoted by $s?$, and that the customer buying it is $c?$. If the operation is to be a success, then $s?$ must be available for sale beforehand:

$$s? \in seating \setminus \mathrm{dom}\, sold$$

Afterwards, the *sold* relation should be modified to indicate that $s?$ has been sold to customer $c?$:

$$sold' = sold \cup \{s? \mapsto c?\}$$

Finally, the collection of seats allocated for this performance should be unchanged by the operation.

We may encapsulate all of this information in a single schema $Purchase_0$, representing the successful purchasing of seat $s?$ by customer $c?$:

```
┌─ Purchase₀ ──────────────────────────
│ BoxOffice
│ BoxOffice'
│ ...
├──────────
│ s? ∈ seating \ dom sold
│ sold' = sold ∪ {s? ↦ c?}
│ seating' = seating
└──────────────────────────────────────
```

□

Some operations, such as the one described in the example above, involve either input to the system or output from it. To model such operations, we include additional components in the declaration part of the operation schema. The predicate part can then relate the values of these components to the states before and after the operation. For example, the schema

```
┌─ Operation ──────────────────────────
│ State
│ State'
│ i? : I
│ o! : O
├──────────
│ ...
└──────────────────────────────────────
```

includes an input component of type I and an output component of type O.

There is a simple convention concerning input and output. If a component represents an input, then its name should end with a query (?); if it represents output, then its name should end with a shriek (!). It should be emphasised that these are not decorations, but part of the component name.

Example 12.7 The operation of purchasing a seat requires two inputs: the name of the seat, and the name of the customer. We model these as two input components $s?$ and $c?$, of types *Seat* and *Customer*, respectively. The operation of successfully purchasing a seat is described by

$$
\begin{array}{|l}
\text{\_\_ } \mathit{Purchase}_0 \text{ \_\_\_\_\_\_\_\_\_\_\_\_} \\
\mathit{BoxOffice} \\
\mathit{BoxOffice}' \\
s? : \mathit{Seat} \\
c? : \mathit{Customer} \\
\hline
s? \in \mathit{seating} \setminus \operatorname{dom} \mathit{sold} \\
\mathit{sold}' = \mathit{sold} \cup \{s? \mapsto c?\} \\
\mathit{seating}' = \mathit{seating} \\
\hline
\end{array}
$$

The effect of this operation is defined only when input $s?$, the seat requested, is available for sale. □

Example 12.8 We may add an output to our description of the purchasing operation, corresponding to the response offered to the customer. This response will be drawn from a free type of responses:

$$\mathit{Response} ::= \mathsf{okay} \mid \mathsf{sorry}$$

and may be declared in a separate schema:

$$
\begin{array}{|l}
\text{\_\_ } \mathit{Success} \text{ \_\_\_\_\_\_\_\_\_\_\_\_} \\
r! : \mathit{Response} \\
\hline
r! = \mathsf{okay} \\
\hline
\end{array}
$$

The effect of a successful purchase may now be modelled as

$$\mathit{Purchase}_0 \wedge \mathit{Success}$$

This produces a schema with two inputs and a single output $r!$, whose value will be okay. □

There is a convention for including two copies of the same schema, one of them decorated with a prime. If *Schema* describes the state of a system, then $\Delta Schema$ is a schema including both *Schema* and *Schema'*: that is,

```
┌─ ΔSchema ─────────────────────
│ Schema
│ Schema'
└───────────────────────────────
```

This schema could be included whenever we wish to describe an operation that may change the state.

Example 12.9 The operation schema $Purchase_0$ could include $\Delta BoxOffice$ in place of *BoxOffice* and *BoxOffice'*:

```
┌─ Purchase₀ ───────────────────
│ ΔBoxOffice
│ ...
├──────────
│ ...
└───────────────────────────────
```

□

Schema decorations are ignored in determining the type of bindings introduced. For example, the bindings

$$\langle\!| a \leadsto x, b \leadsto y |\!\rangle$$

and

$$\langle\!| a' \leadsto v, b' \leadsto w |\!\rangle$$

are of the same schema type. This is essential if a decorated schema is to represent a state of the same system as the undecorated version.

It is therefore possible to equate bindings before and after an operation. Again, there is a convention: we write $\Xi Schema$ to denote the schema that includes *Schema* and *Schema'* and equates their bindings:

```
┌─ ΞSchema ─────────────────────
│ ΔSchema
├──────────
│ θSchema = θSchema'
└───────────────────────────────
```

This schema could be included whenever we wish to describe an operation that does not change the state of the system.

Example 12.10 We may interrogate the box office system to determine the number of seats that are still available for the current performance. This operation may be described by

```
┌─ QueryAvailability ──────────────────
│ ΞBoxOffice
│ available! : ℕ
├──────────
│ available! = free θBoxOffice
└──────────────────────────────────────
```

The output component *available!* is obtained by applying the function *free* to the box office state: see Example 11.15. The inclusion of $\Xi BoxOffice$ confirms that this operation leaves the state unchanged: there are no side effects. □

When we use an abstract data type to model the behaviour of a system, we should include a description of the initial state. This may be seen as the result of an operation, some form of initialisation, that does not refer to the state beforehand. The initial state of a system may be described by a decorated copy of the state schema, representing the state after initialisation.

```
┌─ StateInit ──────────────────────────
│ State′
├──────────
│ ...
└──────────────────────────────────────
```

The predicate part of this schema describes the initial constraints upon the components of the state.

Example 12.11 If we assume that the initial allocation of seats for the current performance has been declared as a global variable

```
│ initial_allocation : ℙ Seat
```

then the initial state of the box office system is described by the following decorated schema:

```
┌─ BoxOfficeInit ──────────────────────
│ BoxOffice′
├──────────
│ seating′ = initial_allocation
│ sold′ = ∅
└──────────────────────────────────────
```

In the initial state, no seats have been sold. □

12.3 Disjunction

Schema disjunction allows us to describe alternatives in the behaviour of a system. We may describe a variety of ways in which a system may evolve, and then combine them to produce a complete description. If S and T are the schemas introduced by

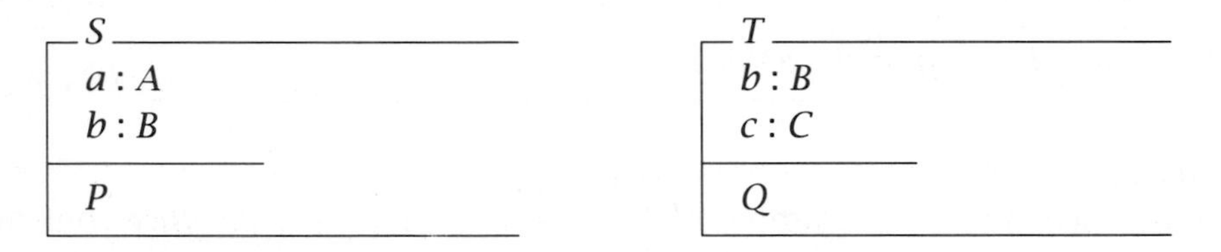

then $S \vee T$ is the schema

$a : A$
$b : B$
$c : C$

$P \vee Q$

As with conjunction, the declaration parts are merged. This time, however, the predicate parts are disjoined.

If the same variable is declared in both schemas, as with b above, then the types must match. If the range of a variable in one schema is a subset of its range in another, then we must move the subrange constraint into the predicate part before combining the schemas. Alternatively, we may choose to normalise both schemas before combination.

Example 12.12 If a customer attempts to purchase a seat from the box office, but the seat requested is not available, then the schema $Purchase_0$ does not apply. To specify what happens in this case, we introduce another schema:

NotAvailable

$\Xi BoxOffice$
$s? : Seat$

$s? \notin seating \setminus \mathrm{dom}\, sold$

This schema applies whenever the seat requested has not been allocated, or has already been sold. The inclusion of $\Xi BoxOffice$ confirms that the state of the system is unchanged.

To indicate that the seat could not be sold, we specify a different response for the customer:

$$\begin{array}{|l}\hline \textit{Failure} \\ r! : \textit{Response} \\ \hline r! = \mathsf{sorry} \\ \hline \end{array}$$

We may then combine the various schemas to produce a complete description of the purchasing operation:

$$\textit{Purchase} \mathrel{\widehat{=}} (\textit{Purchase}_0 \land \textit{Success}) \lor (\textit{NotAvailable} \land \textit{Failure})$$

If the seat requested is available, then the effect of the operation is described by the first disjunct; if it is not, then the second disjunct applies. □

If an operation schema places no constraints upon the state of the system beforehand, then we say that the operation it describes is *total*. Otherwise, the operation is said to be *partial*. This corresponds exactly to the idea of partial and total functions introduced in Chapter 8.

Example 12.13 Having purchased a seat, a customer may decide not to attend the performance. In this case, they may return the seat to the box office. The operation of successfully returning a seat is described by

$$\begin{array}{|l}\hline \textit{Return}_0 \\ \Delta \textit{BoxOffice} \\ s? : \textit{Seat} \\ c? : \textit{Customer} \\ \hline s? \mapsto c? \in \textit{sold} \\ \textit{sold}' = \textit{sold} \setminus \{s? \mapsto c?\} \\ \textit{seating}' = \textit{seating} \\ \hline \end{array}$$

This is a partial operation upon the state of the box office. Its effect is defined only if the seat has been sold to the customer in question: that is, if

$$s? \mapsto c? \in \textit{sold}$$

If this seat has not been sold, or if it has been sold to another customer, then the schema tells us nothing about the consequences of this customer attempting to return it to the box office. The state after this attempt could be any valid state of the system.

To model the effect of an unsuccessful attempt, we introduce another partial operation schema. This will apply only if the seat has not been sold to the customer in question:

NotPossible
$\Xi BoxOffice$
$s? : Seat$
$c? : Customer$

$s? \mapsto c? \notin sold$

The inclusion of $\Xi BoxOffice$ tells us that the state of the box office system is not changed by this operation.

We may combine these partial operations using schema disjunction. The result is a total operation upon the box office state:

$$Return \mathrel{\widehat{=}} (Return_0 \land Success) \lor (NotPossible \land Failure)$$

This describes the effect of attempting to return a seat whatever the current state of the box office. □

12.4 Negation

The negation of a schema introduces the same set of components under a negated constraint. If S is a normalised schema, then its negation $\neg S$ may be obtained by negating the predicate part. For example, if A and B are types and S is introduced by

S
$a : A$
$b : B$

P

then $\neg S$ is the schema

$a : A$
$b : B$

$\neg P$

However, this procedure applies only to normalised schemas.

If the declaration part of a schema contains constraints upon the components, then these constraints must also be negated. Consider the case of *SchemaFour*, a schema introduced in the previous chapter:

SchemaFour

$a : \mathbb{N}$
$c : \mathbb{P}\,\mathbb{N}$

$a \in c \land c \neq \varnothing$

This schema has not been normalised: the declaration part includes the constraint that $a \in \mathbb{N}$ and $c \in \mathbb{P}\,\mathbb{N}$. The negation $\neg SchemaFour$ has a different declaration part:

$a : \mathbb{Z}$
$c : \mathbb{P}\,\mathbb{Z}$

$\neg(a \in \mathbb{N} \land c \in \mathbb{P}\,\mathbb{N} \land a \in c \land c \neq \varnothing)$

This schema is more easily recognised as the negation of the normalised form:

SchemaFourNormalised

$a : \mathbb{Z}$
$c : \mathbb{P}\,\mathbb{Z}$

$a \in \mathbb{N} \land c \in \mathbb{P}\,\mathbb{N} \land a \in c \land c \neq \varnothing$

Where there is constraint information in the declaration part, it is advisable to normalise a schema before calculating its negation.

Example 12.14 The schema *Date* was used to characterise the set of all valid dates in the Gregorian calendar. Its negation, $\neg Date$, describes the set of all bindings of *day* and *month* that do not correspond to a valid date:

$month : Month$
$day : \mathbb{Z}$

$day \notin 1 \mathinner{..} 31 \lor$
$(month \in \{\mathsf{sep}, \mathsf{apr}, \mathsf{jun}, \mathsf{nov}\} \land day > 30) \lor$
$(month = \mathsf{feb} \land day > 29)$

□

Example 12.15 If the box office is no longer in the initial state, then its state may be characterised by the conjunction

$$BoxOffice' \land (\neg BoxOfficeInit)$$

Notice that it is not enough to simply negate the initialisation schema. The schema $\neg BoxOfficeInit$ describes the set of all bindings of *seating* and *sold* that do not match the initial state: this includes bindings that are not valid states of the system. □

12.5 Quantification and hiding

We may quantify over some of the components of a schema while retaining the declarations of the others. If Q is a quantifier and *dec* is a declaration, then the quantified schema

$$Q\ dec \bullet Schema$$

may be obtained from *Schema* by removing those components that are also declared in *dec* and quantifying them with Q in the predicate part. For this schema to be properly defined, every variable declared in *dec* must appear in *Schema* as a component of the same type.

For example, if S is the schema with components a and b of types A and B, introduced under the constraint P,

```
┌─ S ──────────────────
│ a : A
│ b : B
├──────────
│ P
└──────────────────────
```

then $\forall b : B \bullet S$ is the schema

```
┌──────────────────────
│ a : A
├──────────
│ ∀ b : B • P
└──────────────────────
```

and $\exists b : B \bullet S$ is the schema

```
┌──────────────────────
│ a : A
├──────────
│ ∃ b : B • P
└──────────────────────
```

Example 12.16 The friendly box office records the status of the current performance: if the show is a premiere, then seats are sold only to customers who are registered friends of the theatre:

$$
\begin{array}{|l}
\textit{FriendlyBoxOffice} \\
\hline
status : Status \\
friends : \mathbb{P}\, Customer \\
sold : Seat \nrightarrow Customer \\
seating : \mathbb{P}\, Seat \\
\hline
\mathrm{dom}\, sold \subseteq seating \\
status = \mathsf{premiere} \Rightarrow \mathrm{ran}\, sold \subseteq friends \\
\hline
\end{array}
$$

If we precede this schema with a universal quantification of the variable *status*, then we obtain a schema that no longer records the status of the performance:

$$\forall\, status : Status \bullet FriendlyBoxOffice$$

The predicate part of this schema insists that

$$
\begin{array}{l}
\forall\, status : Status \bullet \\
\quad \mathrm{dom}\, sold \subseteq seating \\
\quad status = \mathsf{premiere} \Rightarrow \mathrm{ran}\, sold \subseteq friends
\end{array}
$$

If this quantified expression is to be an invariant of the system, then tickets may be sold only to friends of the theatre, for else the subexpression $status = \mathsf{premiere} \Rightarrow \mathrm{ran}\, sold \subseteq friends$ would be false for one of the values of *status*.

The quantification over *status* has produced a cautious version of the box office system:

$$
\begin{array}{|l}
\textit{CautiousBoxOffice} \\
\hline
friends : \mathbb{P}\, Customer \\
sold : Seat \nrightarrow Customer \\
seating : \mathbb{P}\, Seat \\
\hline
\mathrm{dom}\, sold \subseteq seating \\
\mathrm{ran}\, sold \subseteq friends \\
\hline
\end{array}
$$

It is as if the universal quantification over *status* has forced the system to take a pessimistic view as to the status of the performance: it caters for both possibilities—standard and premiere—by selling only to friends. □

Example 12.17 The operation of successfully returning a ticket to the box office required the name of a customer. We may dispense with this requirement by existentially quantifying over the input component $c?$. The result is an anonymous version of the return operation:

$$\exists\, c? : Customer \bullet Return_0$$

The predicate part of the new schema states that

$$\begin{array}{l} \exists\, c? : Customer \bullet \\ \quad s? \mapsto c? \in sold \land \\ \quad sold' = sold \setminus \{s? \mapsto c?\} \land \\ \quad seating' = seating \end{array}$$

With care, we may rewrite this predicate to make the results of the operation more obvious:

$$\begin{array}{|l} \Delta BoxOffice \\ s? : Seat \\ r! : Response \\ \hline \exists\, c? : Customer \bullet \\ \quad s? \mapsto c? \in sold \land \\ \quad sold' = sold \setminus \{s? \mapsto c?\} \land \\ \quad seating' = seating \end{array}$$

It is as if the existential quantification has forced the system to take an optimistic view as to the identity of the customer. By the one-point rule and the properties of functions, this schema is equivalent to

$$\begin{array}{|l} AnonymousReturn_0 \\ \hline \Delta BoxOffice \\ s? : Seat \\ r! : Response \\ \hline s? \in \mathrm{dom}\, sold \\ sold' = \{s?\} \lhd sold \\ seating' = seating \end{array}$$

For this operation to be properly defined, it is necessary only that the input $s?$ is an element of the domain of $sold$. □

Schema existential quantification is also called *hiding*: the quantified components are no longer visible in the declaration, yet the predicate tells us that they exist. This provides a powerful mechanism for abstraction in the schema language: we may hide any components that are not required at the current level of specification.

This mechanism has its own operator: if *list* is a list of component names, then the schema $Schema \setminus list$ may obtained by existentially quantifying each component in *list* within *Schema*. For example, if S is the schema introduced by

```
┌─ S ──────────────────────
│ a : A
│ b : B
├──────────
│ P
└──────────────────────────
```

then $S \setminus (a)$ is the schema

```
┌──────────────────────────
│ b : B
├──────────
│ ∃ a : A • P
└──────────────────────────
```

Thus hiding is no more than a quick way of writing (and pronouncing) existential quantification over schema components.

Example 12.18 The enhanced box office system included a component that recorded the number of seats available for the current performance. We may abstract away this information by hiding *available* within the schema:

$$EnhancedBoxOffice \setminus (available)$$

The result is a schema with the same components as *BoxOffice*:

```
┌──────────────────────────
│ BoxOffice
├──────────
│ ∃ available : ℕ • available = free θBoxOffice
└──────────────────────────
```

Since *free* is a total function, the number of seats available is always uniquely determined by the values of *seating* and *sold*. This schema is equivalent to the original box office description. □

12.6 Composition

The use of schemas to describe operations begs an interesting question: how does one describe the effect of one operation followed by another? Alternatively, we might ask: if an operation schema characterises a relation between states of the system, then how does one represent the composition of two such relations? The answer in both cases is *schema composition*.

If *OpOne* and *OpTwo* are operation schemas, each including primed and unprimed copies of a state schema *State*, then the schema composition

$$OpOne \mathbin{⨾} OpTwo$$

describes the change in state that results when operation *OpOne* is followed by operation *OpTwo*.

In *OpOne*, the components of *State'* represent the state of the system immediately after the operation. In the composition above, this is also the state of the system immediately before *OpTwo*. We introduce a new schema to represent this intermediate state: *State''*.

The schema composition relates the state immediately before *OpOne* to the state immediately after *OpTwo*, and *State''* is hidden:

$$\begin{aligned} OpOne \mathbin{⨾} OpTwo \;=\; & \exists\, State'' \bullet \\ & \quad \exists\, State' \bullet [OpOne;\ State'' \mid \theta State' = \theta State''] \\ & \quad \land \\ & \quad \exists\, State \bullet [OpTwo;\ State'' \mid \theta State = \theta State''] \end{aligned}$$

The relationship between $\theta State$ and $\theta State''$ is described by *OpOne*; that between $\theta State''$ and $\theta State'$ is described by *OpTwo*.

For the composition to be defined, both schemas must refer to the same state. For any primed component in *OpOne*, there must be an unprimed component of the same name in *OpTwo*. For example, suppose that *OpOne* and *OpTwo* are introduced by

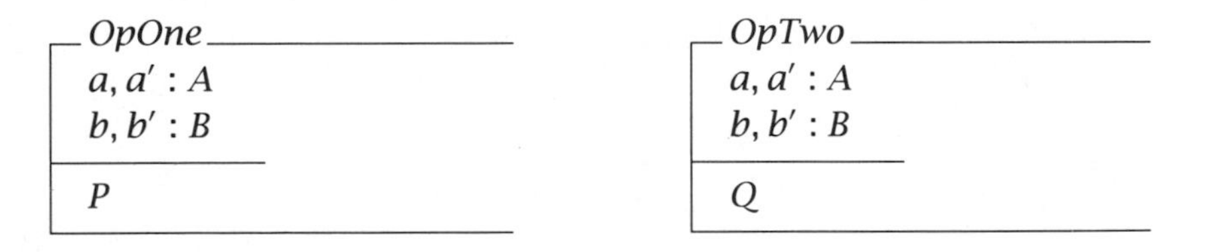

The state components in each operation are the same, so their schema composition will be well defined.

The composition of *OpOne* and *OpTwo* may be calculated using schema existential quantification, as above, or by renaming the state components corresponding to the intermediate state:

$$OpOne \fatsemi OpTwo \ = \\ (OpOne[a''/a', b''/b'] \land OpTwo[a''/a, b''/b]) \setminus (a'', b'')$$

The components representing the intermediate state, a'' and b'' are then hidden. If we were to expand this schema, we would see that the composition is equivalent to:

$$\begin{array}{|l}
a, a' : A \\
b, b' : B \\
\hline
\exists\, a'', b'' \bullet P[a''/a', b''/b'] \land Q[a''/a, b''/b]
\end{array}$$

Example 12.19 If a customer successfully purchases a seat, and then returns it immediately to the box office, then the state of the system should be unaffected. The combined operation is described by

$$Purchase_0 \fatsemi Return$$

where $Purchase_0$ and *Return* are as defined above. The result that we might hope to establish can be expressed as

$$\frac{Purchase_0 \fatsemi Return}{\Xi BoxOffice}$$

This is an inference in which the composition is used as a declaration: introducing a collection of components under the stated constraint. The schema $\Xi BoxOffice$ is used only as a predicate. □

Chapter 13

Promotion

In this chapter we describe an important technique for structuring formal descriptions. It is called *promotion*, and it allows us to compose and factor specifications. It has also been called *framing*, because it is evocative of placing a frame around part of a specification: only what is inside the frame may change; what is outside must remain unaffected.

We begin the chapter with three different examples of the technique: a game, a mail system, and a data array. We then give a formal definition of promotion, and distinguish between two varieties: free and constrained. The chapter ends with two further examples of promotion: a free promotion of a booking system, and a constrained promotion within a priority stack.

13.1 Factoring operations

Large software systems often contain multiple, indexed instances of the same component. A database may contain a number of records, a computer system may have several users, a data network may consist of a number of switching nodes. If this is the case, then there will exist a uniform relationship between the system state and the state of each indexed component.

This relationship allows us to link certain changes in system state to changes in the state of indexed components. We may *factor* a global operation into a local operation and a mixed operation, the latter expressing the relationship between local and global state. This is a useful separation of concerns; the two factors may be specified and analysed in isolation. We have used the structuring information in the design of the system to simplify our formal description.

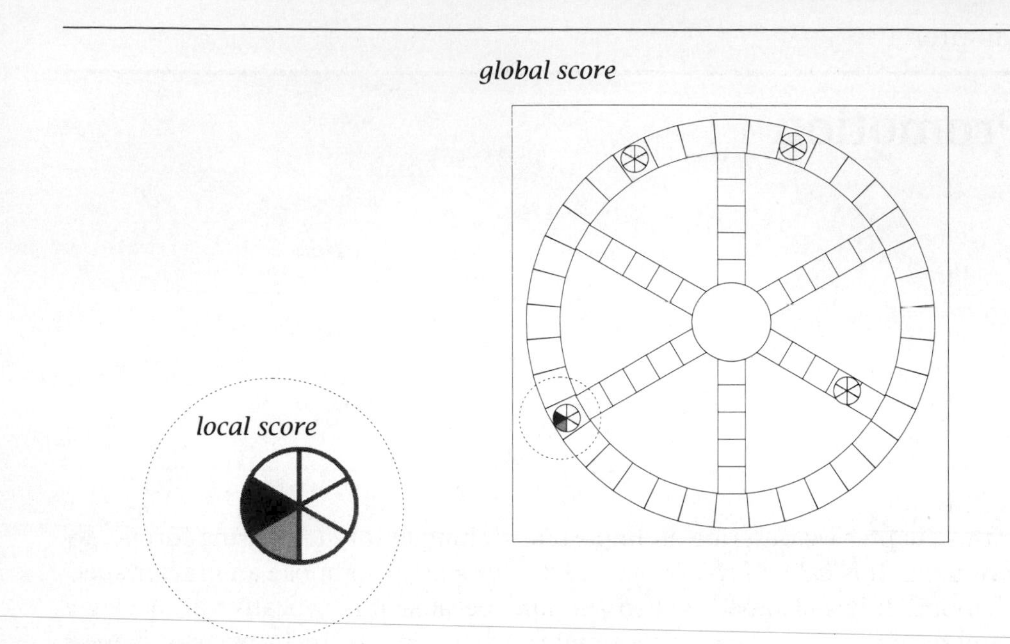

Figure 13.1: A game in progress

Example 13.1 In the game of Trivial Pursuit™, the players collect tokens of various colours—red, green, yellow, blue, brown, and pink—the aim being to collect one token of each colour. There are no teams: each player maintains an individual score. A player's score may be modelled using a schema type

$$\begin{array}{|l}
\textit{LocalScore} \\ \hline
s : \mathbb{P}\, \textit{Colour} \\ \hline
\end{array}$$

where *Colour* is the set of colours mentioned above.

The overall state of play at any point during the game is given by a binding of the following schema type:

$$\begin{array}{|l}
\textit{GlobalScore} \\ \hline
\textit{score} : \textit{Players} \rightarrow\!\!\!\!\!\!+\; \textit{LocalScore} \\ \hline
\end{array}$$

Here, a partial function called *score* associates each player with an object of type *LocalScore*. Figure 13.1 shows a situation in which one of the players has collected exactly two tokens.

Players are awarded tokens if and when they provide correct answers to questions on various subjects; the colour awarded depends upon the choice of subject. If a player $p?$ earns a token of colour $c?$, then the effect upon the state of play is described by the following operation schema:

AnswerGlobal

$\Delta GlobalScore$
$p? : Player$
$c? : Colour$

$p? \in \operatorname{dom} score$
$\{p?\} \ntriangleleft score' = \{p?\} \ntriangleleft score$
$(score'\ p?).s = (score\ p?).s \cup \{c?\}$

Provided that $p?$ is indeed part of the current game, the function *score* is updated to reflect the new score associated with $p?$.

An alternative approach would involve factoring this operation into a local operation—

AnswerLocal

$\Delta LocalScore$
$c? : Colour$

$s' = s \cup \{c?\}$

—and a schema expressing the relationship between global and local states—

Promote

$\Delta GlobalScore$
$\Delta LocalScore$
$p? : Player$

$p? \in \operatorname{dom} score$
$\theta LocalScore = score\ p?$
$score' = score \oplus \{p? \mapsto \theta LocalScore'\}$

—in which a change in *GlobalScore* and a change in *LocalScore* are linked by the identity of the player involved.

If we conjoin the *AnswerLocal* and *Promote* schemas, then we obtain a schema that describes an operation upon the global state:

$\exists \Delta LocalScore \bullet AnswerLocal \wedge Promote$

The local state is uniquely determined by the function *score*, so there is no need to record this information at the global level. The existential quantification hides it, yielding a predicate part

$$\begin{array}{l} \exists \Delta LocalScore \bullet \\ \quad p? \in \mathrm{dom}\, score \\ \quad \theta LocalScore = score\ p? \\ \quad score' = score \oplus \{p? \mapsto \theta LocalScore'\} \\ \quad s' = s \cup \{c?\} \end{array}$$

We may rewrite this as

$$\begin{array}{l} \exists s, s' : \mathbb{P}\, Colour \bullet \\ \quad p? \in \mathrm{dom}\, score \\ \quad \langle\!| s \mapsto s |\!\rangle = score\ p? \\ \quad score' = score \oplus \{p? \mapsto \langle\!| s \mapsto s' |\!\rangle\} \\ \quad s' = s \cup \{c?\} \end{array}$$

and hence as

$$\begin{array}{l} \exists s, s' : \mathbb{P}\, Colour \bullet \\ \quad p? \in \mathrm{dom}\, score \\ \quad (score\ p?).s = s \\ \quad score' = score \oplus \{p? \mapsto \langle\!| s \mapsto s \cup \{c?\} |\!\rangle\} \end{array}$$

to obtain a schema equivalent to *AnswerGlobal*:

$$\begin{array}{|l} \Delta GlobalScore \\ p? : Player \\ c? : Colour \\ \hline p? \in \mathrm{dom}\, score \\ \{p?\} \lhd score' = \{p?\} \lhd score \\ (score'\ p?).s = (score\ p?).s \cup \{c?\} \end{array}$$

□

In the above example, there is little to choose between the two approaches, although the factored description makes it easier to see the effect of the operation upon the local state. However, as we define more operations, and add more information to the local state, the advantages of the factored approach become obvious.

The relationship between the global state and the collection of local states need not be functional. There may be several components with the same index, in which case the association between indices and components can be modelled as a relation.

Example 13.2 An electronic mail system consists of several instances of the component *MailBox*. Each instance may be associated with one or more addresses from the set *Address*. A user of the system may have more than one address, and an address may be associated with more than one user.

```
MailSystem
  address : Person ↔ Address
  mailbox : Address ⇸ MailBox
```

The association between users and addresses is given by a relation *address*, and the association between addresses and mailboxes is given by the partial function *mailbox*.

Figure 13.2 shows a mail system with three users: Carolyn, Denise, and Edward. Each user has a personal mailbox, with an appropriate address. Carolyn and Denise share ownership of the system administrator's mailbox with address *admin*. Edward has two mail addresses, *edward* and *edwardc*, but they both refer to the same mailbox, */usr/spool/mail/edward*.

A mailbox is modelled by a schema type with three components. The first is a sequence of type *Message*, representing the mail messages stored in the box. The others are time stamps:

```
MailBox
  mail : seq Message
  new_mail, last_read : TimeStamp
```

Of these, *new_mail* records the time of arrival of the latest mail message, and *last_read* records the last time that mail in the box was read.

A typical object of type *MailBox* might be

$$\langle\!|\, mail \leadsto \langle m_1, m_2, m_3 \rangle,\ new\_mail \leadsto \text{Tue 14 Feb, 11.00 a.m.}\ last\_read \leadsto \text{Sun 12 Feb, 12.30 p.m.} \,|\!\rangle$$

This tells us that the box holds three messages—m_1, m_2, and m_3—the last of

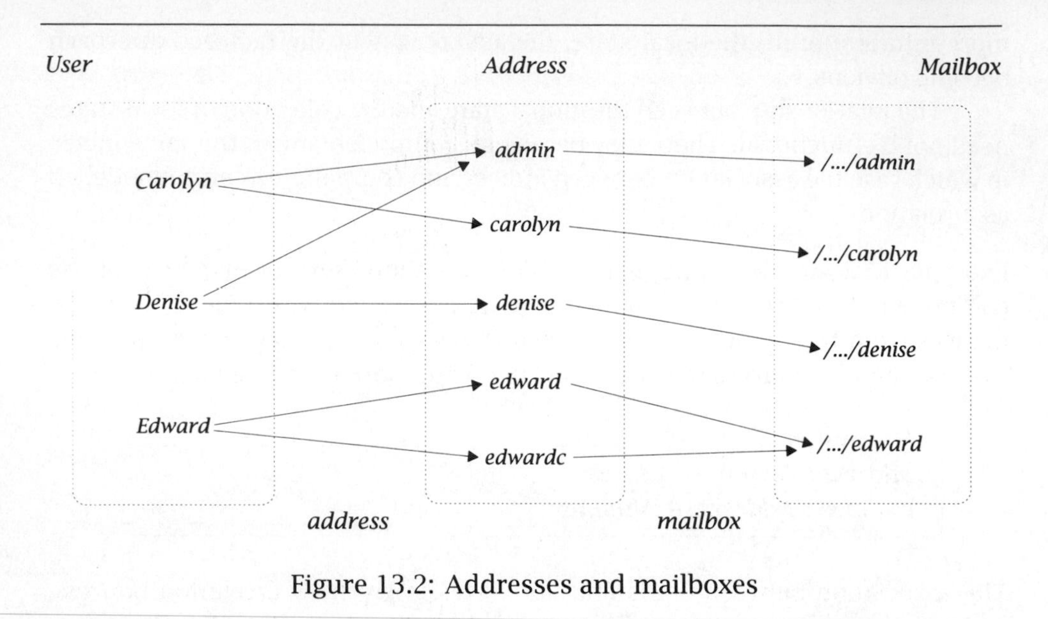

Figure 13.2: Addresses and mailboxes

which arrived at 11.00 a.m. on Tuesday 14th February. It states also that mail in this box was last read at 12.30 p.m. on Sunday 12th February.

If a message $m?$ arrives at time $t?$ for user $u?$, then it will be added to one of the mailboxes belonging to $u?$. These components are taken as inputs to the following operation schema, which describes the effect upon the global state:

ReceiveSystem

$$\Delta MailSystem$$
$$u? : User$$
$$m? : Message$$
$$t? : TimeStamp$$
$$a! : Address$$

$$u? \mapsto a! \in address$$
$$address' = address$$
$$a! \in \operatorname{dom} mailbox$$
$$\{a!\} \ndres mailbox' = \{a!\} \ndres mailbox$$
$$(mailbox'\ a!).mail = (mailbox\ a!).mail \frown \langle m? \rangle$$
$$(mailbox'\ a!).new\_mail = t?$$
$$(mailbox'\ a!).last\_read = (mailbox\ a!).last\_read$$

The address used, $a!$, is provided as an output to the operation. The value of *address* and the contents of the other mailboxes—given by $\{a!\} \ntriangleleft mailbox$—are left unchanged.

Again, we may choose an alternative approach, factoring global operations such as *ReceiveSystem* into two parts. The first part, which is the same for each operation, expresses the link between local and global changes of state:

Promote

$\Delta MailSystem$
$\Delta MailBox$
$u? : User$
$a! : Address$

$u? \mapsto a! \in address$
$address' = address$
$a! \in \mathrm{dom}\ mailbox$
$\theta MailBox = mailbox\ a!$
$mailbox' = mailbox \oplus \{a! \mapsto \theta MailBox'\}$

The link is made by identifying the user *u*? and the address *a*! involved in the operation. The local state is given by *mailbox a*!, where $u? \mapsto a!$ is an element of the *address* relation. This is the only part of the global state that will change; this is the frame in which the operation will take place.

The second part of the factorisation is a schema that describes the effect of adding mail to a single mailbox:

ReceiveBox

$\Delta MailBox$
$m? : Message$
$t? : TimeStamp$

$mail' = mail \frown \langle m? \rangle$
$new\_mail' = t?$
$last\_read' = last\_read$

The incoming message is added to the end of the sequence *mail*, and the *new_mail* is set to *t*?. The other time stamp remains unchanged.

If we conjoin these two schemas, and abstract away the components of the local state, as in

$$\exists \Delta MailBox \bullet ReceiveBox \wedge Promote$$

then we obtain a schema that is logically equivalent to the global operation *ReceiveSystem*. □

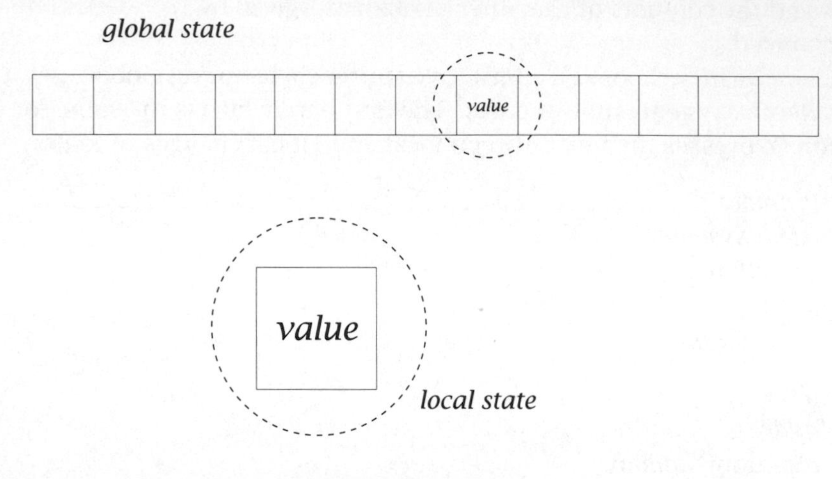

Figure 13.3: A data array

In some systems, the components may be indexed sequentially; in this case, the relationship between the global and local states may be based upon a sequence, rather than a simple function or relation.

Example 13.3 In a model of a data array, each element may be represented by an object of schema type *Data*, where

```
┌─ Data ─────────────────────────
│ value : Value
└────────────────────────────────
```

The state of the array is represented by an object of schema type with a single component, a sequence of *Data* elements:

```
┌─ Array ────────────────────────
│ array : seq Data
└────────────────────────────────
```

The relationship between the state of the array—the global state—and the state of a data element—the local state—is illustrated in Figure 13.3.

If an operation upon the array affects but a single element, then we may express it as the product of two schemas: a local operation schema and a promotion schema. For example, the operation of assigning a new value to a data element could be described as

$$\exists \Delta Data \bullet AssignData \wedge Promote$$

where the local operation schema is introduced by

$$\begin{array}{|l}
\textit{AssignData} \\
\hline
\Delta Data \\
new? : Value \\
\hline
value' = new? \\
\hline
\end{array}$$

and the promotion schema, which makes the link between global and local states using the index of the data, is introduced by

$$\begin{array}{|l}
\textit{Promote} \\
\hline
\Delta Array \\
\Delta Data \\
index? : \mathbb{N} \\
\hline
index? \in \operatorname{dom} array \\
\{index?\} \mathbin{\lhd\!\!\!-} array = \{index?\} \mathbin{\lhd\!\!\!-} array' \\
array\ index? = \theta Data \\
array'\ index? = \theta Data' \\
\hline
\end{array}$$

Once again, the promotion schema describes the *frame*, while the local operation schema describes the *effect*. □

13.2 Promotion

When a global operation is defined in terms of a local operation upon a indexed component, as in each of the examples above, we say that the local operation has been *promoted*. Formally, suppose that we have

- a state schema *Local*, that describes a copy of the local state;
- a state schema *Global*, that describes a copy of the global state;
- a local operation schema *LocalOperation*, that contains decorated and undecorated copies of the state schema *Local*;
- a promotion schema *Promote*, that contains decorated and undecorated copies of both *Local* and *Global*.

Then the promotion schema *promotes* the local operation to

$$\exists \Delta Local \bullet Promote \land LocalOperation$$

which operates on the global state *Global*.

Example 13.4 A global box office system keeps track of bookings for a number of performances. The record of seats allocated and tickets sold for each performance is represented by an object of schema type *BoxOffice*. These objects are indexed by a function on *Performance*, the set of all possible performances:

$$\begin{array}{|l}
\textit{GlobalBoxOffice} \\
\hline
announced : \mathbb{P}\ Performance \\
booking : Performance \nrightarrow BoxOffice \\
\hline
\mathrm{dom}\ booking \subseteq announced \\
\hline
\end{array}$$

As well as booking, the system maintains a set called *announced* for reference purposes. The two components are connected: any performance for which we are booking must have been announced. On the other hand, some performances may have been announced but have not yet started booking.

A booking operation is an operation upon the global box office system that involves the sale or return of a seat. These operations may be factored using promotion. We define a promotion schema:

$$\begin{array}{|l}
\textit{Promote} \\
\hline
\Delta GlobalBoxOffice \\
\Delta BoxOffice \\
p? : Performance \\
\hline
p? \in \mathrm{dom}\ booking \\
\theta BoxOffice = booking\ p? \\
\theta BoxOffice' = booking'\ p? \\
\{p?\} \ndres booking' = \{p?\} \ndres booking \\
announced' = announced \\
\hline
\end{array}$$

This tells us the relationship between the local state of a box office system and the global state in such an operation, given that we are talking about performance $p?$. Such local operations do not affect the list of performances that have been announced.

We may promote the local operation of buying a ticket to a global operation simply by conjoining the schema above with *Purchase*:

$$GlobalPurchase_0 \mathrel{\widehat{=}} \exists \Delta BoxOffice \bullet Purchase \land Promote$$

A single box office has changed—the one identified by input $p?$—and the effect of this change is described by the operation schema *Purchase*.

The promotion schema identifies input $p?$ with a unique performance; if we expand the *GlobalPurchase* schema, then the existential quantification can be eliminated. The result is a schema equivalent to the following:

$$
\begin{array}{l}
\Delta GlobalBoxOffice \\
p? : Performance \\
s? : Seat \\
c? : Customer \\
r! : Response \\
\hline
p? \in \mathrm{dom}\, booking \\
(\,(\, s? \in booking\ p?.seating \setminus \mathrm{dom}\, booking\ p?.sold \land \\
\quad booking\ p?.sold' = booking\ p?.sold \cup \{s? \mapsto c?\} \land \\
\quad r! = okay) \\
\;\lor \\
\;(\, s? \notin booking\ p?.seating \setminus \mathrm{dom}\, booking\ p?.sold \land \\
\quad booking\ p?.sold' = booking\ p?.sold \land \\
\quad r! = sorry\,)\,) \\
\{p?\} \lhd booking' = \{p?\} \lhd booking \\
announced' = announced
\end{array}
$$

Even where the indexing relation is functional, the advantages of structuring our descriptions using promotion should be obvious. □

Of course, the promotion schema is used only in factoring operations which may be described in terms of their effect within an indexed frame. Other operations upon the global state will not be factorised in this way.

Example 13.5 The $GlobalPurchase_0$ operation defined above is not total: it describes only those situations in which the performance in question is already booking. We may wish to add the following alternative:

$$
\begin{array}{l}
\underline{\quad NotYetBooking \quad} \\
\Xi GlobalBoxOffice \\
p? : Performance \\
r! : Response \\
\hline
p? \in announced \setminus \mathrm{dom}\, booking \\
r! = not\_yet\_booking
\end{array}
$$

This describes the situation in which—although the performance in question has been announced—the office is not accepting bookings. □

Example 13.6 We may instruct the box office system to start accepting bookings for a performance $p?$:

$$
\begin{array}{|l}
\multicolumn{1}{l}{\textit{StartBooking}} \\
\Delta GlobalBoxOffice \\
p? : Performance \\
\hline
p? \in announced \\
p? \notin \mathrm{dom}\, booking \\
booking' = booking \cup \{p? \mapsto \theta BoxOfficeInit'\} \\
announced' = announced
\end{array}
$$

A performance cannot start booking unless it has been announced; neither can it start booking more than once. □

13.3 Free and constrained promotion

A promotion is said to be *free* if and only if the promotion schema satisfies

$$(\exists\, Local' \bullet \exists\, Global' \bullet Promote) \Rightarrow (\forall\, Local' \bullet \exists\, Global' \bullet Promote)$$

That is, provided that the update is possible at all, it is possible for all outcomes of the local state.

In a free promotion, neither the promotion schema nor the global state invariant should place constraints upon the component variables of the local state. Accordingly, we would not expect to find explicit mention of the components of *Local* in the expression $\exists\, Global' \bullet Promote$.

Where this is the case, extended forms of the one-point rules may be used to prove that the promotion is free:

$$\frac{\exists\, S \bullet \theta S = t \wedge P}{P[t/\theta S] \wedge t \in S}$$

provided that θS is not free in t, and no component of S appears free in P

$$\frac{P[t/\theta S] \wedge t \in S}{\forall\, S \bullet \theta S = t \wedge P}$$

provided that θS is not free in t, and no component of S appears free in P

That is, if the binding of S that satisfies P is known to be t, then every instance of θS may be replaced with t and the existential quantifier eliminated.

Example 13.7 The data array description of Example 13.3 is an example of a free promotion. The schema $\exists Data' \bullet \exists Array' \bullet Promote$ asserts that the index chosen as input is a valid index for the array—$index? \in \operatorname{dom} array$—and does not constrain the value stored at that index, apart from identifying it as $array\ index?$. The promotion is thus independent of the actual value stored at the index; provided that the index is valid, the promotion will work: it is *free.*

To see this in terms of the implication that was used to characterise a free promotion, we consider the expression

$$\exists Data' \bullet \exists Array' \bullet Promote$$

That is, there is at least one local after state with a global after state satisfying the promotion condition. Expanding the constraint of *Promote*, we obtain

$$\begin{array}{l} \exists Data' \bullet \exists Array' \bullet \\ \quad index? \in \operatorname{dom} array \\ \quad \{index?\} \mathbin{⩤} array = \{index?\} \mathbin{⩤} array' \\ \quad array\ index? = \theta Data \\ \quad array'\ index? = \theta Data' \end{array}$$

The last conjunct of the quantified expression identifies the binding of the local after state: it is equal to $array'\ index?$. Applying the extended form of the existential one-point rule, we obtain

$$\begin{array}{l} \exists Array' \bullet \\ \quad index? \in \operatorname{dom} array \\ \quad \{index?\} \mathbin{⩤} array = \{index?\} \mathbin{⩤} array' \\ \quad array\ index? = \theta Data \\ \quad array'\ index? \in \{Data \bullet \theta Data\} \end{array}$$

This predicate tells us that $array'\ index?$ is an element of the local state space, but does not constrain it in any way. Using the universal one-point rule, we may infer that

$$\begin{array}{l} \forall Data';\ \exists Array' \bullet \\ \quad index? \in \operatorname{dom} array \\ \quad \{index?\} \mathbin{⩤} array = \{index?\} \mathbin{⩤} array' \\ \quad array\ index? = \theta Data \\ \quad array'\ index? = \theta Data' \end{array}$$

Whatever the local state after promotion, some global state must exist. □

A promotion that is not free is said to be *constrained.* In general, constrained promotions are not as elegant: they lack the modularity that freeness implies. However, there are situations in which a constrained promotion is the natural solution.

Example 13.8 We wish to model a *stack* of data objects, each of which contains a piece of data and a priority value:

$$\begin{array}{|l}
\textit{PriData} \\
\hline
\textit{priority} : \mathbb{N} \\
\textit{data} : \textit{Data} \\
\hline
\end{array}$$

The objects in the stack are ordered with respect to their priority values. If object *a* has a lower index than object *b*—if it is nearer the top of the stack—then it must have a higher priority value:

$$\begin{array}{|l}
\textit{Stack} \\
\hline
\textit{stack} : \operatorname{seq} \textit{PriData} \\
\hline
\forall\, i, j : \operatorname{dom} \textit{stack} \mid i < j \bullet (\textit{stack}\ i).\textit{priority} \geq (\textit{stack}\ j).\textit{priority} \\
\hline
\end{array}$$

At any time, only the data object with the highest priority may be operated upon: that is, the object at the head of the stack. Our promotion schema includes this condition:

$$\begin{array}{|l}
\textit{Promote} \\
\hline
\Delta \textit{Stack} \\
\Delta \textit{PriData} \\
\hline
\textit{stack} \neq \langle\rangle \\
\theta \textit{PriData} = \textit{head stack} \\
\textit{stack}' = \langle \theta \textit{PriData}' \rangle \frown \textit{tail stack} \\
\hline
\end{array}$$

The constraint of the promotion schema states that the stack must be non-empty, and that any change is made to the object at the head of the sequence.

In this description, the global state invariant refers to a component of the indexed local state: the priority value. In an *arbitrary* operation, there may be local after states which violate the global state invariant. Consider the case in which the stack contains two objects:

$$\textit{stack} = \langle \langle\!| \textit{priority} \leadsto 3, \textit{data} \leadsto a |\!\rangle, \langle\!| \textit{priority} \leadsto 2, \textit{data} \leadsto b |\!\rangle \rangle$$

In an operation, the state of the first object may change to

$$\langle\!| \mathit{priority} \leadsto 3, \mathit{data} \leadsto c |\!\rangle$$

so at least one after state exists, but after states such as

$$\langle\!| \mathit{priority} \leadsto 1, \mathit{data} \leadsto c |\!\rangle$$

which are disallowed. Hence

$$\exists\, \mathit{PriData}' \bullet \exists\, \mathit{Stack}' \bullet \mathit{Promote} \not\Rightarrow \forall\, \mathit{PriData}' \bullet \exists\, \mathit{Stack}' \bullet \mathit{Promote}$$

and the promotion is constrained. Having observed this, we might decide to strengthen the predicate part of *Promote* in the hope of achieving a free promotion, or we may decide that the existing promotion is an entirely suitable description of our system. □

Chapter 14

Preconditions

The construction of an abstract data type presents two important proof opportunities. The first involves a demonstration that the various requirements upon the data type are consistent and not contradictory. The second involves a demonstration that each operation is never applied outside its domain, in a situation for which the results of the operation are not defined.

If the language of schemas is used to construct the data type, then these opportunities present themselves as simple mathematical tasks. To show that the requirements are consistent, we have only to show that the constraint part of the state schema is satisfiable. This is usually achieved by proving an *initialisation theorem*: we show that an initial state, at least, exists.

To show that the operations are never applied outside their domain, we must investigate their *preconditions*. These may be calculated from the operation schemas using the one-point rule. In this chapter, we explain the procedure for calculating preconditions, and show how it may be simplified by the use of structuring techniques such as promotion.

14.1 The initialisation theorem

In the previous chapters we have seen how the behaviour of a system may be described in terms of an abstract data type. The state of the system was modelled as an object of schema type, the predicate part of which represented a state invariant: a list of requirements that should be true in any valid state.

Clearly, if this includes a contradiction, then the data type description is vacuous: it is impossible to fulfil the requirements, therefore no state exists. To check that this is not the case, and that our specification is of some use, it is enough to establish that at least one state exists.

If the description is to be useful, then there must also exist an initial state. As we saw in Example 12.11, this is usually characterised by a decorated schema, representing the state after initialisation. This is an obvious candidate for our proof of consistency.

Suppose that *State* describes the state of the system, and that *StateInit* characterises the initial state. If we can prove that

$$\exists\, State' \bullet StateInit$$

then we have shown that an initial state exists, and hence also that the requirements upon the state components are consistent. This result is called the *initialisation theorem* for the data type.

Example 14.1 In the case of the box office system, the initial state was characterised by

```
┌─ BoxOfficeInit ─────────────────────
│ BoxOffice'
├──────────
│ seating' = initial_allocation
│ sold' = ∅
└─────────────────────────────────────
```

The initialisation theorem is therefore

$$\exists\, BoxOffice' \bullet BoxOfficeInit$$

□

The initialisation theorem is an easy one to prove, unless there are complicated initial conditions. Most often, the initial state is described uniquely with a number of equations, so the proof strategy is simple: eliminate the quantified variables. One this has been done, the truth of the predicate should follow immediately from the properties of the mathematical objects involved.

Example 14.2 In the case of the box office, we may proceed as follows:

$$\begin{array}{ll} \exists\, BoxOffice' \bullet BoxOfficeInit & \\ \quad \Leftrightarrow \exists\, BoxOffice' \bullet & \text{[definition of } BoxOfficeInit\text{]} \\ \qquad\quad [BoxOffice' \mid & \\ \qquad\qquad seating' = initial\_allocation \land & \\ \qquad\qquad sold' = emptyset] & \end{array}$$

$$\Leftrightarrow \exists\, BoxOffice' \bullet \quad seating' = initial\_allocation \land \quad sold' = \varnothing \qquad \text{[schema quantification]}$$

$$\Leftrightarrow \exists\, seating' : \mathbb{P}\, Seat \bullet \quad \exists\, sold' : Seat \twoheadrightarrow Customer \bullet \quad \operatorname{dom} sold' \subseteq seating' \land \quad seating' = initial\_allocation \land \quad sold' = \varnothing \qquad \text{[definition of } BoxOffice'\text{]}$$

$$\Leftrightarrow initial\_allocation \in \mathbb{P}\, Seat \land \quad \varnothing \in Seat \twoheadrightarrow Customer \qquad \text{[one-point rule, twice]}$$

The proof may be completed by recalling the axiomatic definition of constant *initial_allocation*, which is indeed of type $\mathbb{P}\, Seat$, and expanding the definition of the generic symbol $\twoheadrightarrow$. □

14.2 Precondition investigation

The *precondition* of an operation schema describes the set of states for which the outcome of the operation is properly defined. If *Operation* is an operation schema, then we write

$$\text{pre } Operation$$

to denote the precondition of *Operation*. This is another schema, and is obtained from *Operation* by hiding any components that correspond to the state after the operation, and any outputs that happen to be present.

If the state of the system in question is modelled by a schema *State*, and *outputs* is the list of outputs associated with the operation, then the following equation defines the precondition schema:

$$\text{pre } Operation \;=\; \exists\, State' \bullet Operation \setminus outputs$$

This schema characterises the collection of *before* states and inputs for which some *after* state can be shown to exist.

Example 14.3 The precondition of the operation schema $Purchase_0$, which describes the effect of a successful purchase, is given by

$$\text{pre } Purchase_0$$

$$= \exists\, BoxOffice' \bullet Purchase_0 \qquad \text{[definition of pre]}$$

$$= [BoxOffice;\ s? : Seat;\ c? : Customer \mid \qquad \text{[definition of } BoxOffice'\text{]}$$
$$\exists\, seating' : \mathbb{P}\, Seat;$$
$$sold' : Seat \twoheadrightarrow Customer \mid$$
$$\operatorname{dom} sold' \subseteq seating' \bullet$$
$$s? \in seating \setminus \operatorname{dom} sold$$
$$sold' = sold \cup \{s? \mapsto c?\}$$
$$seating' = seating]$$

$$= [BoxOffice;\ s? : Seat;\ c? : Customer \bullet \qquad \text{[one-point rule, twice]}$$
$$\operatorname{dom}(sold \cup \{s? \mapsto c?\} \subseteq seating \bullet$$
$$s? \in seating \setminus \operatorname{dom} sold]$$

$$= [BoxOffice;\ s? : Seat;\ c? : Customer \bullet \qquad \text{[property of `dom']}$$
$$s? \in seating \setminus \operatorname{dom} sold]$$

The predicate part of $Purchase_0$ identifies an after state that satisfies the state invariant *only if* the chosen seat $s?$ has been allocated and not sold. The effect of $Purchase_0$ is defined only when

$$s? \in seating \setminus \operatorname{dom} sold$$

Notice that the actual precondition includes additional declaration and constraint information. The effect of the operation is properly defined only if the initial values of *seating* and *sold* satisfy the constraint of *BoxOffice* and $s?$ is an element of *Seat*. □

In many cases, the precondition for an operation may be obvious to the writer of the specification. For example, the precondition of $Purchase_0$—see the above example—was sufficiently obvious to be included in the operation schema. In general, we might wish to concentrate upon what the operation is supposed to do, and calculate the precondition later. In the specification process, such cross-checking can be useful.

Example 14.4 A simple control system monitors the entry and exit of vehicles from a car park. It maintains a count of the number of vehicles presently inside; this count should never exceed *capacity*, an integer number greater than zero:

CarPark

$count : \mathbb{N}$

$count \leqslant capacity$

We may define an operation $Exit_0$ that describes the successful departure of a car from the parking area:

$$
\begin{array}{|l}
\multicolumn{1}{l}{\_\_ Exit_0 \_\_\_\_\_\_\_\_} \\
\Delta CarPark \\
\hline
count' = count - 1 \\
\hline
\end{array}
$$

It might seem that this schema would apply to all states of the system, in that we are not placing any explicit constraint upon *count*. However,

$$
\begin{array}{ll}
\text{pre } Exit_0 & \\
\quad = \exists\, CarPark' \bullet Exit_0 & [\text{definition of } Exit_0] \\
\quad = [\, CarPark \mid \exists\, count' : \mathbb{N} \mid & [\text{definition of } CarPark'] \\
\qquad\qquad count' \leqslant capacity \bullet count' = count - 1\,] & \\
\quad = [\, CarPark \mid count - 1 \in \mathbb{N}\,] & [\text{one-point rule}]
\end{array}
$$

Because of the state invariant, this operation should be restricted to those states in which the *count* variable is strictly greater than 0. The effect upon other states is undefined. By calculating the precondition, we have identified a possible source of error.

To see why $Exit_0$ alone might be an unsatisfactory description of the exit operation, suppose that there is a way for cars to enter the car park unobserved. In this case, the function that implements the exit operation may be called while the value of *count* is 0. The subsequent value of *count*, according to $Exit_0$, conflicts with our choice of data representation: anything could happen.

Now that the problem has been detected, we may choose to totalise the operation using a second schema to describe the effect of a car leaving when the system believes that the car park is empty:

$$
\begin{array}{|l}
\multicolumn{1}{l}{\_\_ ExtraCar \_\_\_\_\_\_\_\_} \\
\Xi CarPark \\
r! : Report \\
\hline
count = 0 \\
r! = extra\_car \\
\hline
\end{array}
$$

Assuming that a suitable type of reports is introduced, we may define

$$Exit \mathrel{\widehat{=}} Exit_0 \lor ExtraCar$$

and be sure that all of the possibilities are catered for. □

14.3 Calculation and simplification

The process of calculating preconditions is both straightforward and routine. Indeed, much of the hard work can be carried out using some form of theorem prover or mechanical proof assistant. Suppose that we wish to find the precondition of the following operation schema:

```
┌─ Operation ─────────────────────────
│ Declaration
├─────────────
│ Predicate
└─────────────────────────────────────
```

where *Declaration* represents the declaration part of *Operation*, and *Predicate* the predicate part. To calculate the precondition of *Operation*,

1. divide *Declaration* into three parts:
   - *Before* containing only inputs and before components (unprimed state components)
   - *After* containing only outputs and after components (primed state components)
   - *Mixed* containing all other declarations and inclusions
2. if *Mixed* is not empty, expand every schema mentioned in *Mixed*; add all input and before components to *Before*; add all output and after components to *After*. As there may be several levels of schema inclusion, repeat this step until *Mixed* is empty.
3. the precondition of *Operation* is then

```
┌─────────────────────────────────────
│ Before
├─────────────
│ ∃ After •
│      Predicate
└─────────────────────────────────────
```

Example 14.5 To see how this recipe for preconditions may be applied, consider the following state schema definitions:

```
┌─ S ──────────────        ┌─ T ──────────────
│ a : ℕ                    │ S
│ b : ℕ                    │ c : ℕ
├──────────                ├──────────
│ a ≠ b                    │ b ≠ c
└──────────────────        └──────────────────
```

and suppose that we wish to calculate the precondition of the following operation schema:

$$
\begin{array}{|l}
\textit{Increment} \\
\hline
\Delta T \\
in? : \mathbb{N} \\
out! : \mathbb{N} \\
\hline
a' = a + in? \\
b' = b \\
c' = c \\
out! = c \\
\hline
\end{array}
$$

The first step of our recipe requires that we divide the declaration part of the schema into three parts:

$$Before = \{\text{`}in? : \mathbb{N}\text{'}\}$$

$$After = \{\text{`}out! : \mathbb{N}\text{'}\}$$

$$Mixed = \{\text{`}\Delta T\text{'}\}$$

The second step requires us to empty the third part, *Mixed*, by expanding schema definitions and separating input, output, before and after components. The result is

$$Before = \{\text{`}in? : \mathbb{N}\text{'}, \text{`}T\text{'}\}$$

$$After = \{\text{`}out! : \mathbb{N}\text{'}, \text{`}T'\text{'}\}$$

$$Mixed = \{\}$$

The precondition of *Increment* is then given by

$$
\begin{array}{|l}
\hline
T \\
in? : \mathbb{N} \\
\hline
\exists\, out! : \mathbb{N};\ T' \bullet \\
\qquad a' = a + in? \\
\qquad b' = b \\
\qquad c' = c \\
\qquad out! = c \\
\hline
\end{array}
$$

□

As we can see from the last example, the precondition schema obtained after the third stage of the recipe may be quite complicated. It is usually possible to simplify the predicate part of a precondition schema using the one-point rule. For a precondition schema

$$\begin{array}{|l}
\textit{Before} \\
\hline
\exists \textit{After} \bullet \\
\qquad \textit{Predicate}
\end{array}$$

we may proceed as follows:

4. expand any schemas in *After* that contain equations identifying outputs or after components

5. expand any schemas in *After* that refer to outputs or after components for which we already have equations

6. if *Predicate* contains an equation identifying a component declared in *After*, then use the one-point rule to eliminate that component; repeat this step as many times as possible

7. if $\textit{After}_1$ and $\textit{Predicate}_1$ are what remains of *After* and *Predicate*, then the precondition is now

$$\begin{array}{|l}
\textit{Before} \\
\hline
\exists \textit{After}_1 \bullet \\
\qquad \textit{Predicate}_1
\end{array}$$

Example 14.6 The precondition of *Increment*, calculated in the last example, can be greatly simplified using the remaining part of the recipe. Its predicate part is currently

$$\begin{array}{l}
\exists \, out! : \mathbb{N}; \ T' \bullet \\
\qquad a' = a + in? \\
\qquad b' = b \\
\qquad c' = c \\
\qquad out! = c
\end{array}$$

Looking at Step 5 of the recipe, we expand T', as it contains a declaration of an after component for which we have an equation:

$$\begin{array}{l} \exists\, out! : \mathbb{N};\ S';\ c' : \mathbb{N} \mid b' \neq c' \bullet \\ \quad a' = a + in? \\ \quad b' = b \\ \quad c' = c \\ \quad out! = c \end{array}$$

The same is true of S', so we follow this step again:

$$\begin{array}{l} \exists\, out! : \mathbb{N};\ a' : \mathbb{N};\ b' : \mathbb{N};\ c' : \mathbb{N} \mid a' \neq b' \land b' \neq c' \bullet \\ \quad a' = a + in? \\ \quad b' = b \\ \quad c' = c \\ \quad out! = c \end{array}$$

There are no more schemas to expand, so we proceed to Step 6. The one-point rule can be applied four times, yielding the predicate

$$\begin{array}{l} a + in? \neq b \\ b \neq c \\ a + in? \in \mathbb{N} \\ b \in \mathbb{N} \\ c \in \mathbb{N} \end{array}$$

This is as far as the recipe takes us. However, all but one of these conjuncts follow immediately from the declarations in the precondition schema:

$$\begin{array}{l} in? : \mathbb{N} \\ T \end{array}$$

Removing the redundant information from our predicate, we obtain the final simplified form of 'pre *Increment*':

$$\begin{array}{|l} in? : \mathbb{N} \\ T \\ \hline a + in? \neq b \end{array}$$

□

14.4 Structure and preconditions

The process of calculating preconditions can be further simplified by considering the structure of an operation. If an operation schema is defined to be the disjunction of several partial operations, or if an operation is defined using promotion, then we may be able to save time and effort by factoring out part of the calculation.

The simplest case is that of disjunction. If an operation schema *Op* is defined to be the disjunction of two or more operation schemas, then we may make use of the fact that the precondition operator 'pre' distributes through disjunction. For example, if

$$Op \mathrel{\widehat{=}} Op_1 \lor Op_2$$

then we may conclude that

$$\text{pre } Op = \text{pre } Op_1 \lor \text{pre } Op_2$$

This result follows immediately from the definition of 'pre', given the following theorem of our predicate calculus:

$$\exists A \bullet P \lor Q \Leftrightarrow \exists A \bullet P \lor \exists A \bullet Q$$

Existential quantification distributes through disjunction.

Example 14.7 The *Purchase* operation was defined as a disjunction of two partial operations

$$\begin{aligned} Purchase \mathrel{\widehat{=}} & (Purchase_0 \land Success) \\ & \lor \\ & (NotAvailable \land Failure) \end{aligned}$$

Using the distributive property of 'pre', we may observe that

$$\begin{aligned} \text{pre } Purchase = & \text{ pre } (Purchase_0 \land Success) \\ & \lor \\ & \text{ pre } (NotAvailable \land Failure) \end{aligned}$$

We may calculate the preconditions of the two partial operations—$Purchase_0 \land Success$ and $NotAvailable \land Failure$—separately, and combine them to obtain the precondition of *Purchase*. □

The 'pre' operator does not necessarily distribute through conjunction. If $Op \mathrel{\widehat=} Op_1 \land Op_2$ then pre Op may not be equivalent to pre $Op_1 \land$ pre Op_2. However, this *will* be the case whenever one of the schemas contributes nothing to the precondition.

Example 14.8 In Example 12.8, the schema *Success* was defined to be

$$
\begin{array}{|l}
\hline
\textit{Success} \\
r! : \textit{Response} \\
\hline
r! = \textit{okay} \\
\hline
\end{array}
$$

This schema imposes no constraint upon the before components of the box office state, neither does it describe any input. It therefore makes no contribution to the precondition of an operation, and we may observe that

$$\text{pre}\ (\textit{Purchase}_0 \land \textit{Success}) \ = \ \text{pre}\ \textit{Purchase}_0$$

□

If an operation is defined using a free promotion, then its precondition may be expressed in terms of the precondition of a local operation. If *Promote* is a free promotion, then the equivalence

$$\exists\, \textit{Local}' \bullet \exists\, \textit{Global}' \bullet \textit{Promote} \Leftrightarrow \forall\, \textit{Local}' \bullet \exists\, \textit{Global}' \bullet \textit{Promote} \qquad (*)$$

must hold; this follows from the definition at the start of Section 13.3. Now consider the precondition of *GOp*, the promotion of a local operation *LOp*:

$$
\begin{array}{ll}
\text{pre}\ \textit{GOp} & \\
\quad \Leftrightarrow \exists\, \textit{Global}' \bullet \textit{GOp} & [\text{definition of 'pre'}] \\
\quad \Leftrightarrow \exists\, \textit{Global}' \bullet \exists\, \Delta \textit{Local} \bullet \textit{Promote} \land \textit{LOp} & [\text{definition of } \textit{GOp}] \\
\quad \Leftrightarrow \exists\, \Delta \textit{Local} \bullet \exists\, \textit{Global}' \bullet \textit{Promote} \land \textit{LOp} & [\text{property of } \exists] \\
\quad \Leftrightarrow \exists\, \Delta \textit{Local} \bullet (\exists\, \textit{Global}' \bullet \textit{Promote}) \land \textit{LOp} & \\
 & [\textit{Global}' \text{ does not appear in } \textit{LOp}] \\
\quad \Leftrightarrow \exists\, \textit{Local} \bullet (\exists\, \textit{Local}';\ \textit{Global}' \bullet \textit{Promote}) \land \exists\, \textit{Local}' \bullet \textit{LOp} & \\
 & [\text{free promotion}] \\
\quad \Leftrightarrow \exists\, \textit{Local} \bullet \text{pre}\ \textit{Promote} \land \text{pre}\ \textit{LOp} & [\text{definition of 'pre', twice}]
\end{array}
$$

The equivalence justified by the phrase 'free promotion' can be derived from the equivalence labelled '$*$' using the proof rules for existential introduction and universal elimination.

The result that we have established can be stated as follows: under a free promotion, the precondition of a global operation is a conjunction of two preconditions—the precondition of the local operation, and the precondition of the promotion. We might say that the precondition of the local operation has itself been promoted.

Example 14.9 The description of a data array in Example 13.3 included a global operation *AssignIndex* defined by

$$AssignIndex \mathrel{\widehat=} \exists \Delta Data \bullet AssignData \land Promote$$

This is a free promotion, so the precondition of *AssignIndex* is given by

$$\mathrm{pre}\ AssignIndex = \exists Data' \bullet \mathrm{pre}\ Promote \land \mathrm{pre}\ AssignData$$

The local operation *AssignData* is total: the constraint part of pre *AssignData* is simply *true* precondition. The promotion schema *Promote* was defined by

```
┌─ Promote ─────────────────────────────
│ ΔArray
│ ΔData
│ index? : ℕ
├──────────
│ index? ∈ dom array
│ {index?} ⩤ array = {index?} ⩤ array′
│ array index? = θData
│ array′ index? = θData′
└───────────────────────────────────────
```

The precondition of *Promote* adds the constraint $index? \in \mathrm{dom}\, array$. The precondition of *AssignIndex* is therefore

```
┌───────────────────────────────────────
│ Array
│ Data
│ index? : ℕ
├──────────
│ index? ∈ dom array
└───────────────────────────────────────
```

□

The separation of concerns afforded by the free promotion is not possible where the promotion is constrained. In such cases, the precondition of a promoted operation is calculated by first conjoining the local operation and the promotion schema and then applying the existential quantifier.

Example 14.10 In the prioritised data stack of Example 13.8, we propose a local operation that sets the priority of the top element to 100:

$$
\begin{array}{|l}
\textit{SetPriority} \\
\hline
\Delta \textit{PriData} \\
\hline
\textit{priority}' = 100 \\
\textit{data}' = \textit{data} \\
\hline
\end{array}
$$

We may promote this operation to the global operation

$$\textit{SetPriorityStack} \mathrel{\widehat{=}} \exists \Delta \textit{PriData} \bullet \textit{SetPriority} \land \textit{Promote}$$

where the promotion schema *Promote* is defined by

$$
\begin{array}{|l}
\textit{Promote} \\
\hline
\Delta \textit{Stack} \\
\Delta \textit{PriData} \\
\hline
\textit{stack} \neq \langle\rangle \\
\theta \textit{PriData} = \textit{head stack} \\
\textit{stack}' = \langle \theta \textit{PriData}' \rangle \frown \textit{tail stack} \\
\hline
\end{array}
$$

This insists that the stack is non-empty. We may calculate the precondition of *SetPriorityStack* as follows:

$$
\begin{array}{ll}
\text{pre } \textit{SetPriorityStack} & \\
\quad \Leftrightarrow \exists \textit{Stack}' \bullet \textit{SetPriorityStack} & [\text{definition of 'pre'}] \\
\quad \Leftrightarrow \exists \textit{Stack}' \bullet \exists \Delta \textit{PriData} \bullet \textit{Promote} \land \textit{SetPriority} & \\
& [\text{definition of } \textit{SetPriorityStack}] \\
\quad \Leftrightarrow \exists \Delta \textit{Local} \bullet \quad \exists \textit{Global}' \bullet \textit{Promote} \land \textit{LOp} & [\text{property of } \exists] \\
\quad \Leftrightarrow \exists \Delta \textit{PriData} \bullet (\exists \textit{Stack}' \bullet \textit{Promote}) \land \textit{SetPriority} & \\
& [\textit{Stack}' \text{ does not appear in } \textit{SetPriority}]
\end{array}
$$

At this point, we calculate the value of $\exists \textit{Stack}' \bullet \textit{Promote}$, and obtain

$$
\begin{array}{|l}
\hline
\textit{Stack} \\
\Delta \textit{PriData} \\
\hline
\textit{stack} \neq \langle\rangle \\
\theta \textit{PriData} = \textit{head stack} \\
\forall j : \text{dom tail } \textit{stack} \bullet \theta \textit{PriData}'.\textit{priority} \geq (\textit{stack } j).\textit{priority} \\
\hline
\end{array}
$$

In conjunction with *SetPriority*, this yields

$$
\begin{array}{|l}
Stack \\
\Delta PriData \\
\hline
stack \neq \langle\rangle \\
\theta PriData = head\ stack \\
\theta PriData'.priority = 100 \\
\theta PriData'.data = \theta PriData.data \\
\forall j : \mathrm{dom}\ \mathrm{tail}\ stack \bullet \theta PriData'.priority \geq (stack\ j).priority
\end{array}
$$

Following on from the argument above, we may obtain the precondition of *SetPriorityStack* by quantifying this schema with $\exists \Delta PriData$, yielding

$$
\begin{array}{|l}
Stack \\
\hline
stack \neq \langle\rangle \\
\forall j : \mathrm{dom}\ \mathrm{tail}\ stack \bullet 100 \geq (stack\ j).priority
\end{array}
$$

For the operation to be defined: the stack must be non-empty; every priority value in the tail of the stack must be less than 100; the stack must be ordered according to decreasing priority values.

A very different result would be obtained by factoring the precondition calculation as if it were a free promotion. The constraint part of pre *SetPriority* is simply *true*: there is no restriction at the level of the data objects. The schema

$$\exists PriData' \bullet \mathrm{pre}\ Promote \land \mathrm{pre}\ SetPriority$$

is equivalent to

$$
\begin{array}{|l}
Stack \\
\hline
stack \neq \langle\rangle
\end{array}
$$

This schema that omits an essential part of the precondition: the constraint that every object in the tail of the stack has a priority lower than 100.

The missing constraint appears when we combine the information from the local operation—that the new priority value is 100—with the invariant property of the global state. If we hide the new priority value before combining the two schemas, then this information is lost. □

Operation	Precondition
BoxOfficeInit	*true*
$Purchase_0$	$s? \in seating \setminus \mathrm{dom}\, sold$
NotAvailable	$s? \notin seating \setminus \mathrm{dom}\, sold$
Success	*true*
Purchase	*true*
$Return_0$	$c? \mapsto s? \in sold$
NotPossible	$c? \mapsto s? \notin sold$
Failure	*true*
Return	*true*

Table 14.1: Preconditions in the box office system

Any investigation of the initialisation and preconditions of a specification should be properly recorded. A useful convention, followed by many practitioners, involves tabulating the results of the investigation. In such a table, we may find related partial operations listed together: any overall precondition is then easily established.

Example 14.11 In our theatre box office system, the constraint part of the initialisation schema is simply *true*. No initial input is required: the initial value of *seating* is simply that of some global variable *initial_allocation*.

The *Purchase* and *Return* operations were both total. Each is the disjunction of two partial operations, *Purchase* being defined by

$$Purchase \;\widehat{=}\; (Purchase_0 \land Success) \lor (NotAvailable \land Failure)$$

and *Return* by

$$Return \;\widehat{=}\; (Return_0 \land Success) \lor (NotPossible \land Failure)$$

Each total operation involves two inputs—$s?$ and $c?$—and a single output—$r!$. Having calculated the preconditions, we may collect the results together in a single table: see Table 14.1. □

Chapter 15

A File System

In this chapter, we present the first of several case studies using Z. We show how the schema notation can be used to specify a simple file system: representing concrete data structures and a set of operations upon them. We show also how the preconditions of the various operations can be calculated, and how the description of a single file can be promoted to an indexed component of a file system.

15.1 A programming interface

We will begin by setting down exactly what it is that we intend to model. In this case, it is the programming interface to a file system. This is a list of operations upon the file system, complete with a description of their intended effects. For example: the operation create may be used to create a new file, and the operation read may be used to obtain data from an existing file.

We may divide the operations into two groups: those that affect the data within a single file, and those that affect the file system as a whole. At the file level, there are four operations:

- read: used to read a piece of data from a file;
- write: used to write a piece of data to a file;
- add: used to add a new piece of data to a file;
- delete: used to delete a piece of data from a file.

The operations add and write are quite different. The first will extend the file to accommodate the new data, while the second will overwrite an existing part of the file.

The remainder of the programming interface consists of operations upon the file system. We will consider four of these:

- create: used to create a new file;
- destroy: used to destroy an existing file;
- open: used to make a file available for reading and writing of data;
- close: used to make a file unavailable for reading and writing.

Of these, the first two may be seen as *file management* operations, while the others may be seen as *file access* operations upon the file system.

15.2 Operations upon files

We will represent each file using a relation between storage *keys* with *data* elements. For the purposes of this specification, we may suppose that keys and data are drawn from basic types:

$$[Key, Data]$$

In more elaborate descriptions, there may be more to a file than simply its contents. To keep our specification both flexible and extensible, we use a schema to describe the structure of a file:

File

$contents : Key \pfun Data$

A file should not associate the same key with two different pieces of data, hence the requirement that the relation *contents* should be a partial function.

When a file is initialised, it contains no data, so the value of *contents* should be the empty function. The following schema describes the initial state of a file:

FileInit

$File'$

$contents' = \emptyset$

The schema *File* corresponds to a set of bindings, each with a single component *contents*. The schema *FileInit* corresponds to a much smaller set of bindings, the singleton set $\{\langle\!| contents \leadsto \emptyset |\!\rangle\}$.

To describe an operation which may change the contents of a file, we will include two copies of the file state:

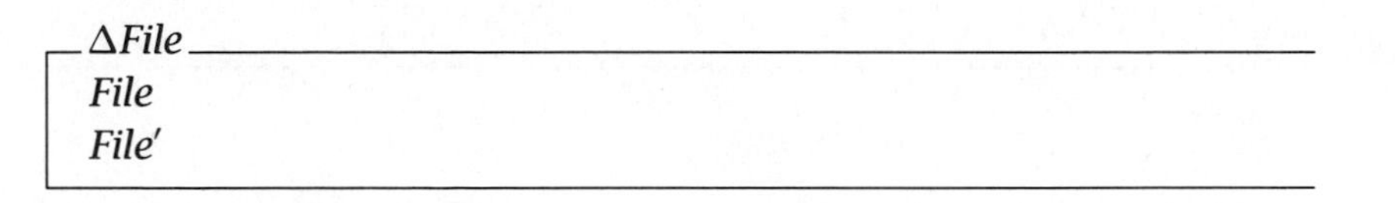

If an operation leaves the contents of a file unchanged, then we will add the condition that the binding remains the same:

$\Xi File$
$\Delta File$

$\theta File = \theta File'$

This schema will be included whenever an operation merely interrogates the file state.

A successful read operation requires an existing key as input and provides the corresponding datum as output:

$Read_0$
$\Xi File$
$k? : Key$
$d! : Data$

$k? \in \operatorname{dom} contents$
$d! = contents\ k?$

There are no side effects to this operation.

A successful write operation replaces the datum stored under an existing key, and provides no output:

$Write_0$
$\Delta File$
$k? : Key$
$d? : Data$

$k? \in \operatorname{dom} contents$
$contents' = contents \oplus \{k? \mapsto d?\}$

The old value of *contents* is updated with a maplet associating $k?$ with a second input $d?$.

A successful add operation has a complementary precondition. This time, the key $k?$ must not be in the domain of *contents*:

$$
\begin{array}{|l}
\multicolumn{1}{l}{\_ Add_0 \_\_\_\_\_\_\_\_\_\_\_\_\_\_\_\_\_\_\_\_} \\
\Delta File \\
k? : Key \\
d? : Data \\
\hline
k? \notin \operatorname{dom} contents \\
contents' = contents \cup \{k? \mapsto d?\} \\
\hline
\end{array}
$$

Again, there is no output from this operation.

Finally, a successful delete operation requires only that the key in question exists. A single input is required, and the state of the file will change:

$$
\begin{array}{|l}
\multicolumn{1}{l}{\_ Delete_0 \_\_\_\_\_\_\_\_\_\_\_\_\_\_\_\_\_\_\_\_} \\
\Delta File \\
k? : Key \\
\hline
k? \in \operatorname{dom} contents \\
contents' = \{k?\} \lhd contents \\
\hline
\end{array}
$$

The effect of removing the key is modelled using domain co-restriction: the maplet starting at $k?$ is removed from *contents*.

15.3 A more complete description

Thus far, we have described only *partial* operations upon files. For each operation, there are circumstances in which the effect upon the file state is not fully defined. For example, we have not explained what happens if an attempt is made to add data using a key that is already in use. We will now extend our description to cover every eventuality.

We will add a type of reports to our formal specification, allowing us to provide some output whether or not the operation is successful:

$$Report ::= \mathsf{key\_in\_use} \mid \mathsf{key\_not\_in\_use} \mid \mathsf{okay}$$

A failed operation upon the file state will always produce a report as output. It will prove convenient to include the following schema:

$$
\begin{array}{|l}
\hline
\textit{KeyError} \\
\textit{File} \\
k? : \textit{Key} \\
r! : \textit{Report} \\
\hline
\end{array}
$$

An error may arise because the specified key is not in use,

$$
\begin{array}{|l}
\hline
\textit{KeyNotInUse} \\
\textit{KeyError} \\
\hline
k? \notin \mathrm{dom}\ \textit{contents} \\
r! = \mathsf{key\_not\_in\_use} \\
\hline
\end{array}
$$

or because the specified key *is* in use,

$$
\begin{array}{|l}
\hline
\textit{KeyInUse} \\
\textit{KeyError} \\
\hline
k? \in \mathrm{dom}\ \textit{contents} \\
r! = \mathsf{key\_in\_use} \\
\hline
\end{array}
$$

A successful operation will always produce a report of the same value:

$$
\begin{array}{|l}
\hline
\textit{Success} \\
r! : \textit{Report} \\
\hline
r! = \mathsf{okay} \\
\hline
\end{array}
$$

We are now ready to define a collection of total operations: schemas in which the state before may be any valid file state:

$$
\begin{aligned}
\textit{Read} &\mathrel{\widehat{=}} (\textit{Read}_0 \land \textit{Success}) \lor \textit{KeyNotInUse} \\
\textit{Write} &\mathrel{\widehat{=}} (\textit{Write}_0 \land \textit{Success}) \lor \textit{KeyNotInUse} \\
\textit{Add} &\mathrel{\widehat{=}} (\textit{Add}_0 \land \textit{Success}) \lor \textit{KeyInUse} \\
\textit{Delete} &\mathrel{\widehat{=}} (\textit{Delete}_0 \land \textit{Success}) \lor \textit{KeyNotInUse}
\end{aligned}
$$

The four operations *Read*, *Write*, *Add*, and *Delete* have been built up in a structured fashion from small components. This avoids any duplication of effort, allowing us to factor out common aspects of the design, and results in a clearer, more comprehensible specification.

In larger case studies and industrial applications, a structured approach is essential if the reader is not to be overwhelmed by detail. As an indication of the amount of information that might be involved, consider the following schema, an expanded version of the operation schema used to describe the read operation:

$$
\begin{array}{|l}
\hline
contents, contents' : Key \twoheadrightarrow Data \\
k? : Key \\
d! : Data \\
r! : Report \\
\hline
(\, k? \in \mathrm{dom}\, contents \land \\
\quad d! = contents\, k? \land \\
\quad contents' = contents \land \\
\quad r! = \mathsf{okay} \,) \\
\lor \\
(\, k? \notin \mathrm{dom}\, contents \land \\
\quad contents' = contents \land \\
\quad r! = \mathsf{key\_not\_in\_use} \,) \\
\hline
\end{array}
$$

The output $d!$ can take any value if the specified key is not in use.

15.4 A file system

A file system contains a number of files indexed using a set of names. In this specification, we will regard the set of names is a basic type:

$$[Name]$$

In our description of the system, we will consider two aspects of a file system state: the collection of named files known to the system, and the set of files that are currently *open*:

$$
\begin{array}{|l}
\hline
\textit{System} \\
\hline
file : Name \twoheadrightarrow File \\
open : \mathbb{P}\, Name \\
\hline
open \subseteq \mathrm{dom}\, file \\
\hline
\end{array}
$$

It is important that the system should not associate the same name with two different files: *file* must always be functional.

When the file system is initialised, there are no files. The partial function *file* is empty, as is the set *open*. As the state invariant insists that every open file is also recorded in *file*, it is enough to insist that $file = \varnothing$:

$$
\begin{array}{|l}
\textit{SystemInit} \\
\hline
System' \\
\hline
file' = \varnothing \\
\hline
\end{array}
$$

Again, the following pair of schemas will be useful when we come to describe file system operations:

$$\Delta System \mathrel{\widehat{=}} [System; \ System']$$

$$\Xi System \mathrel{\widehat{=}} [\Delta System \mid \theta System = \theta System']$$

Both of these schemas insist that the state invariant is preserved: *file* must remain functional, and *open* must remain within its domain.

Since the state of our file system includes indexed copies of *File*, we may choose to promote the operations defined above. The local state is described by *File*, the global state is described by *System*, and the promotion is characterised by the schema

$$
\begin{array}{|l}
\textit{Promote} \\
\hline
\Delta System \\
\Delta File \\
n? : Name \\
\hline
n? \in open \\
file \ n? = \theta File \\
file' \ n? = \theta File' \\
\{n?\} \mathbin{⩤} file = \{n?\} \mathbin{⩤} file' \\
open' = open \\
\hline
\end{array}
$$

which uses the indexing function *file* to explain the relationship between local and global states.

We define four operations using this promotion:

$$KeyRead_0 \mathrel{\widehat{=}} \exists \Delta File \bullet Read \wedge Promote$$

$$KeyWrite_0 \mathrel{\widehat{=}} \exists \Delta File \bullet Write \wedge Promote$$

$$KeyAdd_0 \mathrel{\widehat{=}} \exists \Delta File \bullet Add \wedge Promote$$

$$KeyDelete_0 \mathrel{\widehat{=}} \exists \Delta File \bullet Delete \wedge Promote$$

Although each local operation is total, the file in question may not be open. The resulting global operations are partial.

The operations open and close do not change the name of any file, neither do they add or remove files from the system. They may be described as file access operations, in that they may change the availability of a file for reading and writing. In the formal descriptions of these operations, we will find the following schema useful:

$$
\begin{array}{|l}
\hline
\textit{FileAccess} \\
\Delta \textit{System} \\
n? : \textit{Name} \\
\hline
n? \in \operatorname{dom} \textit{file} \\
\textit{file}' = \textit{file} \\
\hline
\end{array}
$$

This schema describes an operation upon the file system in which the indexing function *file* is left unchanged. It insists also that the input component $n?$ describes a file that is known to the system.

A successful open operation adds a name to the list of open files.

$$
\begin{array}{|l}
\hline
\textit{Open}_0 \\
\textit{FileAccess} \\
\hline
n? \notin \textit{open} \\
\textit{open}' = \textit{open} \cup \{n?\} \\
\hline
\end{array}
$$

This operation is strictly partial. An open operation will fail if the name supplied denotes a file that is already open. This possibility is excluded above.

A successful close operation removes a name from the list of open files:

$$
\begin{array}{|l}
\hline
\textit{Close}_0 \\
\textit{FileAccess} \\
\hline
n? \in \textit{open} \\
\textit{open}' = \textit{open} \setminus \{n?\} \\
\hline
\end{array}
$$

Again, this operation is strictly partial. A close operation will fail if the name supplied does not denote an open file. This possibility is excluded above.

The remaining operations, create and destroy, are file management operations. They may change the list of files known to the system, but they should not affect the list of open files. As with *FileAccess*, we may use a single schema to describe the information that is common to both operations:

$$
\begin{array}{|l}
\hline
\textit{FileManage} \\
\Delta \textit{System} \\
n? : \textit{Name} \\
\hline
\textit{open}' = \textit{open} \\
\hline
\end{array}
$$

This schema insists that the set of open files is preserved.

A successful create operation adds a new name to the list of files known to the system:

$$
\begin{array}{|l}
\hline
\textit{Create}_0 \\
\textit{FileManage} \\
\hline
n? \notin \operatorname{dom} \textit{file} \\
\textit{file}' = \textit{file} \cup \{ n? \mapsto \theta \textit{FileInit} \} \\
\hline
\end{array}
$$

Immediately after this operation, the state of the file associated with name $n?$ is described by the binding $\theta \textit{FileInit}$. That is, $n?$ is associated with a binding of schema type *File* in which *contents* is bound to the empty set.

A successful destroy operation removes a name from the list of files, domain co-restricting the function *file*:

$$
\begin{array}{|l}
\hline
\textit{Destroy}_0 \\
\textit{FileManage} \\
\hline
n? \in \operatorname{dom} \textit{file} \\
\textit{file}' = \{ n? \} \lhd \textit{file} \\
\hline
\end{array}
$$

We require that the name $n?$ already exists.

We might also wish to insist that $n?$ is not an element of *open*, thus preventing the destruction of open files. However, this condition is already enforced by the predicate part of *FileManage*—which insists that this operation should not affect the list of open files—acting in combination with our state invariant $\textit{open} \subseteq \operatorname{dom} \textit{file}$. If we cannot remove $n?$ from *open*, then we cannot remove $n?$ from the domain of *file*.

We will now extend our free type of report messages to take account of the errors that may occur in file access and file management operations:

$$
\begin{aligned}
\textit{Report} ::= \; & \mathsf{key\_in\_use} \mid \mathsf{key\_not\_in\_use} \mid \mathsf{okay} \mid \mathsf{file\_exists} \mid \\
& \mathsf{file\_does\_not\_exist} \mid \mathsf{file\_is\_open} \mid \mathsf{file\_is\_not\_open}
\end{aligned}
$$

This definition replaces the one given earlier.

If an error occurs, then the system state will be left unchanged:

FileError
$$\Xi System$$
$$n? : Name$$
$$r! : Report$$

This information will be common to each of the error cases that we encounter in specifying operations at the system level.

If we attempt to create a file using a name that is already in use, we will receive a report complaining that a file with that name exists:

FileExists
$$FileError$$

$$n? \in \operatorname{dom} file$$
$$r! = \mathsf{file\_exists}$$

Conversely, if we attempt to destroy a file using a name that is not in use, we will receive a report complaining that the file does not exist:

FileDoesNotExist
$$FileError$$

$$n? \notin \operatorname{dom} file$$
$$r! = \mathsf{file\_does\_not\_exist}$$

Sometimes a file will be open when it should be closed,

FileIsOpen
$$FileError$$

$$n? \in open$$
$$r! = \mathsf{file\_is\_open}$$

and sometimes a file will be closed when it should be open,

FileIsNotOpen
$$FileError$$

$$n? \in \operatorname{dom} file$$
$$n? \notin open$$
$$r! = \mathsf{file\_is\_not\_open}$$

We are now ready to describe the interface to the file system. There are four operations involving the contents of files: *KeyRead*, *KeyWrite*, *KeyAdd*, and *KeyDelete*. In each case, if the file exists and is open, then the effect of the operation is described by a promoted file operation:

$$KeyRead \mathrel{\widehat{=}} KeyRead_0 \lor FileIsNotOpen \lor FileDoesNotExist$$

$$KeyWrite \mathrel{\widehat{=}} KeyWrite_0 \lor FileIsNotOpen \lor FileDoesNotExist$$

$$KeyAdd \mathrel{\widehat{=}} KeyAdd_0 \lor FileIsNotOpen \lor FileDoesNotExist$$

$$KeyDelete \mathrel{\widehat{=}} KeyDelete_0 \lor FileIsNotOpen \lor FileDoesNotExist$$

We may complete the definitions of the access and management operations using a similar combination of error cases:

$$Open \mathrel{\widehat{=}} (Open_0 \land Success) \lor FileIsOpen \lor FileDoesNotExist$$

$$Close \mathrel{\widehat{=}} (Close_0 \land Success) \lor FileIsNotOpen \lor FileDoesNotExist$$

$$Create \mathrel{\widehat{=}} (Create_0 \land Success) \lor FileExists$$

$$Destroy \mathrel{\widehat{=}} (Destroy_0 \land Success) \lor FileDoesNotExist \lor FileIsOpen$$

This completes our formal description of the file system.

15.5 Formal analysis

A formal description of a programming interface is useful indeed: it provides a clear, unambiguous account of the operations available, and explains their effects upon the state. It raises a number of important issues—should we able to destroy an open file?—and acts as a source document to resolve the uncertainties inherent in our natural language explanation of the file system's behaviour.

However, there may be errors or contradictions *within* this formal description. There may be conflicting assumptions about system behaviour, in which case our formal design may be impossible to implement. Alternatively, there may be hidden assumptions within an operation schema, leading to circumstances in which the effect of the operation is not explained.

Accordingly, we should undertake some formal analysis. Without too much effort, it is possible to conduct an investigation of our formal design. We begin by checking that our state invariant contains no contradictions. We may establish this by proving the initialisation theorem

$$\exists\, SystemInit \bullet true$$

That is, that there exists a binding of *file* and *open* which satisfies the constraint part of *SystemInit*.

An outline proof of the theorem is easily constructed. Expanding the schema definition of *SystemInit* and applying the one-point rule to *file'*, we find ourselves with an existential statement concerning the empty set. This is easily divided into two statements—labelled [2] and [3] below—about '$\mathbb{P}$' and 'dom', which we may take as valid or prove at our leisure:

$$\dfrac{\dfrac{}{\varnothing \in \mathit{Name} \nrightarrow \mathit{File}}[1] \qquad \dfrac{\dfrac{}{\varnothing \in \mathbb{P}\,\mathit{Name}}[2] \quad \dfrac{}{\varnothing \subseteq \operatorname{dom}\varnothing}[3]}{\begin{array}{l}\exists\, \mathit{open}' : \mathbb{P}\,\mathit{Name} \mid \\ \qquad \mathit{open}' \subseteq \operatorname{dom}\varnothing \bullet \mathit{true}\end{array}}[\exists\text{-intro}]}{\dfrac{\begin{array}{l}\exists\, \mathit{file}' : \mathit{Name} \nrightarrow \mathit{File};\ \mathit{open}' : \mathbb{P}\,\mathit{Name} \mid \\ \qquad \mathit{open}' \subseteq \operatorname{dom}\mathit{file}' \wedge \mathit{file}' = \varnothing \bullet \mathit{true}\end{array}}{\exists\, \mathit{SystemInit} \bullet \mathit{true}}[\text{definition}]}[\text{one-point rule}]$$

However, the result labelled [1] is not immediate. The empty relation is an element of $\mathit{Name} \nrightarrow \mathit{File}$ only if this set is not empty. For this to be the case, there must be at least one element of *File*. It is enough to show that

$$\exists\, \mathit{FileInit} \bullet \mathit{true}$$

This time, the proof is even easier to construct:

$$\dfrac{\dfrac{\dfrac{}{\varnothing \in \mathit{Key} \nrightarrow \mathit{Data}}[4]}{\exists\, \mathit{contents}' : \mathit{Key} \nrightarrow \mathit{Data} \mid \mathit{contents}' = \varnothing \bullet \mathit{true}}[\text{one-point rule}]}{\exists\, \mathit{FileInit} \bullet \mathit{true}}[\text{definition}]$$

As *Key* and *Data* are basic types, we know that they cannot be empty. Hence the empty relation is an element of $\mathit{Key} \nrightarrow \mathit{Data}$, and an initial state exists. Since *Name* is also a given type, we may infer that $\mathit{Name} \nrightarrow \mathit{File}$ is non-empty, and that condition [1] holds. Our formal requirements are thus consistent: they contain no contradictions.

The second part of our investigation involves calculating the precondition of each operation. As an example, consider the operation *KeyRead*, defined by

$$\mathit{KeyRead} \mathrel{\widehat{=}} \mathit{KeyRead}_0 \vee \mathit{FileDoesNotExist} \vee \mathit{FileIsNotOpen}$$

Since the 'pre' operator distributes through disjunction, we know that

$$\begin{array}{l}\operatorname{pre} \mathit{KeyRead} \Leftrightarrow \\ \qquad \operatorname{pre} \mathit{KeyRead}_0 \vee \operatorname{pre} \mathit{FileDoesNotExist} \vee \operatorname{pre} \mathit{FileIsNotOpen}\end{array}$$

If we recall the definition of *FileDoesNotExist*, we may observe that its precondition is equivalent to

$$\begin{array}{|l} System \\ n? : Name \\ \hline \exists\, r! : Report \bullet \\ \quad n? \notin \mathrm{dom}\, file \\ \quad r! = \mathsf{file\_is\_not\_open} \end{array}$$

Using the one-point rule, we may rewrite the predicate part of this schema as $n? \notin \mathrm{dom}\, file$. Similarly, we may establish that pre *FileIsNotOpen* has the constraint $n? \in \mathrm{dom}\, file \land n? \notin open$.

The first disjunct requires a little more work. The operation $KeyRead_0$ was defined by promoting the local operation *Read*:

$$KeyRead_0 \mathrel{\widehat{=}} \exists\, \Delta File \bullet Read \land Promote$$

The combination of *System*, *File*, and *Promote* makes for a free promotion. We can prove this by starting with the schema

$$\exists\, File' \bullet \exists\, System' \bullet Promote$$

and applying the definition of *Promote* to yield

$$\begin{array}{l} [\, n? : Name \mid \\ \quad \exists\, File' \bullet \exists\, System' \bullet \\ \quad\quad n? \in open \\ \quad\quad file\; n? = \theta File \\ \quad\quad file'\; n? = \theta File' \\ \quad\quad \{n?\} \lhd file = \{n?\} \lhd file' \\ \quad\quad open' = open \,] \end{array}$$

The extended form of the one-point rule for existential quantification, introduced in Chapter 13, can be applied to the predicate part of this schema. The result is

$$\begin{array}{l} \exists\, System' \bullet \\ \quad n? \in open \\ \quad file\; n? = \theta File \\ \quad file'\; n? \in \{\, File \bullet \theta File \,\} \\ \quad \{n?\} \lhd file = \{n?\} \lhd file' \\ \quad open' = open \end{array}$$

We may follow this with an application of the universal one-point rule to yield:

$$\begin{array}{l} \forall\, File' \bullet \exists\, System' \bullet \\ \quad n? \in open \\ \quad file\, n? = \theta File \\ \quad file'\, n? = \theta File' \\ \quad \{n?\} \ndres file = \{n?\} \ndres file' \\ \quad open' = open \end{array}$$

This establishes the truth of the schema implication

$$\exists\, File' \bullet \exists\, System' \bullet Promote \;\Rightarrow\; \forall\, File' \bullet \exists\, System' \bullet Promote$$

and confirms that the promotion is free.

The precondition of $KeyRead_0$ is given by

$$\text{pre}\, KeyRead_0 \;=\; \exists\, Local \bullet \text{pre}\, Read \land \text{pre}\, Promote$$

Expanding the precondition schema 'pre *Read*', we find that its predicate part is simply *true*. The remaining predicate information is contributed by the promotion schema, which insists that the file in question is listed as open:

$$\text{pre}\, KeyRead_0 \;\Leftrightarrow\; n? \in open$$

The precondition of $KeyRead_0$ is then

$$\begin{array}{|l} System \\ n? : Name \\ \hline n? \in open \end{array}$$

and the precondition of *KeyRead* is

$$\begin{array}{|l} System \\ n? : Name \end{array}$$

That is, *KeyRead* is a total operation.

We may document the results of our analysis in a table of preconditions: see Table 15.1. For each operation, we list the partial operations used in its definition, together with their preconditions. In every case, the disjunction of these preconditions is *true*; our operations are total.

Operation		Precondition
KeyRead	$KeyRead_0$	$n? \in open$
	FileIsNotOpen	$n? \in (\mathrm{dom}\, file) \setminus open$
	FileDoesNotExist	$n? \notin \mathrm{dom}\, file$
	KeyRead	*true*
KeyWrite	$KeyWrite_0$	$n? \in open$
	FileIsNotOpen	$n? \in (\mathrm{dom}\, file) \setminus open$
	FileDoesNotExist	$n? \notin \mathrm{dom}\, file$
	KeyWrite	*true*
KeyAdd	$KeyAdd_0$	$n? \in open$
	FileIsNotOpen	$n? \in (\mathrm{dom}\, file) \setminus open$
	FileDoesNotExist	$n? \notin \mathrm{dom}\, file$
	KeyAdd	*true*
KeyDelete	$KeyDelete_0$	$n? \in open$
	FileIsNotOpen	$n? \in (\mathrm{dom}\, file) \setminus open$
	FileDoesNotExist	$n? \notin \mathrm{dom}\, file$
	KeyDelete	*true*
Open	$Open_0$	$n? \in (\mathrm{dom}\, file) \setminus open$
	FileIsOpen	$n? \in open$
	FileDoesNotExist	$n? \notin \mathrm{dom}\, file$
	Open	*true*
Close	$Close_0$	$n? \in open$
	FileIsNotOpen	$n? \in (\mathrm{dom}\, file) \setminus open$
	FileDoesNotExist	$n? \notin \mathrm{dom}\, file$
	Close	*true*
Create	$Create_0$	$n? \notin \mathrm{dom}\, file$
	FileExists	$n? \in \mathrm{dom}\, file$
	Create	*true*
Destroy	$Destroy_0$	$n? \in (\mathrm{dom}\, file) \setminus open$
	FileIsOpen	$n? \in open$
	FileDoesNotExist	$n? \notin \mathrm{dom}\, file$
	Destroy	*true*

Table 15.1: Summary of results

Chapter 16

Data Refinement

Writing a formal specification is a worthwhile activity in its own right: there is much to be gained from a good understanding and a simple description. However, we may also wish to develop a specification in such a way that it leads us towards a suitable implementation. This process of development is called *refinement*.

We may refine a formal specification by adding more information. For example, we might be more precise about how data is to be stored, or about how certain calculations are to be carried out. Clearly, it is important that our new, more detailed description is consistent with our original specification: the refinement must be correct.

In this chapter we explain what it means for one partial relation to refine another. Then, using the concepts of forwards and backwards simulation, we develop a theory of refinement for abstract data types, including a set of rules for proving correctness.

16.1 Refinement

The *Concise Oxford Dictionary* (8th edition) contains the following definition:

> **refinement** *n.* Refining or being refined; fineness of feeling or taste, polished manners etc.; subtle or ingenious manifestation *of*, piece of elaborate arrangement, *(all the refinements of reasoning, torture; a countermine was a refinement beyond their skill)*; instance of improvement *(up)on*; piece of subtle reasoning, fine distinction.

Although the bit about subtle reasoning is amusing, the relevant words here are 'instance of improvement upon'. For us, refinement is all about *improving* specifications.

The process of improvement involves the removal of *nondeterminism*, or uncertainty. An abstract specification may leave design choices unresolved; a refinement may resolve some of these choices, and eliminate some of the nondeterminism. Several refinement steps may be performed, each removing another degree of uncertainty, until the specification approaches executable program code.

Example 16.1 A resource manager allocates identical but numbered resources to client programs or users. Using a set of numbers to describe the free resources, the state of the system is characterised by the following schema:

```
┌─ ResourceManager ──────────────────────
│ free : 𝔽 ℕ
└────────────────────────────────────────
```

Any resource that is currently free may be allocated. The effect of an allocation is described by the following operation schema:

```
┌─ Allocate ─────────────────────────────
│ ΔResourceManager
│ r! : Resource
├──────────
│ r! ∈ free ∧ free' = free \ {r!}
└────────────────────────────────────────
```

If there is more than one resource free, then this specification is nondeterministic. It is also partial: we have not explained what is to be done if there are no resources left to be allocated.

This specification may be refined by another in which we decide that, should there be more than one resource free, the resource with the lowest number should be allocated first. In this new specification, the effect of an allocation is described by

```
┌─ Allocate₁ ────────────────────────────
│ ΔResourceManager
│ r! : Resource
├──────────
│ r! = min free ∧ free' = free \ {r!}
└────────────────────────────────────────
```

This specification is deterministic, provided that there is at least one resource to allocate. It is still partial.

A further refinement might explain that the resources are modelled by an array of bits, one bit per resource. A resource is free if the corresponding bit is set to 0. Assuming a suitable definition for 'array of', we may define

ResourceManager$_2$
free$_2$: array of *Bit*

where *Bit* is the set containing just 0 and 1.

The effect of an allocation is determined by searching for the first bit that is set to 0, starting from the lowest position. When this bit is found, it is set to 1 and its index is returned. If there are no 0 bits, an error report is generated. This specification respects the decision made in the previous refinement step: that the lowest numbered resource should be allocated. It is also total: the effect of an allocation is described in all circumstances.

Any client who is happy with the first specification will also be happy with the third. Of course, this two-step development could have been performed in a single, more complicated step in which the free set was implemented by the array directly, an allocation used the lowest index with an unset bit, and the specification was strengthened to add the error-handling. □

Example 16.2 When the Parliament of the European Union passes legislation, it does so in the form of a European directive. Each of the member countries is then required to enact the legislation, and in the United Kingdom this is done by passing an Act of Parliament. Regulatory authorities, such as the Health and Safety Executive, produce regulations, which they then seek to enforce. These legal instruments are so arranged that compliance with the regulations implies compliance with the Act, and compliance with the Act implies compliance with the directive. It is usually the case that the regulations are rather more strict than the original directive, because the legislation has been through two stages of interpretation, each taking into account considerations peculiar to the United Kingdom. We might say that the Act is a refinement of the directive, and that the regulations are a refinement of the Act. □

Example 16.3 For reasons that we are unable to explain, we would like to raise a million pounds sterling. One way to do this would be to raise the money in the United States of America. However, there is a problem with exchange rate fluctuations. At the time of writing, the exchange rate was £1.00 = $1.45, so we would need to raise $1,450,000 in the United States. If the exchange rate changes so that there is parity between the currencies, then we would have to raise only $1,000,000; and if it changes so that there are two US dollars for each pound sterling, then we would need to raise $2,000,000.

To place a bound on the amount of US dollars we need to raise, we place a bound on the exchange rate. In our lifetime, the pound has never exceeded \$2.40 in value. We can safely assume that, in the week in which we need to earn the money, £1.00 ≤ \$2.40. A suitable refinement of our plan, therefore, might involve raising \$2,400,000: we are then sure to achieve our target.

This particular form of refinement is called *data refinement*, in that we are changing the representation of data (money) from pounds to dollars. In the specification, any amount over £1,000,000 is acceptable; the implementation is stronger in insisting on over \$2,400,000. It may be that this implementation is infeasible, in that it requires too much. □

16.2 Relations and nondeterminism

We obtain a simple definition of refinement if we restrict our attention to total relations. If R and S are total relations, then R refines S exactly when $R \subseteq S$. Wherever S relates the same element x to two distinct elements y_1 and y_2, R may remove a degree of uncertainty by omitting either $x \mapsto y_1$ or $x \mapsto y_2$.

To decide if one *partial* relation refines another, we may consider their *totalised* versions. To do this, we augment the source and target of each relation with a distinguished element $\perp$, denoting undefinedness. We may then add a set of pairs to any partial relation ρ, associating any element outside the domain of ρ with every element of the augmented target.

If ρ is a partial relation between types X and Y, then we may totalise ρ by adding the following set of pairs:

$$\{x : X^{\perp};\ y : Y^{\perp} \mid x \notin \operatorname{dom} \rho \bullet x \mapsto y\}$$

where $X^{\perp}$ and $Y^{\perp}$ denote the augmented versions of the source and target.

For convenience, we will use the expression $\overline{s}$ to denote the complement of a set s in its type. For example, if s is a set of type $\mathbb{P}\,X$, then

$$\overline{s} = \{\, x : X \mid x \notin s \,\}$$

We will write $\overset{\bullet}{\rho}$ to denote the totalised form of ρ, where

$$\overset{\bullet}{\rho} \in X^{\perp} \leftrightarrow Y^{\perp}$$

and

$$\overset{\bullet}{\rho} = \rho \cup (\overline{\operatorname{dom} \rho}^{\perp} \times Y^{\perp})$$

The expression $\overset{\bullet}{\rho}$ can be pronounced 'ρ-dot'.

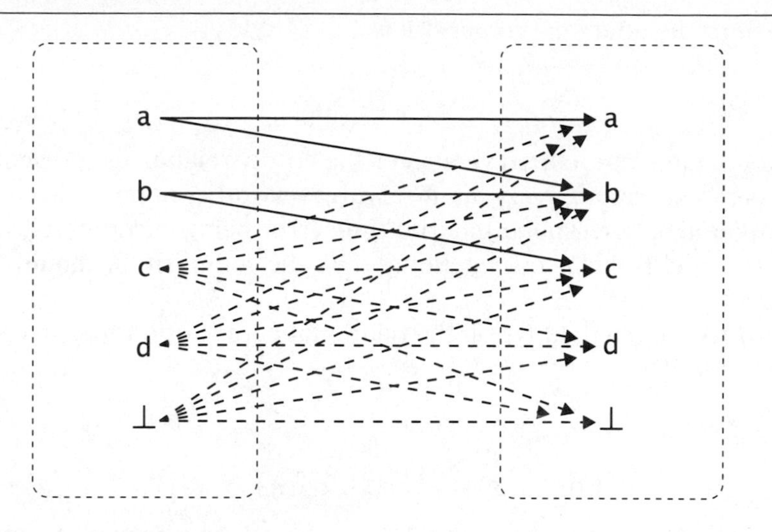

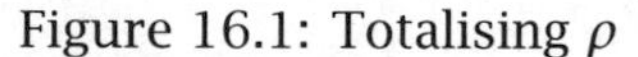
Figure 16.1: Totalising ρ

Example 16.4 If we define a free type L by

$$L ::= \mathsf{a} \mid \mathsf{b} \mid \mathsf{c} \mid \mathsf{d}$$

and a relation ρ by

$$\rho == \{\mathsf{a} \mapsto \mathsf{a}, \mathsf{a} \mapsto \mathsf{b}, \mathsf{b} \mapsto \mathsf{b}, \mathsf{b} \mapsto \mathsf{c}\}$$

then the totalised version of ρ is given by

$$\begin{aligned} \dot{\rho} == \{&\mathsf{a} \mapsto \mathsf{a}, \mathsf{a} \mapsto \mathsf{b}, \mathsf{b} \mapsto \mathsf{b}, \mathsf{b} \mapsto \mathsf{c}, \\ &\mathsf{c} \mapsto \bot, \mathsf{c} \mapsto \mathsf{a}, \mathsf{c} \mapsto \mathsf{b}, \mathsf{c} \mapsto \mathsf{c}, \mathsf{c} \mapsto \mathsf{d}, \\ &\mathsf{d} \mapsto \bot, \mathsf{d} \mapsto \mathsf{a}, \mathsf{d} \mapsto \mathsf{b}, \mathsf{d} \mapsto \mathsf{c}, \mathsf{d} \mapsto \mathsf{d}, \\ &\bot \mapsto \bot, \bot \mapsto \mathsf{a}, \bot \mapsto \mathsf{b}, \bot \mapsto \mathsf{c}, \bot \mapsto \mathsf{d}\} \end{aligned}$$

This extension is shown in Figure 16.1. □

Totalising relations in this way captures the view of operations that we have described in this book: an operation ρ behaves as specified when used within its precondition—its domain; outside its precondition, anything may happen. The role of $\bot$ is to ensure that undefinedness is propagated through relational composition. To see this, suppose that κ_0 denotes the constant function that maps every number to 0:

$$\kappa_0 == \{ z : \mathbb{Z} \bullet z \mapsto 0 \}$$

and consider the relational composition

$$\dot{\varnothing} \mathbin{⨟} \dot{\kappa}_0$$

The first component—a lifted version of the empty relation—represents undefinedness by associating every number with every other number: in computing terms, this might correspond to a run-time error being encountered whatever the initial value. If this is our intention, then the composition should have the same effect.

With the augmented types, the relational composition has precisely this interpretation:

$$\begin{aligned}
&\dot{\varnothing} \mathbin{⨟} \dot{\kappa}_0 \\
&\quad = (\varnothing \cup (\overline{\mathrm{dom}\,\varnothing}^{\perp} \times \mathbb{Z}^{\perp})) \mathbin{⨟} (\kappa_0 \cup (\overline{\mathrm{dom}\,\kappa_0}^{\perp} \times \mathbb{Z}^{\perp})) && \text{[dot]} \\
&\quad = (\overline{\varnothing}^{\perp} \times \mathbb{Z}^{\perp}) \mathbin{⨟} (\kappa_0 \cup (\overline{\mathbb{Z}}^{\perp} \times \mathbb{Z}^{\perp})) && \text{[properties of } \cup \text{ and dom]} \\
&\quad = (\mathbb{Z}^{\perp} \times \mathbb{Z}^{\perp}) \mathbin{⨟} (\kappa_0 \cup (\varnothing^{\perp} \times \mathbb{Z}^{\perp})) && \text{[properties of } \overline{}\text{]} \\
&\quad = ((\mathbb{Z}^{\perp} \times \mathbb{Z}^{\perp}) \mathbin{⨟} \kappa_0) \cup ((\mathbb{Z}^{\perp} \times \mathbb{Z}^{\perp}) \mathbin{⨟} (\{\perp\} \times \mathbb{Z}^{\perp})) && \text{[property of } \times\text{]} \\
&\quad = \kappa_0 \cup (\mathbb{Z}^{\perp} \times \mathbb{Z}^{\perp}) && \text{[properties of } \times\text{]} \\
&\quad = \mathbb{Z}^{\perp} \times \mathbb{Z}^{\perp} && \text{[property of } \cup\text{]}
\end{aligned}$$

Without the addition of an undefined element, we find that the composition recovers from the original undefinedness and behaves exactly as κ_0:

$$\begin{aligned}
&\dot{\varnothing} \mathbin{⨟} \dot{\kappa}_0 \\
&\quad = (\varnothing \cup (\overline{\mathrm{dom}\,\varnothing} \times \mathbb{Z})) \mathbin{⨟} (\kappa_0 \cup (\overline{\mathrm{dom}\,\kappa_0} \times \mathbb{Z})) && \text{[dot without } \perp\text{]} \\
&\quad = (\overline{\varnothing} \times \mathbb{Z}) \mathbin{⨟} (\kappa_0 \cup (\overline{\mathbb{Z}} \times \mathbb{Z})) && \text{[properties of } \cup \text{ and dom]} \\
&\quad = (\mathbb{Z} \times \mathbb{Z}) \mathbin{⨟} (\kappa_0 \cup (\varnothing \times \mathbb{Z})) && \text{[properties of } \overline{}\text{]} \\
&\quad = (\mathbb{Z} \times \mathbb{Z}) \mathbin{⨟} (\kappa_0 \cup \varnothing) && \text{[property of } \times\text{]} \\
&\quad = (\mathbb{Z} \times \mathbb{Z}) \mathbin{⨟} \kappa_0 && \text{[property of } \cup\text{]} \\
&\quad = \kappa_0 && \text{[property of } ⨟\text{]}
\end{aligned}$$

With our interpretation of operations, this is overly generous; it suggests that a run-time error can be avoided by adding a *subsequent* operation.

Having decided upon totalisation using $\perp$, we may derive the conditions for one partial relation to be a correct refinement of another. If σ and ρ are two partial relations of the same type, then σ refines ρ precisely when $\dot{\sigma}$ is a subset of $\dot{\rho}$. This is true if and only if the domain of σ is at least as big as that of ρ and σ agrees with ρ on $\mathrm{dom}\,\rho$.

The first of these conditions insists that σ is at least as defined as ρ, while the second insists that σ respects the information contained in ρ. Thus we may refine a relation by enlarging the domain, or by removing alternatives.

Example 16.5 If ρ is as defined in Example 16.4, and σ is defined by

$$\sigma == \{\mathsf{a} \mapsto \mathsf{a}, \mathsf{b} \mapsto \mathsf{b}, \mathsf{b} \mapsto \mathsf{c}, \mathsf{c} \mapsto \mathsf{c}\}$$

then σ is a refinement of ρ. It has both extended the domain and resolved some of the nondeterminism. That is,

$$\begin{aligned} \operatorname{dom} \sigma &= \{\mathsf{a}, \mathsf{b}, \mathsf{c}\} \\ &\supseteq \{\mathsf{a}, \mathsf{b}\} \\ &= \operatorname{dom} \rho \end{aligned}$$

and

$$\begin{aligned} \operatorname{dom} \rho \lhd \sigma &= \{\mathsf{a} \mapsto \mathsf{a}, \mathsf{b} \mapsto \mathsf{b}, \mathsf{b} \mapsto \mathsf{c},\} \\ &\subseteq \rho \end{aligned}$$

Equivalently, we might observe that $\overset{\bullet}{\sigma} \subseteq \overset{\bullet}{\rho}$, since

$$\begin{aligned} \overset{\bullet}{\sigma} = \{&\mathsf{a} \mapsto \mathsf{a}, \mathsf{b} \mapsto \mathsf{b}, \mathsf{b} \mapsto \mathsf{c}, \mathsf{c} \mapsto \mathsf{c}, \mathsf{d} \mapsto \bot, \mathsf{d} \mapsto \mathsf{a}, \mathsf{d} \mapsto \mathsf{b}, \mathsf{d} \mapsto \mathsf{c}, \mathsf{d} \mapsto \mathsf{d}, \\ &\bot \mapsto \bot, \bot \mapsto \mathsf{a}, \bot \mapsto \mathsf{b}, \bot \mapsto \mathsf{c}, \bot \mapsto \mathsf{d}\} \end{aligned}$$

and each of these pairs is present in $\overset{\bullet}{\rho}$. □

Example 16.6 If the relation τ is defined by

$$\tau == \{\mathsf{a} \mapsto \mathsf{a}, \mathsf{c} \mapsto \mathsf{c}\}$$

then τ is not a refinement of ρ, as

$$\operatorname{dom} \rho = \{\mathsf{a}, \mathsf{b}, \mathsf{c}\} \not\subseteq \{\mathsf{a}, \mathsf{c}\} = \operatorname{dom} \tau$$

We can remove pairs to reduce nondeterminism, but not at the expense of restricting the domain. □

Example 16.7 We may corrupt a bit—an element of the set $\{0, 1\}$—by changing its value:

$$\begin{array}{|l} \sim : Bit \rightarrow Bit \\ \hline \sim 0 = 1 \\ \sim 1 = 0 \end{array}$$

The relation *corruptsto* associates two sequences of bits if the second is no longer than the first, and no two adjacent bits have been corrupted:

$$\_corruptsto\_ : \text{seq}\,Bit \leftrightarrow \text{seq}\,Bit$$

$$\begin{array}{l}\forall\, bs, bs' : \text{seq}\,Bit \bullet \\ \quad bs \; corruptsto \; bs' \Leftrightarrow \\ \qquad \#bs' \leq \#bs \land \forall\, i : 1 \mathrel{..} \#bs' - 1 \bullet \\ \qquad\qquad bs\; i \neq bs'\; i \Rightarrow bs(i+1) = bs'(i+1)\end{array}$$

For example,

$$\langle 1,1,0,1,1,1,0,0 \rangle \; corruptsto \; \langle 0,1,0,0,1 \rangle$$

$$\langle 1,0,0,0,1,1 \rangle \; corruptsto \; \langle 1,0,1,0,0,1 \rangle$$

The relation *changesto* associates two sequences of bits if the second is no longer than the first and every bit with an odd index has been corrupted:

$$\_changesto\_ : \text{seq}\,Bit \leftrightarrow \text{seq}\,Bit$$

$$\begin{array}{l}\forall\, bs, bs' : \text{seq}\,Bit \bullet \\ \quad bs \; changesto \; bs' \Leftrightarrow \\ \qquad \#bs' \leq \#bs \land \forall\, i : 1 \mathrel{..} (\#bs' - 1) \bullet \\ \qquad\qquad i \in \{\, n : \mathbb{N}_1 \bullet 2 * n \,\} \Rightarrow bs\; i = bs'\; i \land \\ \qquad\qquad i \in \{\, n : \mathbb{N} \bullet 2 * n + 1 \,\} \Rightarrow bs\; i \neq bs'\; i\end{array}$$

For example,

$$\langle 1,1,0,1,1,1,0,0 \rangle \; changesto \; \langle 0,1,1,1,0 \rangle$$

$$\langle 1,0,0,0,1,1 \rangle \; changesto \; \langle 0,0,1,0,0,1 \rangle$$

In moving from *corruptsto* to *changesto*, we have traded the fact that in every output pair of bits, at least one is correct, for the fact that in every output pair of bits exactly one is correct.

The second relation is a refinement of the first: both are total relations on seq *Bit*, and *changesto* resolves all of the nondeterminism present in the definition of *corruptsto*. If we are content with the behaviour of *corruptsto*, then we will be content with that of *changesto*. Indeed, we may be more so, as every bit with an even index is guaranteed to be correct. □

16.3 Data types and data refinement

For our purposes, a data type comprises a space of values—or states—and an indexed collection of operations. Any use of the data type in a global state G must start with an *initialisation* and end with a matching *finalisation*. A data type $\mathcal{X}$ is thus a tuple $(X, xi, xf, \{ i : I \bullet xo_i \})$, where

- X is the space of values;
- $xi \in G \leftrightarrow X$ is an initialisation;
- $xf \in X \leftrightarrow G$ is a finalisation;
- $\{ i : I \bullet xo_i \}$ is an indexed collection of operations, such that $xo_i \in X \leftrightarrow X$

Both xi and xf are total, but each xo_i may be partial.

For our purposes, a *program* is a sequence of operations upon a data type. It may be seen as a relation between input and output, recorded by the initialisation and finalisation steps at the beginning and end of this sequence. For example, the sequence $di \fatsemi do_1 \fatsemi do_2 \fatsemi df$ is a program that uses the data type $\mathcal{D} = (D, di, df, \{do_1, do_2\})$.

The choice of data representation within the data type is not relevant to the overall behaviour of the program; it is encapsulated by initialisation and finalisation. Thus programs may be parameterised by data types: the above example could be written as $P(\mathcal{D})$, where

$$P(\mathcal{X}) \;=\; xi \fatsemi xo_1 \fatsemi xo_2 \fatsemi xf$$

and $\mathcal{X}$ is a variable data type with a suitable index set.

If two abstract data types $\mathcal{A}$ and $\mathcal{C}$ use the same index set for their operations, then they will support the same selection of programs: for every program $P(\mathcal{A})$, there must be a corresponding program $P(\mathcal{C})$. What is more, any two programs $P(\mathcal{A})$ and $P(\mathcal{C})$ will be comparable, since they have the same source and target sets.

We may find that the effect of $P(\mathcal{C})$ is defined whenever the effect of $P(\mathcal{A})$ is defined. We may find also that $P(\mathcal{C})$ resolves some of the nondeterminism present in $P(\mathcal{A})$. If this is the case for *every* choice of P, then it is reasonable to say that $\mathcal{C}$ is a refinement of $\mathcal{A}$.

As in our theory of refinement for relations, we will find it convenient to consider totalisations. An abstract data type $\mathcal{X}$ may be totalised by augmenting each component:

$$\dot{\mathcal{X}} \;=\; (X^{\perp}, \dot{xi}, \dot{xf}, \{ i : I \bullet \dot{xo}_i \})$$

Since xi and xf are total, the process of totalisation does nothing but augment each of them with the set of pairs $\{\bot\} \times X^{\bot}$.

We are now able to present a suitable definition of refinement for abstract data types. If data types $\mathcal{A}$ and C share the same indexing set, then $\mathcal{A}$ is refined by C if and only if for each program $P(\mathcal{A})$

$$P(\dot{C}) \subseteq P(\dot{\mathcal{A}})$$

If $\mathcal{A}$ and C are both indexed by the set I, then this definition requires us to prove that, for sequences $\langle s_1, s_2, \ldots s_n \rangle$ in $\operatorname{seq} I$,

$$\dot{ci} \fatsemi \dot{co}_{s_1} \fatsemi \dot{co}_{s_2} \fatsemi \cdots \fatsemi \dot{co}_{s_n} \fatsemi \dot{cf} \;\subseteq\; \dot{ai} \fatsemi \dot{ao}_{s_1} \fatsemi \dot{ao}_{s_2} \fatsemi \cdots \fatsemi \dot{ao}_{s_n} \fatsemi \dot{af}$$

In practice, this may be a difficult result to establish. In the next section, we will see how this requirement may be simplified by considering the relationship between abstract and concrete values.

Example 16.8 We may define two data types for handling sequences of bits, $\mathcal{A}$ and C. Each will accept a sequence of bits at initialisation, and deliver another sequence at finalisation. In each case, the state space is defined as a collection of tuples:

$$A == \operatorname{seq} Bit \times Action \times \operatorname{seq} Bit$$
$$C == \operatorname{seq} Bit \times Action \times \operatorname{seq} Bit$$

where Bit is the set containing just 0 and 1, and $Action$ is defined by

$$Action ::= \mathsf{yes} \mid \mathsf{no}$$

The first component of the state tuple represents the unconsumed part of the input sequence, the second indicates whether or not the next bit *must* be faithfully reproduced, and the third represents the accumulated output.

The initialisation and finalisation operations are the same for both data types. Initially, the whole of the input sequence waits to be consumed, the output sequence is empty, and the next bit may be corrupted.

$$\_ai\_ : \operatorname{seq} Bit \leftrightarrow A$$
$$\_ci\_ : \operatorname{seq} Bit \leftrightarrow C$$

$$\forall\, bs : \operatorname{seq} Bit;\; a : A;\; c : C \bullet$$
$$\quad bs\; ai\; a \Leftrightarrow a = (bs, \mathsf{no}, \langle\rangle)$$
$$\quad bs\; ci\; c \Leftrightarrow c = (bs, \mathsf{no}, \langle\rangle)$$

Finally, any remaining input is discarded, as is the action component. The accumulated output sequence is all that remains:

$$
\begin{array}{l}
\_af\_ : A \leftrightarrow \operatorname{seq} Bit \\
\_cf\_ : C \leftrightarrow \operatorname{seq} Bit \\
\hline
\forall bs : \operatorname{seq} Bit;\ a : A;\ c : C \bullet \\
\quad a \mathrel{af} bs \Leftrightarrow bs = a.3 \\
\quad c \mathrel{cf} bs \Leftrightarrow bs = c.3
\end{array}
$$

The effect of this operation is simply to project out the third component of the current state tuple.

Each data type has a single operation. That of $\mathcal{A}$ is nondeterministic: it may choose to act faithfully, appending the next input bit b to the output sequence. However, if the last bit was faithfully reproduced, it may choose to append the corrupted bit $\sim b$ instead.

$$
\begin{array}{l}
\_ao\_ : A \leftrightarrow A \\
\hline
\forall a, a' : A \bullet \\
\quad a \mathrel{ao} a' \Leftrightarrow a'.1 = \operatorname{tail} a.1 \\
\qquad\qquad a.2 = \mathsf{yes} \Rightarrow \\
\qquad\qquad\quad a'.3 = a.3 \frown \langle head\ a.1 \rangle \wedge a'.2 = \mathsf{no} \\
\qquad\qquad a.2 = \mathsf{no} \Rightarrow \\
\qquad\qquad\quad a'.3 = a.3 \frown \langle \sim head\ a.1 \rangle \wedge a'.2 = \mathsf{yes} \\
\qquad\qquad\quad \vee \\
\qquad\qquad\quad a'.3 = a.3 \frown \langle head\ a.1 \rangle \wedge a'.2 = \mathsf{no}
\end{array}
$$

Whenever a bit is corrupted, the action component of the next state is set to yes, indicating that the next bit must be appended faithfully.

In contrast, the operation of C is completely deterministic. It alternates between corruption and fidelity, changing the value of the action component each time it is applied. This has the effect of removing the disjunction from the above definition, leaving the state after fully determined by the state before.

$$
\begin{array}{l}
\_co\_ : C \leftrightarrow C \\
\hline
\forall c, c' : C \bullet \\
\quad c \mathrel{co} c' \Leftrightarrow c'.1 = \operatorname{tail} c.1 \\
\qquad\qquad c.2 = \mathsf{yes} \Rightarrow \\
\qquad\qquad\quad c'.3 = c.3 \frown \langle head\ c.1 \rangle \wedge c'.2 = \mathsf{no} \\
\qquad\qquad c.2 = \mathsf{no} \Rightarrow \\
\qquad\qquad\quad c'.3 = c.3 \frown \langle \sim head\ c.1 \rangle \wedge c'.2 = \mathsf{yes}
\end{array}
$$

The relationship between $\mathcal{A}$ and C is the same as that between *corruptsto* and *changesto* in Example 16.7. That is, C is a refinement of $\mathcal{A}$. To prove this, we must show that

$$ci \mathbin{⨾} cf \subseteq ai \mathbin{⨾} af$$

$$ci \mathbin{⨾} co \mathbin{⨾} cf \subseteq ai \mathbin{⨾} ao \mathbin{⨾} af$$

$$ci \mathbin{⨾} co \mathbin{⨾} co \mathbin{⨾} cf \subseteq ai \mathbin{⨾} ao \mathbin{⨾} ao \mathbin{⨾} af$$

$$\vdots$$

It is easy to show that this reduces to the requirement that $co \subseteq ao$. The result then follows from the definitions of the two operations. □

16.4 Simulations

We obtain a simpler characterisation of refinement if we consider the values produced at each step of a program's execution. If data types $\mathcal{A}$ and C share the same indexing set, then the programs $P(\mathcal{A})$ and $P(C)$ will have the same number of steps: one for each operation involved. We may therefore compare the two programs on a step-by-step basis.

To do this, we must describe the relationship between the representation of data in $\mathcal{A}$ and that in C. We define a relation between the two sets of states: an element of either $A \leftrightarrow C$ or $C \leftrightarrow A$. If ρ is a relation of type $A \leftrightarrow C$, then we may ask the following questions:

- Is ci a subset of $ai \mathbin{⨾} \rho$? That is, can any initialisation of C be matched by taking an initialisation of $\mathcal{A}$ and following it with ρ?
- Is $\rho \mathbin{⨾} cf$ a subset of af? That is, can any finalisation of C be matched by preceding it with ρ and comparing it with a finalisation of $\mathcal{A}$?
- Is $\rho \mathbin{⨾} co_i$ a subset of $ao_i \mathbin{⨾} \rho$, for each index i? That is, can any operation in C be matched by the corresponding operation in $\mathcal{A}$?

If the answer to each question is *yes*, then we say that ρ is a *simulation* for the two data types. The effect of any program step in C can be simulated by a step in $\mathcal{A}$. Therefore, for any program P,

$$P(C) \subseteq P(\mathcal{A})$$

and we are safe to conclude that C is a refinement of $\mathcal{A}$.

To ensure that this definition is applicable to data types with partial operations, we require that the relations and state spaces are augmented to allow

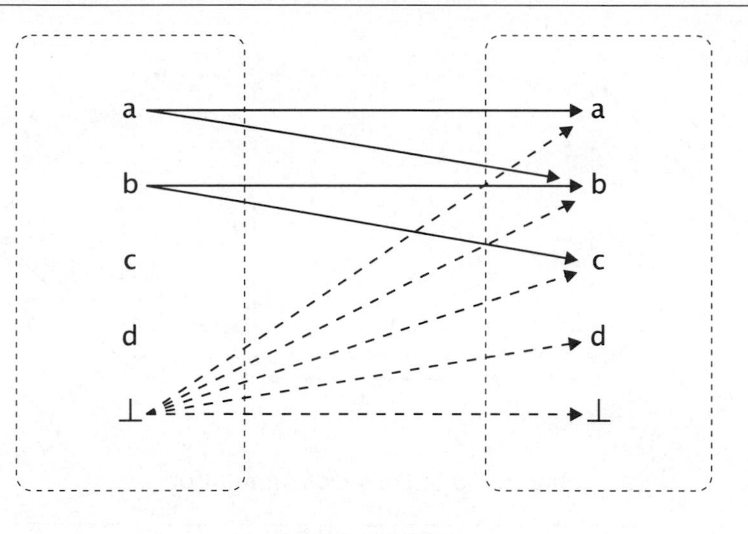

Figure 16.2: Lifting ρ

for undefinedness. It is not necessary to totalise the relation ρ, but it is necessary to propagate undefinedness. We add $\perp$ to its domain and associate it with every element of the target type. If ρ is a relation of type $X \leftrightarrow Y$, then

$$\mathring{\rho} \in X^{\perp} \leftrightarrow Y^{\perp}$$
$$\mathring{\rho} = \rho \cup (\{\perp\} \times Y^{\perp})$$

We say that $\mathring{\rho}$ is the *lifted* form of ρ.

Example 16.9 If we define a free type L by

$$L ::= \mathsf{a} \mid \mathsf{b} \mid \mathsf{c} \mid \mathsf{d}$$

and a relation ρ by

$$\rho == \{\mathsf{a} \mapsto \mathsf{a}, \mathsf{a} \mapsto \mathsf{b}, \mathsf{b} \mapsto \mathsf{b}, \mathsf{b} \mapsto \mathsf{c}\}$$

then the lifted version of ρ is given by

$$\mathring{\rho} == \{\mathsf{a} \mapsto \mathsf{a}, \mathsf{a} \mapsto \mathsf{b}, \mathsf{b} \mapsto \mathsf{b}, \mathsf{b} \mapsto \mathsf{c}, \\ \perp \mapsto \perp, \perp \mapsto \mathsf{a}, \perp \mapsto \mathsf{b}, \perp \mapsto \mathsf{c}, \perp \mapsto \mathsf{d}\}$$

This extension is shown in Figure 16.2. □

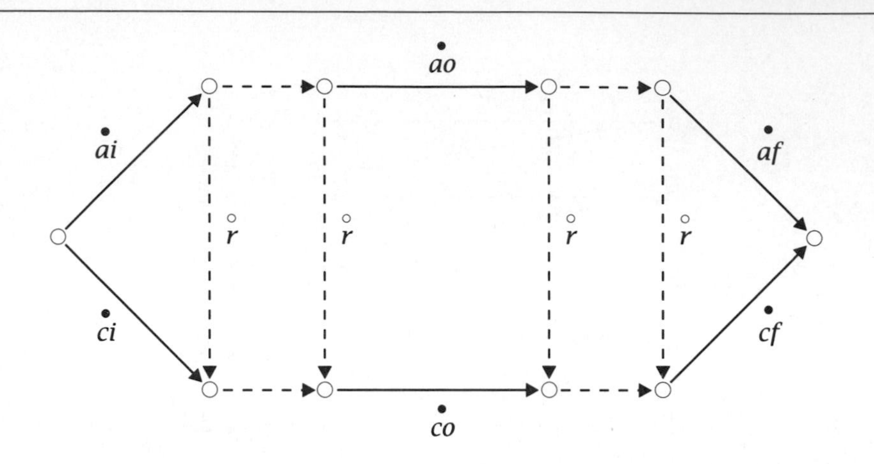

Figure 16.3: Forwards simulation

If data types $\mathcal{A}$ and C share the same indexing set, and r is a relation of type $A \leftrightarrow C$, then r is a *forwards simulation* if

- $\overset{\bullet}{ci} \subseteq \overset{\bullet}{ai} \fatsemi \overset{\circ}{r}$
- $\overset{\circ}{r} \fatsemi \overset{\bullet}{cf} \subseteq \overset{\bullet}{af}$
- $\overset{\circ}{r} \fatsemi \overset{\bullet}{co}_i \subseteq \overset{\bullet}{ao}_i \fatsemi \overset{\circ}{r}$ for each index i

These requirements are illustrated in Figure 16.3. The first insists that the effect of *ci* can be matched by *ai* followed by r, a two-step path around the diagram; the second that the effect of r followed by *cf*, another two-step path, can be matched by *af*; the third that the effect of moving downwards and then across can be matched by moving across and then downwards.

The lower path in the diagram corresponds to a program using data type C. The upper path corresponds to the same program using data type $\mathcal{A}$. Since the effect of each program step can be simulated, it is easy to see that C is a refinement of $\mathcal{A}$.

Valid moves in the concrete data type may be simulated by moves in the abstract data type. The relation r is said to be a *forwards* simulation because, if we consider similar concrete and abstract states, then any valid move forwards to a new concrete state can be matched by a move to a similar abstract state. Since r relates abstract values down to concrete ones—see Figure 16.3—such a relation is sometimes called a *downwards* simulation.

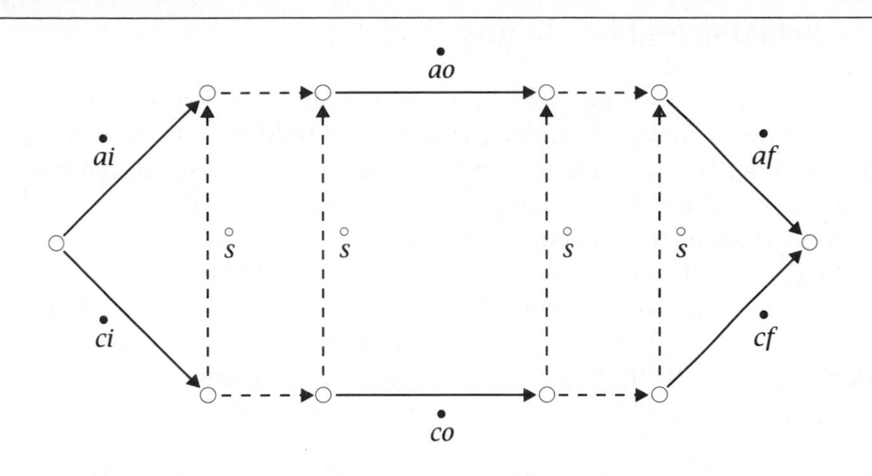

Figure 16.4: Backwards simulation

If data types $\mathcal{A}$ and C share the same indexing set, and s is a relation of type $C \leftrightarrow A$ concrete and abstract states, then s is a *backwards simulation* if

- $\overset{\bullet}{ci} \mathbin{;} \overset{\circ}{s} \subseteq \overset{\bullet}{ai}$
- $\overset{\bullet}{cf} \subseteq \overset{\circ}{s} \mathbin{;} \overset{\bullet}{af}$
- $\overset{\bullet}{co}_i \mathbin{;} \overset{\circ}{s} \subseteq \overset{\circ}{s} \mathbin{;} \overset{\bullet}{ao}_i$ for each index i

The requirements are similar to those for a forwards simulation, except that the position of the simulation is reversed. The first insists that the effect of *ci* followed by s can be matched by *ai*; the second that the effect of *cf* can be matched by s followed by *af*; the third that the effect of moving across and then upwards can be matched by moving upwards and then across.

As before, the lower path in the diagram—Figure 16.4—corresponds to a program using data type C, and the upper path corresponds to the same program using data type $\mathcal{A}$. We have that C is a refinement of $\mathcal{A}$.

Again, valid moves in the concrete data type may be simulated by moves in the abstract data type. The relation r is said to be a *backwards* simulation because, if we consider similar concrete and abstract states, then any valid move to this concrete state from an old concrete state can be matched by a move from a similar abstract state. Since r relates concrete values up to abstract ones—see Figure 16.4—such a relation is sometimes called an *upwards* simulation.

16.5 Relaxing and unwinding

The definitions of forwards and backwards simulation presented above are given in terms of totalised operations and lifted relations. By considering domain and range restrictions, we can obtain an equivalent set of requirements that mention neither totalisation nor lifting. These requirements constitute a more *relaxed* set of rules for data refinement.

We begin with the requirements for forward simulation. Our first *relaxation* uses the fact that, for a total relation ρ, the totalised and lifted forms are identical; there is nothing outside the domain of ρ, so each extension adds the product of $\{\bot\}$ with the target type. Because initialisation is always total, we can argue as follows:

$$\dot{ci} \subseteq \dot{ai} \mathbin{⨾} \mathring{r}$$

$$\Leftrightarrow \mathring{ci} \subseteq \mathring{ai} \mathbin{⨾} \mathring{r} \qquad [ai \text{ and } ci \text{ are both total}]$$

$$\Leftrightarrow ci \subseteq \mathring{ai} \mathbin{⨾} \mathring{r} \ \land\ \{\bot\} \times C^{\bot} \subseteq \mathring{ai} \mathbin{⨾} \mathring{r} \qquad [\text{property of subset}]$$

$$\Leftrightarrow ci \subseteq ai \mathbin{⨾} r \ \land\ \{\bot\} \times C^{\bot} \subseteq \mathring{ai} \mathbin{⨾} \mathring{r} \qquad [\bot \notin \operatorname{dom} ci]$$

$$\Leftrightarrow ci \subseteq ai \mathbin{⨾} r \ \land\ \{\bot\} \times C^{\bot} \subseteq \mathring{ai} \mathbin{⨾} (r \cup \{\bot\} \times C^{\bot}) \qquad [\text{lifting}]$$

$$\Leftrightarrow ci \subseteq ai \mathbin{⨾} r \qquad [\bot \in \operatorname{ran} \mathring{ai}]$$

A similar argument shows that the requirement upon the two finalisation operations can be relaxed to

$$r \mathbin{⨾} cf \ \subseteq\ af$$

In each case, the 'dot' of totalisation and the 'spot' of lifting can be safely removed from the defining condition.

To obtain a suitable relaxation of the third requirement, we consider the following result: if ρ, σ, and τ of relations of type $X \leftrightarrow Z$, $X \leftrightarrow Y$, and $Y \leftrightarrow Z$, respectively, then

$$\rho \subseteq \dot{\sigma} \mathbin{⨾} \mathring{\tau} \ \Leftrightarrow\ (\operatorname{dom} \sigma) \lhd \rho \subseteq \sigma \mathbin{⨾} \tau$$

This may be proved as follows:

$$\rho \subseteq \dot{\sigma} \mathbin{⨾} \mathring{\tau}$$

$$\Leftrightarrow \rho \subseteq (\sigma \cup (\overline{\operatorname{dom} \sigma}^{\bot} \times Y^{\bot})) \mathbin{⨾} \mathring{\tau} \qquad [\text{totalisation}]$$

$$\Leftrightarrow \rho \subseteq (\sigma \mathbin{⨾} \mathring{\tau}) \cup ((\overline{\operatorname{dom} \sigma}^{\bot} \times Y^{\bot}) \mathbin{⨾} \mathring{\tau}) \qquad [\text{distribution}]$$

$$\Leftrightarrow \rho \subseteq (\sigma \mathbin{⨾} \tau) \cup ((\overline{\operatorname{dom}\sigma}^{\perp} \times Y^{\perp}) \mathbin{⨾} \mathring{\tau}) \qquad [\perp \notin \operatorname{ran}\sigma]$$

$$\Leftrightarrow \rho \subseteq (\sigma \mathbin{⨾} \tau) \cup (\overline{\operatorname{dom}\sigma}^{\perp} \times Y^{\perp}) \mathbin{⨾} (\tau \cup \{\perp\} \times Z^{\perp}) \qquad [\text{lifting}]$$

$$\Leftrightarrow \rho \subseteq (\sigma \mathbin{⨾} \tau) \cup (\overline{\operatorname{dom}\sigma}^{\perp} \times Z^{\perp}) \qquad [\text{property of } ⨾]$$

$$\Leftrightarrow (\operatorname{dom}\sigma) \lhd \rho \subseteq \sigma \mathbin{⨾} \tau \qquad [\text{property of relations}]$$

We will call this result 'spot-dot elimination'. Returning to the third requirement for simulation, we proceed as follows:

$$\mathring{r} \mathbin{⨾} \dot{co} \subseteq \dot{ao} \mathbin{⨾} \mathring{r}$$

$$\Leftrightarrow \operatorname{dom} ao \lhd (\mathring{r} \mathbin{⨾} \dot{co}) \subseteq ao \mathbin{⨾} r \qquad [\text{spot-dot elimination}]$$

$$\Leftrightarrow (\operatorname{dom} ao \lhd \mathring{r}) \mathbin{⨾} \dot{co} \subseteq ao \mathbin{⨾} r \qquad [\text{property of } \lhd \text{ and } ⨾]$$

$$\Leftrightarrow (\operatorname{dom} ao \lhd r) \mathbin{⨾} \dot{co} \subseteq ao \mathbin{⨾} r \qquad [\perp \notin \operatorname{dom} ao]$$

$$\Leftrightarrow (\operatorname{dom} ao \lhd r) \mathbin{⨾} (co \cup \overline{\operatorname{dom} co}^{\perp} \times C^{\perp}) \subseteq ao \mathbin{⨾} r \qquad [\text{totalisation}]$$

$$\Leftrightarrow (\operatorname{dom} ao \lhd r) \mathbin{⨾} co \subseteq ao \mathbin{⨾} r \qquad [\text{property of } \subseteq]$$

$$\land$$

$$(\operatorname{dom} ao \lhd r) \mathbin{⨾} (\overline{\operatorname{dom} co}^{\perp} \times C^{\perp}) \subseteq ao \mathbin{⨾} r$$

The first conjunct insists that the effect of *co* is consistent with that of *ao*, wherever *ao* is defined. The second conjunct requires further investigation: since $\perp$ is outside the range of $ao \mathbin{⨾} r$, it is equivalent to the condition that

$$\operatorname{ran}(\operatorname{dom} ao \lhd r) \subseteq \operatorname{dom} co$$

Informally, this requires that the operation *co* is defined for every value that can be reached from the domain of *ao* using relation *r*.

We may also derive a set of relaxed requirements for proving backwards simulation. The requirements upon initialisation and finalisation lose their spots and dots,

$$ci \mathbin{⨾} s \subseteq ai$$

$$cf \subseteq s \mathbin{⨾} af$$

and the third requirement becomes

$$\operatorname{dom}(s \rhd (\operatorname{dom} ao)) \ntriangleleft co \mathbin{⨾} s \subseteq s \mathbin{⨾} ao \quad \land \quad \overline{\operatorname{dom} co} \subseteq \operatorname{dom}(s \rhd (\operatorname{dom} ao))$$

The first conjunct insists that the effect of *co* must be consistent with that of *ao*. The second insists—somewhat awkwardly—that the set of values for which *co* is not defined must be a subset of those for which *ao* is not defined.

F-init-rel-seq	$ci \subseteq ai \mathbin{⨾} r$
F-fin-rel-seq	$r \mathbin{⨾} cf \subseteq af$
F-corr-rel-seq	$(\operatorname{dom} ao) \lhd r \mathbin{⨾} co \subseteq ao \mathbin{⨾} r$ $\operatorname{ran}((\operatorname{dom} ao) \lhd r) \subseteq \operatorname{dom} co$
B-init-rel-seq	$ci \mathbin{⨾} s \subseteq ai$
B-fin-rel-seq	$cf \subseteq s \mathbin{⨾} af$
B-corr-rel-seq	$\operatorname{dom}(s \rhd (\operatorname{dom} ao)) \ntriangleleft co \mathbin{⨾} s \subseteq s \mathbin{⨾} ao$ $\overline{\operatorname{dom} co} \subseteq \operatorname{dom}(s \rhd (\operatorname{dom} ao))$

Table 16.1: Relaxed rules for simulations

These results yield a collection of relaxed proof rules for simulations, collected in Table 16.1. The rules are named according to the type of simulation—F for forwards, B for backwards—and the type of rule: init for initialisation; fin for finalisation; corr for correctness of operations. We add an additional qualifier rel to indicate that we are working within a theory of relations.

These rules may be applied to operations involving input and output only by providing all inputs at initialisation, and delaying all outputs until finalisation. The initial state of a program would include a sequence of inputs—the input values required during execution—and the final state a sequence of outputs. Each rule in Table 16.1 is labelled with the suffix seq to indicate that input and output must be represented in this way.

It is possible to derive an equivalent set of rules in which inputs and outputs may occur at each program step. Suppose that *op* is an operation that involves input and output: a relation of type

$$(State \times Input) \leftrightarrow (State \times Output)$$

In this case, there exists a corresponding operation op_s of type

$$State \times (\operatorname{seq} Input \times \operatorname{seq} Output) \leftrightarrow State \times (\operatorname{seq} Input \times \operatorname{seq} Output)$$

that behaves as follows: the effect of op_s upon the state is that of *op*, given the head of the first sequence as input. Any output from *op* is added to the end of the second sequence. That is,

$$\begin{array}{l} \forall s, s' : State;\ is, is' : \text{seq}\, Input;\ os, os' : \text{seq}\, Output \bullet \\ \quad \forall i : Input;\ o : Output \mid (s, i)\ op\ (s', o) \bullet \\ \qquad (s, (\langle i \rangle \frown is, os))\ op_s\ (s', (is, os \frown \langle o \rangle)) \end{array}$$

In our use of op_s, we may regard the input and output sequences as part of the state information.

To obtain op_s from *op*, we must extract the next value from the input sequence. We define a function that takes a state and a pair of sequences and returns a state, an input, and a new pair of sequences:

$$\begin{array}{l} [State, Input, Output] \\ \hline split : State \times (\text{seq}\, Input \times \text{seq}\, Output) \leftrightarrow \\ \qquad (State \times Input) \times (\text{seq}\, Input \times \text{seq}\, Output) \\ \hline \forall s : State;\ is : \text{seq}\, Input;\ os : \text{seq}\, Output \bullet \\ \quad split(s, (is, os)) = ((s, head\ is), (tail\ is, os)) \end{array}$$

When we apply *split*, the first input is selected, and the results are assembled in a useful combination. The state and next input are presented as a pair, ready for consumption by an operation.

To simplify the process of reasoning about *split*, we derive an equivalent definition that avoids mentioning the arguments of the function. This will require three new operators for manipulating pairs and sequences. The first is a form of parallel composition:

$$\begin{array}{l} [W, X, Y, Z] \\ \hline \_ \parallel \_ : (W \leftrightarrow Y) \times (X \leftrightarrow Z) \to W \times X \leftrightarrow Y \times Z \\ \hline \forall \rho : W \leftrightarrow Y;\ \sigma : X \leftrightarrow Z;\ w : W;\ x : X;\ y : Y;\ z : Z \bullet \\ \quad (w, x) \mapsto (y, z) \in \rho \parallel \sigma \Leftrightarrow w \mapsto y \in \rho \land x \mapsto z \in \sigma \end{array}$$

This allows us to relate a pair of arguments to a pair of results, applying two operations separately and simultaneously.

The second is an operator which duplicates its input:

$$\begin{array}{l} [X] \\ \hline cp : X \rightarrowtail X \times X \\ \hline \forall x : X \bullet cp\, x = (x, x) \end{array}$$

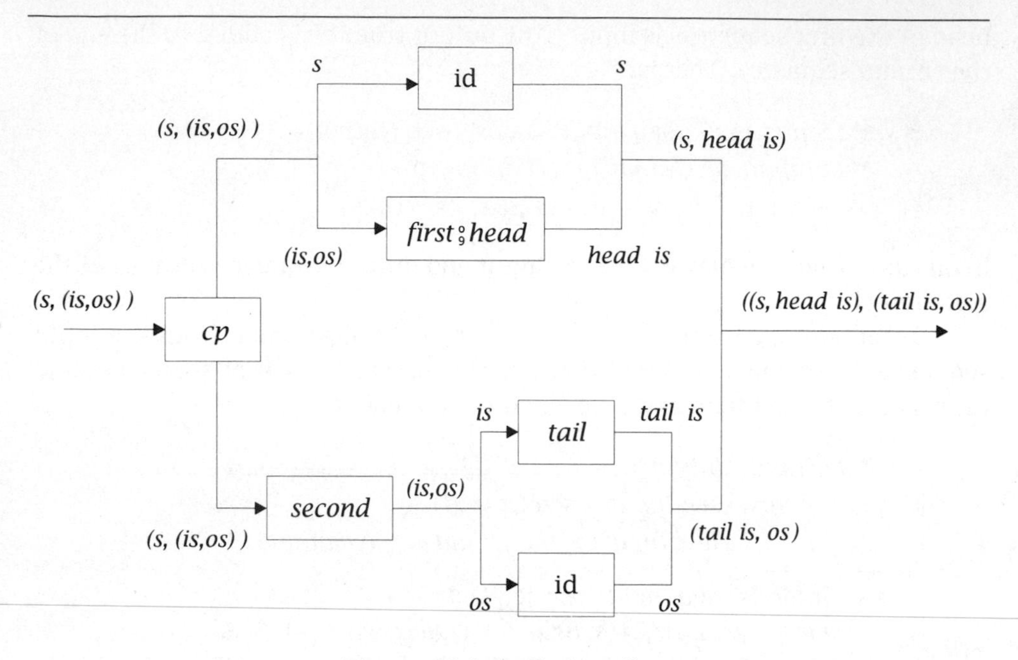

Figure 16.5: *split* data flow

The third operator takes a value-sequence pair and appends the value to the end of the sequence:

$$[X]$$
$$ap : X \times \mathrm{seq}\, X \rightarrowtail \mathrm{seq}\, X$$
$$\forall\, x : X;\ xs : \mathrm{seq}\, X \bullet ap(x, xs) = xs \frown \langle x \rangle$$

Using these combinators, we can define *split* as:

$$split \;=\; cp \fatsemi \; \begin{array}{c} \mathrm{id} \parallel (first \fatsemi head) \\ \parallel \\ second \fatsemi (tail \parallel \mathrm{id}) \end{array}$$

This definition may be explained in terms of data flow, as in the diagram of Figure 16.5. The first operator, *cp*, makes two copies of the input pair. One copy is fed into the parallel combination of 'id' and *first* ⨾ *head*, yielding the first component of the output. The other copy is fed through *second* into the parallel combination of *tail* and 'id', yielding the second component of the output.

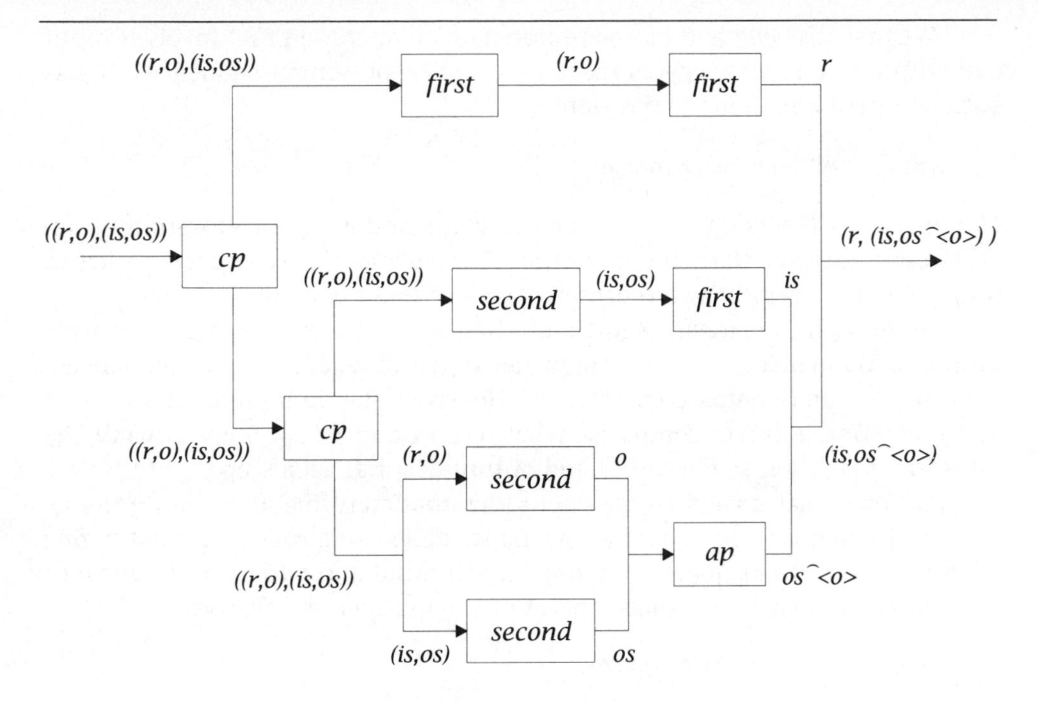

Figure 16.6: *merge* data flow

We will also need a function that adds to the sequence of outputs:

$$[State, Input, Output]$$

$$\begin{array}{l} merge : (State \times Output) \times (\text{seq}\, Input \times \text{seq}\, Output) \rightarrowtail \\ \qquad\qquad State \times (\text{seq}\, Input \times \text{seq}\, Output) \end{array}$$

$$\begin{array}{l} \forall\, s : State;\ o : Output;\ is : \text{seq}\, Input;\ os : \text{seq}\, Output \bullet \\ \quad merge((s, o), (is, os)) = (s, (is, os \frown \langle o \rangle)) \end{array}$$

To simplify the process of reasoning, we observe that

$$\begin{array}{lll} merge & = & cp \,\S\, first \,\S\, first \\ & & \quad \| \\ & & cp \,\S\, second \,\S\, first \\ & & \qquad \| \\ & & \qquad (second \parallel second) \,\S\, ap \end{array}$$

A data flow diagram for this construction is given in Figure 16.6.

We may use *split* and *merge* to translate an operation that involves input and output to one that expects these values to be present as sequences. If ρ is such an operation, then we may define

$$\rho_s = split \mathbin{⨾} (\rho \parallel \mathrm{id}) \mathbin{⨾} merge$$

The operation ρ acts on a pair—a before state, and an input—to produce another pair—an after state, and an output. The *split* and *merge* operators act as translators between the two representations of input and output.

If we wish to compare ρ with another operation σ, in order to verify a proposed refinement, then we might decide to translate σ to a 'sequenced' operation σ_s and compare σ_s with ρ_s. However, the definitions of *split* and *merge* support a direct comparison between ρ and σ: we may *unwind* the rules for simulation so that input and output occur at each step.

Suppose that *ao* and *co* are operations that consume input and produce output. To compare these operations using the existing rules, we must define equivalent operations ao_s and co_s that expect input and output in the form of sequences. We may define these operations using *split* and *merge*:

$$ao_s = split \mathbin{⨾} (ao \parallel \mathrm{id}) \mathbin{⨾} merge$$
$$co_s = split \mathbin{⨾} (co \parallel \mathrm{id}) \mathbin{⨾} merge$$

where 'id' is the identity relation on pairs of input and output sequences.

Furthermore, since r is a relation between states without input and output sequences, we must construct an equivalent relation that acts on the enhanced form of the state. If r is a relation of type

$$AState \leftrightarrow CState$$

then we require a relation r_s of type

$$AState \times (\mathrm{seq}\, Input \times \mathrm{seq}\, Output) \leftrightarrow CState \times (\mathrm{seq}\, Input \times \mathrm{seq}\, Output)$$

in order to compare ao_s and co_s.

For our comparison to make sense, the two operations must have the same type of input and output values. The relation r_s between enhanced states is then defined by

$$r_s = r \parallel \mathrm{id}$$

The rules for the correctness of a forwards simulation—given in Table 16.1—require that

$$(\mathrm{dom}\, ao_s) \lhd r_s \mathbin{⨾} co_s \subseteq ao_s \mathbin{⨾} r_s$$

F-init-rel	$ci \subseteq ai \fatsemi r$
F-corr-rel	$(\mathrm{dom}\, ao) \lhd (r \parallel \mathrm{id}) \fatsemi co \subseteq ao \fatsemi (r \parallel \mathrm{id})$
	$\mathrm{ran}((\mathrm{dom}\, ao) \lhd (r \parallel \mathrm{id})) \subseteq \mathrm{dom}\, co$
B-init-rel	$ci \fatsemi s \subseteq ai$
B-corr-rel	$\mathrm{dom}((s \parallel \mathrm{id}) \rhd (\mathrm{dom}\, ao)) \ntriangleleft co \fatsemi (s \parallel \mathrm{id}) \subseteq (s \parallel \mathrm{id}) \fatsemi ao$
	$\overline{\mathrm{dom}\, co} \subseteq \mathrm{dom}(s \rhd (\mathrm{dom}\, ao))$

Table 16.2: Unwound rules for simulations

The operations co_s and ao_s have the same effect upon the two sequences: they remove a value from one and append a value to the other. The relation r_s has no effect upon the sequences, so this requirement is equivalent to

$$(\mathrm{dom}\, ao) \lhd (r \parallel \mathrm{id}[Input]) \fatsemi co \ \subseteq\ ao \fatsemi (r \parallel \mathrm{id}[Output])$$

Where *ao* is defined, the effect of applying *co* can be matched by applying *ao* and then moving from one state space to the other.

The other condition—that co_s is defined everywhere that ao_s is defined—leads to a second constraint:

$$\mathrm{ran}((\mathrm{dom}\, ao) \lhd (r \parallel \mathrm{id}[Output])) \ \subseteq\ \mathrm{dom}\, co$$

The presence of the identity relation reflects the fact that output is no longer treated as part of the state.

A set of unwound rules for forwards and backwards simulation is presented in Table 16.2. Finalisation is no longer a special case—any program step may produce output—so there are only two rules for each form of simulation. Because these rules may be applied directly, without regarding input and output as special components of the state, we drop the suffix seq from the name of each rule.

Chapter 17

Data Refinement and Schemas

In the previous chapter we presented a theory of data refinement for partial and total relations. In this chapter we see how this theory may be extended to cover specifications written in the schema notation. In essence, each operation schema corresponds to a relation on states. Such an operation is correctly refined if and only if that relation is refined, in the sense already understood. Accordingly, our existing refinements rules can be restated in terms of schemas.

17.1 Relations and schema operations

An operation schema defines an operation upon the state of a system. It does this by describing how the state after the operation is related to the state before. The *meaning* of an operation schema, for our purposes, is thus a relation upon states. This relation need not be total: if the precondition of the schema is not *true*, then there will be states outside the domain.

Where the precondition is not satisfied, the result of the operation is left undefined: anything may happen. For example, an operation that takes the reciprocal of a real number r is specified by the following operation schema:

$$Recip \mathrel{\widehat=} [\, \Delta S \mid r \neq 0 \land r' = 1/r \,]$$

where $S \mathrel{\widehat=} [\, r : \mathbb{R} \,]$. This is a partial operation: when r is zero, it may fail to terminate, and if it does, then the value of r' may be any real number. Ignoring the question of input and output for the moment, the relation corresponding to *Recip* is the totalisation—in the sense of the previous chapter—of the relation:

$$\{\, Recip \bullet \theta S \mapsto \theta S' \,\}$$

If we totalise this, and then simplify the resulting expression, then we get to the true specification of *Recip* ('true' in the sense that it describes all the behaviour of *Recip*, including what happens outside the precondition):

$$\overset{\bullet}{\overbrace{\{\, r, r' : \mathbb{R} \mid r \neq 0 \land r' = 1/r \bullet \theta S \mapsto \theta S' \,\}}}$$

which is the relation:

$$\{\, r, r' : \mathbb{R}^{\perp} \mid r \neq 0 \land r \neq \perp \land r' = 1/r \lor r = 0 \lor r = \perp \bullet \theta S \mapsto \theta S' \,\}$$

This relates any state in which r is strictly positive to one in which it has the reciprocal value. A state in which r is zero, or is undefined, is related to all possible states.

An operation schema may also include input and output components. To represent these, the domain of the corresponding relation will be a Cartesian product of states and inputs, and the range will be a product of states and outputs. If *Op* describes an operation on a state S, then the corresponding relation will be a lifted, totalised version of

$$\{\, Op \bullet (\theta S, i?) \mapsto (\theta S', o!) \,\}$$

That is,

$$\overset{\bullet}{\overbrace{split \operatorname{⨾} (\{\, Op \bullet (\theta S, i?) \mapsto (\theta S', o!) \,\} \parallel \mathrm{id}) \operatorname{⨾} merge}}$$

Using this correspondence, we may translate between the language of schemas and the language of relations. A schema specification S is really a relaxed and unwound relational specification on a data type $\mathcal{D}$.

Suppose now that data types $\mathcal{A}$ and C are described using schemas, the two state schemas being A and C respectively. A proposed simulation between the two data types can itself be expressed as a schema:

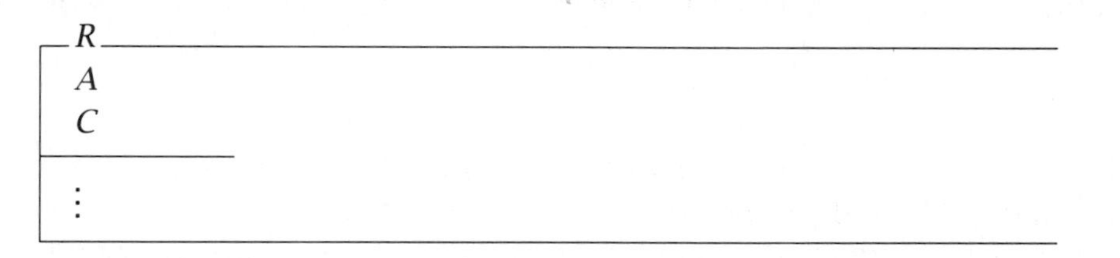

The relationship that this schema records is called a *retrieve* relation: it shows how the representation of data in $\mathcal{A}$—which may be more abstract—can be retrieved from the representation of data in C.

To decide whether or not R is a simulation, we will need to compare operations with the same index; let us consider two such operations, AO and CO, each with a single input $i?$ and a single output $o!$. We will also need to examine the initialisations of $\mathcal{A}$ and C; let us suppose that these are described by schemas AI and CI, respectively.

17.2 Forwards simulation

To apply the existing rules for forwards simulation, we consider the relations that correspond to the retrieve and operation schemas:

$$\begin{aligned} r &= \{ R \bullet \theta A \mapsto \theta C \} \\ ao &= \{ AO \bullet (\theta A, i?) \mapsto (\theta A', o!) \} \\ co &= \{ CO \bullet (\theta C, i?) \mapsto (\theta C', o!) \} \end{aligned}$$

We consider also the sets of states produced at initialisation:

$$\begin{aligned} ai &= \{ AI \bullet \theta A' \} \\ ci &= \{ CI \bullet \theta C' \} \end{aligned}$$

To simplify the process of reasoning about ai and ci, we will regard each as a trivial form of relation, in which the first component of each pair is ignored.

The unwound rules for forwards simulation, presented towards the end of the last chapter, insist that the following condition must hold for the two initialisations:

$$ci \subseteq ai \mathbin{⨾} r$$

We may express this condition in terms of schemas:

$$\begin{aligned} & ci \subseteq ai \mathbin{⨾} r \\ & \quad \Leftrightarrow \forall c : C \bullet c \in ci \Rightarrow c \in ai \mathbin{⨾} r && \text{[by property of } \subseteq] \\ & \quad \Leftrightarrow \forall C \bullet \theta C \in ci \Rightarrow \theta C \in ai \mathbin{⨾} r && \text{[by schema calculus]} \\ & \quad \Leftrightarrow \forall C \bullet \theta C \in ci \Rightarrow && \text{[by property of } ⨾] \\ & \qquad\qquad \exists A \bullet \theta A \in ai \land \theta A \mapsto \theta C \in r \\ & \quad \Leftrightarrow \forall C \bullet \theta C \in \{ CI \bullet \theta C' \} \Rightarrow && \text{[by definition]} \\ & \qquad\qquad \exists A \bullet \theta A \in \{ AI \bullet \theta A' \} \land \\ & \qquad\qquad\quad \theta A \mapsto \theta C \in \{ R \bullet \theta A \mapsto \theta C \} \\ & \quad \Leftrightarrow \forall C' \bullet CI \Rightarrow \exists A' \bullet AI \land R' && \text{[by comprehension]} \end{aligned}$$

F-init	$\forall C' \bullet CI \Rightarrow \exists A' \bullet AI \land R'$
F-corr	$\forall A;\ C \bullet \text{pre}\ AO \land R \Rightarrow \text{pre}\ CO$
	$\forall A;\ C;\ C' \bullet \text{pre}\ AO \land R \land CO \Rightarrow \exists A' \bullet AO \land R'$

Table 17.1: Rules for forwards simulation

The unwound rules insist also that

$$(\text{dom}\ ao) \lhd (r \parallel \text{id}) \operatorname{⨾} co \subseteq ao \operatorname{⨾} (r \parallel \text{id})$$

and that

$$\text{ran}((\text{dom}\ ao) \lhd (r \parallel \text{id})) \subseteq \text{dom}\ co$$

for every pair of operations ao and co. These requirements lead to a pair of conditions upon the corresponding operation schemas.

The first condition is that the concrete operation CO must be defined in any state whose abstract equivalent satisfies the precondition of AO.

$$\forall A;\ C \bullet \text{pre}\ AO \land R \Rightarrow \text{pre}\ CO$$

This tells us that the development step has—if anything—weakened the precondition of the operation.

The second condition tells us that the concrete operation produces results that are consistent with those of the abstract:

$$\begin{aligned} &\forall A;\ C;\ C' \bullet \\ &\quad \text{pre}\ AO \land R \land CO \Rightarrow \exists A' \bullet AO \land R' \end{aligned}$$

Suppose that two concrete states C and C' are related by the concrete operation CO. Suppose also that A, the abstract equivalent of C, lies within the precondition of AO. Then for CO to be a correct refinement of AO, there must be an abstract state A', corresponding to C', that can be reached from A by applying AO. The three conditions are presented together in Table 17.1.

Example 17.1 We require a system that will monitor the access to a building. The system should keep track of the people who are inside the building, and should forbid entry by more than a specified number of people at any time. Let *Staff* be the set of all members of staff:

$$[\,Staff\,]$$

and let *maxentry* be the maximum number of people that may enter the building at any time:

$$\mid\ maxentry : \mathbb{N}$$

We can model the state of our system by recording the names of those currently inside the building; the state invariant restricts the number of people accordingly:

$$ASystem \mathrel{\widehat=} [\ s : \mathbb{P}\ Staff \mid \#s \leq maxentry\ ]$$

Initially, there is no-one in the building; this satisfies the invariant, no matter what the value of *maxentry*:

$$ASystemInit \mathrel{\widehat=} [\ ASystem' \mid s' = \varnothing\ ]$$

A person who is not already recorded as being inside the building may enter it, providing there is enough room:

$$
\begin{array}{|l}
\hline
\textit{AEnterBuilding} \\
\Delta ASystem \\
p? : Staff \\
\hline
\#s < maxentry \\
p? \notin s \\
s' = s \cup \{p?\} \\
\hline
\end{array}
$$

A person who is in the building may leave it:

$$
\begin{array}{|l}
\hline
\textit{ALeaveBuilding} \\
\Delta ASystem \\
p? : Staff \\
\hline
p? \in s \\
s' = s \setminus \{p?\} \\
\hline
\end{array}
$$

A more concrete specification might model the state of the system as an injective sequence: a sequence with no repetitions. The length of this sequence must be less than *maxentry*:

$$CSystem \mathrel{\widehat=} [\, l : \mathrm{iseq}\ Staff \mid \#l \leq maxentry \,]$$

where the generic symbol 'iseq' is as defined in Section 9.2.

The length of l represents the number of people inside the building, since l contains no duplicates. Initially, there is no one in the building:

$$CSystemInit \mathrel{\widehat=} [\, CSystem' \mid l' = \langle\rangle \,]$$

A person who is not already inside the building may enter it, providing there is enough room:

$$\begin{array}{|l}
\textit{CEnterBuilding} \\
\hline
\Delta CSystem \\
p? : Staff \\
\hline
\#l < maxentry \\
p? \notin \mathrm{ran}\, l \\
l' = l \frown \langle p? \rangle \\
\hline
\end{array}$$

A person who is in the building may leave it:

$$\begin{array}{|l}
\textit{CLeaveBuilding} \\
\hline
\Delta CSystem \\
p? : Staff \\
\hline
p? \in \mathrm{ran}\, l \\
l' = l \upharpoonright (Staff \setminus \{p?\}) \\
\hline
\end{array}$$

Although both specifications describe the same system, the first is more abstract: it doesn't record the order in which people enter the building. The use of a sequence certainly makes the second specification a bit more awkward: we have to say that it contains no duplicates. The second specification also makes certain design decisions: for example, new people are appended to the end of the sequence.

We regard the first description as an abstract specification, and the second as a step on the way to producing a design. We intend to implement the set of names using an array, in which the elements will be ordered. We take a design decision to record the names in order of arrival. This decision may be documented using a retrieve relation:

$$
\begin{array}{|l}
\hline
\textit{ListRetrieveSet} \\
\textit{ASystem} \\
\textit{CSystem} \\
\hline
s = \operatorname{ran} l \\
\hline
\end{array}
$$

This is a formal record of the design step. It will help us to demonstrate that the second specification is a correct implementation of the first.

In order to prove that this refinement is correct, we must establish that each of the following statements is a theorem:

$$\forall\ CSystem' \bullet CSystemInit \Rightarrow \\ \quad (\exists\ ASystem' \bullet ASystemInit \Rightarrow ListRetrieveSet')$$

$$\forall\ ASystem;\ CSystem \bullet \text{pre}\ AEnterBuilding \wedge ListRetrieveSet' \Rightarrow \\ \quad \text{pre}\ CEnterBuilding$$

$$\forall\ ASystem;\ CSystem;\ CSystem' \bullet \\ \quad \text{pre}\ AEnterBuilding \wedge ListRetrieveSet \wedge CEnterBuilding \Rightarrow \\ \qquad (\exists\ ASystem' \bullet ListRetrieveSet' \wedge AEnterBuilding)$$

$$\forall\ ASystem;\ CSystem \bullet \text{pre}\ ALeaveBuilding \wedge ListRetrieveSet' \Rightarrow \\ \quad \text{pre}\ CLeaveBuilding$$

$$\forall\ ASystem;\ CSystem;\ CSystem' \bullet \\ \quad \text{pre}\ ALeaveBuilding \wedge ListRetrieveSet \wedge CLeaveBuilding \Rightarrow \\ \qquad (\exists\ ASystem' \bullet ListRetrieveSet' \wedge ALeaveBuilding)$$

□

Example 17.2 We are required to produce a program that finds the average of some numbers. We decide that the program should find the *arithmetic* mean of some *natural* numbers. Our specification describes a simple interface consisting of two operations: an operation *AEnter* that adds a number to our data set and an operation *AMean* that calculates the arithmetic mean of the numbers entered thus far.

The state of the program is modelled using a sequence of natural numbers to represent the data set:

$$AMemory \mathrel{\widehat{=}} [\, s : \text{seq}\, \mathbb{N} \,]$$

The use of a sequence or a bag—rather than a set—is important here, as we may be faced with many copies of the same natural number.

Operation	Precondition
AMemoryInit	*true*
AEnter	*true*
AMean	$s \neq \langle\rangle$

Table 17.2: Specification of the Mean Machine

In the initial state, the sequence of numbers is empty:

$$AMemoryInit \mathrel{\widehat{=}} [\, AMemory' \mid s' = \langle\rangle \,]$$

As each number is entered, it is added to the end of the sequence:

$$\begin{array}{|l}
\textit{AEnter} \\ \hline
\Delta AMemory \\
n? : \mathbb{N} \\ \hline
s' = s \frown \langle n? \rangle \\ \hline
\end{array}$$

The arithmetic mean of a series is its sum divided by its length. The following schema makes it clear exactly what is to be calculated:

$$\begin{array}{|l}
\textit{AMean} \\ \hline
\Xi AMemory \\
m! : \mathbb{R} \\ \hline
s \neq \langle\rangle \\
m! = \dfrac{\sum_{i=1}^{\#s} (s\ i)}{\#s} \\ \hline
\end{array}$$

The result makes sense only if the length of the sequence is strictly positive: this leads us to the precondition recorded in Table 17.2.

It is not necessary to keep the entire sequence of numbers that has been input; there is another way to compute the mean. In a specification we are more concerned with clarity than with efficiency, so the summation over a series is entirely appropriate. We will now consider a design in which only two numbers are stored: the running total and the sample size.

Operation	Precondition
InitCMemory	*true*
CEnter	*true*
CMean	$size \neq 0$

Table 17.3: Design of the Mean Machine

The state comprises two numbers: one natural, one real.

$$CMemory \mathrel{\widehat=} [\, sum : \mathbb{N};\ size : \mathbb{N} \,]$$

In the initial state, both of these are zero.

$$InitCMemory \mathrel{\widehat=} [\, CMemory' \mid sum' = 0 \land size' = 0 \,]$$

When a number is entered, it is added to the running total, and the sample size is increased by one:

$$\begin{array}{|l}
\text{—— } CEnter \text{ ————————} \\
\Delta CMemory \\
n? : \mathbb{N} \\
\hline
sum' = sum + n? \\
size' = size + 1 \\
\hline
\end{array}$$

If at least one number has been entered, then the mean may be obtained by dividing the running total by the sample size. In our design, the effect of this operation is described by

$$\begin{array}{|l}
\text{—— } CMean \text{ ————————} \\
\Xi CMemory \\
m! : \mathbb{R} \\
\hline
size \neq 0 \\
m! = \dfrac{sum}{size} \\
\hline
\end{array}$$

The precondition for this schema is recorded in Table 17.3.

To understand what is being computed by *CMean*, we must consider what happens if we enter a sequence of numbers and divide their sum by the number of entries. The relationship between specification and design should be obvious:

$$
\begin{array}{|l}
\multicolumn{1}{l}{\textit{SumSizeRetrieve}} \\
\hline
\textit{AMemory} \\
\textit{CMemory} \\
\hline
\textit{sum} = \sum_{i=1}^{\#s} (s\,i) \\
\textit{size} = \#s \\
\hline
\end{array}
$$

The retrieve relation is not functional from concrete to abstract, as it was in Example 17.1. Instead, it is functional from abstract to concrete.

The correctness of the design should also be obvious: if we take *CEnter* and *CMean*, and replace *sum* and *size* by the expressions that *Retrieve* gives us for them in terms of *s*, then we obtain the abstract descriptions of these operations. In order to prove this, we must prove that the following are theorems:

$$
\begin{array}{l}
\forall\, CMemory' \bullet CMemoryInit \Rightarrow \\
\quad (\exists\, AMemory' \bullet AMemoryInit \Rightarrow SumSizeRetrieve')
\end{array}
$$

$$
\forall\, AMemory;\ CMemory \bullet \text{pre } AEnter \wedge SumSizeRetrieve' \Rightarrow \text{pre } CEnter
$$

$$
\begin{array}{l}
\forall\, AMemory;\ CMemory;\ CMemory' \bullet \\
\quad \text{pre } AEnter \wedge SumSizeRetrieve \wedge CEnter \Rightarrow \\
\qquad (\exists\, AMemory' \bullet SumSizeRetrieve' \wedge AEnter)
\end{array}
$$

$$
\forall\, AMemory;\ CMemory \bullet \text{pre } AMean \wedge SumSizeRetrieve' \Rightarrow \text{pre } CMean
$$

$$
\begin{array}{l}
\forall\, AMemory;\ CMemory;\ CMemory' \bullet \\
\quad \text{pre } AMean \wedge SumSizeRetrieve \wedge CMean \Rightarrow \\
\qquad (\exists\, AMemory' \bullet SumSizeRetrieve' \wedge AMean)
\end{array}
$$

We may now translate our design into the *refinement calculus*—the subject of the next chapter—using a mixture of program code and *specification statements*. Briefly, the specification statement $w : [\, pre, post \,]$ describes a program that must terminate if started in any state satisfying *pre*, yielding a state satisfying *post*, while changing only those variables mentioned in *w*.

The result of our translation is shown below. The body of the procedure *enter* comprises a specification which insists that the global variable *sum* must be increased by the value of the $n?$, and that *size* must be incremented.

$$
\begin{array}{l}
\mathsf{var}\ sum, size : \mathbb{N} \bullet \\
\quad \ldots \\
\quad \mathsf{proc}\ enter\,(\mathsf{val}\ n? : \mathbb{N}); \\
\qquad sum, size : [\, true, sum' = sum + n? \land size' = size + 1 \,]; \\
\quad \mathsf{proc}\ mean\,(\mathsf{res}\ m! : \mathbb{R}); \\
\qquad m! : [\, size \neq 0, m! = sum / size \,]
\end{array}
$$

The body of the procedure *mean* comprises another specification that insists that $m!$ must have the final value $sum/size$. In this case, the implementor may assume that the value of *size* is not 0.

We may fill in some detail by refining the specification statements into a target programming language: in this case, Pascal. The result is a program that correctly implements our original specification:

```
PROGRAM MeanMachine(input,output);
  VAR
    n,sum,size: 0..maxint;
    m: real;
  PROC Enter(n: 0..maxint);
    BEGIN
      sum := sum + n;
      size := size + 1
    END;
  PROC Mean(VAR m: real);
    BEGIN
      m := sum / size
    END;
  BEGIN
    sum := 0;
    size := 0;
    WHILE NOT eof DO
      BEGIN
        read(n);
        Enter(n)
      END;
    Mean(m);
    write(m)
  END.
```

□

Example 17.3 We wish to use a dictionary to check the spelling of words. If the word is in the dictionary, then it is considered to be spelt correctly; if not, then it is considered to be spelt incorrectly. Abstractly, the dictionary is simply a set of words

$$ADict \mathrel{\widehat{=}} [\, ad : \mathbb{P}\, Word \,]$$

The task of implementing the dictionary efficiently is a searching problem. One solution is to keep the dictionary in a sorted order, and employ a binary search method. This design is recorded by the following schema:

$$\begin{array}{|l}
\multicolumn{1}{l}{CDict_1} \\ \hline
cd_1 : \mathrm{iseq}\, Word \\ \hline
\forall\, i, j : \mathrm{dom}\, cd_1 \mid i \leq j \bullet (cd_1\, i) \leq_W (cd_1\, j) \\ \hline
\end{array}$$

The words are kept (without duplicates) in a sequence in ascending order. We have taken that $\leq_W$ is the ordering on *Word*.

Alternatively, we could divide the words according to length, and a search would proceed by looking at only those words of the same length as the word we are checking, thus cutting down the search space.

$$\begin{array}{|l}
\multicolumn{1}{l}{CDict_2} \\ \hline
cd_2 : \mathrm{seq}(\mathbb{P}\, Word) \\ \hline
\forall\, i : \mathrm{dom}\, cd_2 \bullet \forall\, w : (cd_2\, i) \bullet \#w = i \\ \hline
\end{array}$$

This design starts by introducing a sequence of sets of words, with each of the sets containing only words of a particular length: the first set has words of length 1, the second of length 2, and so on.

As a third alternative, suppose that we are more interested in space efficiency. In this case, we might choose to exploit the common prefixes in the dictionary. As an example, suppose that our dictionary were rather sparsely filled with the following words: *and*, *ant*, *bee*, *can*, and *cat*. Instead of storing all 15 letters, we need store only 11 of them. The data structure that we have in mind is a tree. At its root there are three branches, one for a, one for b, and one for c. Below each of these branches, there is another prefix tree.

If $X \twoheadrightarrow_1 Y$ denotes the set of all non-empty functions between X and Y, then the free type of prefix trees is given by

$$\begin{aligned}
WordTree ::= {} & \mathsf{tree}\langle\!\langle Letter \twoheadrightarrow_1 WordTree \rangle\!\rangle \mid \\
& \mathsf{treeNode}\langle\!\langle Letter \twoheadrightarrow WordTree \rangle\!\rangle
\end{aligned}$$

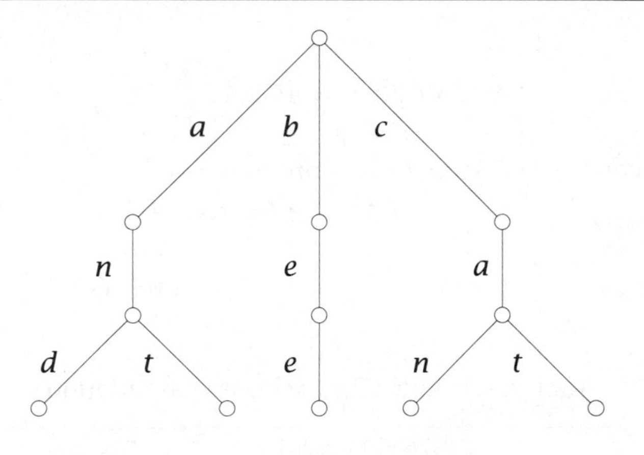

Figure 17.1: A word tree

The use of two injections—tree and treeNode—means that we can capture proper prefixes.

With this definition, the design of the dictionary can be described by the following schema:

$$CDict_3 \mathrel{\widehat{=}} [\, cd_3 : WordTree \,]$$

Our five-word dictionary—illustrated in Figure 17.1—may be expressed formally as a *WordTree*:

$$\begin{array}{l} \mathsf{tree}\,\{a \mapsto \mathsf{tree}\{n \mapsto \mathsf{tree}\{d \mapsto \mathsf{treeNode}\,\varnothing, t \mapsto \mathsf{treeNode}\,\varnothing\}\}, \\ \quad b \mapsto \mathsf{tree}\{e \mapsto \mathsf{tree}\{e \mapsto \mathsf{treeNode}\,\varnothing\}\}, \\ \quad c \mapsto \mathsf{tree}\{a \mapsto \mathsf{tree}\{n \mapsto \mathsf{treeNode}\,\varnothing, t \mapsto \mathsf{treeNode}\,\varnothing\}\} \\ \quad \} \end{array}$$

As a final example, consider a little dictionary which contains only the words *tin* and *tiny*. This has the representation as a word tree which is linear:

$$\mathsf{tree}\{t \mapsto \mathsf{tree}\{i \mapsto \mathsf{tree}\{n \mapsto \mathsf{treeNode}\{y \mapsto \mathsf{treeNode}\,\varnothing\}\}\}\}$$

The injection treeNode is used to mark a node that contains the end of a word, even if it is a proper prefix of another word.

Each of the three designs—$CDict_1$, $CDict_2$, and $CDict_3$—forms the basis for a correct data refinement of *ADict*. □

B-init	$\forall A; C \bullet CI \land R \Rightarrow AI$
B-corr	$\forall C \bullet (\forall A \bullet R \Rightarrow \text{pre } AO) \Rightarrow$ $\forall A'; C' \bullet CO \land R' \Rightarrow \exists A \bullet R \land AO$
	$\forall C \bullet (\forall A \bullet R \Rightarrow \text{pre } AO) \Rightarrow \text{pre } CO$

Table 17.4: Rules for backwards simulation

17.3 Backwards simulation

Some valid refinements cannot be proved correct using forwards simulation. We may characterise these as refinements in which the resolution of nondeterminism is postponed. Where this is the case, backwards simulation should be used instead. In backwards simulation, it is as if the abstract system can simulate the concrete one by being able to anticipate its actions.

As in the case of forwards simulation, the rules for the refinement of relations—presented at the end of the previous chapter—give rise to a corresponding set of conditions for the refinement of specifications. For any initial concrete state, the equivalent abstract state(s) must be initial abstract states

$$\forall C'; A' \bullet CI \land R' \Rightarrow AI$$

Whatever abstract equivalent A' we choose, it must meet the constraints of initialisation AI.

If operation CO is to correctly implement abstract operation AO, then it must work whenever AO is guaranteed to work.

$$\forall C \bullet (\forall A \bullet R \Rightarrow \text{pre } AO) \Rightarrow \text{pre } CO$$

Finally, for any abstract equivalent A' of the after state C', there must be an abstract equivalent A of the before state C such that A and A' are correctly related: that is, related by AO.

$$\forall C \bullet (\forall A \bullet R \Rightarrow \text{pre } AO) \Rightarrow (\forall A'; C' \bullet CO \land R' \Rightarrow (\exists A \bullet R \land AO))$$

These rules are summarised in Table 17.4.

Example 17.4 The Phoenix is a cinema whose box office works as follows. A customer may telephone and ask for a ticket. The box office clerk decides if there is an unsold ticket so as to accommodate the request. If there is, then a note is made to reserve a ticket for the caller. When the customer arrives, the box office clerk allocates an unsold ticket which identifies the seat.

We contrast this procedure with that of the Apollo theatre. At the Apollo, a customer may telephone and ask for a ticket. The box office clerk decides if there is an unsold ticket so as to accommodate the request. If there is, then one is allocated and put to one side for the caller. When the customer arrives, the clerk presents the allocated ticket which identifies the seat.

The customer cannot tell the difference between the two booking procedures. The point at which the ticket is allocated—and a nondeterministic choice of seat number is made—cannot be detected by the caller. The transaction appears the same in each case: the customer telephones the box office, arrives at the place of entertainment, obtains a ticket, and takes the indicated seat.

The Phoenix maintains a pool of tickets, drawn from a given set

$[Ticket]$

We will concentrate on the activities of a single customer, keeping track not only of the pool of unused tickets, but also of whether or not this customer has booked a ticket. The state of the Phoenix box office is then

Phoenix

$ppool : \mathbb{P}\ Ticket$
$bkd : Booked$

where *Booked* is the free type

$Booked ::= \mathsf{yes} \mid \mathsf{no}$

The booking operation requires that the customer has not already booked, and that there is a ticket to be allocated:

PBook

$\Delta Phoenix$

$bkd = \mathsf{no}$
$ppool \neq \varnothing$
$bkd' = \mathsf{yes}$
$ppool' = ppool$

A successful arrival requires that the customer has booked and that a ticket has been left for them:

$$
\begin{array}{|l}
\textit{PArrive} \\
\hline
\Delta \textit{Phoenix} \\
t! : \textit{Ticket} \\
\hline
\textit{bkd} = \mathsf{yes} \\
\textit{ppool} \neq \varnothing \\
\textit{bkd}' = \mathsf{no} \\
t! \in \textit{ppool} \\
\textit{ppool}' = \textit{ppool} \setminus \{t!\} \\
\hline
\end{array}
$$

Afterwards, the record is updated to say that there is no booking, a ticket is allocated, and the pool of tickets is updated accordingly.

Our model of the Apollo system requires a more sophisticated form of ticket. We employ a free type with a constant null, representing the absence of a ticket, and an embedded copy of the basic type *Ticket*.

$$\textit{ATicket} ::= \mathsf{null} \mid \mathsf{ticket}\langle\langle \textit{Ticket} \rangle\rangle$$

The state of the Apollo box office contains a pool of ordinary tickets, and a possibly-null ticket:

$$
\begin{array}{|l}
\textit{Apollo} \\
\hline
\textit{apool} : \mathbb{P}\, \textit{Ticket} \\
\textit{tkt} : \textit{ATicket} \\
\hline
\end{array}
$$

The booking operation requires that no ticket has already been reserved by the customer, and that the pool is not empty.

$$
\begin{array}{|l}
\textit{ABook} \\
\hline
\Delta \textit{Apollo} \\
\hline
\textit{tkt} = \mathsf{null} \\
\textit{apool} \neq \varnothing \\
\textit{tkt}' \neq \mathsf{null} \\
\mathsf{ticket}^{\sim}\, \textit{tkt}' \in \textit{apool} \\
\textit{apool}' = \textit{apool} \setminus \{\mathsf{ticket}^{\sim}\, \textit{tkt}'\} \\
\hline
\end{array}
$$

Afterwards, a single ticket is removed from the pool and reserved in the state component *tkt*.

A successful arrival operation requires that the customer has reserved a ticket. This ticket is then issued, and the pool remains unchanged.

$$
\begin{array}{|l}
\hline
\textit{AArrive} \\
\Delta \textit{Apollo} \\
t! : \textit{Ticket} \\
\hline
\textit{tkt} \neq \mathsf{null} \\
\textit{tkt}' = \mathsf{null} \\
t! = \mathsf{ticket}^{\sim}\ \textit{tkt} \\
\textit{apool}' = \textit{apool} \\
\hline
\end{array}
$$

The relationship between the two systems may be documented by the following retrieve relation:

$$
\begin{array}{|l}
\hline
\textit{ApolloPhoenixRetr} \\
\textit{Phoenix} \\
\textit{Apollo} \\
\hline
\textit{bkd} = \mathsf{no} \Rightarrow \textit{tkt} = \mathsf{null} \wedge \textit{ppool} = \textit{apool} \\
\textit{bkd} = \mathsf{yes} \Rightarrow \textit{tkt} \neq \mathsf{null} \wedge \textit{ppool} = \textit{apool} \cup \{\mathsf{ticket}^{\sim}\ \textit{tkt}\} \\
\hline
\end{array}
$$

We put forward two conjectures:

- The Phoenix system is data refined by the Apollo system.
- The Apollo system is data refined by the Phoenix system.

The first of these can be proved using forwards simulation; the second cannot. To see why, consider the following statement:

$$
\begin{array}{l}
\mathrm{pre}\ \textit{AArrive} \wedge \textit{ApolloPhoenixRetr} \wedge \textit{PArrive} \vdash \\
\qquad \exists\, \textit{Apollo}' \bullet \textit{ApolloPhoenixRetr}' \wedge \textit{AArrive}
\end{array}
$$

To prove this, we must show that $t! = \mathsf{ticket}^{\sim}\ \textit{tkt}$: one of the predicates of *AArrive*. The most that we can deduce from the antecedents is that $t! \in \textit{apool} \cup \{\mathsf{ticket}^{\sim}\ \textit{tkt}\}$. This is not enough. Notice that when we prove the refinement the other way around, the proof will work as expected.

As the reader will have guessed, we need the backwards simulation rules in order to be able to prove the second conjecture. Our troublesome predicate asks the very question that backwards simulation sets out to answer: that is, is there a state that the abstract operation could have started in that would have led to this situation? □

Example 17.5 The game of Mastermind™ was popular some twenty years ago. In this game, one player chooses a code of six coloured pegs, and the others tries to guess what this code is. The guesser is allowed a number of attempts; the setter replies to each attempt by stating how many of the guess's pegs are of the correct colour, and how many of these are in the correct order.

In the specification of an electronic version of Mastermind™, we might state that a random sequence is chosen when the system is switched on. An implementation may do exactly this, or it may postpone the choice until the first attempt is made. Since there is no way to detect that the choice has not already been made, this would be a valid refinement of the specification, provable using backwards simulation.

An implementation might also choose to postpone the choice until the last possible moment. The system could then maintain a set of codes—consistent with the answers it has given the user thus far—and leave the decision about the 'real' code until it has no room left to manoeuver. Of course, delaying the choice of code is against the spirit of the game, but with this interface there is no way to detect the 'fraud': our cheating implementation is a correct refinement of the specification. □

Example 17.6 Here is another example of a refinement which requires the backwards rules; it also has a novel twist. It concerns a greatly simplified model of a vending machine, which dispenses drinks in response to three-digit codes typed in by its users. The specification abstracts from the detail of the digits being input one-by-one, and requires instead that the sequence is entered atomically. This kind of abstraction, where the level of atomicity in the system is changed, is useful in describing many similar interfaces, such as that used in telephone systems.

We begin with a few global definitions. The free type *Status* is used to signal the success or failure of the current interaction with the machine, and to keep track of whether a transaction is in progress; *Digits* are those numbers between 0 and 9; and $\mathrm{seq}_3[X]$ is the set of sequences of Xs whose length is exactly 3.

$$
\begin{array}{l}
\mathit{Status} ::= \mathsf{yes} \mid \mathsf{no} \\
\mathit{Digits} == 0 \mathinner{..} 9 \\
\mathrm{seq}_3[X] == \{\, s : \mathrm{seq}\, X \mid \#s = 3 \,\}
\end{array}
$$

The state of our specification contains two boolean variables; these indicate whether it is in use, and whether the current transaction will be successful or not.

$$
\mathit{VMSpec} \mathrel{\widehat=} [\, \mathit{busy}, \mathit{vend} : \mathit{Status} \,]
$$

Initially, both variables are set to no:

$$VMSpecInit \mathrel{\widehat{=}} [\, VMSpec' \mid busy' = vend' = \mathsf{no} \,]$$

A user interacts by inputting a three-digit sequence, and then collecting the drink, if the numbers were correctly chosen. We have abstracted from the need to pay, and even from the kind of drink that gets dispensed. The first part of the transaction is to choose the drink.

$$\begin{array}{|l}
\textit{Choose} \\ \hline
\Delta VMSpec \\
i? : \mathrm{seq}_3\ Digit \\ \hline
busy = \mathsf{no} \\
busy' = \mathsf{yes} \\ \hline
\end{array}$$

Note that the value of *vend* is left undetermined by the operation: its value is nondeterministically chosen. The end of the transaction simply signals whether the transaction is successful or not:

$$\begin{array}{|l}
\textit{VendSpec} \\ \hline
\Delta VMSpec \\
o! : Status \\ \hline
busy' = \mathsf{no} \\
o! = vend \\ \hline
\end{array}$$

At the design level, digits are entered separately. All we actually need to record is the number of digits entered. Initially, there is no transaction in progress:

$$VMDesign \mathrel{\widehat{=}} [\, digits : 0 \mathinner{..} 3 \,]$$

$$VMDesignInit \mathrel{\widehat{=}} [\, VMDesign' \mid digits' = 0 \,]$$

A transaction starts with a user punching in the first digit:

$$\begin{array}{|l}
\textit{FirstPunch} \\ \hline
\Delta VMDesign \\
d? : Digit \\ \hline
digits = 0 \\
digits' = 1 \\ \hline
\end{array}$$

and continues with the user punching in further digits:

$$
\begin{array}{|l}
\hline
\textit{NextPunch} \\
\Delta \textit{VMDesign} \\
d? : \textit{Digit} \\
\hline
(0 < \textit{digits} < 3 \land \textit{digits}' = \textit{digits} + 1) \lor \\
(\textit{digits} = 0 \land \textit{digits}' = \textit{digits}) \\
\hline
\end{array}
$$

Notice that *NextPunch* is ineffective unless a transaction is in progress. The operation *VendDesign*, which describes the act of dispensing the drink, chooses the output *o*! nondeterministically:

$$
\begin{array}{|l}
\hline
\textit{VendDesign} \\
\Delta \textit{VMDesign} \\
o! : \textit{Status} \\
\hline
\textit{digits}' = 0 \\
\hline
\end{array}
$$

It should be clear that there is a refinement between the abstract and concrete systems that we have presented. Suppose that we want the drink referred to by the digit-sequence 238. Abstractly, the transaction proceeds by invoking the *Choose* operation with input 238; next, we invoke the *VendSpec* operation, and receive the indication *o*! telling us whether we were successful.

Concretely, the transaction proceeds by invoking the *FirstPunch* operation with input 2; then *NextPunch* with input 3; then *NextPunch* with input 8; then we invoke the *VendDesign* operation, and receive the indication *o*! telling us whether we were successful.

There are three differences between the two systems: they have a different set of operation names; they have different types of inputs; and they make the nondeterministic choice at different times.

If we are to prove the refinement, then we must explain the correspondence between the two sets of operations. We want the two *Vend* operations to correspond, and for the abstract *Choose* operation to be related to the concrete *FirstPunch* operation. There is no operation in the abstract interface that corresponds to the concrete *NextPunch* operation, but instead, we relate it to the identity on the abstract state. To summarise:

$$
\begin{array}{r l}
\textit{VMSpecInit} & \text{is refined by } \textit{VMDesignInit} \\
\textit{Choose} & \text{is refined by } \textit{FirstPunch} \\
\Xi \textit{VMSpec} & \text{is refined by } \textit{NextPunch} \\
\textit{VendSpec} & \text{is refined by } \textit{VendDesign}
\end{array}
$$

The difference in the types of inputs means that we cannot use the proof rules that we have derived from the definition of refinement. However, recall that our treatment of inputs and outputs started by considering them as distinguished items of state. In fact, it is not necessary for the two operations to have the same inputs and outputs. To see this, consider the retrieve relation described the following schema:

$$
\begin{array}{|l}
\textit{RetrieveVM} \\
\hline
\textit{VMSpec} \\
\textit{VMDesign} \\
\hline
\textit{busy} = \mathsf{no} \Leftrightarrow \textit{digits} = 0 \\
\hline
\end{array}
$$

To prove the forwards simulation correctness rule for *Choose–FirstPunch*: we must prove the following:

$$
\begin{array}{l}
\forall\, \textit{VMSpec};\ \textit{VMDesign};\ \textit{VMDesign}' \bullet \\
\quad \mathrm{pre}\ \textit{Choose} \wedge \textit{RetrieveVM} \wedge \textit{FirstPunch} \Rightarrow \\
\qquad \exists\, \textit{VMSpec}' \bullet \textit{RetrieveVM}' \wedge \textit{Choose}
\end{array}
$$

It is sufficient to prove

$$
\begin{array}{l}
\forall\, \textit{busy}, \textit{vend} : \textit{Status};\ \textit{digits}, \textit{digits}' : 0 \mathinner{..} 3;\ i? : \mathrm{seq}_3\, \textit{Digit};\ d? : \textit{Digit} \bullet \\
\quad \textit{busy} = \mathsf{no} \wedge \\
\quad \textit{busy} = \mathsf{no} \Leftrightarrow \textit{digits} = 0 \wedge \\
\quad \textit{digits} = 0 \wedge \textit{digits}' = 1 \Rightarrow \\
\qquad \exists\, \textit{busy}', \textit{vend}' : \textit{Status} \bullet \\
\qquad\qquad \textit{busy}' = \mathsf{no} \Leftrightarrow \textit{digits}' = 0 \wedge \textit{busy}' = \mathsf{yes}
\end{array}
$$

which is clearly true.

The difference in the point at which the nondeterministic choice is made is more interesting. In the abstract system, this choice is made at the beginning of the transaction, in the operation *Choose*. In the concrete system, the decision is delayed until the end of the transaction, during the operation *VendDesign*. This postponement of nondeterminism is characteristic of backwards refinement, and will mean that we will fail in our attempt to show that this refinement is a forwards simulation.

If the vending machine made more use of the digits offered by the user as input, then the retrieve relation might be more interesting; as it is, all that the retrieve relation can do is to identify what it means to be in a transaction in the abstract and concrete states. Consider the forwards simulation correctness rule for the operation of vending:

$$\begin{array}{l} \forall\, VMSpec;\ VMDesign;\ VMDesign' \bullet \\ \quad \text{pre}\ VendSpec \land RetrieveVM \land VendDesign \Rightarrow \\ \qquad \exists\, VMSpec' \bullet RetrieveVM' \land VendSpec \end{array}$$

To prove this, we must establish that

$$\begin{array}{l} \forall\, busy, vend : Status;\ digits, digits' : 0\,..\,3;\ o! : Status \bullet \\ \quad busy = \mathsf{no} \Leftrightarrow digits = 0 \land \\ \quad digits' = 0 \Rightarrow \\ \qquad \exists\, busy', vend' : Status \bullet \\ \qquad busy' = \mathsf{no} \Leftrightarrow digits' = 0 \land busy' = \mathsf{no} \land o! = vend \end{array}$$

This is clearly false. Thus, this is not a forwards simulation; it is however, a backwards simulation. In the implementation, the choice is made later, only after all the digits have been punched. It is as if the specification can prophesy the future. □

Example 17.7 A simple distributed operating system allows users to store files in a shared file store. A natural specification of this system might contain a mapping from names to files.

$$AFS \mathrel{\widehat=} [\, afs : Name \pfun File \,]$$

Initially, there are no files:

$$AFSInit \mathrel{\widehat=} [\, AFS' \mid afs' = \varnothing \,]$$

Files may be read from the file store:

$$\begin{array}{|l} \textit{Read} \\ \hline \Xi AFS \\ n? : Name \\ f! : File \\ \hline n? \in \text{dom}\, afs \\ f! = afs\, n? \\ \hline \end{array}$$

or stored in it:

$$\begin{array}{|l}
\multicolumn{1}{l}{\textit{Store}} \\ \hline
\Delta AFS \\
f? : File \\
n? : Name \\ \hline
afs' = afs \oplus \{n? \mapsto f?\} \\
n? \notin \mathrm{dom}\, afs \\ \hline
\end{array}$$

The atomicity implied by this specification would, of course, be inappropriate for a realistic implementation. It would require that other transactions are halted while the file is stored. At the design level, files are transferred byte by byte to the file store. The atomic steps of this transaction may be interleaved with the actions of other users.

The concrete system contains two mappings: a concrete file system, and a temporary file system. The latter is used to store partial files that are in the process of being transferred over the network. Files are represented as sequences of bytes.

$$\begin{array}{|l}
\multicolumn{1}{l}{\textit{CFS}} \\ \hline
cfs : Name \rightarrowtail\!\!\!\!\!\!\!+\;\; \mathrm{seq}\, Byte \\
tfs : Name \rightarrowtail\!\!\!\!\!\!\!+\;\; \mathrm{seq}\, Byte \\ \hline
\mathrm{dom}\, cfs \cap \mathrm{dom}\, tfs = \varnothing \\ \hline
\end{array}$$

Initially, there are no files:

$$CFSInit \mathrel{\widehat{=}} [\, CFS' \mid cfs' = tfs' = \varnothing \,]$$

The act of storing a file in the distributed file store is performed not by a single operation, but by a transaction. First, the user must *Start* the transaction; *Next* the user must transfer the file byte by byte; and finally the user must *Stop* the transaction.

The transaction is started by making a reservation in the temporary file store:

$$\begin{array}{|l}
\multicolumn{1}{l}{\textit{Start}} \\ \hline
\Delta CFS \\
n? : Name \\ \hline
n? \notin \mathrm{dom}\, cfs \cup \mathrm{dom}\, tfs \\
tfs' = tfs \oplus \{n? \mapsto \langle\rangle\} \\
cfs' = cfs \\ \hline
\end{array}$$

The file is accumulated in the temporary file store:

$$
\begin{array}{l}
\textit{Next} \\
\hline
\Delta CFS \\
n? : Name \\
b? : Byte \\
\hline
n? \in \operatorname{dom} tfs \\
tfs' = tfs \oplus \{n? \mapsto (tfs\ n?) \frown \langle b? \rangle\} \\
cfs' = cfs \\
\hline
\end{array}
$$

When the transaction is finalised, it is transferred to the concrete file system:

$$
\begin{array}{l}
\textit{Stop} \\
\hline
\Delta CFS \\
n? : Name \\
\hline
n? \in \operatorname{dom} tfs \\
tfs' = \{n?\} \mathbin{⩤} tfs \\
cfs' = cfs \oplus \{n? \mapsto tfs\ n?\} \\
\hline
\end{array}
$$

The retrieve relation is simply the conversion between the abstract type of a file and its representation as a sequence of bytes:

$$
\mid\ retr\_file : \operatorname{seq} Byte \rightarrow File
$$

$$
\begin{array}{l}
\textit{RetrieveACFS} \\
\hline
AFS \\
CFS \\
\hline
afs = cfs \mathbin{⨾} retr\_file \\
\hline
\end{array}
$$

There is a forwards simulation between the following two systems

$$(AFS, AFSInit, \Xi AFS, \Xi AFS, Store, Read)$$
$$(CFS, CFSInit, Start, Next, Stop, Read)$$

and a backwards simulation between

$$(AFS, AFSInit, Store, \Xi AFS, \Xi AFS, Read)$$
$$(CFS, CFSInit, Start, Next, Stop, Read)$$

□

Chapter 18

Functional Refinement

When the relations used in refining or structuring our specifications turn out to be functions, then our proof obligations can be simplified. If the retrieve relation is functional, then we may employ a different set of proof rules; we may even be able to proceed by calculation. If the state description involves a functional promotion, then the promotion of the refinement is the refinement of the promotion. In this chapter we examine these simplifications, and show how they may be applied to the refinement of specifications.

18.1 Retrieve functions

Suppose that we have a data type $\mathcal{A}$, and a forwards simulation which is a *total* function from concrete to abstract: that is, we have a retrieve relation $f^{\sim}$, where f is a total function. In this case, the proof rule for correctness may be simplified, using a cancellation law for relational composition. If R and S are relations, and f is a total function, then

$$R \subseteq S \mathbin{⨾} f^{\sim} \Leftrightarrow R \mathbin{⨾} f \subseteq S$$

The proof of this cancellation law is instructive, and we present it here:

$$\begin{aligned}
& R \subseteq S \mathbin{⨾} f^{\sim} \\
\Leftrightarrow\ & \forall x : X;\ y : Y \bullet x \mapsto y \in R \Rightarrow x \mapsto y \in S \mathbin{⨾} f^{\sim} && \text{[by def of } \subseteq\text{]} \\
\Leftrightarrow\ & \forall x : X;\ y : Y \bullet && \text{[by def of } ⨾\text{]} \\
& \qquad x \mapsto y \in R \Rightarrow \exists z : Z \bullet x \mapsto z \in S \land z \mapsto y \in f^{\sim} \\
\Leftrightarrow\ & \forall x : X;\ y : Y \bullet && \text{[by def of } {}^{\sim}\text{]} \\
& \qquad x \mapsto y \in R \Rightarrow \exists z : Z \bullet x \mapsto z \in S \land y \mapsto z \in f
\end{aligned}$$

F-init-func-rel	$ci \mathbin{;} f \subseteq ai$
F-fin-func-rel	$f^{\sim} \mathbin{;} cf \subseteq af$
F-corr-func-rel	$\operatorname{dom} ao \lhd f^{\sim} \mathbin{;} co \mathbin{;} f \subseteq ao$
	$\operatorname{ran}((\operatorname{dom} ao) \lhd f^{\sim}) \subseteq \operatorname{dom} co$

Table 18.1: Rules for retrieve functions

$$
\begin{aligned}
&\Leftrightarrow \forall x : X;\ y : Y \bullet x \mapsto y \in R \Rightarrow \exists z : Z \bullet x \mapsto z \in S \land z = f(y) && [f \text{ is total}]\\
&\Leftrightarrow \forall x : X;\ y : Y \bullet x \mapsto y \in R \Rightarrow f(y) \in Z \land x \mapsto f(y) \in S && [\text{by } \exists\text{-opr}]\\
&\Leftrightarrow \forall x : X;\ y : Y \bullet x \mapsto y \in R \Rightarrow x \mapsto f(y) \in S && [f \text{ is total}]\\
&\Leftrightarrow \forall x : X;\ y : Y \bullet f(y) \in Z \land x \mapsto y \in R \Rightarrow x \mapsto f(y) \in S && [f \text{ is total}]\\
&\Leftrightarrow \forall x : X;\ y : Y;\ z : Z \bullet z = f(y) \land x \mapsto y \in R \Rightarrow x \mapsto z \in S && [\text{by } \forall\text{-opr}]\\
&\Leftrightarrow \forall x : X;\ y : Y;\ z : Z \bullet x \mapsto y \in R \land y \mapsto z \in f \Rightarrow x \mapsto z \in S && [f \text{ is total}]\\
&\Leftrightarrow \forall x : X;\ z : Z \bullet && [\text{by pred calc}]\\
&\qquad (\exists y : Y \bullet x \mapsto y \in R \land y \mapsto z \in f) \Rightarrow x \mapsto z \in S\\
&\Leftrightarrow \forall x : X;\ z : Z \bullet x \mapsto z \in R \mathbin{;} f \Rightarrow x \mapsto z \in S && [\text{by def of } \mathbin{;}]\\
&\Leftrightarrow R \mathbin{;} f \subseteq S && [\text{by def of } \subseteq]
\end{aligned}
$$

It is, in fact, not necessary to insist that f is total; the weaker condition that $\operatorname{ran} R \subseteq \operatorname{dom} f$ is enough.

Now consider the correctness rule for forwards simulation, but with the inverse of a total function f for the retrieve relation. We must prove that

$$\operatorname{dom} ao \lhd f^{\sim} \mathbin{;} co \subseteq ao \mathbin{;} f^{\sim}$$

Using the cancellation law, we see that this is equivalent to

$$\operatorname{dom} ao \lhd f^{\sim} \mathbin{;} co \mathbin{;} f \subseteq ao$$

In practice, the transformed rule is simpler to prove than the the original. A similar transformation may be made to the rule for initialisation. The rules for refinement with a total retrieve function are presented in Table 18.1.

F-func	$\forall C \bullet \exists_1 A \bullet R$
F-init-func	$\forall A'; C' \bullet CI \land R' \Rightarrow AI$
F-corr-func	$\forall A; A'; C; C' \bullet \text{pre } AO \land R \land CO \land R' \Rightarrow AO$
	$\forall A; C \bullet \text{pre } AO \land R \Rightarrow \text{pre } CO$

Table 18.2: Rules for functional refinement

18.2 Functional refinement

The new rules for the refinement of relations give rise to a set of rules for the functional refinement of specifications. Any application of these rules will require a proof that the retrieve relation is a total function: that is,

$$\forall C \bullet \exists_1 A \bullet R$$

Once this requirement has been established, we are left with the rules shown in Table 18.2. Notice that these are easier to apply that those given at the end of the previous chapter.

If we are able to present a set of equations that defines each abstract component as a total function of concrete components, then our retrieve relation must be a function. The resulting form of retrieve relation is quite common in realistic specifications.

Example 18.1 In Example 17.1, the retrieve relation was defined by an equation expressing the abstract component—a set—as a total function of the concrete component—a list.

```
┌─ ListRetrieveSet ──────────────────
│ ASystem
│ CSystem
├──────────
│ s = ran l
└────────────────────────────────────
```

This retrieve relation is a total, surjective function from concrete to abstract; that is, every concrete list represents exactly one abstract set, and every set is so represented. The proof of this follows immediately from the observation that *ListRetrieveSet* is essentially just ran, which is itself a total, surjective function.

Since the retrieve relation is a total function, we could have proved the simpler set of proof obligations:

$$\forall\ CSystem \bullet \exists_1\ ASystem \bullet ListRetrieveSet$$

$$\forall\ CSystem';\ ASystem' \bullet CSystemInit \land ListRetrieveSet' \Rightarrow ASystemInit$$

$$\forall\ ASystem;\ CSystem \bullet \text{pre}\ AEnterBuilding \land ListRetrieveSet \Rightarrow \\ \quad \text{pre}\ CEnterBuilding$$

$$\forall\ ASystem;\ ASystem';\ CSystem;\ CSytems' \bullet \\ \quad \text{pre}\ AEnterBuilding \land \\ \quad ListRetrieveSet \land \\ \quad CEnterBuilding \land \\ \quad ListRetrieveSet' \\ \qquad \Rightarrow AEnterBuilding$$

$$\forall\ ASystem;\ CSystem \bullet \text{pre}\ ALeavebuilding \land ListRetrieveSet \Rightarrow \\ \quad \text{pre}\ CLeaveBuilding$$

$$\forall\ ASystem;\ ASystem';\ CSystem;\ CSytems' \bullet \\ \quad \text{pre}\ ALeaveBuilding \land \\ \quad ListRetrieveSet \land \\ \quad CLeaveBuilding \land \\ \quad ListRetrieveSet' \\ \qquad \Rightarrow ALeaveBuilding$$

□

18.3 Calculating data refinements

One way of developing an implementation from a specification is to write down the description of the concrete state, record the retrieve relation, and then *calculate* the rest of the concrete system. This is easily done if the retrieve relation is a total surjective function from concrete to abstract.

The result of this calculation is the *weakest* refinement of the specification, with respect to the retrieve relation, if there is any refinement at all. Let's call this refinement $\mathcal{W}$; it is the weakest refinement in the sense that it is a refinement of $\mathcal{A}$ ($\mathcal{A} \sqsubseteq \mathcal{W}$) and that, for every other C which is also a refinement of $\mathcal{A}$ using the forwards simulation $f^{\sim}$, we have that $\mathcal{W} \sqsubseteq C$.

F-init-calc-rel	$wi == ai \fatsemi f^{\sim}$
F-corr-calc-rel	$wo == f \fatsemi ao \fatsemi f^{\sim}$

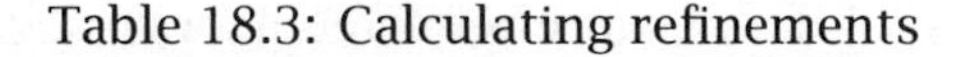

Table 18.3: Calculating refinements

How can we find $\mathcal{W}$? Consider one of its operations *wo*, a refinement of the abstract operation *ao*; it may be calculated from the identity

$$wo \;==\; f \fatsemi ao \fatsemi f^{\sim}$$

To see how this works, observe that the definition chosen for *wo* solves the forwards simulation inequality *exactly*. The result is the largest relation that is a refinement of *ao*.

$$\begin{aligned}
& f^{\sim} \fatsemi wo \\
&= f^{\sim} \fatsemi f \fatsemi ao \fatsemi f^{\sim} && \text{[by definition]} \\
&= \mathrm{id}[\mathrm{ran}\, f] \fatsemi ao \fatsemi f^{\sim} && \text{[by relational calculus]} \\
&= ao \fatsemi f^{\sim} && \text{[since } f \text{ is surjective]}
\end{aligned}$$

Again, notice that, rather than insisting that f is surjective, the weaker condition that $\mathrm{dom}\, ao \subseteq \mathrm{ran}\, f$ would suffice. The rules for calculating refinements are given in Table 18.3.

To see how this extends to specifications, suppose that we have an abstract state described by the schema A, an initialisation

$$AI \mathrel{\widehat{=}} [\, A' \mid p \,]$$

and an operation

$$AO \mathrel{\widehat{=}} [\, \Delta A \mid q \,]$$

Suppose further that we have a total surjective function f from the concrete state C to A which is used in the retrieve relation

$$F \mathrel{\widehat{=}} [\, A;\ C \mid \theta A = f(\theta C) \,]$$

F-init-calc	$CI \mathrel{\widehat=} CI \mathbin{;} F'$
F-corr-calc	$CO \mathrel{\widehat=} F \mathbin{;} AO \mathbin{;} F'$

Table 18.4: Calculating refinements with schemas

If this is the case, then the weakest refinement with respect to f is given by the initialisation

$$CI \mathrel{\widehat=} CI \mathbin{;} F' \quad = \quad [\, C' \mid p[f(\theta C')/\theta A']\,]$$

and the operation

$$CO \mathrel{\widehat=} F \mathbin{;} AO \mathbin{;} F' \quad = \quad [\, \Delta C \mid q[f(\theta C), f(\theta C')/\theta A, \theta A']\,]$$

For completeness, these definitions are summarised in Table 18.4.

Example 18.2 As *ListRetrieveSet* is a total surjective function, we could have calculated the weakest refinement, which is strictly weaker than our concrete system in the previous example.

This would have avoided the decision to put newcomers at the end of the list. Recall that the specification $s' = s \cup \{p?\}$. The retrieve relation states that $s = \operatorname{ran} l$, and the dashed counterpart, so we can calculate the weakest refinement as $\operatorname{ran} l' = \operatorname{ran} l \cup \{p?\}$. This requires that the right elements are in the list, without prescribing their order.

Similarly, it would have avoided the design decision to preserve the order of the list after the leave operation, requiring merely that the right elements are present. We can see from this the value of calculating the weakest refinement: we make exactly the design step recorded in the retrieve relation. □

Example 18.3 In Example 17.2, the retrieve relation *SumSizeRetrieve* is a total, surjective function, but it goes from abstract to concrete. That is, every abstract sequence can be reduced to a unique sum and size—sequences are finite—and every pair of numbers *sum* and *size* can be expressed in the more abstract form of a sequence. Thus, the retrieve relation cannot be used to simplify the refinement proof obligations, nor can it be used to calculate the weakest refinement in the manner that we have shown. □

Example 18.4 We wish to build a temperature sensor as part of some larger piece of equipment. We might encapsulate the recording of the temperature in the following Fahrenheit abstract data type. Fahrenheit temperatures range from absolute zero up to a maximum temperature of 5000°F. Since absolute zero is −459.4°F, we define

$$°F == \{ f : \mathbb{R} \mid -459.4 \leq f \leq 5000 \}$$

Our temperature store keeps track of one value:

$$\begin{array}{|l} \textit{FTemp} \\ \hline f : °F \\ \hline \end{array}$$

Standard temperature is 65°F:

$$\textit{StdTemp} == 65$$

and this is used to provide a default value at initialisation-time:

$$\begin{array}{|l} \textit{FTempInit} \\ \hline \textit{FTemp}' \\ \hline f' = \textit{StdTemp} \\ \hline \end{array}$$

The temperature can always be incremented, provided that the value does not go below the maximum:

$$\begin{array}{|l} \textit{FTInc} \\ \hline \Delta \textit{FTemp} \\ \hline f \leq 4999 \\ f' = f + 1 \\ \hline \end{array}$$

Similarly, the temperature can always be decremented, provided that the value does not go below the minimum:

$$\begin{array}{|l} \textit{FTDec} \\ \hline \Delta \textit{FTemp} \\ \hline f \geq -458.4 \\ f' = f - 1 \\ \hline \end{array}$$

At the design stage, the internal representation need not be kept in Fahrenheit: it could easily be maintained in Celsius. Celsius values are those above absolute zero, which is $-273°$C. For convenience, we choose a maximum value of 2760°C.

$$Celsius == \{ t : \mathbb{R} \mid -273 \leq t \leq 2760 \}$$

$$CTemp \mathrel{\widehat{=}} [c : C]$$

The retrieve relation between these representations is well-known:

$$\begin{array}{|l}
\hline RetrieveFC \\
FTemp \\
CTemp \\
\hline
f = (9/5) * c + 32 \\
\hline
\end{array}$$

The schema *RetrieveFC*, regarded as a relation from *CTemp* to *FTemp*, is a total bijection: each Celsius temperature corresponds to exactly one Fahrenheit value. We can therefore use *RetrieveFC* to calculate a refinement.

We begin with the concrete initialisation:

$$\begin{array}{|l}
\hline
CTemp' \\
\hline
(9/5) * c' + 32 = StdTemp \\
\hline
\end{array}$$

We may rewrite the predicate part of this schema to make the initial value of c' more explicit:

$$\begin{array}{|l}
\hline CTempInit \\
CTemp' \\
\hline
c' = (5/9) * (StdTemp - 32) \\
\hline
\end{array}$$

The concrete version of the increment operation is described by the following schema:

$$\begin{array}{|l}
\hline
\Delta CTemp \\
\hline
(9/5) * c + 32 \leq 4999 \\
(9/5) * c' + 32 = (9/5) * c + 32 + 1 \\
\hline
\end{array}$$

Again, we may rewrite the predicate part:

$$
\begin{array}{|l}
\textit{CTInc} \\
\hline
\Delta \textit{CTemp} \\
\hline
c \leq 2759 * (4/9) \\
c' = c + (5/9) \\
\hline
\end{array}
$$

Finally, the concrete version of the decrement operation is

$$
\begin{array}{|l}
\hline
\Delta \textit{CTemp} \\
\hline
(9/5) * c + 32 \geq -458.4 \\
(9/5) * c' + 32 = (9/5) * c + 32 - 1 \\
\hline
\end{array}
$$

which may be rewritten as

$$
\begin{array}{|l}
\textit{CTDec} \\
\hline
\Delta \textit{CTemp} \\
\hline
c > 272 * (4/9) \\
c' = c - (5/9) \\
\hline
\end{array}
$$

Given the new representation, we can calculate the refinement. The calculation is straightforward, although the results may need to be simplified before they are used; this is typical of the calculational approach. □

18.4 Refining promotion

Promotion is a powerful tool for structuring specifications; it allows us to construct multi-layer descriptions of large systems. An important feature of promotion, one not discussed in Chapter 13, is that it is monotonic with respect to refinement. This result may be summarised as 'the refinement of a promotion is the promotion of the refinement'. If our specification includes a promoted abstract data type, we can refine this data type independently, while preserving its relationship with the rest of the system.

The simplest form of promotion uses a function to index a data type S, whose operations are then promoted. Suppose that the enclosing data type is P, and that the state of P is described by

$$P \mathrel{\widehat{=}} [\, f : I \rightarrow\!\!\!\!\!\rightarrow S \,]$$

A suitable promotion schema might be

$$
\begin{array}{|l}
\hline
\textit{Promote} \\
\Delta S \\
\Delta P \\
i? : I \\
\hline
i? \in \operatorname{dom} f \\
\theta S = f(i?) \\
f' = f \oplus \{ i? \mapsto \theta S' \} \\
\hline
\end{array}
$$

If SO is an operation of S, then it may be promoted in the usual way: that is,

$$PO \mathrel{\widehat{=}} \exists \Delta S \bullet Promote \land SO$$

To model this form of promotion in the relational calculus, we define three operators. The first applies a function to an argument; the second is a prefix version of overriding; the third is a curried version of relational image:

$$
\begin{array}{|l}
\hline
[X, Y] \\
apply : (X \to Y) \times X \to Y \\
ovr : ((X \to Y) \times X) \times Y \to X \to Y \\
img : (X \leftrightarrow Y) \to \mathbb{P} X \to \mathbb{P} Y \\
\hline
\forall f : X \to Y ; \; x : X \bullet apply(f, x) = f(x) \\
\forall f : X \to Y ; \; x : X ; \; y : Y \bullet ovr((f, x), y) = f \oplus \{ x \mapsto y \} \\
\forall R : X \leftrightarrow Y ; \; S : \mathbb{P} X \bullet (img\, R) S = R (\!| S |\!) \\
\hline
\end{array}
$$

If op is an operation on a data type $\mathcal{D}$, then we can promote it to an operation $\Phi(op)$ on a data type $\Phi(\mathcal{D})$ whose space of values is $I \to D$, for some indexing set I. The definition of $\Phi(op)$ is given by

$$\Phi(op) \;==\; cp \mathbin{;} \begin{array}{c} \mathrm{id} \\ \| \\ apply \mathbin{;} op \end{array} \mathbin{;} ovr$$

where cp and $\|$ are as defined in Chapter 16.

If the data types $\mathcal{A}$ and C are linked by a forwards simulation ρ, then the retrieve relation between promoted data types $\Phi(\mathcal{A})$ and $\Phi(C)$ is identified by the following equation:

$$r \;=\; img(\mathrm{id} \parallel \rho)$$

We will now demonstrate that r defines a forwards simulation from A to C, and thus that $\Phi(C)$ refines $\Phi(\mathcal{A})$. Consider the correctness condition for a matching pair of operations *ao* and *co*:

$$(r \parallel \mathrm{id}) \fatsemi \Phi(co) \subseteq \Phi(ao) \fatsemi r$$

Observe that each side is a relation drawn from $A \times I \leftrightarrow A$; we require the index of that part of the state which is being updated.

We may rewrite the left-hand side of this inequation using to the laws of the relational calculus, the definitions of *apply* and *ovr*, and the properties of our retrieve and promotion relations.

$$
\begin{array}{ll}
(r \parallel \mathrm{id}) \fatsemi \Phi(co) & \\[1em]
= (r \parallel \mathrm{id}) \fatsemi cp \fatsemi \begin{array}{c}\mathrm{id}\\ \parallel \\ apply \fatsemi co\end{array} \fatsemi ovr & [\text{by definition of } \Phi(co)] \\[2em]
\subseteq cp \fatsemi \begin{array}{c}r \parallel \mathrm{id}\\ \parallel \\ r \parallel \mathrm{id}\end{array} \fatsemi \begin{array}{c}\mathrm{id}\\ \parallel \\ apply \fatsemi co\end{array} \fatsemi ovr & [\text{property of } cp] \\[2em]
= cp \fatsemi \begin{array}{c}(r \parallel \mathrm{id}) \fatsemi \mathrm{id}\\ \parallel \\ (r \parallel \mathrm{id}) \fatsemi apply \fatsemi co\end{array} \fatsemi ovr & [\text{abiding property}] \\[2em]
= cp \fatsemi \begin{array}{c}r \parallel \mathrm{id}\\ \parallel \\ (img(\mathrm{id} \parallel \rho) \parallel \mathrm{id}) \fatsemi apply \fatsemi co\end{array} \fatsemi ovr & [\mathrm{id} \text{ unit}] \\[2em]
= cp \fatsemi \begin{array}{c}r \parallel \mathrm{id}\\ \parallel \\ apply \fatsemi \rho \fatsemi co\end{array} \fatsemi ovr & [\text{property of } apply] \\[2em]
\subseteq cp \fatsemi \begin{array}{c}r \parallel \mathrm{id}\\ \parallel \\ apply \fatsemi ao \fatsemi \rho\end{array} \fatsemi ovr & [\text{since } \mathcal{A} \sqsubseteq C] \\[2em]
= cp \fatsemi \begin{array}{c}\mathrm{id} \fatsemi (r \parallel \mathrm{id})\\ \parallel \\ apply \fatsemi ao \fatsemi \rho\end{array} \fatsemi ovr & [\mathrm{id} \text{ unit}] \\[2em]
= cp \fatsemi \begin{array}{c}\mathrm{id}\\ \parallel \\ apply \fatsemi ao\end{array} \fatsemi \begin{array}{c}r \parallel \mathrm{id}\\ \parallel \\ \rho\end{array} \fatsemi ovr & [\text{abiding property}]
\end{array}
$$

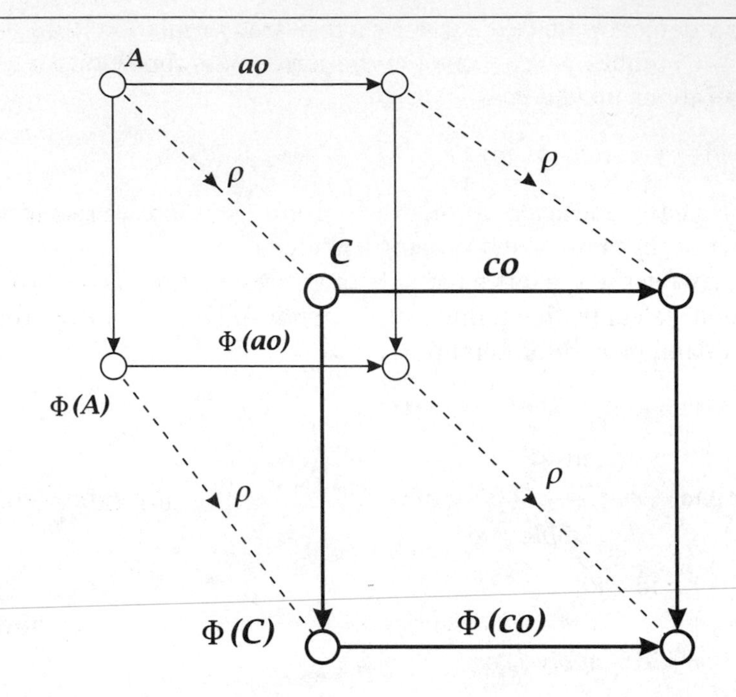

Figure 18.1: Refining promotion

$$= cp \fatsemi \begin{array}{c} \mathrm{id} \\ \| \\ apply \fatsemi ao \end{array} \fatsemi \begin{array}{c} img(\mathrm{id} \parallel \rho) \parallel \mathrm{id} \\ \| \\ \rho \end{array} \fatsemi ovr \qquad [\text{definition of } r]$$

$$= cp \fatsemi \begin{array}{c} \mathrm{id} \\ \| \\ apply \fatsemi ao \end{array} \fatsemi ovr \fatsemi img(\mathrm{id} \parallel \rho) \qquad [\text{property of } ovr]$$

$$= cp \fatsemi \begin{array}{c} \mathrm{id} \\ \| \\ apply \fatsemi ao \end{array} \fatsemi ovr \fatsemi r \qquad [\text{definition of } r]$$

$$= \Phi(ao) \fatsemi r \qquad [\text{definition of } \Phi(ao)]$$

This shows that the promotion of *co* correctly refines the promotion of *ao*, as in Figure 18.1. The application of this should be obvious: we may specify an abstract data type, and then calculate its promotion. When we come to refine the abstract data type, the same calculation promotes the more concrete data type into a correct refinement of the promoted system.

Example 18.5 The simple temperature sensor may be used in situations where there is more than one temperature to record. As a specification, we may take the obvious promotion of the Fahrenheit data type. If *Ind* represent the set of indices used to refer to the individual temperatures, then the state consists of a total function:

$$FTDisplay \mathrel{\widehat{=}} [\, fd : Ind \rightarrow FTemp \,]$$

The promotion of each operation is simple:

$$\begin{array}{|l} \textit{FTPromote} \\ \hline \Delta FTDisplay \\ \Delta FTemp \\ i? : Ind \\ \hline \theta FTemp = fd\ i? \\ fd' = fd \oplus \{ i? \mapsto \theta FTemp' \} \\ \hline \end{array}$$

The promoted operations are

$$FTDisplayInc \mathrel{\widehat{=}} \exists \Delta FTemp \bullet FTPromote \land FTInc$$
$$FTDisplayDec \mathrel{\widehat{=}} \exists \Delta FTemp \bullet FTPromote \land FTDec$$

The concrete state of the new system is described by

$$CTDisplay \mathrel{\widehat{=}} [\, cd : Ind \rightarrow CTemp \,]$$

with the following promotion:

$$\begin{array}{|l} \textit{CTPromote} \\ \hline \Delta CTDisplay \\ \Delta CTemp \\ i? : Ind \\ \hline \theta CTemp = cd\ i? \\ cd' = cd \oplus \{ i? \mapsto \theta CTemp' \} \\ \hline \end{array}$$

The refined, promoted operations are

$$CTDisplayInc \mathrel{\widehat{=}} \exists \Delta CTemp \bullet CTPromote \land CTInc$$
$$CTDisplayDec \mathrel{\widehat{=}} \exists \Delta CTemp \bullet CTPromote \land CTDec$$

□

Chapter 19

Refinement Calculus

We have seen that an abstract specification may be refined until a suitable concrete design is reached. Such a design may be translated into an abstract programming notation and then refined further, to yield a description in the language of guarded commands. This description may be translated into a standard programming language.

Specification (schemas)

⇘ *refinement*

Design (schemas)

⇘ *translation*

Algorithm (abstract program)

⇘ *refinement*

Code (guarded commands)

⇘ *translation*

Code (programming language)

The abstract programming notation that we will use is a *refinement calculus* for the schema language. In this chapter, we will see how to translate schemas into *specification statements*, and how to refine these statements towards executable program code.

19.1 The specification statement

In our formal specifications, we use schemas to describe operations upon an abstract data type. An alternative approach involves the use of *specification statements*: abstract programs consisting of a precondition, a postcondition, and a list of variables.

If *frame* is a list of variables, and *precondition* and *postcondition* are both predicates upon the state, then

$$frame : [\, precondition,\ postcondition \,]$$

is a specification statement. It describes an operation that that begins in a state satisfying *precondition* and ends in a state satisfying *postcondition*. Only those variables listed in *frame* are affected.

Example 19.1 In Example 12.10, we used a schema to describe an operation with a single output: the number of free seats remaining in the box office. This operation could also be described by the following specification statement:

$$available! : [\, true,\ available! = free(\theta BoxOffice) \,]$$

The operation changes the value of *available*! so that it is equal to the value of $free(\theta BoxOffice)$. □

If a specification statement refers to a variable that is not declared in its frame, then it must leave the value of that variable unchanged.

Example 19.2 The following specification statement describes the operation of finding an approximate root for a function—a value m such that $f(m)$ is close to zero—within a particular interval $[a, b]$. It will fail if no such value exists:

$$m : \left[\begin{array}{c} f(a) * f(b) \leq 0 \\ a \leq b \end{array} ,\ \begin{array}{c} -0.1 < f(m') < 0.1 \\ a \leq m' \leq b \end{array} \right]$$

The operation is not allowed to change a, b, or f in order to achieve the desired result: these variables are not included in the frame. □

A specification statement as a program that terminates if started when *precondition* is true, modifies only those variables in *frame*, and produces a result satisfying *postcondition*. We can combine this program with others, using the constructs of the guarded command language: if ··· fi, do ··· od, begin ··· end, and '; '.

If the precondition of a specification statement is *false*, then there is no guarantee that the corresponding program will terminate. The specification statement abort is an extreme example of this:

$$\mathsf{abort} \;=\; w : [\, \mathit{false},\ \mathit{true} \,]$$

This represents a program that may fail to terminate whatever the initial state. Even if it does terminate, we can say nothing about the final state.

Another statement that may produce any result is choose w. In this case, the program is guaranteed to terminate, but may do anything to the values of variables in w:

$$\mathsf{choose}\ w \;=\; w : [\, \mathit{true},\ \mathit{true} \,]$$

The special case in which there are no variables to modify—the list w is empty—is described by skip:

$$\mathsf{skip} \;=\; [\, \mathit{true},\ \mathit{true} \,]$$

This is guaranteed to terminate, but can change nothing.

The statement magic describes an impossible program: a program guaranteed to terminate and establish the postcondition *false*:

$$\mathsf{magic} \;=\; w : [\, \mathit{true},\ \mathit{false} \,]$$

Notice that this program cannot be described by an operation schema: in the schema language, an impossible constraint leads to a false precondition.

19.2 Assignment

A program in the refinement calculus may consist of a mixture of specification statements and code. For example, the following program is the sequential composition of a specification statement and an assignment:

$$x, y : \left[\begin{array}{ll} x = X & x' = X - Y \\ y = Y\ , & y' = X \end{array} \right] ; \quad x := y - x$$

Any specification statement may be *refined* towards code, using a number of simple laws. An application of the refinement calculus may involve a number of refinements, beginning with a single specification statement, and ending with a program consisting only of guarded commands.

If a program P is correctly refined by another program Q, then we write $P \sqsubseteq Q$: pronounced 'P is refined by Q'. Naturally, refinement is transitive:

$$P \sqsubseteq Q \land Q \sqsubseteq R \Rightarrow P \sqsubseteq R$$

In our use of the refinement calculus, each refinement step will correspond to the application of a law involving the $\sqsubseteq$ symbol.

A simple way to refine a specification statement is to strengthen the post-condition: we are then agreeing to do more than was originally required.

Law 19.1 (strengthen postcondition) If $post_2$ is stronger than $post_1$ whenever pre is true—that is, if

$$pre \land post_2 \Rightarrow post_1$$

—then

$$w : [\, pre, post_1 \,] \sqsubseteq w : [\, pre, post_2 \,]$$

□

Example 19.3 Since $x < 0.01 \Rightarrow x < 0.1$, we have that

$$m : \left[\begin{array}{cc} f(a) * f(b) \leq 0 & -0.1 < f(m') < 0.1 \\ a \leq b & , \quad a \leq m' \leq b \end{array} \right]$$

$$\sqsubseteq \quad \text{(strengthen postcondition)}$$

$$m : \left[\begin{array}{cc} f(a) * f(b) \leq 0 & -0.01 < f(m') < 0.01 \\ a \leq b & , \quad a \leq m' \leq b \end{array} \right]$$

The refinement step has produced a more deterministic program, one that insists upon a closer approximation. □

Another simple way to refine a specification statement is to weaken the precondition: we have broadened the terms of our guarantee with respect to termination.

Law 19.2 (weaken precondition) If $pre_1 \Rightarrow pre_2$ then

$$w : [\, pre_1, post \,] \sqsubseteq w : [\, pre_2, post \,]$$

□

Example 19.4 Since

$$f(a) * f(b) \leq 0 \wedge a \leq b \Rightarrow f(a) * f(b) \leq 0$$

we have that

$$m : \left[\begin{array}{c} f(a) * f(b) \leq 0 \\ a \leq b \end{array} , \begin{array}{c} -0.01 < f(m') < 0.01 \\ a \leq m' \leq b \end{array} \right]$$

$$\sqsubseteq \quad \text{(weaken precondition)}$$

$$m : \left[\begin{array}{c} f(a) * f(b) \leq 0 \\ \end{array} , \begin{array}{c} -0.01 < f(m') < 0.01 \\ a \leq m' \leq b \end{array} \right]$$

We now require an implementation to produce a correct result even when a and b fail to describe an interval. This may be too much to ask: if $b < a$, then the postcondition will not be satisfiable. □

A specification statement is said to be *feasible* if and only if, whenever the precondition holds, there is an instantiation of the frame variables which satisfies the postcondition. For example, if the frame contains x and y of types X and Y respectively, *pre* is the precondition, and *post* is the postcondition, then

$$pre \Rightarrow \exists x' : X; y' : Y \bullet post$$

If a specification is infeasible, then we will not be able to refine it to code.

Example 19.5 If $a = 1$, $b = -3$, and $f(x) = x$, then it is certainly true that

$$f(a) * f(b) \leq 0$$

but there can be no m' such that $a \leq m' \leq b$. Hence the implication

$$f(a) * f(b) \leq 0 \Rightarrow \\ \quad \exists m' : \mathbb{R} \bullet -0.01 < f(m') < 0.01 \wedge a \leq m' \leq b$$

is false, and the specification statement

$$m : \left[\begin{array}{c} f(a) * f(b) \leq 0 \\ \end{array} , \begin{array}{c} -0.01 < f(m') < 0.01 \\ a \leq m' \leq b \end{array} \right]$$

is infeasible. □

In the refinement calculus, program variables may be introduced using a declaration and a constraint; we call the constraint an *invariant*, as it must be true whenever the variables are used. The start of a declaration is marked by the symbol begin, the start of the corresponding variable scope by •, and the end of a scope by the symbol end.

Law 19.3 (introduce local block) If x is a variable that does not appear in frame w, and *inv* is a predicate on x, then

$$w : [\, pre,\ post \,] \sqsubseteq \begin{array}{l} \mathsf{begin} \\ \quad \mathsf{var}\ x : T \mid inv \bullet \\ \qquad w, x : [\, pre,\ post \,] \\ \mathsf{end} \end{array}$$

Where the scope of the declaration is clear, we may choose to omit the begin and end symbols. □

Example 19.6

$$m : \left[\begin{array}{ll} f(a) * f(b) \le 0 & -0.1 < f(m') < 0.1 \\ a \le b & ,\quad a \le m' \le b \end{array} \right]$$

$$\sqsubseteq \quad \text{(introduce local block)}$$

$$\begin{array}{l} \mathsf{begin} \\ \quad \mathsf{var}\ x, y \bullet \\ \qquad x, y, m : \left[\begin{array}{ll} f(a) * f(b) \le 0 & -0.1 < f(m') < 0.1 \\ a \le b & ,\quad a \le m' \le b \end{array} \right] \\ \mathsf{end} \end{array}$$

□

We require some way of distinguishing between the value of a variable before an operation, and the value of that same variable afterwards. If x is a variable that appears in the frame, we write x to denote its value beforehand, and x' to denote its value afterwards. There is no need to decorate variables that are not in the frame, as they cannot be changed by the operation.

A postcondition may include free occurrences of both decorated and undecorated after variables, as in the statement

$$x : [\, true,\ x' < x \,]$$

which requires that x be decreased: its value afterwards must be strictly less than its value before.

If there is a substitution of decorated variables that makes the postcondition an immediate consequence of the precondition, then we may refine the specification statement to an assignment.

Law 19.4 (assignment introduction) If E is an expression with the same type as w such that

$$pre \Rightarrow post[E/w', x/x']$$

then

$$w, x : [\, pre, post \,] \sqsubseteq w := E$$

□

Variables that are not assigned to have the same value after the operation as before, hence the substitution of x for x' above.

Example 19.7 Since $(x' = x + 1)[x + 1/x']$ we have

$$x : [\, true, x' = x + 1 \,] \sqsubseteq x := x + 1$$

□

If the current values of the variables in the frame are enough to make the postcondition true, then the specification statement can be replaced by skip.

Law 19.5 (skip introduction) If $pre \Rightarrow post[w/w']$ then

$$w : [\, pre, post \,] \sqsubseteq \mathsf{skip}$$

□

Example 19.8 Since $x = 5 \wedge y = x^3 \Rightarrow x = 5$, we have that

$$x, y : [\, x = 5 \wedge y = x^3, x' = 5 \,]$$

$$\sqsubseteq \mathsf{skip}$$

□

19.3 Logical constants

It is often convenient to introduce fresh mathematical variables to represent certain values. For example, in the following program we use variables X and Y to represent the initial values of x and y:

$$x, y : \left[\begin{array}{ll} x = X & x' = X - Y \\ y = Y \ , & y' = X \end{array} \right] ; \ x := y - x$$

The variables X and Y will not form part of the final code; they are merely a logical device. They are called *logical constants*, and may be declared as follows:

begin con $X : T \bullet prog$ end

This declaration introduces a logical constant named X, which ranges over T. Its scope is delimited by the local block begin $\cdots$ end.

Example 19.9 The following composition of specification statements describes a program that must strictly increase the value of variable x twice:

begin
    con $X \bullet x : [\, x = X,\ x' > X \,]$
end;
begin
    con $X \bullet x : [\, x = X,\ x' > X \,]$
end

The scope of each logical constant is important. The following statement describes a program with quite different behaviour:

begin
    con $X \bullet x : [\, x = X,\ x' > X \,];\ \ x : [\, x = X,\ x' > X \,]$
end

□

Logical constants are used to give names to things that already exist. A simple example is the way in which they may be used to fix the before value of a variable: for example,

begin con $X \bullet x : [\, x = X,\ x' > X \,]$ end

The variable X takes a value that makes subsequent *preconditions* true, if possible. Within the scope of X, there is only one precondition, $x = X$, and X takes on this value: namely, the value of x before the specification statement. This particular statement is equivalent to

$$\text{begin con } X \bullet x : [\, true,\ x' > x \,] \text{ end}$$

More generally, we can introduce a logical constant in much the same way as we would introduce an existential quantifier.

Law 19.6 (introduce logical constant) If $pre_1 \Rightarrow (\exists\, C : T \bullet pre_2)$, and C is a fresh name, then

$$w : [\, pre_1,\ post \,] \quad \sqsubseteq \quad \left\{ \begin{array}{l} \text{begin} \\ \qquad \text{con } C : T \bullet w : [\, pre_2,\ post \,] \\ \text{end} \end{array} \right.$$

□

Conversely, if a logical constant is no longer mentioned in a program, then we can eliminate its declaration. This corresponds to the elimination of an existential quantifier.

Law 19.7 (eliminate logical constant) If C occurs nowhere in *prog*, then

$$\left. \begin{array}{l} \text{begin} \\ \qquad \text{con } C : T \bullet prog \\ \text{end} \end{array} \right\} \quad \sqsubseteq \quad prog$$

□

Logical constants are rarely found in programming languages, and are certainly not the kind of constant that one finds in C. In order to declare a more conventional constant, one can introduce a state variable which has an invariant that says that it never changes. For example, one might wish to declare a constant whose value is a fixed approximation to π. This is done by introducing a variable, and then constraining it to be constant:

$$\begin{array}{l} \text{begin} \\ \qquad \text{var } pi : \mathbb{R} \mid pi = 22/7 \bullet \\ \qquad\qquad \vdots \\ \text{end} \end{array}$$

19.4 Sequential composition

A specification statement describes a task: change the values of the variables in the frame so that the postcondition is achieved. It is often possible to divide this task into two smaller tasks, to be performed sequentially. Instead of proceeding directly from *pre* to *post*, we use one program to move from *pre* to an intermediate result *mid*. A second program can then be used to move from *mid* to *post*.

The intermediate result *mid* is characterised by a predicate upon the variables in the frame. Without loss of generality, suppose that x is the only variable that is changed during the first task. The first program is then

$$x : [\, pre,\ mid \,]$$

To obtain the precondition and postcondition for the second program, some substitutions are necessary.

In the precondition of the second program, we use x to refer to the value of x when that program starts. This is precisely the value of that variable when the first program finishes, represented by x' in *mid*. The precondition might also make reference to the value of x when the first program starts, represented by x in *mid*. To avoid confusion, we will replace this value with a logical constant X.

The postcondition is similar to *post*, except that we can no longer use x to refer to the value of x when the first program starts. We must replace x with the same logical constant X. The second program is then

$$w, x : [\, mid[X/x, x/x'],\ post[X/x] \,]$$

Notice that the second task may involve changing variables other than x.

Law 19.8 (sequential composition introduction) For fresh constants X,

$$w, x : [\, pre,\ post \,] \quad \sqsubseteq \quad \left\{ \begin{array}{l} \mathsf{begin} \\ \quad \mathsf{con}\ X \bullet \\ \quad\quad x : [\, pre,\ mid \,]; \\ \quad\quad w, x : [\, mid[X/x, x/x'],\ post[X/x] \,] \\ \mathsf{end} \end{array} \right.$$

The predicate *mid* must not contain before variables other than x. □

Example 19.10

$$x : [\, true,\ x' = x + 2 \,]$$

$\sqsubseteq$ (sequential composition introduction)

con X •

$x : [\, true,\ x' = x + 1 \,];$

$x : [\, x = X + 1,\ x' = X + 2 \,]$

□

Example 19.11 Suppose that we want to swap two variables without using a third variable to store the intermediate value. Suitable code might be developed as follows:

$x, y : [\, true,\ x' = y \land y' = x \,]$

$\sqsubseteq$ (sequential composition introduction)

con $X_1, Y_1 : \mathbb{Z}$ •

$x, y : [\, true,\ x' = x - y \land y' = x \,];$ [◁]

$x, y : \left[\begin{array}{ll} x = X_1 - Y_1 & x' = Y_1 \\ y = X_1 & ,\ y' = X_1 \end{array} \right]$ [†]

$\sqsubseteq$ (sequential composition introduction)

con X_2, Y_2 •

$x, y : [\, true,\ x' = x - y \land y' = y \,];$ [◁]

$x, y : \left[\begin{array}{ll} x = X_2 - Y_2 & x' = X_2 - Y_2 \\ y = Y_2 & ,\ y' = X_2 \end{array} \right]$ [‡]

$\sqsubseteq$ (assignment introduction)

$x := x - y$

‡

$\sqsubseteq$ (assignment introduction)

$y := x + y$

†

$\sqsubseteq$ (assignment introduction)

$x := y - x$

Note the use of marginal markers. The ◁ symbol always points to the next part of the program to be refined. Other marginal markers refer to parts of the program whose development proceeds at a later point.

The development is recorded as a flattened tree of refinements. It is not difficult to see how the tree may be walked in order to extract the code from the development. If we do this, we obtain

$$x, y : [\, x = X \land y = Y,\ x = Y \land y = X \,]$$

$$\sqsubseteq$$

```
begin con X₁, Y₁ : ℤ •
    begin con X₂, Y₂ •
        x := x − y ;
        y := x + y
    end ;
    x := y − x
end
```

$$\sqsubseteq$$

$$x := x - y\ ;$$
$$y := x + y\ ;$$
$$x := y - x$$

□

If we want to introduce a sequential composition where the *mid* and *post* predicates make no reference to the before variables, then a simpler version of the rule may be used:

Law 19.9 (simple sequential composition) If the predicates *mid* and *post* make no reference to before variables, then

$$w, x : [\, pre,\ post \,] \quad \sqsubseteq \quad x : [\, pre,\ mid \,]\ ;\ \ w, x : [\, mid[x/x'],\ post \,]$$

□

We will often wish to introduce a sequential composition and then reduce one of the two statements to an assignment. There are two ways in which this can be done, corresponding to the following pair of derived rules.

Law 19.10 (leading assignment)

$$w, x : [\, pre[E/x],\ post[E/x] \,] \quad \sqsubseteq \quad x := E\ ;\ \ w, x : [\, pre,\ post \,]$$

□

Law 19.11 (following assignment)

$$w, x : [\, pre,\ post \,] \ \sqsubseteq \ w : [\, pre,\ post[E/x'] \,] \ ; \ \ x := E$$

□

These rules are easy to apply. First we decide upon the assignment that is to be performed, then we calculate the new specification statement.

19.5 Conditional statements

In our abstract programming notation, the *language of guarded commands*, a conditional statement takes the following form:

$$\begin{array}{l} \mathsf{if} \ \ G_1 \rightarrow com_1 \\ \square \ \ G_2 \rightarrow com_2 \\ \quad \vdots \\ \square \ \ G_n \rightarrow com_n \\ \mathsf{fi} \end{array}$$

Each branch $G_i \rightarrow com_i$ is a guarded command: G_i is the guard, and com_i is the command. When this conditional is activated the guards $G_1, G_2, \ldots, G_n$ are evaluated, and one of the commands whose guard is true is executed. If no guard is true, then the program aborts.

Law 19.12 (conditional introduction) If $pre \Rightarrow (G_1 \lor G_2 \lor \ldots \lor G_n)$ then

$$w : [\, pre,\ post \,] \ \sqsubseteq \ \left\{ \begin{array}{l} \mathsf{if} \ \ G_1 \rightarrow w : [\, G_1 \land pre,\ post \,] \\ \square \ \ G_2 \rightarrow w : [\, G_2 \land pre,\ post \,] \\ \vdots \\ \square \ \ G_n \rightarrow w : [\, G_n \land pre,\ post \,] \\ \mathsf{fi} \end{array} \right.$$

□

If the specification is required to terminate, then the conditional must not abort: the precondition must establish that at least one guard is true. Furthermore, whichever branch is taken must implement the specification, under the assumption that the corresponding guard is true.

We will also employ a generalised form of the conditional statement, in which the indexing variable may take any finite range:

$$\mathsf{if} \ \ i : S \ \square \ G_i \rightarrow com_i \ \mathsf{fi}$$

where S is a finite set.

Law 19.13 (generalised conditional introduction) If $pre \Rightarrow \exists\, i : S \bullet G_i$ and S is a finite set, then

$$w : [\, pre,\ post\,] \ \sqsubseteq\ \textsf{if}\ \ i : S \ \square\ G_i \rightarrow w : [\, G_i \wedge pre,\ post\,]\ \textsf{fi}$$

□

Example 19.12 Given two variables x and y, we may develop a program that will ensure that $x \le y$, by preserving their values, or swapping them if necessary:

$$x, y : \left[\begin{array}{c} x \le y \wedge x' = x \wedge y' = y \\ \vee \\ true\ ,\ y \le x \wedge x' = y \wedge y' = x \end{array}\right]$$

$\sqsubseteq$ (conditional introduction)

$$\begin{array}{llr} \textsf{if}\ \ x \le y \rightarrow x, y : \left[\begin{array}{c} x \le y \wedge x' = x \wedge y' = y \\ \vee \\ x \le y\ ,\ y \le x \wedge x' = y \wedge y' = x \end{array}\right] & & [\triangleleft] \\ \square\ \ y \le x \rightarrow x, y : \left[\begin{array}{c} x \le y \wedge x' = x \wedge y' = y \\ \vee \\ y \le x\ ,\ y \le x \wedge x' = y \wedge y' = x) \end{array}\right] & & [\dagger] \\ \textsf{fi} & & \end{array}$$

$\sqsubseteq$ (strengthen postcondition)

$x, y : [\, x \le y,\ x \le y \wedge x' = x \wedge y' = y\,]$

$\sqsubseteq$ (skip introduction)

skip

We complete the development with

†

$\sqsubseteq$ (strengthen postcondition)

$x, y : [\, y \le x,\ y \le x \wedge x' = y \wedge y' = x\,]$

$\sqsubseteq$ (assignment introduction)

$x, y := y, x$

Notice that the disjunction of the guards is true, thus validating the introduction of the conditional. The program is

$$\begin{array}{l} \text{if } x \leq y \rightarrow \text{skip} \\ \Box\ y \leq x \rightarrow x, y := y, x \\ \text{fi} \end{array}$$

□

To end this section, we present a pair of laws for manipulating the frame in a specification statement. If we drop the name of a variable from the frame, then it cannot change; thus, we may remove the after decoration from any of its occurrences in the postcondition.

Law 19.14 (contract frame)

$$w, x : [\, pre,\ post\,] \sqsubseteq w : [\, pre,\ post[x/x']\,]$$

□

Conversely, we can expand the frame of a statement by adding additional variables. These new variables may not be changed by the postcondition.

Law 19.15 (expand frame)

$$w : [\, pre,\ post\,] = w, x : [\, pre,\ post \wedge x' = x\,]$$

□

19.6 Iteration

In our language of guarded commands, the iteration construct is similar in form to the conditional statement:

$$\begin{array}{l} \text{do } G_1 \rightarrow com_1 \\ \Box\ G_2 \rightarrow com_2 \\ \quad \vdots \\ \Box\ G_n \rightarrow com_n \\ \text{od} \end{array}$$

When this statement is reached, the guards are evaluated and one of the commands whose guard is true is executed. This is repeated until no guard is true, at which point the statement terminates.

To see how a refinement law for this construct may be formulated, suppose that *inv* is an invariant property of the loop: that is, a predicate that must be true before and after every iteration. Suppose further that G represents the disjunction of guards: the condition that must be true if the statement is not to terminate immediately. Such a loop may refine a specification statement that includes *inv* in the precondition, and $inv \wedge \neg G$ in the postcondition.

For the refinement to be correct, the loop must be guaranteed to terminate. It is enough to identify a *variant* for the loop: an integer-valued function that must decrease with each iteration, but which never passes zero. If V is such a function, then the loop

$$\text{do } G \rightarrow w : [\, inv \wedge G,\ inv[w'/w] \wedge 0 \leq V[w'/w] < V \,] \text{ od}$$

will refine the statement $w : [\, inv,\ inv[w'/w] \wedge \neg G[w'/w] \,]$. More formally, we have the following law:

Law 19.16 (loop introduction)

$$w : \left[\begin{array}{ll} & \neg G[w'/w] \\ inv \;, & inv[w'/w] \end{array}\right] \sqsubseteq \left\{\begin{array}{l} \text{do} \\ \quad G \rightarrow \\ \qquad w : \left[\begin{array}{ll} G & inv[w'/w] \\ inv \;, & 0 \leq V[w'/w] < V \end{array}\right] \\ \text{od} \end{array}\right.$$

□

Example 19.13 Suppose that we have an injective sequence s of integer values, one of which is our *target*, and we want to establish where in the sequence it lies. If we want to put the *target*'s index into the variable i, then we can specify this task as

$$i : [\, target \in \operatorname{ran} s,\ s(i') = target \,]$$

As we don't have any information on how the members of s are arranged, we shall have to search s, and we may as well do a linear search, starting at the beginning and working up.

Consider the variant for the loop that will be required. Since we know that the *target* appears in the sequence, we know that $\#s$ is an upper bound for the total number of iterations, and in practice, we hope to do better than this. We can actually give a precise value to the number of iterations required by using a logical constant to name the position we are looking for. Since

$$target \in \operatorname{ran} s \Rightarrow \exists I : \mathbb{Z} \bullet s(I) = target$$

we can refine our specification to

$$
\begin{array}{l}
\textsf{begin} \\
\quad \textsf{con}\, I : 1\,..\,\#s \bullet \\
\qquad\quad i : [\, s(I) = \mathit{target},\ s(i') = \mathit{target}\,] \\
\textsf{end}
\end{array}
$$

Our variant will be $I - i$, and our invariant will be that I indexes the *target*, and that we haven't passed it by: $s(I) = \mathit{target} \wedge i \leq I$.

In order to set up the pattern for the loop introduction rule, we split the specification in two, thus:

$$
\begin{array}{l}
i : [\, s(I) = \mathit{target},\ s(I) = \mathit{target} \wedge i' \leq I\,]; \\
i : [\, s(I) = \mathit{target} \wedge i \leq I,\ s(i') = \mathit{target}\,]
\end{array}
$$

The first specification statement is easily disposed of using the assignment introduction rule, to yield $i := 1$. We may then strengthen the postcondition of the second to obtain

$$
i : \left[\begin{array}{cc} & s(i') = \mathit{target} \\ s(I) = \mathit{target} & s(I) = \mathit{target} \\ i \leq I & ,\quad i' \leq I \end{array} \right]
$$

Now the specification matches the pattern for the application of the loop rule, we turn the handle, and out pops

$$
\begin{array}{l}
\textsf{do} \\
\quad s(i) \neq \mathit{target} \rightarrow \\
\qquad\qquad i : \left[\begin{array}{cc} s(I) = \mathit{target} & s(I) = \mathit{target} \\ i \leq I & i' \leq I \\ s(i) \neq \mathit{target} & ,\ 0 \leq I - i' < I - i \end{array} \right] \\
\textsf{od}
\end{array}
$$

The body of the loop is implemented by the assignment $i := i + 1$. Summarising all this, we have the (entirely obvious) program

$$
\begin{array}{l}
i := 1;\ \ \textsf{do} \\
\qquad\qquad s(i) \neq \mathit{target} \rightarrow \\
\qquad\qquad\qquad i := i + 1 \\
\qquad\ \ \textsf{od}
\end{array}
$$

In this development, the use of a logical constant was a useful device in developing the variant and the invariant for the loop. Once it was clear what these were, the appropriate pattern was set up by splitting the specification into two, the first part becoming the initialisation, and the second part becoming the loop itself; the invariant defined what the *mid* predicate should be. The postcondition was then strengthened so that it contained the invariant, and the remainder formed the (negated) guard. □

Example 19.14 Suppose that we wish to initialise an integer array so that every entry is zero. An array may be modelled mathematically as a total function from a set of indices to values (in this case, numbers):

$$ar : (1..n) \rightarrow \mathbb{N}$$

The initialisation operation has the task of assigning the value 0 to every element in the array. Its specification is given by

$$Init \;=\; ar : [\, true,\ \operatorname{ran} ar' = \{0\} \,]$$

Our first step in developing the code for this rather simple operation is to use an obvious transformation of the postcondition:

$$Init \;=\; ar : [\, true,\ \forall j : 1..n \bullet ar'\, j = 0 \,]$$

The reason for this is that we intend to implement the operation using a loop, and the universal quantifier points to the way that the loop might be developed. One strategy for loop development is to take such a quantified expression, and replace a constant by a variable. The following shorthand helps us in doing this:

$$zeroed(i, ar) \;=\; \forall j : 1..i \bullet ar\, j = 0$$

The development of the code now follows. The refinement calculus should be used with a light touch, rather than in this heavy-handed manner; however, we go into greater detail so that the reader may follow our reasoning.

$$ar : [\, true,\ zeroed(n, ar') \,]$$

$$\sqsubseteq$$

$$\mathsf{var}\ j \mid 1 \leq j \leq n + 1 \bullet$$
$$\quad j, ar : [\, true,\ zeroed(n, ar') \,]$$

The variable j will be used as a loop counter; thus it will range from the smallest element in the domain of ar to just after the highest.

$\sqsubseteq$ (simple sequential composition)

$$j, ar : [\, true,\ zeroed(j' - 1, ar')\,]; \qquad [\lhd]$$

$$j, ar : [\, zeroed(j - 1, ar),\ zeroed(n, ar')\,] \qquad [\dagger]$$

We introduce the semicolon in order to choose the loop invariant. At the beginning of the loop, and after each iteration, we will have zeroed all the blocks up, but not including j. The specification statement before the semicolon must establish the invariant, and the one after must be developed into the loop.

$\sqsubseteq$ (assignment introduction)

$$j := 1$$

If we set j to 1, then we have zeroed no blocks.

Our development continues with a refinement of $\dagger$:

$\dagger$

$\sqsubseteq$ (strengthen postcondition)

$$j, ar : [\, zeroed(j - 1, ar),\ zeroed(j' - 1, ar') \land j' = n + 1\,]$$

Provided that $zeroed(j' - 1, ar') \land j' = n + 1 \Rightarrow zeroed(n, ar')$.

Having added the invariant to the postcondition, we can apply the loop introduction rule:

$\sqsubseteq$ (loop introduction)

$$\text{do } j \neq n + 1 \rightarrow$$

$$j, ar : \left[\begin{array}{cc} j \neq n + 1 & 0 \leq n - j' + 1 < n - j + 1 \\ zeroed(j - 1, ar)\ , & zeroed(j' - 1, ar') \end{array} \right]$$

$$\text{od}$$

The function $n - j + 1$ is our variant: when we enter the loop with $j = 1$, we have n more iterations to perform:

$\sqsubseteq$ (following assignment)

$$ar : \left[\begin{array}{c} j \neq n + 1 \\ zeroed(j - 1, ar)\ ,\ zeroed(j, ar') \end{array} \right]; \qquad [\lhd]$$

$$j := j + 1$$

In the implementation of the body of the loop, we shall need to increment j. Since we started j with the value 1, the assignment to j must be done at the end of the loop.

The only thing left to do is to free the next element of *ar*, that is, the jth element:

$\sqsubseteq$ (assignment introduction)

$$ar := ar \oplus \{j \mapsto 0\}$$

There are several small proof obligations to be fulfilled: the more significant ones are

- $zeroed(0, ar)$
- $zeroed(j - 1, ar) \wedge j = n + 1 \Rightarrow zeroed(n, ar)$
- $j \neq n + 1 \wedge zeroed(j - 1, ar) \Rightarrow j \neq n + 1 \wedge zeroed(j, ar \oplus \{j \mapsto 0\})$

The first and third predicates are simple properties of *zeroed*, and the second follows from the properties of equality. Summarising our development, we have that shown that *Init* is refined by

```
begin
    var j | 1 ≤ j ≤ n + 1 •
        j := 1;
        do j ≠ n + 1 →
            ar := update(ar, j, 0);
            j := j + 1
        od
end
```

This might be translated into Modula2 as

```
PROCEDURE Init ;
  BEGIN
    FOR j := 1 TO n DO ar[j] := 0
  END
```

□

Example 19.15 We would like to develop an algorithm that converts numbers from a base β to the base 10. For an $n+1$ digit number, a solution that requires more than n multiplications is not acceptable.

Take as an example the following binary number: 10011100. It is well known that it may be converted to the decimal number calculated from the following expression:

$$1 * 2^7 + 0 * 2^6 + 0 * 2^5 + 1 * 2^4 + 1 * 2^3 + 1 * 2^2 + 0 * 2^1 + 0 * 2^0$$
$$= 156$$

Clearly, the calculation has used a polynomial to relate binary to decimal numbers. To express this, suppose for convenience that the number in base β is presented in an array of n elements, with each digit in a separate element, and with a_1 representing the least significant digit. The elements of the array represent the coefficients of a polynomial of degree $n - 1$:

$$a_1 + a_2 * \beta + a_3 * \beta^2 + \cdots + a_n * \beta^{n-1}$$

How should we develop some code that will evaluate this polynomial for a particular value of β? A straightforward approach might be to adapt some code that simply sums the elements of an array. If we insert into each location i in the array the value of the expression $a_i * \beta^{i-1}$, then this solution will be correct; however, it is far from optimal.

A more efficient algorithm may be developed if we recall from numerical analysis the method known as *Horner's rule.* This is based on the identity:

$$\begin{aligned} & a_1 + a_2 * \beta + a_3 * \beta^2 + \cdots + a_n * \beta^{n-1} \\ & \quad = a_1 + \beta * (a_2 + \beta * (\cdots \beta * (a_{n-2} + \beta * (a_{n-1} + \beta * a_n)) \cdots)) \end{aligned}$$

The intended algorithm starts from the high-order coefficients and works downwards. Clearly this requires fewer multiplications than the straightforward approach. As a formal specification, let's take the recurrence relation that a numerical analyst would use:

$$\textstyle\sum_{i=1}^{n} a_i * \beta^{i-1} = H_{1,n}$$

where

$$\begin{aligned} H_{n,n} &= a_n \\ H_{i,n} &= a_i + \beta * H_{i+1,n} \qquad \text{for } i < n \end{aligned}$$

Now, suppose that we have a number in base β with digits $a_n a_{n-1} \ldots a_2 a_1$, then our algorithm must satisfy the specification

$$d : [\, \mathit{true},\ d' = \textstyle\sum_{i=1}^{n} a_i * \beta^{i-1} \,]$$

and our specification can be rewritten as

$$d : [\, \mathit{true},\ d' = H_{1,n} \,]$$

The strategy for calculating the code for this algorithm is quite clear: we can develop a loop which varies the first index of H. It is easy enough to establish $H_{n,n}$, and we want to end up with $H_{1,n}$, so the loop counter is decreasing, and the invariant will involve $d = H_{j,n}$, for loop counter j.

$d : [\, true,\ d' = H_{1,n}\,]$

$\sqsubseteq$

var $j : 1\,..\,n$ •

$d, j : [\, true,\ d' = H_{1,n}\,]$

$\sqsubseteq$ (sequential composition introduction)

$d, j : [\, true,\ d' = H_{j',n}\,]$; [◁]

$d, j : [\, d = H_{j,n},\ d' = H_{1,n}\,]$ [†]

$\sqsubseteq$ (assignment introduction)

$d, j := a_n, n$

The statement labelled † may be further refined:

†

$\sqsubseteq$ (strengthen postcondition)

$d, j : [\, d = H_{j,n},\ d' = H_{1,n} \wedge j' = 1\,]$

$\sqsubseteq$ (strengthen postcondition)

$d, j : [\, d = H_{j,n},\ d' = H_{j',n} \wedge j' = 1\,]$

The second refinement is, of course, an equivalence. We are now ready to introduce a loop:

$\sqsubseteq$ (loop introduction)

do

$j \neq 1 \rightarrow$

$$d, j : \left[\begin{array}{ll} j \neq 1 & 0 \leq j' < j \\ d = H_{j,n}\ , & d' = H_{j',n} \end{array}\right]$$

od

The body of the loop is equivalent to the specification statement

$$d, j : [\, \begin{pmatrix} j \neq 0 \\ d = H_{j+1,n} \end{pmatrix} [j-1/j],\ \begin{pmatrix} 0 \leq j' \leq j \\ d' = H_{j',n} \end{pmatrix} [j-1/j]\,]$$

which may be further refined as follows:

$\sqsubseteq$ (leading assignment)

$j := j - 1;$

$$d, j : \left[\begin{array}{c} j \neq 0 \\ d = H_{j+1,n} \end{array} , \begin{array}{c} 0 \leq j' \leq j \\ d' = H_{j',n} \end{array} \right]$$

$\sqsubseteq$ (contract frame)

$$d : \left[\begin{array}{c} j \neq 0 \\ d = H_{j+1,n} \end{array} , \begin{array}{c} 0 \leq j \leq j \\ d' = H_{j,n} \end{array} \right]$$

$\sqsubseteq$ (strengthen postcondition)

$d : [j \neq 0 \wedge d = H_{j+1,n},\ d' = a_j + \beta * H_{j+1,n}]$

$\sqsubseteq$ (strengthen postcondition)

$d : [j \neq 0 \wedge d = H_{j+1,n},\ d' = a_j + \beta * d]$

$\sqsubseteq$ (assignment introduction)

$d := a_j + \beta * d$

Thus, we have derived the program text

```
begin
    var j : 1 .. n •
        d, j := a_n, n;
        do j ≠ 1 →
            j := j − 1;
            d := a_j + x * d
        od
end
```

which corresponds to the following procedure:

```
PROCEDURE Translate ;
  BEGIN
    d := a[n] ;
    FOR j := n DOWNTO 1 DO
      d := a[j] + x * d
  END
```

□

Chapter 20

A Telecommunications Protocol

This chapter describes a case study in using abstraction and refinement. The subject of the study is a telecommunications protocol, Signalling System No. 7, an international standard for signalling between telephone exchanges.

We begin with an abstract specification of the protocol. This may then serve as an independent correctness criterion for a subsequent refinement. The abstraction explains the service offered by the protocol; the refinement explains how this is to be achieved.

20.1 Specification: the external view

Let M be the set of messages that the protocol handles. The abstract specification of this protocol is quite small, and we call it the *external view*:

$$
\begin{array}{|l}
\textit{Ext} \\
\hline
\textit{in}, \textit{out} : \operatorname{seq} M \\
\hline
\exists\, s : \operatorname{seq} M \bullet \textit{in} = s \frown \textit{out} \\
\hline
\end{array}
$$

The state comprises two sequences: the messages that have come in and those that have gone out. We will use these sequences to keep track of the message traffic handled by the protocol.

As we shall see, messages will be added to the left-hand end of these sequences, so that the oldest messages are to be found towards the right. The invariant states that the *out* sequence is a *suffix* of the *in* sequence: the protocol must deliver messages without corruption or re-ordering. The missing messages are in flight, as it were, in the system. For example, a suitable pair of sequences satisfying this invariant would be

$$in = \langle m_5, m_4, m_3, m_2, m_1 \rangle \qquad out = \langle m_3, m_2, m_1 \rangle$$

This models the situation in which five messages have been input to the protocol, three have been output, and two are still in flight.

Initially, no messages have been sent:

$$ExtInit \mathrel{\widehat=} [\, Ext' \mid in' = \langle\rangle \,]$$

This forces both *InFlight* and *out* to be empty.

We will model two operations, describing the transmission and reception of messages. New messages are added to the *in* sequence:

Transmit

$$\Delta Ext$$
$$m? : M$$

$$in' = \langle m? \rangle \frown in$$
$$out' = out$$

Messages are received from the in-flight stream, which might not have reached the destination. Thus, either the output sequence gets one longer (and by the state invariant, this must be the next message in sequence), or there is no message available in flight:

Receive

$$\Delta Ext$$

$$in' = in$$
$$\#out' = \#out + 1 \lor out' = out$$

There are many other operations relevant to trunk signalling, but these two will serve to illustrate our refinement.

20.2 Design: the sectional view

The published description of Signalling System No. 7 is a rather large document; the specification that we have just produced is exceedingly small. We have obtained this economy through the use of *abstraction*, demonstrating that the specifications of large systems need not themselves be large. The abstraction of the specification is linked to the detail of the implementation by means of data refinement.

As an aid to understanding, we introduce a *sectional view.* Suppose that *SPC* is the set of signalling point codes, identifying points in the network. A sectional view describes the *route* that the messages must take: a non-empty sequence of *SPC*s, without repetition. Each section in this route may receive and send messages; those which have been received but not yet sent are said to be in the section.

The description is formalised in the following specification:

$$
\begin{array}{l}
\textit{Section} \\
\hline
\textit{route} : \mathrm{iseq}\ \textit{SPC} \\
\textit{rec}, \textit{ins}, \textit{sent} : \mathrm{seq}(\mathrm{seq}\ M) \\
\hline
\textit{route} \neq \langle\rangle \\
\#\textit{route} = \#\textit{rec} = \#\textit{ins} = \#\textit{sent} \\
\textit{rec} = \textit{ins} \mathbin{\widehat{=}} \textit{sent} \\
\textit{front sent} = \textit{tail rec} \\
\hline
\end{array}
$$

where *ins* represents the sequence of messages currently inside this section, *rec* represents the sequence of messages that have been received, and *sent* represents the sequence of messages that have been sent.

The expression $\textit{ins} \mathbin{\widehat{=}} \textit{sent}$ denotes the pair-wise concatenation of the two sequences. Thus, if we have that

$$\textit{rec} = \textit{ins} \mathbin{\widehat{=}} \textit{sent}$$

then we must also have, for appropriate i, that

$$\textit{rec}\ i = (\textit{ins}\ i) \frown (\textit{sent}\ i)$$

Pairwise concatenation is defined as follows:

$$
\begin{array}{l}
[X] \\
\hline
\_ \mathbin{\widehat{=}} \_ : \mathrm{seq}(\mathrm{seq}\ X) \times \mathrm{seq}(\mathrm{seq}\ X) \rightarrowtail \mathrm{seq}(\mathrm{seq}\ X) \\
\hline
\forall s, t : \mathrm{seq}(\mathrm{seq}\ X) \mid \#s = \#t \bullet \\
\quad \forall i : \mathrm{dom}\ s \bullet \\
\qquad (s \mathbin{\widehat{=}} t) i = (s\ i) \frown (t\ i) \\
\hline
\end{array}
$$

That is, the pairwise concatenation of any two sequences of sequences is the sequence obtained by concatenating each element of the first sequence with the corresponding element of the second.

We now rewrite our operations in terms of the new viewpoint. We leave the *route* component unspecified in the initialisation: the resulting specification may then be strengthened to provide the initialisation for any particular route:

$$
\begin{array}{|l}
\multicolumn{1}{l}{\textit{SectionInit}} \\
\hline
\textit{Section}' \\
\hline
\forall\, i : \operatorname{dom} \textit{route} \bullet \\
\qquad \textit{rec}\ i = \textit{ins}\ i = \textit{sent}\ i = \langle\rangle \\
\hline
\end{array}
$$

In *Transmit*, the new message is received by the first section in the route; that is, it is added to the sequence *head rec*:

$$
\begin{array}{|l}
\multicolumn{1}{l}{\textit{STransmit}} \\
\hline
\Delta \textit{Section} \\
m? : M \\
\hline
\textit{route}' = \textit{route} \\
\textit{head rec}' = \langle m? \rangle \frown (\textit{head rec}) \\
\textit{tail rec}' = \textit{tail rec} \\
\textit{ins}' = \textit{ins} \\
\textit{sent}' = \textit{sent} \\
\hline
\end{array}
$$

The *Receive* operation should be delivering the message to the output from the protocol. In the sectional view, this means transferring it to *last sent*. But where should this message come from? The answer is that it comes from within the previous section:

$$
\begin{array}{|l}
\multicolumn{1}{l}{\textit{SReceive}} \\
\hline
\Delta \textit{Section} \\
\hline
\textit{route}' = \textit{route} \\
\textit{rec}' = \textit{rec} \\
\textit{front ins}' = \textit{front ins} \\
\textit{last ins}' = \textit{front}(\textit{last ins}) \\
\textit{front sent}' = \textit{front sent} \\
\textit{last sent}' = \langle \textit{last}(\textit{last ins}) \rangle \frown (\textit{last sent}) \\
\hline
\end{array}
$$

In the external view, messages arrive at the destination nondeterministically. In the sectional view, the nondeterminism is explained by the progress of the message through the series of sections: For this to make sense, we must add an operation which moves messages through the series of sections in the route.

We call this operation *Daemon*, and it chooses nondeterministically a section i, which will make progress. *Daemon* transfers the oldest message in i's section to the following section, $i + 1$. Nothing else changes. The successful part of this operation is:

$$
\begin{array}{l}
\textit{Daemon}_0 \\
\hline
\Delta \textit{Section} \\
\hline
\exists\, i : 1 \mathrel{..} \#\textit{route} - 1 \mid \\
\quad \textit{ins}\; i \neq \langle\rangle \bullet \\
\quad \textit{ins}'\; i = \textit{front}(\textit{ins}\; i) \\
\quad \textit{ins}'(i+1) = \langle \textit{last}(\textit{ins}\; i) \rangle \frown \textit{ins}(i+1) \\
\quad \forall\, j : \operatorname{dom} \textit{route} \mid j \neq i \wedge j \neq i+1 \bullet \textit{ins}'\; j = \textit{ins}\; j \\
\hline
\end{array}
$$

This operation is not part of the user interface. The user cannot invoke *Daemon*, but it is essential to our understanding of the system and to its correctness. How do such operations fit into our view of specification?

We imagine such operations as *daemons* that work in the background, invoked nondeterministically. It should be clear that we could dispense with such operations, but only by adding the required degree of nondeterminism to the remainder of our specification. The important thing about a daemon is that its effects are *invisible* from an abstract point of view. In this specification, the sectional operation *Daemon* corresponds to the external operation $\Xi \textit{Ext}$.

We should remark that the specification of the abstract state does not insist that messages actually arrive, since it is possible to satisfy the specification trivially by insisting that $\textit{out} = \langle\rangle$. This problem could be addressed by adding an integer-valued *variant* to the state to measure the progress of a message through the system. We could then add a constraint to each operation to insist that the variant is decreased while the message is in flight. This would then be enough to guarantee delivery.

20.3 Relationship between external and sectional views

We should prove that two views that we have of our protocol are consistent, both internally and with one another. In our description of the external view, we insisted that the protocol should deliver messages without corruption or re-ordering. To retrieve the external view from the sectional view, we have only to observe that the head of *rec* corresponds to the sequence *in*; the last of *sent* corresponds to the sequence *out*; and the distributed concatenation of *ins* corresponds to the discrepancy between them.

The consistency of the external view is summed up by the predicate part of the schema *Ext*:

$$\exists s : \text{seq}\, M \bullet in = s \frown out$$

There must be some sequence of messages *s* which, when prefixed to the sequence *out*, produces the sequence *in*.

The consistency of the sectional view depends on the same property holding true in terms of the concrete model. That is, with *head rec* in place of *in*, *last sent* in place of *out*, and the contents of all the sections, in order, in place of the existentially quantified variable *s*.

The following inference asserts that this property holds in *Section*:

$$\frac{Section}{head\ rec = (\frown / \ ins) \frown (last\ sent)}$$

We may prove this by induction upon the length of the route, *#route*. The base case requires that the result holds for $\#route = 1$:

$$\begin{aligned}
&(\frown / \ ins) \frown (last\ sent) \\
&\quad = (\frown / \langle ins\ 1 \rangle) \frown (last\ \langle sent\ 1 \rangle) && [\#route = \#ins = \#sent = 1] \\
&\quad = (ins\ 1) \frown (sent\ 1) && [\text{by definition of } \frown /] \\
&\quad = rec\ 1 && [\text{from } Section] \\
&\quad = head\ rec && [\text{by definition of } head]
\end{aligned}$$

The inductive step involves the assumption that

$$head(front\ rec) = (\frown / (front\ ins)) \frown (last(front\ sent))$$

and proceeds as follows:

$$\begin{aligned}
&(\frown / \ ins) \frown (last\ sent) \\
&\quad = (\frown / ((front\ ins) \frown \langle last\ ins \rangle)) \frown (last\ sent) && [\#ins = \#route > 1] \\
&\quad = (\frown / (front\ ins)) \frown (last\ ins) \frown (last\ sent) && [\text{by the definition of } \frown /] \\
&\quad = (\frown / (front\ ins)) \frown (last\ rec) && [\text{from } Section] \\
&\quad = (\frown / (front\ ins)) \frown (last\ (tail\ rec)) && [\#rec = \#route > 1] \\
&\quad = (\frown / (front\ ins)) \frown (last\ (front\ sent)) && [\text{from } Section] \\
&\quad = head(front\ rec) && [\text{by the induction hypothesis}] \\
&\quad = head\ rec && [\text{by a property of } head]
\end{aligned}$$

The sectional view is more detailed than the external view, and our the above result helps to demonstrate that it is in some way a *refinement*. The proof of the theorem is simple, increasing our confidence in our abstractions. We can explain the refinement by documenting the retrieve relation:

$$
\begin{array}{|l}
\textit{RetrieveExtSection} \\
\hline
\textit{Ext} \\
\textit{Section} \\
\hline
\textit{in} = \textit{head rec} \\
\textit{out} = \textit{last sent} \\
\hline
\end{array}
$$

This may be used to prove that the various operations on the concrete sectional view are correct with respect to their corresponding abstractions. Notice that the retrieve relation is actually functional from concrete to abstract. We must prove that the retrieve relation is a total function:

$$\forall \textit{Section} \bullet \exists_1 \textit{Ext} \bullet \textit{RetrieveExtSection}$$

We must prove that the initialisation is correct,

$$\forall \textit{Ext}'; \textit{Section}' \bullet \textit{SectionInit} \land \textit{RetrieveExtSection}' \Rightarrow \textit{ExtInit}$$

that the transmit and receive operations are correct,

$$\forall \textit{Ext}; \textit{Section} \bullet \text{pre } \textit{Transmit} \land \textit{RetrieveExtSection}' \Rightarrow \text{pre } \textit{STransmit}$$

$$\begin{array}{l}\forall \textit{Ext}; \textit{Ext}'; \textit{Section}; \textit{Section}' \bullet \\ \quad \text{pre } \textit{Transmit} \land \textit{RetrieveExtSection} \land \textit{STransmit} \land \\ \qquad \textit{RetrieveExtSection}' \Rightarrow \\ \qquad\quad \textit{Transmit}\end{array}$$

$$\forall \textit{Ext}; \textit{Section} \bullet \text{pre } \textit{Receive} \land \textit{RetrieveExtSection}' \Rightarrow \text{pre } \textit{SReceive}$$

$$\begin{array}{l}\forall \textit{Ext}; \textit{Ext}'; \textit{Section}; \textit{Section}' \bullet \\ \quad \text{pre } \textit{Receive} \land \textit{RetrieveExtSection} \land \textit{SReceive} \land \textit{RetrieveExtSection}' \Rightarrow \\ \qquad \textit{Receive}\end{array}$$

and that the daemon is correct:

$$\forall \textit{Ext}; \textit{Section} \bullet \text{pre } \Xi \textit{Ext} \land \textit{RetrieveExtSection}' \Rightarrow \text{pre } \textit{Daemon}$$

$$\begin{array}{l}\forall \textit{Ext}; \textit{Ext}'; \textit{Section}; \textit{Section}' \bullet \\ \quad \text{pre } \Xi \textit{Ext} \land \textit{RetrieveExtSection} \land \textit{Daemon} \land \textit{RetrieveExtSection}' \Rightarrow \\ \qquad \Xi \textit{Ext}\end{array}$$

20.4 Enriching the model

The additional detail in the sectional view allows us to introduce concepts that were not relevant in the external view. For example, we may wish to add a new signalling point to the route. This operation has no relevance at the higher level, and cannot be expressed in terms of the abstract model.

To describe such an operation, we require an operator on sequences that allows us to *insert* an additional element after a given point: for example,

$$\langle a, b, d, e, f \rangle \; insert \; (2, c) \;=\; \langle a, b, c, d, e, f \rangle$$

Such an operator may be defined by

$$
\begin{array}{l}
[X] \\
\hline
\_insert\_ : \mathrm{seq}\, X \times (\mathbb{N} \times X) \to \mathrm{seq}\, X \\
\hline
\forall\, s : \mathrm{seq}\, X;\; i : \mathbb{N};\; x : X \bullet \\
\qquad s \; insert \; (i, x) = (1 \mathinner{..} i) \lhd s \frown \langle x \rangle \frown squash((1 \mathinner{..} i) \mathbin{⩤} s)
\end{array}
$$

where *squash* takes a function and yields a valid sequence, as in Chapter 9.

The *InsertSection* operation inserts a new *SPC* after a given point in the route. The new section has no messages in it, but it is glued into the route by making its input stream the output stream of the preceding section, and its output stream the input stream of the following section:

$$
\begin{array}{l}
\textit{InsertSection} \\
\hline
\Delta Section \\
s?, new? : SPC \\
\hline
s? \in \mathrm{ran}(front\; route) \\
new? \notin \mathrm{ran}\; route \\
\\
\exists\, i : 1 \mathinner{..} (\#route - 1) \mid \\
\qquad i = route^{\sim}\; s? \bullet \\
\qquad\qquad route' = route\; insert\; (i, new?) \\
\qquad\qquad rec' = rec\; insert\; (i, sent\; i) \\
\qquad\qquad ins' = ins\; insert\; (i, \langle\rangle) \\
\qquad\qquad sent' = sent\; insert\; (i, rec\; i + 1)
\end{array}
$$

To end the chapter, we prove a useful result about our design: messages in transit are unaffected by the insertion of a new section. If *ins* and *ins'* are related according to the definition of *InsertSection* above, then

$$
\begin{aligned}
& {}^\frown/\, ins' \\
&= {}^\frown/\,(ins\ insert\ (i, \langle\rangle)) && [InsertSection] \\
&= {}^\frown/\,((1\,..\,i \lhd ins) \frown \langle\langle\rangle\rangle \frown (squash(1\,..\,i \ntriangleleft ins))) && [\text{definition of } insert] \\
&= {}^\frown/\,(1\,..\,i) \lhd s \frown \\
&\quad {}^\frown/\,\langle\langle\rangle\rangle \frown \\
&\quad {}^\frown/\, squash((1\,..\,i) \ntriangleleft ins) && [\text{definition of } {}^\frown/] \\
&= {}^\frown/\,(1\,..\,i \lhd ins) \frown \\
&\quad \langle\rangle \frown \\
&\quad {}^\frown/\, squash(1\,..\,i \ntriangleleft ins) && [\text{definition of } {}^\frown/] \\
&= {}^\frown/\,(1\,..\,i \lhd ins) \frown \\
&\quad {}^\frown/\, squash(1\,..\,i \ntriangleleft ins) && [\text{property of } \langle\rangle] \\
&= {}^\frown/\,((1\,..\,i \lhd ins) \frown squash(1\,..\,i \ntriangleleft ins)) && [\text{property of } {}^\frown/] \\
&= {}^\frown/\, ins && [\text{properties of } \lhd \text{ and } \ntriangleleft]
\end{aligned}
$$

This shows that messages in transit are not affected by the insertion of a new signalling point in the route. That is, the lower-level operation of manipulating the route in this way is invisible at the higher level of abstraction. The operation is therefore a daemon; this is important for the integrity of the abstraction.

Chapter 21

An Operating System Scheduler

In this chapter we describe a case study in the specification and design of a piece of software. The accent is on rigorous development, and we try to keep the overt formality to a minimum. An important aspect is the use of an auxiliary data type and its refinement; this is a common practice in large projects, where re-use is important.

The subject of the study is a *scheduler*: the component of an operating system that determines which process should be run, and when. We describe the service that the scheduler provides to the remainder of the operating system: the way in which it controls access to a processor. We then describe an implementation that provides this service.

21.1 Processes

The purpose of an operating system is to allow many processes to share the resources of a computer. In our system, there is a single processor to be shared, and this is made available to one process at a time. We say that a process is *running* when it is making use of the processor. The purpose of a scheduler is to determine which process is running, and when.

Processes must be created before they may be scheduled, and may be destroyed after they have served their purpose. While they exist, they may occupy one of three states:

Current Since there is a single processor, at any time, there will be at most one process running. We will call this the *current* process.

Ready There may be several processes that are waiting to use the processor. These processes are said to be *ready*.

Blocked There may be some processes that are waiting, not for the processor, but for a different resource or event. These processes are said to be *blocked.*

While a process is running it has exclusive use of the processor. At some point, control will be passed to the kernel. This may happen because the current process has issued a service call, or it may be that the kernel interrupts it. Whatever, the scheduler will be asked to dispatch another process.

21.2 Specification

Our system will deal with up to n processes, where n is a natural number.

$$| \; n : \mathbb{N}$$

Each process will be associated with a *process identifier*, or *pid*. For our purposes, a pid can be represented by a number between 1 and n.

$$PId == 1 \mathrel{..} n$$

Zero is used to represent the 'null process': a marker that says that there is no process where this value is found.

$$nullPId == 0$$

An 'optional pid' can be either a true pid or the null pid:

$$OptPId == PId \cup \{nullPId\}$$

The abstract state of the scheduler classifies every process in one of four ways: a process is either the current process, or it is ready, blocked, or free. There might not be a current process:

$$
\begin{array}{|l}
\hline
\textit{AScheduler} \\
\hline
current : OptPId \\
ready : \mathbb{P}\, PId \\
blocked : \mathbb{P}\, PId \\
free : \mathbb{P}\, PId \\
\hline
\langle \{current\} \setminus \{nullPId\}, \\
\quad ready, \\
\quad blocked, \\
\quad free \rangle \text{ partition } PId \\
\hline
\end{array}
$$

The free set describes those process identifiers that are not currently in use. Initially, all process identifiers are free, and there is no current process:

$$
\begin{array}{|l}
\hline
\multicolumn{1}{l}{\textit{ASchedulerInit}} \\
\textit{AScheduler}' \\
\hline
\textit{current}' = \textit{nullPId} \\
\textit{ready}' = \varnothing \\
\textit{blocked}' = \varnothing \\
\textit{free}' = \textit{PId} \\
\hline
\end{array}
$$

If there is no current process, then any process that is ready may be dispatched to the processor:

$$
\begin{array}{|l}
\hline
\multicolumn{1}{l}{\textit{ADispatch}} \\
\Delta \textit{AScheduler} \\
p! : \textit{PId} \\
\hline
\textit{current} = \textit{nullPId} \\
\textit{ready} \neq \varnothing \\
\textit{current}' \in \textit{ready} \\
\textit{ready}' = \textit{ready} \setminus \{\textit{current}'\} \\
\textit{blocked}' = \textit{blocked} \\
\textit{free}' = \textit{free} \\
p! = \textit{current}' \\
\hline
\end{array}
$$

Any process which is dispatched is permitted to execute for a period of time before being interrupted. When this time period expires, it is returned to the set of ready processes:

$$
\begin{array}{|l}
\hline
\multicolumn{1}{l}{\textit{ATimeOut}} \\
\Delta \textit{AScheduler} \\
p! : \textit{PId} \\
\hline
\textit{current} \neq \textit{nullPId} \\
\textit{current}' = \textit{nullPId} \\
\textit{ready}' = \textit{ready} \cup \{\textit{current}\} \\
\textit{blocked}' = \textit{blocked} \\
\textit{free}' = \textit{free} \\
p! = \textit{current} \\
\hline
\end{array}
$$

The role of the *nullPId* value as place-holder should now be obvious.

If the current becomes blocked, it is removed and added to the set of blocked processes:

$$
\begin{array}{|l}
\multicolumn{1}{l}{\textit{ABlock}} \\
\hline
\Delta AScheduler \\
p! : PId \\
\hline
current \neq nullPId \\
current' = nullPId \\
ready' = ready \\
blocked' = blocked \cup \{current\} \\
free' = free \\
p! = current \\
\hline
\end{array}
$$

A blocked process may be woken up. This is the system signalling that the required resource is now available. The woken process must wait its turn for scheduling, so it is added to the set of ready processes:

$$
\begin{array}{|l}
\multicolumn{1}{l}{\textit{AWakeUp}} \\
\hline
\Delta AScheduler \\
p? : PId \\
\hline
p? \in blocked \\
current' = current \\
ready' = ready \cup \{p?\} \\
blocked' = blocked \setminus \{p?\} \\
free' = free \\
\hline
\end{array}
$$

When a process is created, an identifier must be assigned from the set of free identifiers. Clearly, the free set must be non-empty for this to be possible:

$$
\begin{array}{|l}
\multicolumn{1}{l}{\textit{ACreate}} \\
\hline
\Delta AScheduler \\
p! : PId \\
\hline
free \neq \emptyset \\
current' = current \\
ready' = ready \cup \{p!\} \\
blocked' = blocked \\
free' = free \setminus \{p!\} \\
p! \in free \\
\hline
\end{array}
$$

At the end of its life, a process may be destroyed. If the designated process is the current process, then afterwards there is no current process, and the process identifier becomes available for further use.

$$
\begin{array}{|l}
\hline
\textit{ADestroyCurrent} \\
\Delta \textit{AScheduler} \\
p? : \textit{PId} \\
\hline
p? = \textit{current} \\
\textit{current}' = \textit{nullPId} \\
\textit{ready}' = \textit{ready} \\
\textit{blocked}' = \textit{blocked} \\
\textit{free}' = \textit{free} \cup \{p?\} \\
\hline
\end{array}
$$

If the process is ready, it is destroyed and the identifier becomes available for further use:

$$
\begin{array}{|l}
\hline
\textit{ADestroyReady} \\
\Delta \textit{AScheduler} \\
p? : \textit{PId} \\
\hline
p? \in \textit{ready} \\
\textit{current}' = \textit{current} \\
\textit{ready}' = \textit{ready} \setminus \{p?\} \\
\textit{blocked}' = \textit{blocked} \\
\textit{free}' = \textit{free} \cup \{p?\} \\
\hline
\end{array}
$$

The designated process might be a blocked process; again, it is destroyed, and the identifier becomes available again:

$$
\begin{array}{|l}
\hline
\textit{ADestroyBlocked} \\
\Delta \textit{AScheduler} \\
p? : \textit{PId} \\
\hline
p? \in \textit{blocked} \\
\textit{current}' = \textit{current} \\
\textit{ready}' = \textit{ready} \\
\textit{blocked}' = \textit{blocked} \setminus \{p?\} \\
\textit{free}' = \textit{free} \cup \{p?\} \\
\hline
\end{array}
$$

The destroy operation comprises these three cases:

$$\textit{ADestroy} \mathrel{\widehat=} \textit{ADestroyCurrent} \lor \textit{ADestroyReady} \lor \textit{ADestroyBlocked}$$

21.3 Chains

Our scheduler is a piece of low-level system software, and its implementation may use only very simple facilities. We intend to write a program with a simple data structure using an array and a few counters. If we were using a high-level programming language, we might well use a linked list implemented with pointers. As it is, we must implement our linked list directly.

A *chain* is a finite injection from *PId* to *PId* with a unique start and a unique end. The start of a chain is a pid that is in the domain of the injection but not the range; the end is a pid that is in the range but not the domain. We will include both the start and the end of a chain as components in a schema that characterises the data type of chains. For convenience, we will include another component, *set*, to identify the set of all pids that appear in the chain, including the start and the end:

$$
\begin{array}{|l}
\textit{Chain} \\
\hline
\textit{start}, \textit{end} : \textit{OptPId} \\
\textit{links} : \textit{PId} \rightarrowtail\!\!\!\!\!\!\twoheadrightarrow \textit{PId} \\
\textit{set} : \mathbb{F}\,\textit{PId} \\
\hline
\textit{set} = \operatorname{dom} \textit{links} \cup \operatorname{ran} \textit{links} \cup (\{\textit{start}\} \setminus \{\textit{nullPId}\}) \\
\textit{links} = \varnothing \Rightarrow \textit{start} = \textit{end} \\
\textit{links} \neq \varnothing \Rightarrow \\
\qquad \{\textit{start}\} = (\operatorname{dom} \textit{links}) \setminus \operatorname{ran} \textit{links} \\
\qquad \{\textit{end}\} = (\operatorname{ran} \textit{links}) \setminus \operatorname{dom} \textit{links} \\
\forall\, e : \textit{set} \mid e \neq \textit{start} \bullet \textit{start} \mapsto e \in \textit{links}^{+}
\end{array}
$$

The final part of the data type invariant insists that the elements of the chain are connected, in the sense that every one may be reached from the start pid by applying the function *links* a finite number of times. This is enough to guarantee the uniqueness of the *start* and *end* elements.

For convenience, we use the null pid to represent the start and end points of an empty chain. With the above invariant, it is the case that

$$\textit{set} = \varnothing \Rightarrow \textit{start} = \textit{nullPId} \wedge \textit{end} = \textit{nullPId}$$

The initial state of a chain is described by the following schema:

$$
\begin{array}{|l}
\textit{ChainInit} \\
\hline
\textit{Chain}' \\
\hline
\textit{start}' = \textit{nullPIdend}' = \textit{nullPId}
\end{array}
$$

We will define three operations on elements of this data type. The first describes the effect of pushing an element onto the end of a chain. There are two cases to consider. If there is no end point, then the injection must be empty, and the new element will become the end point:

$$
\begin{array}{l}
\textit{PushEmpty} \\
\hline
\Delta \textit{Chain} \\
p? : \textit{PId} \\
\hline
\textit{end} = \textit{nullPId} \\
\textit{end}' = p? \\
\textit{links}' = \textit{links} \\
\hline
\end{array}
$$

If there is an end point, then we update the chain so that the end points to the new element:

$$
\begin{array}{l}
\textit{PushNonEmpty} \\
\hline
\Delta \textit{Chain} \\
p? : \textit{PId} \\
\hline
\textit{end} \neq \textit{nullPId} \\
\textit{links}' = \textit{links} \cup \{\textit{end} \mapsto p?\} \\
\hline
\end{array}
$$

A successful push operation is then

$$\textit{Push} \mathrel{\widehat{=}} \textit{PushEmpty} \lor \textit{PushNonEmpty}$$

Our second operation describes the effect of popping an element from the front of a chain; this will be successful if there is at least one element present. Again, there are two cases to consider. If the chain has only one element—if *links* must be empty but *start* is not null—then the new start will be null:

$$
\begin{array}{l}
\textit{PopSingleton} \\
\hline
\Delta \textit{Chain} \\
p! : \textit{PId} \\
\hline
\textit{start} \neq \textit{nullPId} \\
\textit{links} = \varnothing \\
\textit{start}' = \textit{nullPId} \\
\textit{links}' = \textit{links} \\
p! = \textit{start} \\
\hline
\end{array}
$$

Notice that the new value of *end* is determined by the state invariant.

If there is more than one element in the chain, then the start element is provided as output, and the start point moved along the chain.

$$
\begin{array}{|l}
\textit{PopMultiple} \\
\hline
\Delta Chain \\
p! : PId \\
\hline
links \neq \varnothing \\
start' = links\ start \\
links' = \{start\} \lhd links \\
p! = start \\
\hline
\end{array}
$$

A successful pop operation is then

$$Pop \mathrel{\widehat=} PopSingleton \lor PopMultiple$$

Our third operation describes the effect of deleting an element from a chain. If this element is the first element in the chain, then the delete operation has an effect that is similar to *Pop*:

$$
\begin{array}{|l}
\textit{DeleteStart} \\
\hline
\Delta Chain \\
p? : PId \\
\hline
p? = start \\
\exists\, p! : PId \bullet Pop \\
\hline
\end{array}
$$

Notice how we simply ignore the popped element, hiding the output from the *Pop* operation within an existential quantification.

If the designated element is at the end of the chain, then the effect is different. The last link in the chain simply disappears:

$$
\begin{array}{|l}
\textit{DeleteEnd} \\
\hline
\Delta Chain \\
p? : PId \\
\hline
p? \neq start \\
p? = end \\
links' = links \rhd \{end\} \\
\hline
\end{array}
$$

The disappearance is described by range subtraction; the data type invariant is enough to determine the new value of *end*.

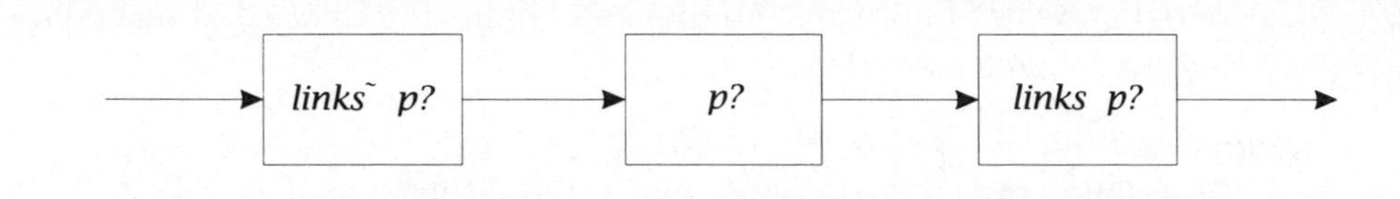

Figure 21.1: A middle element

If the designated element is in the chain, but at neither end, then the effect is different again. Consider the situation pictured in Figure 21.1. The previous element—which is identified as $links^{\sim}\ p?$—will be mapped to the next element—which is identified as $links\ p?$. In the following schema, $p?$ itself is removed using domain restriction:

$$
\begin{array}{l}
\textit{DeleteMiddle} \\
\hline
\Delta Chain \\
p? : PId \\
\hline
p? \neq start \\
p? \neq end \\
p? \in set \\
links' = \{p?\} \ntriangleleft links \oplus \{links^{\sim}\ p? \mapsto links\ p?\} \\
\hline
\end{array}
$$

A successful delete operation is then

$$Delete \mathrel{\widehat{=}} DeleteStart \lor DeleteMiddle \lor DeleteEnd$$

21.4 Design

We will now formulate a design for the scheduler based upon the chain data type. Our design will involve three chains: one each for the sets of ready, blocked, and free processes.

$$
\begin{array}{l}
ReadyChain \mathrel{\widehat{=}} \\
\quad Chain[rstart / start, rend / end, rlinks / links, rset / set]
\end{array}
$$

$$
\begin{array}{l}
BlockedChain \mathrel{\widehat{=}} \\
\quad Chain[bstart / start, bend / end, blinks / links, bset / set]
\end{array}
$$

$$
\begin{array}{l}
FreeChain \mathrel{\widehat{=}} \\
\quad Chain[fstart / start, fend / end, flinks / links, fset / set]
\end{array}
$$

The initial states of the ready and blocked chains are defined in terms of the initialisation schema *ChainInit*:

$$ReadyChainInit \mathrel{\widehat=} ChainInit[rstart'/start', rend'/end', rlinks'/links', rset'/set']$$

$$BlockedChainInit \mathrel{\widehat=} ChainInit[bstart'/start', bend'/end', blinks'/links', bset'/set']$$

The free chain, however, is initially full:

```
┌─ FreeChainFull ──────────────────────
│ FreeChain
├──────────────
│ fset' = PId
└──────────────────────────────────────
```

We will require push and pop operations on the ready and free chains, and push and delete operations on the blocked chain. We may define these by renaming the components of the corresponding operations on *Chain*:

$$PushReadyChain \mathrel{\widehat=} Push[rstart/start, rend/end, rlinks/links, rset/set, rstart'/start', rend'/end', rlinks'/links', rset'/set']$$

$$PopReadyChain \mathrel{\widehat=} Pop[rstart/start, rend/end, rlinks/links, rset/set, rstart'/start', rend'/end', rlinks'/links', rset'/set']$$

$$DeleteReadyChain \mathrel{\widehat=} Delete[rstart/start, rend/end, rlinks/links, rset/set, rstart'/start', rend'/end', rlinks'/links', rset'/set']$$

$$PushBlockedChain \mathrel{\widehat=} Push[bstart/start, bend/end, blinks/links, bset/set, bstart'/start', bend'/end', blinks'/links', bset'/set']$$

$$DeleteBlockedChain \mathrel{\widehat=} Delete[bstart/start, bend/end, blinks/links, bset/set, bstart'/start', bend'/end', blinks'/links', bset'/set']$$

$$PushFreeChain \mathrel{\widehat=} Push[fstart/start, fend/end, flinks/links, fset/set, fstart'/start', fend'/end', flinks'/links', fset'/set']$$

$$PopFreeChain \mathrel{\widehat=} Pop[fstart/start, fend/end, flinks/links, fset/set, fstart'/start', fend'/end', flinks'/links', fset'/set']$$

The state of the concrete scheduler comprises the three chains, together with an optional current process:

CScheduler

$$
\begin{array}{|l}
\hline
ReadyChain \\
BlockedChain \\
FreeChain \\
current : OptPId \\
chainstore : PId \rightarrow OptPId \\
\hline
\langle \{current\} \setminus \{nullPId\}, rset, bset, fset \rangle \text{ partition } PId \\
rlinks = rset \lhd chainstore \rhd rset \\
blinks = bset \lhd chainstore \rhd bset \\
flinks = fset \lhd chainstore \rhd fset \\
current \neq nullPId \Rightarrow chainstore\ current = nullPId \\
\hline
\end{array}
$$

It is also useful to identify the working space used: the component *chainstore* is the union of the three chain functions, plus an optional map to *nullPId*.

Initially, there is no current process, and all chains are empty:

CSchedulerInit

$$
\begin{array}{|l}
\hline
CScheduler' \\
ReadyChainInit \\
BlockedChainInit \\
FreeChainFull \\
\hline
current' = nullPId \\
\hline
\end{array}
$$

When a process is dispatched to the processor, the ready chain is popped; the result becomes the current process.

CDispatch

$$
\begin{array}{|l}
\hline
\Delta CScheduler \\
p! : PId \\
\Xi BlockedChain \\
\Xi FreeChain \\
\hline
current = nullPId \\
rset \neq \varnothing \\
PopReadyChain \\
current' = p! \\
\hline
\end{array}
$$

When the current process times out, it is pushed onto the ready chain. If there is no such process, this is impossible.

CTimeOut

$\Delta CScheduler$
$p! : PId$
$\Xi BlockedChain$
$\Xi FreeChain$

$current \neq nullPId$
$PushReadyChain[p!/p?]$
$current' = nullPId$
$p! = current$

When the current process is blocked, it is pushed onto the blocked chain. Again, if there is no such process, this is impossible.

CBlock

$\Delta CScheduler$
$p! : PId$
$\Xi ReadyChain$
$\Xi FreeChain$

$current \neq nullPId$
$PushBlockedChain[p!/p?]$
$current' = nullPId$
$p! = current$

When a blocked process is woken up, it is pushed onto the ready chain:

CWakeUp

$\Delta CScheduler$
$p? : PId$
$\Xi FreeChain$

$p? \in bset$
$DeleteBlockedChain$
$PushReadyChain$
$current' = current$

For this operation to be successful, it must be applied only when the process identifier in question is present in the blocked chain.

When a process is created, an identifier is popped off the free chain and pushed onto the ready chain.

$$
\begin{array}{|l}
\textit{CCreate} \\
\hline
\Delta CScheduler \\
p! : PId \\
\Xi BlockedChain \\
\hline
fset \neq \varnothing \\
current' = current \\
PopFreeChain \\
PushReadyChain[p!/p?] \\
\hline
\end{array}
$$

Since *PushReadyChain* expects an identifier as input, we use schema renaming to capture the effect of process creation: the identifier in question is not chosen by the environment of the scheduler, but is instead supplied as output.

If the current process is destroyed, then the ready and blocked chains are unaffected. The process identifier is pushed onto the free chain:

$$
\begin{array}{|l}
\textit{CDestroyCurrent} \\
\hline
\Delta CScheduler \\
p? : PId \\
\Xi ReadyChain \\
\Xi BlockedChain \\
\hline
p? = current \\
current' = nullPId \\
PushFreeChain \\
\hline
\end{array}
$$

If a process is destroyed when ready, then the current process and the blocked chain are unaffected. The appropriate identifier is deleted from the ready chain and pushed onto the free chain:

$$
\begin{array}{|l}
\textit{CDestroyReady} \\
\hline
\Delta CScheduler \\
p? : PId \\
\Xi BlockedChain \\
\hline
p? \in rset \\
current' = current \\
DeleteReadyChain \\
PushFreeChain \\
\hline
\end{array}
$$

If a process is destroyed when blocked, then the current process is again unaffected. The identifier is deleted from the blocked chain and pushed onto the free chain:

$$
\begin{array}{|l}
\hline
\textit{CDestroyBlocked} \\
\Delta \textit{CScheduler} \\
p? : \textit{PId} \\
\Xi \textit{ReadyChain} \\
\hline
p? \in \textit{bset} \\
\textit{current}' = \textit{current} \\
\textit{DeleteBlockedChain} \\
\textit{PushFreeChain} \\
\hline
\end{array}
$$

21.5 Correctness of the design step

To see how the abstract and concrete descriptions are related, consider the following abstract state:

$$\textit{current} = 3$$

$$\textit{ready} = \{2, 4, 6\}$$

$$\textit{blocked} = \{5, 7\}$$

$$\textit{free} = \{1, 8, 9, 10\}$$

There are many concrete states that correspond to this; one possibility is

$$
\begin{array}{l}
\textit{current} = 3 \\
\textit{chainstore} \\
\quad = \{1 \mapsto 8, 2 \mapsto 6, 3 \mapsto 0, 4 \mapsto 2, 5 \mapsto 0, \\
\qquad 6 \mapsto 0, 7 \mapsto 5, 8 \mapsto 9, 9 \mapsto 10, 10 \mapsto 0\}
\end{array}
$$

$$
\begin{array}{l}
\textit{rstart} = 4 \\
\textit{rend} = 6 \\
\textit{rlinks} = \{4 \mapsto 2, 2 \mapsto 6\} \\
\textit{rset} = \{2, 4, 6\}
\end{array}
$$

$$
\begin{array}{l}
\textit{bstart} = 7 \\
\textit{bend} = 7 \\
\textit{blinks} = \{7 \mapsto 5\} \\
\textit{bset} = \{5, 7\}
\end{array}
$$

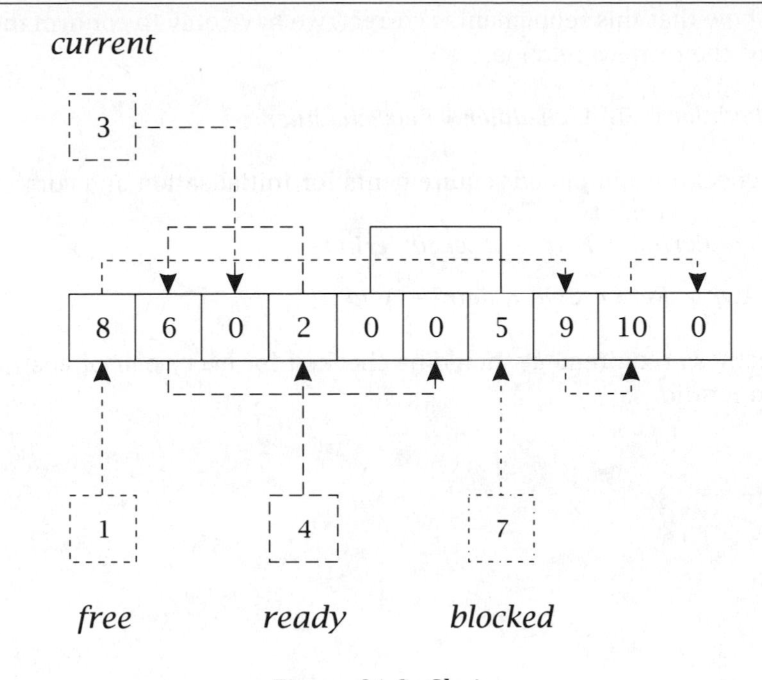

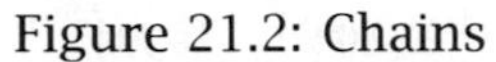

Figure 21.2: Chains

$$fstart = 1$$
$$fend = 10$$
$$flinks = \{1 \mapsto 8, 8 \mapsto 9, 9 \mapsto 10\}$$
$$fset = \{1, 8, 9, 10\}$$

This configuration is illustrated in Figure 21.2.

The connection between the concrete and abstract descriptions is described by the following schema:

```
┌─ RetrScheduler ──────────────────────
│ AScheduler
│ CScheduler
├──────────────
│ ready = rset
│ blocked = bset
│ free = fset
└──────────────────────────────────────
```

This is a functional refinement: the retrieve relation is functional from concrete to abstract.

To show that this refinement is correct, we have only to confirm the functionality of the retrieve relation,

$$CScheduler \vdash \exists_1 AScheduler \bullet RetrScheduler$$

and then check the simplified requirements for initialisation and correctness:

$$CSchedulerInit \land Retr' \vdash ASchedulerInit$$

$$\text{pre } AOp \land Retr \land COp \land Retr' \vdash AOp$$

The correctness requirement should be checked for every pair of abstract and concrete operations.

Chapter 22

A Bounded Buffer Module

In this chapter we present a rigorous development of a *bounded buffer*: a finite data store that behaves as a first-in first-out queue. We begin by describing the behaviour of the module as an abstract data type, using the language of schemas. This is refined to another description that is more suggestive of a programming language implementation. This description is then translated into the refinement calculus and refined to code.

22.1 Specification

A bounded buffer is a data store that may hold a finite number of values. It behaves as a first-in first-out queue: values leave in the order in which they arrive. We will develop a programming language implementation of a bounded buffer with three operations:

- `BufferInit`, an initialisation
- `BufferIn`, providing input to the buffer
- `BufferOut`, accepting output from the buffer

Each of these operations will be described at three levels of abstraction: as part of a specification, as part of a design, and as part of an implementation.

At the specification level, the state of a bounded buffer will include three components:

- *buffer*: a sequence of values
- *size*: the number of values present
- *max_size*: an indication of the buffer's capacity

The sequence *buffer*, and the state itself, will use a generic parameter X to refer to the type of values to be stored:

$$
\begin{array}{l}
\text{\_\_}\mathit{Buffer}[X]\text{\_\_\_\_\_\_\_\_} \\
\mathit{buffer} : \operatorname{seq} X \\
\mathit{size} : \mathbb{N} \\
\mathit{max\_size} : \mathbb{N} \\
\hline
\mathit{size} = \#\mathit{buffer} \\
\mathit{size} \leq \mathit{max\_size}
\end{array}
$$

The number of values present is equal to the length of the sequence, and must never exceed the maximum buffer size.

At initialisation, the bounded buffer is empty: *buffer* is equal to the empty sequence and *size* is zero:

$$
\begin{array}{l}
\text{\_\_}\mathit{BufferInit}[X]\text{\_\_\_\_\_\_\_\_} \\
\mathit{Buffer}'[X] \\
\hline
\mathit{buffer}' = \langle\rangle
\end{array}
$$

The value of *max_size* is left unconstrained: a suitable value should be chosen when the buffer is instantiated.

The capacity of the buffer cannot be changed after instantiation; this fact is recorded as an invariant in the following schema:

$$
\begin{array}{l}
\text{\_\_}\mathit{UpdateBuffer}[X]\text{\_\_\_\_\_\_\_\_} \\
\mathit{Buffer}[X] \\
\mathit{Buffer}'[X] \\
\hline
\mathit{max\_size}' = \mathit{max\_size}
\end{array}
$$

If the buffer is not full, an item may be inserted:

$$
\begin{array}{l}
\text{\_\_}\mathit{BufferIn}_0[X]\text{\_\_\_\_\_\_\_\_} \\
\mathit{UpdateBuffer}[X] \\
x? : X \\
\hline
\mathit{size} < \mathit{max\_size} \\
\mathit{buffer}' = \mathit{buffer} \frown \langle x? \rangle
\end{array}
$$

The new value is appended to the end of sequence *buffer*.

Extracting an item is possible only if the buffer is not empty; the value obtained is the one at the head of *buffer*:

$$
\begin{array}{|l}
\hline
\textit{BufferOut}_0[X] \\
\textit{UpdateBuffer}[X] \\
x! : X \\
\hline
\textit{buffer} \neq \langle\rangle \\
\textit{buffer}' = \textit{tail buffer} \\
x! = \textit{head buffer} \\
\hline
\end{array}
$$

These schemas represent partial operations: they describe the effect of a successful insertion and a successful extraction, respectively.

To provide a more informative interface to our data type, we consider a pair of error cases, each with its own report. We introduce a free type of reports with three elements:

$$\textit{Report} ::= \mathsf{ok} \mid \mathsf{full} \mid \mathsf{empty}$$

ok will be used to indicate a favourable outcome to an operation, full will be used to indicate that the buffer is full, and empty will be used to indicate that the buffer is empty.

We include a successful report as the single output component in a schema with no constraint:

$$
\begin{array}{|l}
\hline
\textit{Success} \\
\textit{report}! : \textit{Report} \\
\hline
\textit{report}! = \mathsf{ok} \\
\hline
\end{array}
$$

while the other reports are associated with predicates upon the current state.

The error report full may be obtained only if *size* is equal to *max_size*:

$$
\begin{array}{|l}
\hline
\textit{BufferInError}[X] \\
\Xi \textit{Buffer}[X] \\
\textit{report}! : \textit{Report} \\
\hline
\textit{size} = \textit{max\_size} \\
\textit{report}! = \mathsf{full} \\
\hline
\end{array}
$$

The inclusion of $\Xi \textit{Buffer}[X]$ indicates that the state of the buffer is unchanged by this operation.

Operation	Precondition
BufferInit	*true*
$BufferIn_0$	$size < max\_size$
BufferInError	$size = max\_size$
BufferIn	*true*
$BufferOut_0$	$buffer \neq \langle\rangle$
BufferOutError	$buffer = \langle\rangle$
BufferOut	*true*

Table 22.1: Preconditions in the bounded buffer specification

The report empty may be obtained only if the sequence *buffer* is equal to the empty sequence:

```
┌─ BufferOutError[X] ─────────────────────
│ ΞBuffer[X]
│ report! : Report
├─────────────
│ buffer = ⟨⟩
│ report! = empty
└─────────────────────────────────────────
```

Again, the state of the buffer is left unchanged.

We may define total versions of the input and output operations:

$$BufferIn[X] \mathrel{\widehat{=}} (BufferIn_0[X] \land Success) \lor BufferInError[X]$$

$$BufferOut[X] \mathrel{\widehat{=}} (BufferOut_0[X] \land Success) \lor BufferOutError[X]$$

A simple precondition analysis will confirm that the input operation will be successful unless the buffer is full, and that the output operation will be successful unless the buffer is empty.

The preconditions associated with these operations are summarised in Table 22.1. Notice that the input operation is total on valid states of the system, as the remaining possibility—that the current buffer size is greater than the capacity—is outlawed by the state invariant.

22.2 Design

We may now present a more concrete description of the bounded buffer: a design for implementation. Our description is based upon the idea of a circular array: an array in which the two ends are considered to be joined. We will maintain two indices into this array, a bottom and a top, to delimit the values that are of interest. This part of the array is then a concrete representation of the bounded buffer.

The size of the array will correspond to the capacity of the bounded buffer that it represents. Because of this, we need some way of distinguishing between the case in which the buffer is empty—the two indices coincide—and the case in which the buffer is full—again, the two indices coincide. Accordingly, we maintain a separate record of the number of values stored.

At the design level, there are five components in the state schema:

- *array*: a sequence of values
- *max_size*: the capacity of the buffer
- *bot*: the index of the first value stored
- *top*: the index of the last value stored
- *size*: the number of values stored

Although the circular array is modelled as a sequence, this sequence will be used in a way that reflects our design intentions:

$$
\begin{array}{|l}
\textit{Array}[X] \\
\hline
\textit{array} : \operatorname{seq} X \\
\textit{max\_size} : \mathbb{N} \\
\textit{bot}, \textit{top} : \mathbb{N} \\
\textit{size} : \mathbb{N} \\
\hline
\textit{bot} \in 1 \mathrel{..} \textit{max\_size} \\
\textit{top} \in 1 \mathrel{..} \textit{max\_size} \\
\textit{size} \in 0 \mathrel{..} \textit{max\_size} \\
\#\textit{array} = \textit{max\_size} \\
\textit{size} \bmod \textit{max\_size} = (\textit{top} - \textit{bot} + 1) \bmod \textit{max\_size} \\
\hline
\end{array}
$$

When the buffer is full, we have $size = max\_size$; when the buffer is empty, we have $size = 0$. In either of these two extremes, it is the case that

$$top + 1 \bmod max\_size = bot$$

As in the specification, we will insist that the capacity of the buffer cannot be changed after installation:

$$
\begin{array}{|l}
\hline
\textit{UpdateArray}[X] \\
\textit{Array}[X] \\
\textit{Array}'[X] \\
\hline
max\_size' = max\_size \\
\hline
\end{array}
$$

Since *max_size* is included as part of the design state, the invariant property is exactly the same.

22.3 A retrieve relation

The connection between concrete and abstract states is a simple one. If we cut the circular buffer immediately below the *bot* mark, and then straighten it out, we will find that the first *size* elements are the same as those in the abstract buffer. Alternatively, if we shift the circular buffer so that *bot* occurs at position 1, then trim away the waste, then we have the abstract buffer.

To help us in writing the retrieve relation, we introduce a shift operator on sequences: $\_ \ll \_$. We can shift an empty sequence indefinitely, but it will still be empty.

$$n \ll \langle\rangle = \langle\rangle$$

If we shift a sequence by no places at all, then we leave it unchanged:

$$0 \ll s = s$$

If we shift a non-empty sequence by one place, the first becomes the last:

$$1 \ll (\langle x \rangle \frown s) = s \frown \langle x \rangle$$

A suitable generic definition would be

$$
\begin{array}{|l}
\hline\hline
[X] \\
\_ \ll \_ : \mathbb{N} \times \operatorname{seq} X \rightarrow \operatorname{seq} X \\
\hline
\forall n : \mathbb{N};\ x : X;\ s : \operatorname{seq} X \bullet \\
\quad n \ll \langle\rangle = \langle\rangle \land \\
\quad 0 \ll s = s \land \\
\quad (n+1) \ll (\langle x \rangle \frown s) = n \ll (s \frown \langle x \rangle) \\
\hline
\end{array}
$$

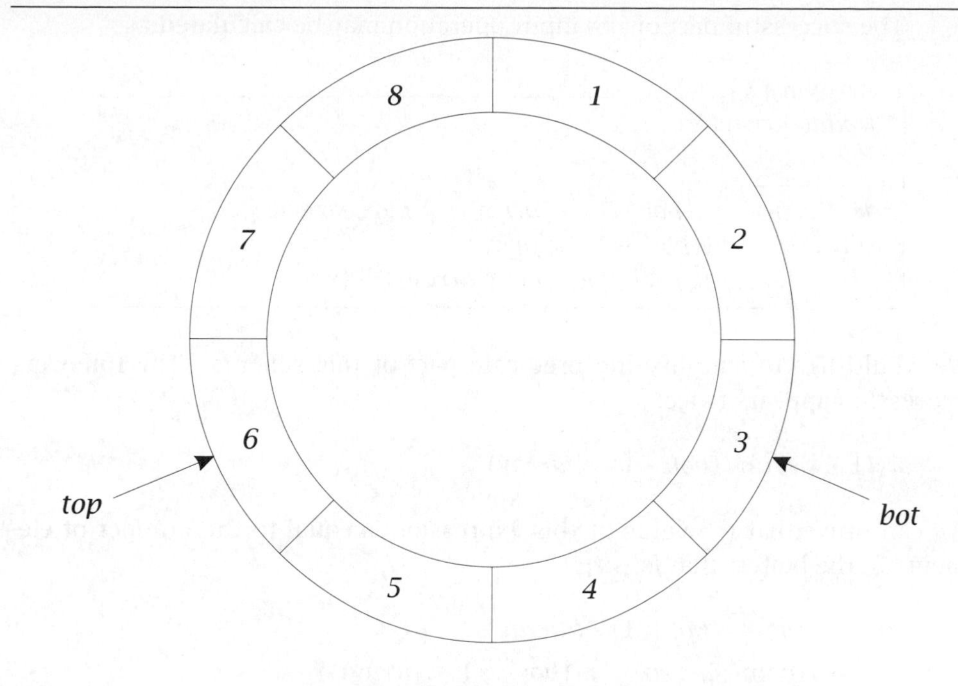

Figure 22.1: A circular array with pointers

Returning to the retrieve relation, consider the circular buffer shown in Figure 22.1. To extract the abstract object represented by this buffer, we may shift the concrete sequence by two places, and then restrict the result to the indices 1 . . 4. That is, we extract

$$\begin{aligned}
&(1 \,..\, 4) \lhd (2 \ll \langle 1, 2, 3, 4, 5, 6, 7, 8 \rangle) \\
&= (1 \,..\, 4) \lhd \langle 3, 4, 5, 6, 7, 8, 1, 2 \rangle \\
&= \langle 3, 4, 5, 6 \rangle
\end{aligned}$$

In general we have the retrieve relation

RetrieveBuffer[*X*]
Buffer[*X*]   *Array*[*X*]
$buffer = (1 \,..\, size) \lhd ((bot - 1) \ll array)$

Notice that the retrieve relation is a total, surjective function, so that we can calculate the data refinement.

The successful part of the input operation may be calculated as

$$
\begin{array}{|l}
\textit{ArrayIn}_0[X] \\
\hline
\textit{UpdateArray}[X] \\
x? : X \\
\hline
\#((1 \mathinner{..} size) \lhd ((bot - 1) \ll array)) < max\_size \\
((1 \mathinner{..} size') \lhd ((bot' - 1) \ll array')) \\
\quad = ((1 \mathinner{..} size) \lhd ((bot - 1) \ll array)) \frown \langle x? \rangle \\
\hline
\end{array}
$$

We would like to simplify the predicate part of this schema. The following expression appears twice:

$$\#((1 \mathinner{..} size) \lhd ((bot - 1) \ll array))$$

We can prove that the value of this expression is equal to the number of elements in the buffer: that is, *size*.

$$
\begin{aligned}
&\#((1 \mathinner{..} size) \lhd ((bot - 1) \ll array)) \\
&\quad = \#(\mathrm{dom}((1 \mathinner{..} size) \lhd ((bot - 1) \ll array))) && \text{[the size of a function = the size of its domain]} \\
&\quad = \#((1 \mathinner{..} size) \cap \mathrm{dom}((bot - 1) \ll array)) && \text{[property of domain restriction]} \\
&\quad = \#((1 \mathinner{..} size) \cap \mathrm{dom}\, array) && \text{[property of shifting]} \\
&\quad = \#((1 \mathinner{..} size) \cap (1 \mathinner{..} max\_size)) && \text{[consequence of the state invariant]} \\
&\quad = \#(\max\{1, 1\} \mathinner{..} \min\{size, max\_size\}) && \text{[property of intervals]} \\
&\quad = \#(1 \mathinner{..} \min\{size, max\_size\}) && \text{[maximum of a singleton set]} \\
&\quad = \#(1 \mathinner{..} size) && \text{[consequence of the state invariant]} \\
&\quad = size - 1 + 1 && \text{[property of intervals]} \\
&\quad = size && \text{[arithmetic]}
\end{aligned}
$$

To simplify the second predicate in the schema, we will make use of a simple property of sequences. If we consider the expression

$$(1 \mathinner{..} m \lhd s) \frown \langle x \rangle$$

we notice that, if $m \leq \# s$, the constructed sequence has $m + 1$ elements, and also that its $m + 1^{\text{th}}$ element is x. Thus for any $m \leq \# s$, we have

$$(1 \mathinner{..} m \lhd s) \frown \langle x \rangle \;=\; (1 \mathinner{..} m + 1) \lhd (s \oplus \{m + 1 \mapsto x\})$$

The overriding operator ensures that the last element in the sequence is x.

We may now simplify the second predicate:

$$\begin{aligned}
&(1 \mathinner{..} size') \lhd (bot' - 1 \ll array') = \\
&\qquad ((1 \mathinner{..} size) \lhd (bot' - 1 \ll array)) \frown \langle x? \rangle
\end{aligned}$$

$$\begin{aligned}
\Leftrightarrow\ &(1 \mathinner{..} size') \lhd (bot' - 1 \ll array') = \\
&\qquad (1 \mathinner{..} size + 1) \lhd ((bot - 1 \ll array) \oplus \{size + 1 \mapsto x?\})
\end{aligned}$$

[property of sequences]

$$\begin{aligned}
\Leftarrow\ &size' = size + 1 \land \\
&bot' - 1 \ll array' = (bot - 1 \ll array) \oplus \{size + 1 \mapsto x?\}
\end{aligned}$$

[property of domain restriction]

$$\begin{aligned}
\Leftrightarrow\ &size' = size + 1 \land \\
&bot' - 1 \ll array' = \\
&\qquad bot - 1 \ll (array \\
&\qquad\qquad \oplus \\
&\qquad\qquad \{(size + 1 + bot - 1 - 1 \mathrm{\ mod\ } \# array) + 1 \mapsto x?\}
\end{aligned}$$

[property of shifting]

$$\begin{aligned}
\Leftarrow\ &size' = size + 1 \land bot' = bot \land \\
&array' = array \oplus \{(size + bot - 1 \mathrm{\ mod\ } \# array) + 1 \mapsto x?\}
\end{aligned}$$

[arithmetic and a property of shifting]

$$\begin{aligned}
\Leftrightarrow\ &size' = size + 1 \land bot' = bot \land \\
&array' = array \oplus \{(size + bot - 1 \mathrm{\ mod\ } max_size) + 1 \mapsto x?\}
\end{aligned}$$

[consequence of the state invariant]

$$\begin{aligned}\Leftrightarrow\ & size' = size + 1 \land bot' = bot \land \\ & array' = \\ & \quad array \\ & \quad \oplus \\ & \quad \{(size \bmod max\_size + bot - 1 \bmod max\_size) + 1 \mapsto x?\}\end{aligned}$$

[arithmetic]

$$\begin{aligned}\Leftrightarrow\ & size' = size + 1 \land bot' = bot \land \\ & array' = \\ & \quad array \\ & \quad \oplus \\ & \quad \{((top - bot + 1) \bmod max\_size + bot - 1 \bmod max\_size) + 1 \\ & \quad\ \mapsto \\ & \quad\ x?\}\end{aligned}$$

[the state invariant]

$$\begin{aligned}\Leftrightarrow\ & size' = size + 1 \land \\ & bot' = bot \land \\ & array' = array \oplus \{(top - bot + 1 + bot - 1 \bmod max\_size) + 1 \mapsto x?\}\end{aligned}$$

[arithmetic]

$$\begin{aligned}\Leftrightarrow\ & size' = size + 1 \land \\ & bot' = bot \land \\ & array' = array \oplus \{(top \bmod max\_size) + 1 \mapsto x?\}\end{aligned}$$

[arithmetic]

$$\begin{aligned}\Leftarrow\ & size' = size + 1 \land \\ & bot' = bot \land \\ & top' = (top \bmod max\_size) + 1 \land \\ & array' = array \oplus \{top' \mapsto x?\}\end{aligned}$$

[property of equality]

The first step in the derivation is contingent upon $size \leq \#array$, which is a consequence of the state invariant.

We have found a stronger condition that shows how we can update the concrete state to achieve the abstract effect. The *size* of the buffer is increased by 1; *bot* is unchanged; *top* is moved one place; and the new element is added at the new *top* of the buffer.

The result of our calculation is a concrete operation schema that describes the effect of a successful input:

$$
\begin{array}{|l}
\hline
\textit{ArrayIn}_0[X] \\
\textit{UpdateArray}[X] \\
x? : X \\
\hline
\textit{size} < \textit{max\_size} \\
\textit{size}' = \textit{size} + 1 \\
\textit{bot}' = \textit{bot} \\
\textit{top}' = (\textit{top} \bmod \textit{max\_size}) + 1 \\
\textit{array}' = \textit{array} \oplus \{\textit{top}' \mapsto x?\} \\
\hline
\end{array}
$$

The error case for the concrete operation is easily calculated. A simple substitution into the abstract schema yields:

$$
\begin{array}{|l}
\hline
\textit{ArrayInError}[X] \\
\Xi\textit{Array}[X] \\
\textit{report}! : \textit{Report} \\
\hline
\#((1 \mathinner{\ldotp\ldotp} \textit{size}) \lhd ((\textit{bot} - 1) \ll \textit{array})) = \textit{max\_size} \\
\textit{report}! = \mathsf{full} \\
\hline
\end{array}
$$

The calculation that we performed earlier has given us a simplification of the first predicate:

$$
\begin{array}{|l}
\hline
\textit{ArrayInError}[X] \\
\Xi\textit{Array}[X] \\
\textit{report}! : \textit{Report} \\
\hline
\textit{size} = \textit{max\_size} \\
\textit{report}! = \mathsf{full} \\
\hline
\end{array}
$$

The total form of the input operation is then described by

$$
\begin{array}{l}
\textit{ArrayIn}[X] \mathrel{\widehat{=}} \\
\quad (\textit{ArrayIn}_0[X] \\
\quad\ \wedge \\
\quad\ \textit{Success}) \\
\quad \vee \\
\quad \textit{ArrayInError}[X]
\end{array}
$$

A similar calculation yields the concrete form of the output operation:

$$
\begin{array}{|l}
\hline
\textit{ArrayOut}_0[X] \\
\textit{UpdateArray}[X] \\
x! : X \\
\hline
1 \mathinner{..} \textit{size} \lhd (\textit{bot} - 1 \ll \textit{array}) \neq \langle\rangle \\
(1 \mathinner{..} \textit{size}' \lhd (\textit{bot}' - 1 \ll \textit{array}')) = \\
\quad \textit{tail}\,(1 \mathinner{..} \textit{size} \lhd (\textit{bot} - 1 \ll \textit{array})) \\
x! = \textit{head}\,(1 \mathinner{..} \textit{size} \lhd (\textit{bot} - 1 \ll \textit{array})) \\
\hline
\end{array}
$$

The first predicate is easily simplified:

$$1 \mathinner{..} \textit{size} \lhd (\textit{bot} - 1 \ll \textit{array}) \neq \langle\rangle$$

$$\Leftrightarrow \#(1 \mathinner{..} \textit{size} \lhd (\textit{bot} - 1 \ll \textit{array})) \neq 0$$

[property of sequences]

$$\Leftrightarrow \textit{size} \neq 0$$

[previous calculation]

To simplify the second predicate, we observe that the right-hand expression may be rewritten as follows:

$$\textit{tail}\,(1 \mathinner{..} \textit{size} \lhd (\textit{bot} - 1 \ll \textit{array}))$$

$$= \textit{squash}\,(2 \mathinner{..} \textit{size} \lhd (1 \mathinner{..} \textit{size} \lhd (\textit{bot} - 1 \ll \textit{array})))$$

[definition of *tail*]

$$= \textit{squash}\,(2 \mathinner{..} \textit{size} \lhd (\textit{bot} - 1 \ll \textit{array}))$$

[property of domain restriction]

$$= \textit{squash}\,(1 \mathinner{..} \textit{size} - 1 \lhd (1 \ll (\textit{bot} - 1 \ll \textit{array})))$$

[by a property of shifting]

$$= \textit{squash}\,(1 \mathinner{..} \textit{size} - 1 \lhd (\textit{bot} \ll \textit{array}))$$

[property of shifting]

$$= 1 \mathinner{..} \textit{size} - 1 \lhd (\textit{bot} \ll \textit{array})$$

[property of squashing]

The second predicate may then be simpified:

$$1 \mathinner{..} size' \lhd (bot' - 1 \ll array') = tail\,(1 \mathinner{..} size \lhd (bot - 1 \ll array)$$

$$\Leftrightarrow 1 \mathinner{..} size' \lhd (bot' - 1 \ll array') = 1 \mathinner{..} size - 1 \lhd (bot \ll array)$$

[previous calculation]

$$\Leftarrow size > 0 \land size' = size - 1 \land \\ bot' = (bot \bmod max\_size) + 1 \land \\ array' = array$$

[property of equality]

The right-hand side of the third predicate can be rewritten as follows:

$$head\,(1 \mathinner{..} size \lhd (bot - 1 \ll array))$$

$$= (1 \mathinner{..} size \lhd (bot - 1 \ll array))\,1 \quad \text{[provided that } size \neq 0]$$

$$= (bot - 1 \ll array)\,1 \quad \text{[provided that } size \neq 0]$$

$$= array\ bot \quad \text{[property of shifting]}$$

Provided that the buffer is not empty, we should decrement the *size*; increment *bot*; leave *top* alone; and output the element that was indexed by *bot*.

Using these calculations to simplify the operation schema that describes the concrete output operation, we obtain

$$\begin{array}{|l} \multicolumn{1}{l}{ArrayOut_0[X]} \\ \hline UpdateArray[X] \\ x! : X \\ \hline size \neq 0 \\ size' = size - 1 \\ bot' = (bot \bmod max\_size) + 1 \\ array' = array \\ x! = array\ bot \\ \hline \end{array}$$

The error case is easily calculated:

$$\begin{array}{|l} \multicolumn{1}{l}{ArrayOutError[X]} \\ \hline \Xi Array[X] \\ report! : Report \\ \hline (1 \mathinner{..} size) \lhd ((bot - 1) \ll array) = \langle\rangle \\ report! = \mathsf{empty} \\ \hline \end{array}$$

Again, this may be simplified:

$$
\begin{array}{|l}
\hline
\textit{ArrayOutError}[X] \\
\Xi \textit{Array}[X] \\
\textit{report}! : \textit{Report} \\
\hline
\textit{size} = 0 \\
\textit{report}! = \mathsf{empty} \\
\hline
\end{array}
$$

The robust version of the concrete output operation is then

$$
\begin{aligned}
\textit{ArrayOut}[X] \mathrel{\widehat{=}} & \ \textit{ArrayOut}_0[X] \land \textit{Success} \\
& \lor \\
& \textit{ArrayOutError}[X]
\end{aligned}
$$

22.4 Implementation

Our implementation of the design will be parameterised by the maximum size of the buffer. The global declarations for our bounded buffer module will be

$$
\begin{array}{l}
\mathsf{var}\ \ \textit{ibuffer} : \mathsf{array}\ [1 \mathinner{..} \textit{max\_size}]\ \mathsf{of}\ X; \\
\qquad \textit{bot}, \textit{top} : 1 \mathinner{..} \textit{max\_size}; \\
\qquad \textit{size} : 0 \mathinner{..} \textit{max\_size}; \\
\mathsf{and}\ \textit{size}\ \mathsf{mod}\ \textit{max\_size} = (\textit{top} - \textit{bot} + 1)\ \mathsf{mod}\ \textit{max\_size}
\end{array}
$$

We will begin with the concrete input operation:

$$
\textit{IBufferIn}[X] \mathrel{\widehat{=}} \textit{Array}'[X] : \left[\textit{true}\ ,\ \begin{pmatrix} \textit{ArrayIn}_0[X] \land \textit{Success} \\ \lor \\ \textit{ArrayInError}[X] \end{pmatrix} \right]
$$

The derivation of code is quite simple:

$$
\begin{array}{l}
\textit{IBufferIn}[X] \sqsubseteq \\
\quad \mathsf{if}\ \ \textit{size} < \textit{max\_size} \rightarrow \\
\qquad \textit{Array}'[X] : [\, \textit{size} < \textit{max\_size}, \textit{ArrayIn}_0[X] \land \textit{Success} \,] \qquad [\triangleleft] \\
\quad \Box\ \ \textit{size} = \textit{max\_size} \rightarrow \\
\qquad \textit{Array}'[X] : [\, \textit{size} = \textit{max\_size}, \textit{ArrayInError}[X] \,] \qquad [\dagger] \\
\quad \mathsf{fi}
\end{array}
$$

We refine the first alternative

$$\lhd$$

$\sqsubseteq$ (strengthen postcondition)

$$Array'[X] : \left[size < max\_size \ , \ \begin{array}{r@{\;}l} size' &= size + 1 \\ bot' &= bot \\ top' &= (top \ \mathsf{mod} \ max\_size) + 1 \\ ibuffer' &= ibuffer \oplus \{top' \mapsto x?\} \\ report! &= \mathsf{ok} \end{array} \right]$$

$\sqsubseteq$ (assignment introduction)

$$\begin{array}{l} size := size + 1 \, ; \\ top := (top \ \mathsf{mod} \ max\_size) + 1 \, ; \\ ibuffer := ibuffer \oplus \{top \mapsto x\} \, ; \\ report = \mathsf{ok} \end{array}$$

and then the second alternative:

$$\dagger$$

$\sqsubseteq$ (strengthen postcondition)

$$Array'[X] : \left[size = max\_size \ , \ report! = \mathsf{full} \right]$$

$\sqsubseteq$ (assignment introduction)

$report := \mathsf{full}$

Collecting the code, and encapsulating the input operation as a parameterised procedure with value and result parameters—with the usual programming language interpretation—we have

```
procedure BufferIn[X]
    (val x : X; res report : Report);
    if size < max_size →
        size := size + 1;
        top := (top mod max_size) + 1;
        ibuffer[top] := x;
        report = ok
    □ size = max_size →
        report := full
    fi
```

The following specification statement corresponds closely to the concrete output operation:

$$IBufferOut[X] \mathrel{\widehat{=}} Array'[X] : \left[\; true \; , \; \left(\begin{array}{l} ArrayOut_0[X] \wedge Success \\ \vee \\ ArrayOutError[X] \end{array} \right) \right]$$

This may be refined as follows:

$IBufferOut[X]$

$\sqsubseteq$ (*conditionalintroduction*)

if $size \neq 0 \rightarrow$

$Array'[X] : [\, size \neq 0, \; ArrayOut_0[X] \wedge Success \,]$ [◁]

□ $size = 0 \rightarrow$

$Array'[X] : [\, size = 0, \; ArrayOutError[X] \,]$ [†]

fi

We may refine the first alternative:

◁

$\sqsubseteq$ (strengthen postcondition)

$$Array'[X] : \left[\begin{array}{ll} & size' = size - 1 \\ & bot' = (bot \bmod max\_size) + 1 \\ & array' = array \\ size \neq 0 \; , & report! = \mathsf{ok} \end{array} \right]$$

$\sqsubseteq$ (assignment introduction)

$size := size - 1; \; bot := (bot \bmod max\_size) + 1; \; report! := \mathsf{ok}$

and the second alternative:

†

$\sqsubseteq$ (strengthen postcondition)

$Array'[X] : [\, size = 0, \; report! = \mathsf{empty} \,]$

$\sqsubseteq$ (assignment introduction)

$report! := \mathsf{empty}$

We may collect the code and encapsulate the output operation as a parameterised procedure:

procedure *IBufferOut*
  (res *report* : *ReportType*) ;
  if $size \neq 0 \rightarrow$
    $size := size - 1$;
    $bot := (bot \bmod max\_size) + 1$;
    report! := ok
  $\Box$ $size = 0 \rightarrow$
    report! := empty
  fi

Similarly, we may derive a procedure that accepts a single value and resets the buffer to hold just that value:

procedure *ResetBuffer*[X]
  (val $x : X$) ;
  $bot, top, size, ibuffer[1] := 1, 1, 1, x$

A suitable initialisation for the buffer module is described by the following assignment:

initially $bot, top, size := 1, max\_size, 0$

22.5 Executable code

We may now translate our refinement calculus implementation into executable code. The language chosen is Modula-2:

```
MODULE Buffer;

  EXPORT
    max_size, ReportType, ResetBuffer,
    BufferIn, BufferOut;

  CONST
    max_size = N;

  TYPE
    ReportType = ( OK, Full, Empty );
```

```
VAR
  ibuffer: ARRAY [ 1 .. max_size ] OF X;
  bot, top: 1 .. max_size;
  size: 0 .. max_size;

PROCEDURE ResetBuffer ( x: X );
  BEGIN
    bot := 1;
    top := 1;
    size := 1;
    ibuffer[1] := x
  END;

PROCEDURE BufferIn ( x: X; VAR report: ReportType );
  IF size < max_size THEN
    BEGIN
      size := size + 1;
      top := ( top MOD max_size ) + 1;
      ibuffer[top] := x;
      report = OK
    END
  ELSE report := Full;

PROCEDURE BufferOut ( VAR report: ReportType );
  IF size <> 0 THEN
    BEGIN
      size := size - 1;
      bot := ( bot MOD max_size ) + 1;
      report := OK
    END
  ELSE report := Empty;

BEGIN
  bot := 1;
  top := max_size;
  size := 0
END Buffer;
```

Chapter 23

A Save Area

In this chapter we present the specification and development of a *save area*, a module in an operating system with two operations, *Save* and *Restore*, by means of which records are stored and retrieved in a first-in first-out manner. Such a module may be useful in a check-pointing scheme, for instance, where the current state of a record structure is saved. At a later time, the system can be restored to this state.

Our specification is nondeterministic, delaying a key design decision until a more appropriate stage of development is reached. The development itself is in two parts: a decision is taken to introduce a two-level memory; a representation is chosen for the data structure used in main memory.

The design is produced using calculation. A concrete state is proposed, and its relation to the abstract state is documented. The concrete operations are then calculated from the abstract operations and the retrieve relation. The lowest level of design provides the starting point for the calculation of the code using the refinement calculus.

23.1 Specification

Our specification of the save area will leave abstract the details of the records being manipulated. We introduce a basic type

$[Record]$

to represent the set of all records. Each operation will return a status report; the free type of reports is defined by

$Status ::= \mathsf{ok} \mid \mathsf{full} \mid \mathsf{empty}$

The state of the system comprises a sequence of records:

$$
\begin{array}{|l}
\textit{SaveArea} \\
\hline
\textit{save\_area} : \mathrm{seq}\ \textit{Record} \\
\hline
\end{array}
$$

Initially, no records have been stored and this sequence is empty:

$$
\begin{array}{|l}
\textit{InitSaveArea} \\
\hline
\textit{SaveArea}' \\
\hline
\textit{save\_area}' = \langle\rangle \\
\hline
\end{array}
$$

We will use the sequence as a stack, with the last element as the top of the stack. When a record is stored, it is placed at the end:

$$
\begin{array}{|l}
\textit{Save}_0 \\
\hline
\Delta \textit{SaveArea} \\
\textit{record}? : \textit{Record} \\
\textit{status}! : \textit{Status} \\
\hline
\textit{save\_area}' = \textit{save\_area} \frown \langle \textit{record}? \rangle \\
\textit{status}! = \mathsf{ok} \\
\hline
\end{array}
$$

It is easy to see that $Save_0$ is total, but the *Save* operation may fail: there may not always be enough room to store the new record. We do not have enough state information to predict when this may happen.

We could remedy this by adding a component to describes the amount of store left; this value would be updated every time *save_area* was modified. However, the amount of free space left in the system is influenced by factors other than the size of the records and the number stored. We would need to model the rest of the system in some way.

Following this path leads us away from abstraction and modularity. It is better to admit that we do not know the circumstances—at this level of abstraction—that determine the amount of free space and hence the success or failure of the *Save* operation. Thus the error case for *Save* is described by

$$
\begin{array}{|l}
\textit{SaveFullErr} \\
\hline
\Xi \textit{SaveArea} \\
\textit{status}! : \textit{Status} \\
\hline
\textit{status}! = \mathsf{full} \\
\hline
\end{array}
$$

The complete description of *Save* is then

$$Save \mathrel{\widehat=} Save_0 \lor SaveFullErr$$

This is a *nondeterministic* specification: whenever the operation is used, it may succeed in appending the record and report ok, or it may leave the state unchanged and report full.

It is useful at this point to draw a distinction between a nondeterministic specification, such as this, and a *loose* specification. A loose specification is one in which a constant is introduced with a range of values: for example, we may declare a constant n thus

$$| \; n : \mathbb{N}$$

This constant is then a parameter to the specification.

Suppose that we have another parameterised specification, identical in every way except for the fact that the range of n is restricted:

$$| \; n : 1 \mathrel{..} 10$$

Although we have been more precise about the value of n, this restriction is not a refinement in the sense described above: it is merely a tighter version of the same specification.

A loosely-specified constant is there to be instantiated at any stage of development: we may make this choice during specification, or retain the constant as a parameter of the design. A nondeterministic operation—such as *Save*—involves an internal choice of behaviours: we must propose an implementation that, when will behave accordingly.

The *Restore* operation is wholly deterministic. We can restore a record whenever there is at least one record in *save_area*:

```
┌─ Restore₀ ─────────────────────────────
│ ΔSaveArea
│ r! : Record
│ status! : Status
├────────────
│ save_area ≠ ⟨⟩
│ save_area = save_area' ⁀ ⟨r!⟩
│ status! = ok
└────────────────────────────────────────
```

The last record in the save area is removed from the stack and provided as output; the success of the operation is reported.

Operation		Precondition
Save	$Save_0$	*true*
	SaveFullErr	*true*
	Save	*true*
Restore	$Restore_0$	$save\_area \neq \langle\rangle$
	RestoreEmptyErr	$save\_area = \langle\rangle$
	Restore	*true*

Table 23.1: Preconditions for the save area

However, if *save_area* is empty, then we must return an error message:

```
┌─ RestoreEmptyErr ─────────────────
│ ΞSaveArea
│ status! : Status
├───────────
│ save_area = ⟨⟩
│ status! = empty
└───────────────────────────────────
```

The complete description of *Restore* is then

$$Restore \mathrel{\widehat=} Restore_0 \lor RestoreEmptyErr$$

The preconditions for the operations in this interface are collected in Table 23.1.

23.2 Design

Our first design decision involves the introduction of a two-level memory. Large amounts of data will be saved, and this will quickly exhaust the main memory available to our program. Accordingly, we will employ secondary memory; once the main memory is exhausted, we will copy it here.

Let n be the number of records that we can save in main memory. We insist that the value of n—a parameter to the specification—is at least 1:

```
│ n : ℕ
├───────────
│ n ≥ 1
```

We define two sets of sequences: a *bounded* sequence is one whose length does not exceed n; a *full* sequence is one whose length is exactly n.

$$
\begin{array}{l}
[X] \\
\hline
bseq : \mathbb{P}(\mathrm{seq}\, X) \\
fseq : \mathbb{P}(\mathrm{seq}\, X) \\
\hline
bseq = \{ s : \mathrm{seq}\, X \mid \# s \leq n \} \\
fseq = \{ s : \mathrm{seq}\, X \mid \# s = n \}
\end{array}
$$

Our concrete design employs main and secondary memory: main memory is a bounded sequence of records; secondary memory is a list of full sequences:

$$
\begin{array}{l}
CSaveArea \\
\hline
main : bseq[Record] \\
secondary : \mathrm{seq}(fseq[Record])
\end{array}
$$

We can extract our abstract description using distributed concatenation:

$$
\begin{array}{l}
Retrieve \\
\hline
SaveArea \\
CSaveArea \\
\hline
save\_area = (\frown / \, secondary) \frown main
\end{array}
$$

For a given value of n, there is only one way in which the *save_area* sequence can be split into *main* and *secondary*. Similarly, there is only one way that *main* and *secondary* can be combined to make *save_area*, if order is to be maintained.

The retrieve relation described by this schema is a total bijection, and we may use it to derive an initialisation:

$$
\begin{array}{l}
CSaveArea' \\
\hline
(\frown / \, secondary') \frown main' = \langle\rangle
\end{array}
$$

There is a unique solution to the equation in the predicate part:

$$
\begin{array}{lr}
(\frown / \, secondary') \frown main' = \langle\rangle & \\
\quad \Leftrightarrow \frown / \, secondary' = \langle\rangle \wedge main' = \langle\rangle & \text{[catenation]} \\
\quad \Leftrightarrow secondary' = \langle\rangle \wedge main' = \langle\rangle & \text{[distributed catenation]}
\end{array}
$$

The initialisation of the two-level system is given by

$$\begin{array}{|l}
\textit{InitCSaveArea} \\
\hline
\textit{CSaveArea}' \\
\hline
\textit{main}' = \langle\rangle \\
\textit{secondary}' = \langle\rangle \\
\hline
\end{array}$$

The concrete version of $Save_0$ may be obtained using substitution:

$$\begin{array}{|l}
\hline
\Delta \textit{CSaveArea} \\
\textit{record}? : \textit{Record} \\
\textit{status}! : \textit{Status} \\
\hline
(\frown / \textit{secondary}') \frown \textit{main}' = (\frown / \textit{secondary}) \frown \textit{main} \frown \langle \textit{record}? \rangle \\
\textit{status}! = \mathsf{ok} \\
\hline
\end{array}$$

The first equation in the predicate part of this schema describes the concrete state change associated with this operation. It has two solutions in terms of *main* and *secondary*: either

$$\frown / \textit{secondary}' = (\frown / \textit{secondary}) \frown \textit{main} \quad \wedge \quad \textit{main}' = \langle \textit{record}? \rangle$$

or

$$\frown / \textit{secondary}' = \frown / \textit{secondary} \quad \wedge \quad \textit{main}' = \textit{main} \frown \langle \textit{record}? \rangle$$

From the properties of distributed concatenation, it is easy to see that

$$\begin{array}{l}
\frown / \textit{secondary}' = (\frown / \textit{secondary}) \frown \textit{main} \Leftarrow \\
\quad \textit{secondary}' = \textit{secondary} \frown \langle \textit{main} \rangle
\end{array}$$

The concrete version of $Save_0$ is thus described by

$$\begin{array}{|l}
\hline
\Delta \textit{CSaveArea} \\
\textit{record}? : \textit{Record} \\
\textit{status}! : \textit{Status} \\
\hline
(\textit{main}' = \langle \textit{record}? \rangle \wedge \textit{secondary}' = \textit{secondary} \frown \langle \textit{main} \rangle) \vee \\
\quad (\textit{main}' = \textit{main} \frown \langle \textit{record}? \rangle \wedge \textit{secondary}' = \textit{secondary}) \\
\textit{status}! = \mathsf{ok} \\
\hline
\end{array}$$

However, the invariant property of *CSaveArea*, together with the declarations of *fseq* and *bseq*, allows us to be more explicit about the factors determining the new values of *main* and *secondary*. In the first case,

$$secondary \frown \langle main \rangle \in \text{seq}(fseq[Record])$$

$$\Leftrightarrow secondary \in \text{seq}(fseq[Record]) \land main \in fseq[Record]$$

[property of sequences]

$$\Leftrightarrow main \in fseq[Record]$$

[*CSaveArea* invariant]

$$\Leftrightarrow main \in \text{seq}\, Record \land \#main = n$$

[definition of *fseq*]

$$\Leftrightarrow \#main = n$$

[*CSaveArea* invariant]

and in the second,

$$main \frown \langle record? \rangle \in bseq[Record]$$

$$\Leftrightarrow main \frown \langle record? \rangle \in \text{seq}\, Record \land \#(main \frown \langle record? \rangle) \leq n$$

[definition of *bseq*]

$$\Leftrightarrow main \in \text{seq}\, Record \land \langle record? \rangle \in \text{seq}\, Record \land \#(main \frown \langle record? \rangle) \leq n$$

[property of sequences]

$$\Leftrightarrow \langle record? \rangle \in \text{seq}\, Record \land \#(main \frown \langle record? \rangle) \leq n$$

[*CSaveArea* invariant]

$$\Leftrightarrow record? \in Record \land \#(main \frown \langle record? \rangle) \leq n$$

[property of sequences]

$$\Leftrightarrow \#(main \frown \langle record? \rangle) \leq n$$

[declaration of *record?*]

$$\Leftrightarrow (\#main) + \#\langle record? \rangle \leq n$$

[property of #]

$$\Leftrightarrow (\#main) + 1 \leq n$$

[property of #]

$$\Leftrightarrow \#main < n$$

[property of numbers]

The successful part of our save operation is therefore

$$
\begin{array}{l}
\textit{CSave}_0 \\
\hline
\Delta \textit{CSaveArea} \\
\textit{record?} : \textit{Record} \\
\textit{status!} : \textit{Status} \\
\hline
(\quad \# \textit{main} = n \land \\
\qquad \textit{main}' = \langle \textit{record?} \rangle \land \\
\qquad \textit{secondary}' = \textit{secondary} \frown \langle \textit{main} \rangle \\
\quad \lor \\
\quad \# \textit{main} < n \land \\
\qquad \textit{main}' = \textit{main} \frown \langle \textit{record?} \rangle \land \\
\qquad \textit{secondary}' = \textit{secondary} \quad) \\
\textit{status!} = \mathsf{ok} \\
\hline
\end{array}
$$

The error case is easily calculated:

$$
\begin{array}{l}
\textit{CSaveFullErr} \\
\hline
\Xi \textit{CSaveArea} \\
\textit{status!} : \textit{Status} \\
\hline
\textit{status!} = \mathsf{full} \\
\hline
\end{array}
$$

The complete description of this operation is given by

$$\textit{CSave} \mathrel{\widehat{=}} \textit{CSave}_0 \lor \textit{CSaveFullErr}$$

23.3 Further design

Our second design decision concerns the implementation of main memory storage. A bounded sequence such as *main* can be implemented using a fixed-length array; a suitable representation might be

$$
\begin{array}{l}
[X] \\
\hline
\textit{Array} : \mathbb{P}(\mathbb{N} \twoheadrightarrow X) \\
\hline
\textit{Array} = (1 \mathinner{..} n) \rightarrow X \\
\hline
\end{array}
$$

That is, a fixed-length array can be represented by a total function from the indices to the target type.

Our new design adds an array and a counter to the existing representation of secondary memory:

$$
\begin{array}{|l}
\hline
\textit{CSaveArea1} \\
\textit{array} : \textit{Array}[\textit{Record}] \\
\textit{count} : 0 \mathinner{..} n \\
\textit{secondary} : \mathrm{seq}(\textit{fseq}[\textit{Record}]) \\
\hline
\end{array}
$$

The counter is used to keep track of the number of records stored.

We may retrieve the bounded sequence of the abstract state by discarding any array elements whose indices are greater than the current value of the variable *count*:

$$
\begin{array}{|l}
\hline
\textit{Retrieve1} \\
\textit{CSaveArea} \\
\textit{CSaveArea1} \\
\hline
\textit{main} = (1 \mathinner{..} \textit{count}) \lhd \textit{array} \\
\hline
\end{array}
$$

The resulting retrieve relation is a total surjective function from concrete to abstract, and we may calculate the latest refinement of the save operation:

$$
\begin{array}{|l}
\hline
\Delta \textit{CSaveArea} \\
\textit{record?} : \textit{Record} \\
\textit{status!} : \textit{Status} \\
\hline
(\quad \#((1 \mathinner{..} \textit{count}) \lhd \textit{array}) = n \land \\
\qquad\qquad (1 \mathinner{..} \textit{count}') \lhd \textit{array}' = \langle \textit{record?} \rangle \land \\
\qquad\qquad \textit{secondary}' = \\
\qquad\qquad\qquad \textit{secondary} \frown \langle (1 \mathinner{..} \textit{count}) \lhd \textit{array} \rangle \\
\quad \lor \\
\quad \#((1 \mathinner{..} \textit{count}) \lhd \textit{array}) < n \land \\
\qquad\qquad (1 \mathinner{..} \textit{count}') \lhd \textit{array}' = \\
\qquad\qquad\qquad ((1 \mathinner{..} \textit{count}) \lhd \textit{array}) \frown \langle \textit{record?} \rangle \land \\
\qquad\qquad \textit{secondary}' = \textit{secondary} \quad) \\
\textit{status!} = \mathsf{ok} \\
\hline
\end{array}
$$

It is easy to see that

$$\#((1 \mathinner{..} \textit{count}) \lhd \textit{array}) \; = \; \textit{count}$$

This simplification makes the predicate part more readable:

$$
\begin{array}{l}
\Delta CSaveArea \\
record? : Record \\
status! : Status \\
\hline
(\quad count = n \land \\
\qquad (1 \mathinner{..} count') \lhd array' = \langle record? \rangle \land \\
\qquad secondary' = \\
\qquad\qquad secondary \frown \langle (1 \mathinner{..} count) \lhd array \rangle) \\
\quad \lor \\
\quad count < n \land \\
\qquad (1 \mathinner{..} count') \lhd array' = \\
\qquad\qquad ((1 \mathinner{..} count) \lhd array) \frown \langle record? \rangle \land \\
\qquad secondary' = secondary \quad) \\
status! = \mathsf{ok}
\end{array}
$$

The predicate part includes a disjunction; we proceed by analysing the two cases. In case $count = n$, we have

$$(1 \mathinner{..} count') \lhd array' = \langle record? \rangle$$

We may infer that $(1 \mathinner{..} count') \lhd array'$ is a singleton sequence. Hence

$$count' = 1$$

and $array'$ may take any value as long as its first element is $record?$. $secondary'$ must take the value

$$secondary \frown \langle (1 \mathinner{..} n) \lhd array \rangle$$

which, since $\operatorname{dom} array$ is by definition $1 \mathinner{..} n$, is simply

$$secondary \frown \langle array \rangle$$

In case $count < n$, we have

$$(1 \mathinner{..} count') \lhd array' = ((1 \mathinner{..} count) \lhd array) \frown \langle record? \rangle$$

This tells us that these two sequences have the same length, and hence that $count' = count + 1$.

We may then observe that

$$
\begin{aligned}
&(1 \mathbin{..} count') \lhd array' = ((1 \mathbin{..} count) \lhd array) \frown \langle record? \rangle \\
&\quad \Leftrightarrow (1 \mathbin{..} (count + 1)) \lhd array' = \\
&\qquad\quad = ((1 \mathbin{..} count) \lhd array) \frown \langle record? \rangle \\
&\hfill [\text{since } count' = count + 1] \\
&\quad \Leftrightarrow (1 \mathbin{..} (count + 1)) \lhd array' = \\
&\qquad\quad ((1 \mathbin{..} count) \lhd array) \oplus \\
&\qquad\qquad \{\#((1 \mathbin{..} count) \lhd array) + 1 \mapsto record?\} \\
&\hfill [\text{property of } \frown] \\
&\quad \Leftrightarrow (1 \mathbin{..} (count + 1)) \lhd array' = \\
&\qquad\quad ((1 \mathbin{..} count) \lhd array) \oplus \{count + 1 \mapsto record?\} \\
&\hfill [\text{since } count' = count + 1] \\
&\quad \Leftrightarrow (1 \mathbin{..} (count + 1)) \lhd array' = \\
&\qquad\quad (1 \mathbin{..} (count + 1)) \lhd (array \oplus \{count + 1 \mapsto record?\}) \\
&\hfill [\text{by a property of } \oplus]
\end{aligned}
$$

There are many solutions for $array'$, but an obvious one is

$$array' = array \oplus \{count + 1 \mapsto record?\}.$$

Our new operation has been simplified to

$$
\begin{array}{|l}
\hline
CCSave_0 \\
\hline
\Delta CSaveArea1 \\
record? : Record \\
status! : Status \\
\hline
(\quad count = n \land \\
\qquad\quad count' = 1 \land \\
\qquad\quad array'\ 1 = record? \land \\
\qquad\quad secondary' = secondary \frown \langle array \rangle \\
\quad \lor \\
\quad count < n \land \\
\qquad\quad count' = count + 1 \land \\
\qquad\quad array' = array \oplus \{count + 1 \mapsto record?\} \land \\
\qquad\quad secondary' = secondary \quad) \\
status! = \mathsf{ok} \\
\hline
\end{array}
$$

The error case is simple:

$$\begin{array}{|l}
\hline
\textit{CCSaveFullErr} \\
\Xi CSaveArea1 \\
status! : Status \\
\hline
status! = \mathsf{full} \\
\hline
\end{array}$$

and the complete definition of the save operation is

$$CCSave \mathrel{\widehat{=}} CCSave_0 \lor CCSaveFullErr$$

23.4 Refinement to code

Before we move into the refinement calculus, we break the $CCSave_0$ operation into its component disjuncts: the secondary memory update

$$\begin{array}{|l}
\hline
\textit{CCUpdateSM} \\
\Delta CSaveArea1 \\
record? : Record \\
status! : Status \\
\hline
count = n \\
count' = 1 \\
array'\ 1 = record? \\
secondary' = secondary \frown \langle array \rangle \\
status! = \mathsf{ok} \\
\hline
\end{array}$$

and the main memory update

$$\begin{array}{|l}
\hline
\textit{CCUpdateMM} \\
\Delta CSaveArea1 \\
record? : Record \\
status! : Status \\
\hline
count < n \\
count' = count + 1 \\
array' = array \oplus \{count + 1 \mapsto record?\} \\
secondary' = secondary \\
status! = \mathsf{ok} \\
\hline
\end{array}$$

If we define *save* to be the refinement calculus equivalent of *CCSave*:

$$save \mathrel{\widehat{=}} CSaveArea1, status! : [\ true,\ CCSave\ ]$$

then

$$save = CSaveArea1, status! : \left[\begin{array}{rl} & CCUpdateMM \\ & \vee \\ & CCUpdateSM \\ & \vee \\ true\ , & CCSaveFullErr \end{array}\right]$$

We may refine this specification statement using the refinement rule for conditional introduction, to obtain

$$\begin{array}{ll}
\mathsf{if}\ count < n \rightarrow & \\
\quad CSaveArea1, status! : [\ count < n,\ CCUpdateMM\ ] & [\lhd] \\
\Box\ count = n \rightarrow & \\
\quad CSaveArea1, status! : \left[\begin{array}{rl} & CCUpdateSM \\ & \vee \\ count = n\ , & CCSaveFullEr \end{array}\right] & [\dagger] \\
\mathsf{fi} &
\end{array}$$

The first alternative ($\lhd$) can be rewritten by expanding the definition of the *CCUpdateMM* operation:

$$count, array, status! : \left[\begin{array}{rl} & count' = \\ & \quad count + 1 \\ & array' = \\ & \quad array \oplus \{count + 1 \mapsto record?\} \\ & status! = \\ count < n\ , & \quad \mathsf{ok} \end{array}\right]$$

and then refined by assignment introduction, leaving us with the following assignment statement:

$$count, array, status! := count + 1, array \oplus \{count + 1 \mapsto record?\}, \mathsf{ok}$$

The second alternative (†) can be rewritten as

$$count, array, secondary, status! : \left[count = n\ ,\ \begin{array}{l} count' = 1 \land \\ \quad array'\ 1 = record? \land \\ \quad secondary' = \\ \qquad secondary \frown \langle array \rangle \land \\ \quad status! = \mathsf{ok} \\ \lor \\ count' = count \land \\ \quad array' = array \land \\ \quad secondary' = secondary \land \\ \quad status! = \mathsf{full}) \end{array} \right]$$

and then refined by sequential composition introduction:

$$\mathsf{con}\ X \bullet$$

$$status!, secondary : \left[true\ ,\ \begin{array}{l} status! = \mathsf{ok} \land \\ \quad secondary' = \\ \qquad secondary \frown \langle array' \rangle \\ \lor \\ status! = \mathsf{full} \land \\ \quad secondary' = secondary \end{array} \right] \qquad [\ddagger]$$

$$;$$

$$count, array : \left[\begin{array}{l} status! = \mathsf{ok} \land \\ \quad secondary = \\ \qquad X \frown \langle array \rangle \\ \lor \\ status! = \mathsf{full} \land \\ \quad secondary = X \end{array}\ ,\ \begin{array}{l} count' = 1 \land \\ \quad array'\ 1 = \\ \qquad record? \land \\ \quad secondary' = \\ \qquad X \frown \langle array \rangle \land \\ \quad status! = \mathsf{ok} \\ \lor \\ count' = count \land \\ \quad array' = array \land \\ \quad secondary' = X \land \\ \quad status! = \mathsf{full} \end{array} \right] \qquad [\triangleleft]$$

The precondition suggests to us that we should refinement the second part of the sequential composition using a conditional again, sing the guards *status*! = ok and *status*! = full.

$$
\begin{array}{l}
\textsf{if}\ \ status! = \textsf{ok} \rightarrow \\
\qquad count, array : \left[\begin{array}{ll} & count' = 1 \\ status! = \textsf{ok} & array'\ 1 = record? \\ secondary = & secondary' = X \frown \langle array \rangle \\ \quad X \frown \langle array \rangle\ , & status! = \textsf{ok} \end{array}\right] \qquad [\lhd] \\
\square\ \ status! = \textsf{full} \rightarrow \\
\qquad count, array : \left[\begin{array}{ll} & count' = count \\ & array' = array \\ status! = \textsf{full} & secondary' = X \\ secondary = X\ , & status! = \textsf{full} \end{array}\right] \qquad [] \\
\textsf{fi}
\end{array}
$$

The first alternative may be refined by assignment introduction to obtain

$$count, array := 1, array \oplus \{1 \mapsto record?\}$$

while the second may be refined by skip introduction. We have now removed all the specification statements except ‡, leaving the program

$$
\begin{array}{l}
\textsf{if}\ \ count < n \rightarrow \\
\qquad count, array, status! := count + 1, array \oplus \{count + 1 \mapsto record?\}, \textsf{ok} \\
\square\ \ count = n \rightarrow \\
\qquad status!, secondary : \left[\begin{array}{ll} & status! = \textsf{ok}\ \wedge \\ & \qquad secondary' = secondary \frown \langle array' \rangle \\ & \qquad \vee \\ true\ , & status! = \textsf{full} \wedge secondary' = secondary \end{array}\right] \\
\qquad ; \\
\qquad \textsf{if}\ \ status! = \textsf{ok} \rightarrow \\
\qquad\qquad count, array := 1, array \oplus \{1 \mapsto record?\} \\
\qquad \square\ \ status! = \textsf{full} \rightarrow \\
\qquad\qquad \textsf{skip} \\
\qquad \textsf{fi} \\
\textsf{fi}
\end{array}
$$

The remaining specification statement should look familiar: it is the specification that we started with. Our little program development turns out to be recursive. It describes the interface to main memory in terms of some code and an interface to secondary memory. The two interfaces are described in the same way. Secondary memory could be implemented directly, or we could use a tertiary memory; tertiary memory could be implemented directly, or we could use…

Index

Notation

Resources

There is a world-wide web site associated with this book, containing exercises, solutions, transparencies, and additional material. The address of the site is http://www.comlab.ox.ac.uk/igdp/usingz. If you are unable to gain access, then write to the authors at Oxford University Computing Laboratory, Wolfson Building, Parks Road, Oxford OX1 3QD.

A variety of tools are available for use with the Z notation, but the most useful of these is a type-checking program called *fuzz*. For details, contact the Spivey Partnership, at 10, Warneford Road, Oxford OX4 1LU, or e-mail mike@comlab.oxford.ac.uk.

The authors teach a number of short courses based upon the material in this book; these are part of the Software Engineering Programme at Oxford. For further information, see http://www.comlab.ox.ac.uk/igdp or write to the IGDP Administrator at 1 Wellington Square, Oxford OX1 2JA.

This Book

This book was written during the spring and summer of 1995, using an IBM ThinkPad and a Toshiba T6600 portable. It was edited using Emacs under OS/2, processed using Y&YTeX, and printed using a Monotype Prism PS Plus image-setter. The London Underground map and diagram were supplied on film by the London Transport Museum.

The Toshiba portable was stolen at the end of the summer, together with the corrected drafts of several chapters. If you are offered this machine—the serial number is 064 15 15 6E—then pay no more than £200, and send us the contents of the hard disk.

Emacs was ported to OS/2 by Eberhard Mattes, and is available from any good ftp archive. Y&YTeX is a commercial TeX system that supports outline fonts. It is available from Y&Y at Tuttle's Livery, 45 Walden Street, Concord, MA 01742-2513, USA, or see http://www.yandy.com.

The web site that accompanies this book was produced in collaboration with question, a London-based web production company. For further details, contact Katie Blakstad-Cooke, katie@question.co.uk, or see their web site at http://www.question.co.uk. We would also like to thank Malcolm Harper and Jon Hill for their help in this matter.

Thanks

For inspiration, friendship, practical assistance, and legal advice during the preparation of this book:

Ali Abdallah, James Anderson, Linda Anderson, Laurence Arnold, John Axford, Liz Bailey, Alexandra Barros, Jose Barros, Katie Blakstad-Cooke, Matthew Blakstad-Cooke, Tommaso Bolognesi, Stephen Brien, Sally Brown, Jeremy Bryans, Ana Cavalcanti, Rance Cleaveland, Peter Coesmans, Peter Combey, Denise Cresswell, Mats Daniels, Aled Davies, Tim Denvir, Jeremy Dick, Maureen Doherty, Frankie Elston, Susan Even, Mike Field, Paul Gardiner, Dave Gavaghan, Michael Goldsmith, Sally Goodliffe, Liz Goodman, Josh Guttman, Jackie Harbor, Malcolm Harper, Guy Hart-Davis, Jon Hill, Jane Hillston, Robyn Hitchcock, Tony Hoare, Brendan Hodgson, Andy Holyer, Fleur Howles, Jason Hulance, Dave Jackson, Alan Jeffrey, Marina Jirotka, Liz Johns, Randolph Johnson, Rhona Johnston, Geraint Jones, Mathai Joseph, Mark Josephs, Mike Kalougin, Steve King, Chris Lansley, Stefan Leue, Roger Loader, Lauren Lytle, Grainne Maher, Andrew Martin, David Mayers, Steve McKeever, Jenny McKenzie, Quentin Miller, Andrew Miranker, Swapan Mitra, Carroll Morgan, Andrew Newman, John Nicholls, Nimal Nissanke, Colin O'Halloran, Duncan Oliver, Monica Payne, David Penkower, Divya Prasad, John Quinn, Mike Reed, Phil Richards, Andi Roberts, Bill Roscoe, Peter Ryan, Bahram Sadr-Salek, Bryan Scattergood, Steve Schneider, Jenni Scott, Eleanor Sepanski, Carolyn Shafran, Juliet Short, Alan Shouls, Andrew Simpson, Jane Sinclair, David Skillicorn, Mike Spivey, Vicki Stavridou, Joe Stoy, Bernard Sufrin, Wilson Sutherland, Muffy Thomas, Jacqui Thornton, Pete Verey, Matt Wallis, Imogen Wells, Elaine Welsh, Shirley Williams, Ken Wood, Maureen York, and Ernst Zermelo.

PEYTON JONES, S.L. and LESTER, D., *Implementing Functional Languages*
POMBERGER, G., *Software Engineering and Modula 2*
POTTER, B., SINCLAIR, J., and TILL, D., *An Introduction to Formal Specification and Z*
ROSCOE, A.W. (ed.), *A Classical Mind: Essays in honour of C.A.R. Hoare*
ROZENBERG, G. and SALOMAA, A., *Cornerstones of Undecidability*
RYDEHEARD, D.E. and BURSTALL, R.M., *Computational Category Theory*
SHARP, R., *Principles of Protocol Design*
SLOMAN, M. and KRAMER, J., *Distributed Systems and Computer Networks*
SPIVEY, J.M., *An Introduction to Logic Programming*
SPIVEY, J.M., *The Z. Notation: A reference manual* (2nd edn)
TENNENT, R.D., *Principles of Programming Languages*
TENNENT, R.D., *Semantics of Programming Languages*
WATT, D.A., *Programming Language Concepts and Paradigms*
WATT, D.A., *Programming Language Processors*
WATT, D.A., WICHMANN, B.A. and FINDLAY, W., *ADA: Language and methodology*
WATT, D.A., *Programming Language Syntax and Semantics*
WELSH, J. and ELDER, J., *Introduction to Modula 2*
WELSH, J. and ELDER, J., *Introduction to Pascal* (3rd edn)
WELSH, J. and HAY, A., *A Model Implementation of Standard Pascal*
WIKSTRÖM, A., *Functional Programming Using Standard ML*